Lecture Notes in Artificial Intelligence   1759

Subseries of Lecture Notes in Computer Science
Edited by J. G. Carbonell and J. Siekmann

Lecture Notes in Computer Science
Edited by G. Goos, J. Hartmanis and J. van I   n

Springer
Berlin
Heidelberg
New York
Barcelona
Hong Kong
London
Milan
Paris
Tokyo

Mohammed J. Zaki Ching-Tien Ho (Eds.)

Large-Scale
Parallel Data Mining

Springer

Series Editors

Jaime G. Carbonell, Carnegie Mellon University, Pittsburgh, PA, USA
Jörg Siekmann, University of Saarland, Saarbrücken, Germany

Volume Editors

Mohammed J. Zaki
Computer Science Department
Rensselaer Polytechnic Institute
Troy, NY 12180, USA
E-mail: zaki@cs.rpi.edu

Ching-Tien Ho
K55/B1, IBM Almaden Research Center
650 Harry Road, San Jose, CA 95120, USA
E-mail: ho@almaden.ibm.com

Cataloging-in-Publication Data applied for

Die Deutsche Bibliothek - CIP-Einheitsaufnahme

Large scale parallel data mining / Mohammed J. Zaki ; Ching-Tien Ho (ed.)
- Berlin ; Heidelberg ; New York ; Barcelona ; Hong Kong ; London ;
Milan ; Paris ; Singapore ; Tokyo : Springer, 2000
(Lecture notes in computer science ; Vol. 1759 : Lecture notes in
artificial intelligence)
ISBN 3-540-67194-3

CR Subject Classification (1991): I.2.8, I.2.11, I.2.4, I.2.6, H.3, F.2.2, C.2.4

ISBN 3-540-67194-3 Springer-Verlag Berlin Heidelberg New York

Springer-Verlag is a company in the specialist publishing group BertelsmannSpringer
© Springer-Verlag Berlin Heidelberg 2000
Printed in Germany

Typesetting: Camera-ready by author, data conversion by Christian Grosche
Printed on acid-free paper   SPIN 10719635   06/3142   5 4 3 2 1 0

Preface

With the unprecedented rate at which data is being collected today in almost all fields of human endeavor, there is an emerging economic and scientific need to extract useful information from it. For example, many companies already have data-warehouses in the terabyte range (e.g., FedEx, Walmart). The World Wide Web has an estimated 800 million web-pages. Similarly, scientific data is reaching gigantic proportions (e.g., NASA space missions, Human Genome Project). High-performance, scalable, parallel, and distributed computing is crucial for ensuring system scalability and interactivity as datasets continue to grow in size and complexity.

To address this need we organized the workshop on Large-Scale Parallel KDD Systems, which was held in conjunction with the 5th ACM SIGKDD International Conference on Knowledge Discovery and Data Mining, on August 15th, 1999, San Diego, California. The goal of this workshop was to bring researchers and practitioners together in a setting where they could discuss the design, implementation, and deployment of large-scale parallel knowledge discovery (PKD) systems, which can manipulate data taken from very large enterprise or scientific databases, regardless of whether the data is located centrally or is globally distributed. Relevant topics identified for the workshop included:

- How to develop a rapid-response, scalable, and parallel knowledge discovery system that supports global organizations with terabytes of data.
- How to address some of the challenges facing current state-of-the-art data mining tools. These challenges include relieving the user from time and volume constrained tool-sets, evolving knowledge stores with new knowledge effectively, acquiring data elements from heterogeneous sources such as the Web or other repositories, and enhancing the PKD process by incrementally updating the knowledge stores.
- How to leverage high performance parallel and distributed techniques in all the phases of KDD, such as initial data selection, cleaning and preprocessing, transformation, data-mining task and algorithm selection and its application, pattern evaluation, management of discovered knowledge, and providing tight coupling between the mining engine and database/file server.
- How to facilitate user interaction and usability, allowing the representation of domain knowledge, and to maximize understanding during and after the process. That is, how to build an adaptable knowledge engine which supports business decisions, product creation and evolution, and leverages information into usable or actionable knowledge.

This book contains the revised versions of the workshop papers and it also includes several invited chapters, to bring the readers up-to-date on the recent developments in this field. This book thus represents the state-of-the-art in parallel and distributed data mining methods. It should be useful for both researchers and practitioners interested in the design, implementation, and deployment of large-scale, parallel knowledge discovery systems.

December 1999   Mohammed J. Zaki
                                                                     Ching-Tien Ho

Workshop Chairs

Workshop Chair: Mohammed J. Zaki (Rensselaer Polytechnic Institute, USA)
Workshop Co-Chair: Ching-Tien Ho (IBM Almaden Research Center, USA)

Program Committee

David Cheung (University of Hong Kong, Hong Kong)
Alok Choudhary (Northwestern University, USA)
Alex A. Freitas (Pontifical Catholic University of Parana, Brazil)
Robert Grossman (University of Illinois-Chicago, USA)
Yike Guo (Imperial College, UK)
Hillol Kargupta (Washington State University, USA)
Masaru Kitsuregawa (University of Tokyo, Japan)
Vipin Kumar (University of Minnesota, USA)
Reagan Moore (San Diego Supercomputer Center, USA)
Ron Musick (Lawrence Livermore National Lab, USA)
Srini Parthasarathy (University of Rochester, USA)
Sanjay Ranka (University of Florida, USA)
Arno Siebes (Centrum Wiskunde Informatica, Netherlands)
David Skillicorn (Queens University, Canada)
Paul Stolorz (Jet Propulsion Lab, USA)
Graham Williams (Cooperative Research Center for Advanced Computational Systems, Australia)

Acknowledgements

We would like to thank all the invited speakers, authors, and participants for contributing to the success of the workshop. Special thanks are due to the program committee for their support and help in reviewing the submissions.

Table of Contents

Large-Scale Parallel Data Mining

Mining Frameworks

Associations and Sequences

Classification

Clustering

Parallel and Distributed Data Mining: An Introduction

Mohammed J. Zaki

Computer Science Department
Rensselaer Polytechnic Institute
Troy, NY 12180
zaki@cs.rpi.edu
http://www.cs.rpi.edu/~zaki

Abstract. The explosive growth in data collection in business and scientific fields has literally forced upon us the need to analyze and mine useful knowledge from it. Data mining refers to the entire process of extracting useful and novel patterns/models from large datasets. Due to the huge size of data and amount of computation involved in data mining, high-performance computing is an essential component for any successful large-scale data mining application. This chapter presents a survey on large-scale parallel and distributed data mining algorithms and systems, serving as an introduction to the rest of this volume. It also discusses the issues and challenges that must be overcome for designing and implementing successful tools for large-scale data mining.

1 Introduction

Data Mining and Knowledge Discovery in Databases (KDD) is a new interdisciplinary field merging ideas from statistics, machine learning, databases, and parallel and distributed computing. It has been engendered by the phenomenal growth of data in all spheres of human endeavor, and the economic and scientific need to extract useful information from the collected data. The key challenge in data mining is the extraction of knowledge and insight from massive databases.

Data mining refers to the overall process of discovering new patterns or building models from a given dataset. There are many steps involved in the KDD enterprise which include data selection, data cleaning and preprocessing, data transformation and reduction, data-mining task and algorithm selection, and finally post-processing and interpretation of discovered knowledge [1,2]. This KDD process tends to be highly iterative and interactive.

Typically data mining has the two high level goals of *prediction* and *description* [1]. In prediction, we are interested in building a model that will predict unknown or future values of attributes of interest, based on known values of some attributes in the database. In KDD applications, the description of the data in human-understandable terms is equally if not more important than prediction. Two main forms of data mining can be identified [3]. In *verification-driven* data mining the user postulates a hypothesis, and the system tries to validate it.

M.J. Zaki, C.-T. Ho (Eds.): Large-Scale Parallel Data Mining, LNAI 1759, pp. 1–23, 2000.
© Springer-Verlag Berlin Heidelberg 2000

The common verification-driven operations include query and reporting, multi-dimensional analysis or On-Line Analytical Processing (OLAP), and statistical analysis. *Discovery-driven* mining, on the other hand, automatically extracts new information from data, and forms the main focus of this survey. The typical discovery-driven tasks include association rules, sequential patterns, classification and regression, clustering, similarity search, deviation detection, etc.

While data mining has its roots in the traditional fields of machine learning and statistics, the sheer volume of data today poses the most serious problem. For example, many companies already have data warehouses in the terabyte range (e.g., FedEx, UPS, Walmart). Similarly, scientific data is reaching gigantic proportions (e.g., NASA space missions, Human Genome Project). Traditional methods typically made the assumption that the data is memory resident. This assumption is no longer tenable. Implementation of data mining ideas in high-performance parallel and distributed computing environments is thus becoming crucial for ensuring system scalability and interactivity as data continues to grow inexorably in size and complexity.

Parallel data mining (PDM) deals with tightly-coupled systems including shared-memory systems (SMP), distributed-memory machines (DMM), or clusters of SMP workstations (CLUMPS) with a fast interconnect. Distributed data mining (DDM), on the other hand, deals with loosely-coupled systems such as a cluster over a slow Ethernet local-area network. It also includes geographically distributed sites over a wide-area network like the Internet. The main differences between PDM to DDM are best understood if view DDM as a gradual transition from tightly-coupled, fine-grained parallel machines to loosely-coupled medium-grained LAN of workstations, and finally very coarse-grained WANs. There is in fact a significant overlap between the two areas, especially at the medium-grained level where is it hard to draw a line between them.

In another view, we can think of PDM as an essential component of a DDM architecture. An individual site in DDM can be a supercomputer, a cluster of SMPs, or a single workstation. In other words, each site supports PDM locally. Multiple PDM sites constitute DDM, much like the current trend in meta- or super-computing. Thus the main difference between PDM and DDM is that of scale, communication costs, and data distribution. While, in PDM, SMPs can share the entire database and construct a global mined model, DMMs generally partition the database, but still generate global patterns/models. On the other hand, in DDM, it is typically not feasible to share or communicate data at all; local models are built at each site, and are then merged/combined via various methods.

PDM is the ideal choice in organizations with centralized data-stores, while DDM is essential in cases where there are multiple distributed datasets. In fact, a successful large-scale data mining effort requires a hybrid PDM/DDM approach, where parallel techniques are used to optimize the local mining at a site, and where distributed techniques are then used to construct global or consensus patterns/models, while minimizing the amount of data and results communicated. In this chapter we adopt this unified view of PDM and DDM.

This chapter provides an introduction to parallel and distributed data mining. We begin by explaining the PDM/DDM algorithm design space, and then go on to survey current parallel and distributed algorithms for associations, sequences, classification and clustering, which are the most common mining techniques. We also include a section on recent systems for distributed mining. After reviewing the open challenges in PDM/DDM, we conclude by providing a roadmap for the rest of this volume.

2 Parallel and Distributed Data Mining

Parallel and distributed computing is expected to relieve current mining methods from the sequential bottleneck, providing the ability to scale to massive datasets, and improving the response time. Achieving good performance on today's multiprocessor systems is a non-trivial task. The main challenges include synchronization and communication minimization, work-load balancing, finding good data layout and data decomposition, and disk I/O minimization, which is especially important for data mining.

2.1 Parallel Design Space

The parallel design space spans a number of systems and algorithmic components including the hardware platform, the kind of parallelism exploited, the load balancing strategy, the data layout and the search procedure used.

Distributed Memory Machines vs. Shared Memory Systems. The performance optimization objectives change depending on the underlying architecture. In DMMs synchronization is implicit in message passing, so the goal becomes communication optimization. For shared-memory systems, synchronization happens via locks and barriers, and the goal is to minimize these points. Data decomposition is very important for distributed memory, but not for shared memory. While parallel I/O comes for "free" in DMMs, it can be problematic for SMP machines, which typically serialize I/O. The main challenge for obtaining good performance on DMM is to find a good data decomposition among the nodes, and to minimize communication. For SMP the objectives are to achieve good *data locality*, i.e., maximize accesses to local cache, and to avoid/reduce *false sharing*, i.e., minimize the ping-pong effect where multiple processors may be trying to modify different variables which coincidentally reside on the same cache line. For today's non-uniform memory access (NUMA) hybrid and/or hierarchical machines (e.g., cluster of SMPs), the optimization parameters draw from both the DMM and SMP paradigms.

Another classification of the different architectures comes from the database literature. Here, *shared-everything* refers to the shared-memory paradigm, with a global shared memory and common disks among all the machines. *Shared-nothing* refers to distributed-memory architecture, with a local memory and disk for each processor. A third paradigm called *shared-disks* refers to the mixed case where processors have local memories, but access common disks [4,5].

Task vs. Data Parallelism. These are the two main paradigms for exploiting algorithm parallelism. Data parallelism corresponds to the case where the database is partitioned among P processors. Each processor works on its local partition of the database, but performs the same computation of evaluating candidate patterns/models. Task parallelism corresponds to the case where the processors perform different computations independently, such as evaluating a disjoint set of candidates, but have/need access to the entire database. SMPs have access to the entire data, but for DMMs this can be done via selective replication or explicit communication of the local data. Hybrid parallelism combining both task and data parallelism is also possible, and in fact desirable for exploiting all available parallelism in data mining methods.

Static vs. Dynamic Load Balancing. In static load balancing work is initially partitioned among the processors using some heuristic cost function, and there is no subsequent data or computation movement to correct load imbalances which result from the dynamic nature of mining algorithms. Dynamic load balancing seeks to address this by stealing work from heavily loaded processors and re-assigning it to lightly loaded ones. Computation movement also entails data movement, since the processor responsible for a computational task needs the data associated with that task as well. Dynamic load balancing thus incurs additional costs for work/data movement, but it is beneficial if the load imbalance is large and if load changes with time. Dynamic load balancing is especially important in multi-user environments with transient loads and in heterogeneous platforms, which have different processor and network speeds. These kinds of environments include parallel servers, and heterogeneous, meta-clusters. With very few exceptions, most extant parallel mining algorithms use only a static load balancing approach that is inherent in the initial partitioning of the database among available nodes. This is because they assume a dedicated, homogeneous environment.

Horizontal vs. Vertical Data Layout. The standard input database for mining is a relational table having N rows, also called feature vectors, transactions, or records, and M columns, also called dimensions, features, or attributes. The data layout can be row-wise or column-wise. Many data mining algorithms assume a *horizontal* or row-wise database layout, where they store, as a unit, each transaction (*tid*), along with the attribute values for that transaction. Other methods use a *vertical* or column-wise database layout, where they associate with each attribute a list of all tids (called *tidlist*) containing the item, and the corresponding attribute value in that transaction. Certain mining operations a more efficient using a horizontal format, while others are more efficient using a vertical format.

Complete vs. Heuristic Candidate Generation. The final results of a mining method may be sets, sequences, rules, trees, networks, etc., ranging from simple patterns to more complex models, based on certain search criteria. In the intermediate steps several *candidate* patterns or partial models are evaluated, and the final result contains only the ones that satisfy the (user-specified) input parameters. Mining algorithms can differ in the way new candidates are generated for evaluation. One approach is that of *complete* search, which is guaranteed to generate and test all valid candidates consistent with the data. Note that completeness doesn't mean exhaustive, since pruning can be used to eliminate useless branches in the search space. *Heuristic* generation sacrifices completeness for the sake of speed. At each step, it only examines a limited number (or only one) of "good" branches. *Random* search is also possible. Generally, the more complex the mined model, the more the tendency towards heuristic or greedy search.

Candidate and Data Partitioning. An easy way to discuss the many parallel and distributed mining methods is to describe them in terms of the computation and data partitioning methods used. For example, the database itself can be shared (in shared-memory or shared-disk architectures), partially or totally replicated, or partitioned (using round-robin, hash, or range scheduling) among the available nodes (in distributed-memory architectures).

Similarly, the candidate concepts generated and evaluated in the different mining methods can be shared, replicated or partitioned. If they are shared then all processors evaluate a single copy of the candidate set. In the replicated approach the candidate concepts are replicated on each machine, and are first evaluated locally, before global results are obtained by merging them. Finally, in the partitioned approach, each processor generates and tests a disjoint candidate concept set.

In the sections below we describe parallel and distributed algorithms for some of the typical discovery-driven mining tasks including associations, sequences, decision tree classification and clustering. Table 1 summarizes in list form where each parallel algorithm for each of the above mining tasks lies in the design space. It would help the reader to refer to the table while reading the algorithm descriptions below.

2.2   Association Rules

Given a database of transactions, where each transaction consists of a set of items, association discovery finds all the item sets that frequently occur together, the so called *frequent itemsets*, and also the rules among them. An example of an association could be that, "40% of people who buy Jane Austen's *Pride and Prejudice* also buy *Sense and Sensibility*." Potential application areas include catalog design, store layout, customer segmentation, telecommunication alarm diagnosis, etc.

The Apriori [6] method serves as the base algorithm for the vast majority of parallel association algorithms. Apriori uses a complete, bottom-up search, with a horizontal data layout and enumerates all frequent itemsets. Apriori is an iterative algorithm that counts itemsets of a specific length in a given database pass. The process starts by scanning all transactions in the database and computing the frequent items. Next, a set of potentially frequent *candidate* itemsets

Algorithm	Base Algorithm	Machine	Parallelism	LoadBal	DB Layout	Concepts	Database
Association Rule Mining							
CD, PEAR, PDM, FDM, NPA	Apriori	DMM	Data	Static	Horizontal	Replicated	Partitioned
DD, SPA, IDD	Apriori	DMM	Task	Static	Horizontal	Partitioned	Partitioned
HD	Apriori	DMM	Hybrid	Hybrid	Horizontal	Hybrid	Partitioned
CCPD	Apriori	SMP	Data	Static	Horizontal	Shared	Partitioned
CandD, HPA, HPA-ELD	Apriori	DMM	Task	Static	Horizontal	Partitioned	Partially Replicated
PCCD	Apriori	SMP	Task	Static	Horizontal	Partitioned	Shared
APM	DIC	SMP	Task	Static	Horizontal	Shared	Partitioned
PPAR	Partition	DMM	Task	Static	Horizontal	Replicated	Partitioned
PE, PME, PC, PMC	Eclat, Clique	CLUMPS	Task	Static	Vertical	Partitioned	Partially Replicated
Sequence Mining							
NPSPM	GSP	DMM	Data	Static	Horizontal	Replicated	Partitioned
SPSPM	GSP	DMM	Task	Static	Horizontal	Partitioned	Partitioned
HPSPM	GSP	DMM	Task	Static	Horizontal	Partitioned	Partially Replicated
pSPADE	SPADE	SMP	Task	Dynamic	Vertical	Partitioned	Shared
D-MSDD	MSDD	DMM	Task	Static	Horizontal	Partitioned	Replicated
Decision Tree Classification							
SPRINT, SLIQ/R, SLIQ/D, ScalParC	SLIQ/SPRINT	DMM	Data	Static	Vertical	Replicated	Partitioned
DP-att, DP-rec, PDT	C4.5	DMM	Data	Static	Horizontal	Replicated	Partitioned
MWK	SPRINT	SMP	Data	Dynamic	Vertical	Shared	Shared
SUBTREE	SPRINT	SMP	Hybrid	Dynamic	Vertical	Partitioned	Partitioned
HTF	SPRINT	DMM	Hybrid	Dynamic	Vertical	Partitioned	Partitioned
pCLOUDS	CLOUDS	DMM	Hybrid	Dynamic	Horizontal	Partitioned	Partitioned
Clustering							
P-CLUSTER	K-Means	DMM	Data	Static	Horizontal	Replicated	Partitioned
MAFIA	-	DMM	Task	Static	Horizontal	Partitioned	Partitioned

Table 1. Design Space for Parallel Mining Algorithms: Associations, Sequences, Classification and Clustering.

of length 2 is formed from the frequent items. Another database scan is made to obtain their supports. The frequent itemsets are retained for the next pass, and the process is repeated until all frequent itemsets (of various lengths) have been enumerated.

Other sequential methods for associations that have been parallelized, include DHP [7], which tries to reduce the number of candidates by collecting approximate counts (using hash tables) in the previous level. These counts can be used to rule out many candidates in the current pass that cannot possibly be frequent. The *Partition* algorithm [8] minimizes I/O by scanning the database only twice. It partitions the database into small chunks which can be handled in memory. In the first pass it generates a set of all potentially frequent itemsets, and in the second pass it counts their global frequency. In both phases it uses a vertical database layout. The DIC algorithm [9] dynamically counts candidates of varying length as the database scan progresses, and thus is able to reduce the number of scans.

A completely different design characterizes the equivalence class based algorithms (Eclat, MaxEclat, Clique, and MaxClique) proposed by Zaki et al. [10]. These methods utilize a vertical database format, complete search, a mix of bottom-up and hybrid search, and generate a mix of maximal and non-maximal frequent itemsets. The algorithms utilize the structural properties of frequent itemsets to facilitate fast discovery. The items are organized in a subset lattice search space, which is decomposed into small independent chunks or sub-lattices, which can be solved in memory. Efficient lattice traversal techniques are used, which quickly identify all the frequent itemsets via tidlist intersections.

Replicated or Shared Candidates, Partitioned Database. The candidate concepts in association mining are the frequent itemsets. A common paradigm for parallel association mining is to partition the database in equal-sized horizontal blocks, with the candidate itemsets replicated on all processors. For Apriori-based parallel methods, in each iteration, each processor computes the frequency of the candidate set in its local database partition. This is followed by a sum-reduction to obtain the global frequency. The infrequent itemsets are discarded, while the frequent ones are used to generate the candidates for the next iteration.

Barring minor differences, the methods that follow this data-parallel approach include PEAR [11], PDM [12], Count Distribution (CD) [13], FDM [14], Non-Partitioned Apriori (NPA) [15], and CCPD [16]. CCPD uses shared-memory machines, and thus maintains a shared candidate set among all processors. It also parallelizes the candidate generation.

The other algorithms use distributed-memory machines. PDM, based on DHP, prunes candidates using approximate counts from the previous level. It also does parallelizes candidate generation, at the cost of an extra round of communication. The remaining methods simply replicate the computation for candidate generation. FDM is further optimized to work on distributed sites. It uses novel pruning techniques to minimize the number of candidates, and thus the communication during sum-reduction.

The advantage of replicated candidates and partitioned database, for Apriori-based methods, is that they incur only a small amount of communication. In each iteration only the frequencies of candidate concepts are exchanged; no data is exchanged. These methods thus outperform the pure partitioned candidates approach described in the next section. Their disadvantage is that the aggregate system memory is not used effectively, since the candidates are replicated.

Other parallel algorithms, that use a different base sequential method include APM [17], a task-parallel, shared-memory, asynchronous algorithm, based on DIC. Each processor independently applies DIC to its local partition. The candidate set is shared among processors, but is updated asynchronously when a processor inserts new itemsets.

PPAR [11], a task-parallel, distributed-memory algorithm, is built upon Partition, with the exception that PPAR uses the horizontal data format. Each processor gathers the locally frequent itemsets of all sizes in one pass over their local database (which may be partitioned into chunks as well). All potentially frequent itemsets are then broadcast to other processors. Then each processor gathers the counts of these global candidates in the second local pass. Finally a broadcast is performed to obtain the globally frequent itemsets.

Partitioned Candidates, Partitioned Database. Algorithms implementing this approach include Data Distribution (DD) [13], Simply-Partitioned Apriori (SPA) [15], and Intelligent Data Distribution (IDD) [18]. All three are Apriori-based, and employ task parallelism on distributed-memory machines. Here each processor computes the frequency of a disjoint set of candidates. However, to find the global support each processor must scan the entire database, both its local partition, and other processor's partitions (which are exchanged in each iteration). The main advantage of these methods is that they utilize the aggregate system-wide memory by evaluating disjoint candidates, but they are impractical for any realistic large-scale dataset.

The Hybrid Distribution (HD) algorithm [18] adopts a middle ground between Data Distribution and Count Distribution. It utilizes the aggregate memory, and also minimizes communication. It partitions the P processors into G equal-sized groups. Each of the G groups is considered a super-processor, and applies Count Distribution, while the P/G processors within a group use Intelligent Data Distribution. The database is horizontally partitioned among the G super-processors, and the candidates are partitioned among the P/G processors in a group. HD cuts down the database communication costs by $1/G$.

Partitioned Candidates, Selectively Replicated or Shared Database. A third approach is to evaluate a disjoint candidate set and to selectively replicate the database on each processor. Each processor has all the information to generate and test candidates asynchronously. Methods in this paradigm are Candidate Distribution (CandD) [13], Hash Partitioned Apriori (HPA) [15], HPA-ELD [15], and PCCD [16], all of which are Apriori-based. PCCD uses SMP machines, and accesses a shared-database, but is not competitive with CCPD. Candidate Distribution is also outperformed by Count Distribution. Nevertheless, HPA-ELD, a hybrid between HPA and NPA, was shown to be better than NPA, SPA, and HPA.

Zaki et al. [19] proposed four algorithms, ParEclat (PE), ParMaxEclat (PME), ParClique (PC), and ParMaxClique (PMC), targeting hierarchical systems like clusters of SMP machines. The data is assumed to be vertically partitioned among the SMP machines. After an initial tidlist exchange phase and class scheduling phase, the algorithms proceed asynchronously. In the asynchronous phase each processor has available the classes assigned to it, and the tidlists for all items. Thus each processor can independently generate all frequent itemsets from its classes. No communication or synchronization is required. Further, all available memory of the system is used, no in-memory hash trees are needed, and only simple intersection operations are required for itemset enumeration.

Most of the extant association mining methods use a static load balancing scheme; a dynamic load balancing approach on a heterogeneous cluster has been presented in [20]. For more detailed surveys of parallel and distributed association mining see [21] and the chapter by Joshi et al. in this volume.

2.3   Sequential Patterns

Sequence discovery aims at extracting frequent events that commonly occur over a period of time [22]. An example of a sequential pattern could be that "70% of the people who buy Jane Austen's *Pride and Prejudice* also buy *Emma* within a month". Sequential pattern mining deals with purely categorical domains, as opposed to the real-valued domains used in time-series analysis. Examples of categorical domains include text, DNA, market baskets, etc.

In essence, sequence mining is "temporal" association mining. However, while association rules discover only intra-transaction patterns (itemsets), we now also have to discover inter-transaction patterns (sequences) across related transactions. The set of all frequent sequences is an superset of the set of frequent itemsets. Hence, sequence search is much more complex and challenging than itemset search, thereby necessitating fast parallel algorithms.

Serial algorithms for sequence mining that have been parallelized include GSP [23], MSDD [24], and SPADE [25]. GSP is designed after Apriori. It computes the frequency of candidate sequences of length k in iteration k. The candidates are generated from the frequent sequences from the previous iteration. MSDD discovers patterns in multiple event sequences; it explores the rule space directly instead of the sequence space. SPADE is similar to Eclat. It uses vertical layout and temporal joins to compute frequency. The search space is broken into small memory-resident chunks, which are explored in depth- or breadth-first manner.

Three parallel algorithms based on GSP were presented in [26]. All three methods use the partitioned database approach, and are distributed-memory based. NPSPM (with replicated candidates) is equivalent to NPA, SPSPM (with partitioned candidates) the same as SPA and HPSPM is equivalent to HPA, which have been described above. HPSPM performed the best among the three. A parallel and distributed implementation of MSDD was presented in [27].

A shared-memory, SPADE-based parallel algorithm, utilizing dynamic load balancing is described by Zaki, and new algorithms for parallel sequence mining are also described by Joshi et al. in this volume.

2.4 Classification

Classification aims to assign a new data item to one of several predefined categorical classes [28,29]. Since the field being predicted is pre-labeled, classification is also known as supervised induction. While there are several classification methods including neural networks [30] and genetic algorithms [31], decision trees [32,33] are particularly suited to data mining, since they can be constructed relatively quickly, and are simple and easy to understand. Common applications of classification include credit card fraud detection, insurance risk analysis, bank loan approval, etc.

A decision tree is built using a recursive partitioning approach. Each internal node in the tree represents a decision on an attribute, which splits the database into two or more children. Initially the root contains the entire database, with examples from mixed classes. The split point chosen is the one that best separates or discriminates the classes. Each new node is recursively split in the same manner until a node contains only one or a majority class.

Decision tree classifiers typically use a greedy search over the space of all possible trees; there are simply too many trees to allow a complete search. The search is also biased towards simple trees. Existing classifiers have used both the horizontal and vertical database layouts. In parallel decision tree construction the candidate concepts are the possible split points for all attributes within a node of the expanding tree. For numeric attributes a split point is of the form $A \leq v_i$, and for categorical attributes the test takes the form $A \in \{v_1, v_2, ...\}$, where v_i is a value from the domain of attribute A.

Below we look at some parallel decision tree methods. Recent surveys on parallel and scalable induction methods are also presented in [34,35].

Replicated Tree, Partitioned Database. SLIQ [36] was one of the earliest scalable decision tree classifiers. It uses a vertical data format, called attribute lists, allowing it to pre-sort numeric attributes in the beginning, thus avoiding the repeated sorting required at each node in traditional tree induction. Nevertheless it uses a memory-resident structure called *class-list*, which grows linearly in the number of input records. SPRINT [37] removes this memory dependence, by storing the classes as part of the attribute lists. It uses data parallelism, and a distributed-memory platform.

In SPRINT and parallel versions of SLIQ, the attribute lists are horizontally partitioned among all processors. The decision tree is also replicated on all processors. The tree is constructed synchronously in a breadth-first manner. Each processor computes the best split point, using its local attribute lists, for all the nodes on the current tree level. A round of communication takes place to determine the best split point among all processors. Each processor independently splits the current nodes into new children using the best split point, setting the stage for the next tree level. Since a horizontal record is split in multiple attribute lists, a hash table is used to note which record belongs to which child.

The parallelization of SLIQ follows a similar paradigm, except for the way the class list is treated. SLIQ/R uses a replicated class list, while SLIQ/D uses a distributed class list. Experiments showed that while SLIQ/D is better able to exploit available memory, SLIQ/R was better in terms of performance, but SPRINT outperformed both SLIQ/R and SLIQ/D.

ScalParC [38] is also an attribute-list-based parallel classifier for distributed-memory machines. It is similar in design to SLIQ/D (except that it uses hash tables per node, instead of global class lists). It uses a novel distributed hash table for splitting a node, reducing the communication complexity and memory requirements over SPRINT, making it scalable to larger datasets.

The DP-rec and DP-att [39] algorithms exploit record-based and attribute-based data parallelism, respectively. In record-based data parallelism (also used in SPRINT, ScalParC SLIQ/D and SLIQ/R), the records or attribute lists are horizontally partitioned among the processors. In contrast, in attribute-based data parallelism, the attributes are divided so that each processor is responsible for an equal number of attributes. In both the schemes processors cooperate to expand a tree node. Local computations are performed in parallel, followed by information exchanges to get a global best split point.

Parallel Decision Tree (PDT) [40], a distributed-memory, data-parallel algorithm, splits the training records horizontally in equal-sized blocks, among the processors. It follows a master-slave paradigm, where the master builds the tree, and finds the best split points. The slaves are responsible for sending class frequency statistics to the master. For categorical attributes, each processor gathers local class frequencies, and forwards them to the master. For numeric attributes, each processor sorts the local values, finds class frequencies for split points, and exchanges these with all other slaves. Each slave can then calculate the best local split point, which is sent to the master, who then selects the best global split point.

Shared Tree, Shared Database. MWK (and its precursors BASIC and FWK) [41], a shared-memory implementation based on SPRINT uses this approach. MWK uses dynamic attribute-based data parallelism. Multiple processors co-operate to build a shared decision tree in a breadth-first manner. Using a dynamic scheduling scheme, each processor acquires an attribute for any tree node at the current level, and evaluates the split points, before processing another attribute. The processor that evaluates the last attribute of a tree node, also computes the best split point for that node. Similarly, the attribute lists are split among the children using attribute parallelism.

Hybrid Tree Parallelism. SUBTREE [41] uses dynamic task parallelism (that exists in different sub-trees) combined with data parallelism on shared-memory systems. Initially all processors belong to one group, and apply data parallelism at the root. Once new child nodes are formed, the processors are also partitioned into groups, so that a group of child nodes can be processed in parallel by a processor group. If the tree nodes associated with a processor group become pure (i.e., contain examples from a single class), then these processors join some other active group.

The Hybrid Tree Formulation (HTF) in [42] is very similar to SUBTREE. HTF uses distributed memory machines, and thus data redistribution is required in HTF when assigning a set of nodes to a processor group, so that the processor group has all records relevant to an assigned node.

pCLOUDS [43] is a distributed-memory parallelization of CLOUDS [44]. It does not require attribute lists or the pre-sorting for numeric attributes; instead it samples the split points for numeric attributes followed by an estimation step to narrow the search space for the best split. It thus reduces both computation and I/O requirements. pCLOUDS employs a mixed parallelism approach. Initially, data parallelism is applied for nodes with many records. All small nodes are queued to be processed later using task parallelism. Before processing small nodes the data is redistributed so that all required data is available locally at a processor.

2.5 Clustering

Clustering is used to partition database records into subsets or clusters, such that elements of a cluster share a set of common properties that distinguish them from other clusters [45,46,47,48]. The goal is to maximize intra-cluster and minimize inter-cluster similarity. Unlike classification which has predefined labels, clustering must in essence automatically come up with the labels. For this reason clustering is also called unsupervised induction. Applications of clustering include demographic or market segmentation for identifying common traits of groups of people, discovering new types of stars in datasets of stellar objects, and so on.

The K-means algorithm is a popular clustering method. The idea is to randomly pick K data points as cluster centers. Next, each record or point is assigned to the cluster it is closest to in terms of squared-error or Euclidean distance. A new center is computed by taking the mean of all points in a cluster, setting the stage for the next iteration. The process stops when the cluster centers cease to change. Parallelization of K-means received a lot of attention in the past. Different parallel methods, mainly using hypercube computers, appear in [49,50,51,52]. We do not describe these methods in detail, since they used only small memory-resident datasets.

Hierarchical clustering represents another common paradigm. These methods start with a set of distinct points, each forming its own cluster. Then recursively, two clusters that are close are merged into one, until all points belong to a single cluster. In [49,53], parallel hierarchical agglomerative clustering algorithms were presented, using several inter-cluster distance metrics and parallel computer architectures. These methods also report results on small datasets.

P-CLUSTER [54] is a distributed-memory client-server K-means algorithm. Data is partitioned into blocks on a server, which sends initial cluster centers and data blocks to each client. A client assigns each record in its local block to the nearest cluster, and sends results back to the server. The server then recalculates the new centers and another iteration begins. To further improve performance P-CLUSTER uses that the fact that after the first few iterations only a few records change cluster assignments, and also the centers have less tendency to move in later iterations. They take advantage of these facts to reduce the number of distance calculations, and thus the time of the clustering algorithm.

Among the recent methods, MAFIA [55], is a distributed memory algorithm for subspace clustering. Traditional methods, like K-means and hierarchical clustering, find clusters in the whole data space, i.e., they use all dimensions for distance computations. Subspace clustering focuses on finding clusters embedded in subsets of a high-dimensional space. MAFIA uses adaptive grids (or bins) in each dimension, which are merged to find clusters in higher dimensions. Parallel implementation of MAFIA is similar to association mining. The candidates here are the potentially dense units (the subspace clusters) in k dimensions, which have to be tested if they are truly dense. MAFIA employs task parallelism, where data as well as candidates are equally partitioned among all processors. Each processor computes local density, followed by a reduction to obtain global density.

The paper by Dhillon and Modha in this volume presents a distributed-memory parallelization of K-means, while the paper by Johnson and Kargupta describes a distributed hierarchical clustering method.

2.6   Distributed Mining Frameworks

Recently, there has been an increasing interest in distributed and wide-area data mining systems. The fact that many global businesses and scientific endeavors require access to multiple, distributed, and often heterogeneous databases, underscores the growing importance of distributed data mining.

An ideal platform for DDM is a cluster of machines at a local site, or cluster of clusters spanning a wide area, the so-called computational grids, connected via Internet or other high speed networks. As we noted earlier, PDM is best viewed as a local component within a DDM system. Further the main differences between the two is the cost of communication or data movement, and the fact that DDM must typically handle multiple (possibly heterogeneous) databases. Below we review some recent efforts in developing DDM frameworks.

Most methods/systems for DDM assume that the data is horizontally partitioned among the sites, and is homogeneous (share the same feature space). Each site mines its local data and generates locally valid concepts. These concepts are exchanged among all the sites to obtain the globally valid concepts. The Partition [8] algorithm for association mining is a good example. It is inherently suitable for DDM. Each site can generate locally frequent itemsets at a given threshold level. All local results are combined and then evaluated at each site to obtain the globally frequent itemsets.

Another example is JAM [56,57], a java-based multi-agent system utilizing meta-learning, used primarily in fraud-detection applications. Each agent builds a classification model, and different agents are allowed to build classifiers using different techniques. JAM also provides a set of meta-learning agents for combining multiple models learnt at different sites into a *meta-classifier* that in many cases improves the overall predictive accuracy. Knowledge Probing [58] is another approach to meta-learning. Knowledge probing retains a descriptive model after combining multiple classifiers, rather than treating the meta-classifier as a black-box. The idea is to learn on a separate dataset, the class predictions from all the local classifiers.

PADMA [59] is an agent based architecture for distributed mining. Individual agents are responsible for local data access, hierarchical clustering in text document classification, and web based information visualization. The BODHI [60] DDM system is based on the novel concept of collective data mining. Naive mining of heterogeneous, vertically partitioned, sites can lead to an incorrect global data model. BODHI guarantees correct local and global analysis with minimum communication.

In [61] a new distributed do-all primitive, called D-DOALL, was described that allows easy scheduling of independent mining tasks on a network of workstations. The framework allows incremental reporting of results, and seeks to reduce communication via resource-aware task scheduling principles.

The Papyrus [62] java-based system specifically targets wide-area DDM over clusters and meta-clusters. It supports different data, task and model strategies. For example, it can move models, intermediate results or raw data between nodes. It can support coordinated or independent mining, and various methods for combining local models. Papyrus uses PMML (Predictive Model Markup Language) to describe and exchange mined models. Kensignton [63] is another java-based system for distributed enterprise data mining. It is a three-tiered system, with a client front-end for GUI, and visual programming of data mining tasks. The middle-layer application server provides persistent storage, task execution control, and data management and preprocessing functions. The third-tier implements a parallel data mining service.

Other recent work in DDM includes decision tree construction over distributed databases [64], where the learning agents can only exchange summaries instead of raw data, and the databases may have shared attributes. The main challenge is to construct a decision tree using implicit records rather than materializing a join over all the datasets. The WoRLD system [65] describes an inductive rule-learning program that learns from data distributed over a network. WoRLD also avoids joining databases to create a central dataset. Instead it uses marker-propagation to compute statistics. A marker is a label of a class of interest. Counts of the different markers are maintained with each attribute value, and used for evaluating rules. Markers are propagated among different tables to facilitate distributed learning.

For more information on parallel and distributed data mining see the book by Freitas and Lavington [66] and the edited volume by Kargupta and Chan [67]. Also see [68] for a discussion of cost-effective measures for assessing the performance of a mining algorithm before implementing it.

3 Research Issues and Challenges

In this section we highlight some of the outstanding research issues and a number of open problems for designing and implementing the next-generation large-scale mining methods and KDD systems.

High Dimensionality. Current methods are only able to hand a few thousand dimensions or attributes. Consider association rule mining as an example. The second iteration of the algorithm counts the frequency of all pairs of items, which has quadratic complexity. In general, the complexity of different mining algorithms may not be linear in the number of dimensions, and new parallel methods are needed that are able to handle large number of attributes.

Large Size. Databases continue to increase in size. Current methods are able to (perhaps) handle data in the gigabyte range, but are not suitable for terabyte-sized data. Even a single scan for these databases is considered expensive. Most current algorithms are iterative, and scan data multiple times. For example, it is an open problem to mine all frequent associations in a single pass, although sampling based methods show promise [69,70]. In general, minimizing the number of data scans is paramount. Another factor limiting the scalability of most mining algorithms is that they rely on in-memory data structures for storing potential patterns and information about them (such as candidate hash tree [6] in associations, tid hash table [71] in classification). For large databases these structures will certainly not fit in aggregate system memory. This means that temporary results will have to be written out to disk or the database will have to be divided into partitions small enough to be processed in memory, entailing further data scans.

Data Location. Today's large-scale data sets are usually logically and physically distributed, requiring a decentralized approach to mining. The database may be horizontally partitioned where different sites have different transactions, or it may be vertically partitioned, with different sites having different attributes. Most current work has only dealt with the horizontal partitioning approach. The databases may also have heterogeneous schemas.

Data Type. To-date most data mining research has focused on structured data, as it is the simplest, and most amenable to mining. However, support for other data types is crucial. Examples include unstructured or semi-structured (hyper)text, temporal, spatial and multimedia databases. Mining these is fraught with challenges, but is necessary as multimedia content and digital libraries proliferate at astounding rates. Techniques from parallel and distributed computing will lie at the heart of any proposed scalable solutions.

Data Skew. One of the problems adversely affecting load balancing in parallel mining algorithms is sensitivity to data skew. Most methods partition the database horizontally in equal-sized blocks. However, the number of patterns generated from each block can be heavily skewed, i.e., while one block may contribute many, the other may have very few patterns, implying that the processor responsible for the latter block will be idle most of the time. Randomizing the blocks is one solution, but it is still not adequate, given the dynamic and interactive nature of mining. The effect of skewness on different algorithms needs to be further studied (see [72] for some recent work).

Dynamic Load Balancing. Most extant algorithms use only a static partitioning scheme based on the initial data decomposition, and they assume a homogeneous, dedicated environment. This is far from reality. A typical parallel database server has multiple users, and has transient loads. This calls for an investigation of dynamic load balancing schemes. Dynamic load balancing is also crucial in a heterogeneous environment, which can be composed of meta- and super-clusters, with machines ranging from ordinary workstations to supercomputers.

Incremental Methods. Everyday new data is being collected, and existing data stores are being updated with the new data or purged of the old one. To-date there have been no parallel or distributed algorithms that are incremental in nature, which can handle updates and deletions without having to recompute patterns or rules over the entire database.

Multi-table Mining, Data Layout, and Indexing Schemes. Almost no work has been done on mining over multiple tables or over distributed databases which have different schemas. Data in a warehouse is typically arranged in a star schema, with a central fact table (e.g., point-of-sales data), and associated dimension tables (e.g., product information, manufacturer, etc.). Traditional mining over these multiple tables would first require us to create a large single table that is the join of all the tables. The joined table also has tremendous amounts of redundancy. We need better methods for processing such multiple tables, without having to materialize a single large view. Also, little work has been done on the optimal or near-optimal data layout or indexing schemes for fast data access for mining.

Parallel DBMS/File Systems. To-date most results reported have hand-partitioned the database, mainly horizontally, on different processors. There has been very little study conducted in using a parallel database/file system for managing the partitioned database, and the accompanying striping, and layout issues. Recently there has been increasing emphasis on tight database integration of mining [73,74,75,76], but it has mainly been confined to sequential approaches. Some exceptions include Data Surveyor [77], a mining tool that uses the Monet database server for parallel classification rule induction. Also, generic set-oriented primitive operations were proposed in [78] for classification and clustering. These primitives were fully integrated with a parallel DBMS.

Interaction, Pattern Management, and Meta-level Mining. The KDD process is highly interactive, as the human participates in almost all the steps. For example, the user is heavily involved in the initial data understanding, selection, cleaning, and transformation phases. These steps in fact consume more time than mining *per se*. Moreover, depending on the parameters of the search, mining methods may generate too many patterns to be analyzed directly. One needs methods to allow meta-level queries [79,80,81] on the results, to impose constraints that focus on patterns of interest [82,83], to refine or generalize rules [84,85], etc. Thus there is a need for a complete set of tools that query and mine the pattern/model database as well. Parallel methods can be successful in providing the desired rapid response in all of the above steps.

4   Book Organization

This book contains chapters covering all the major tasks in data mining including parallel and distributed mining frameworks, associations, sequences, clustering and classification. We provide a brief synopsis of each chapter below, organized under four main headings.

4.1   Mining Frameworks

Graham Williams et al. present Data Miner's Arcade, a java-based platform-independent system for integrating multiple analysis and mining tools, using a common API, and providing seamless data access across multiple systems. Components of the DM Arcade include parallel algorithms (e.g., BMARS - multiple adaptive regression B-splines), virtual environments for data visualization, and data management for mining.

Bailey et al. describe the implementation of Osiris, a data server for wide-area distributed data mining, built upon clusters, meta-clusters (with commodity network like Internet) and super-clusters (with high-speed network). Osiris addresses three key issues: What data layout should be used on the server? What tradeoffs are there in moving data or predictive models between nodes? How data should be moved to minimize latency; what protocols should be used? Experiments were performed on a wide-area system linking Chicago and Washington via the NSF/MCI vBNS network.

Parthasarathy et al. present InterAct, an active mining framework for distributed mining. Active mining refers to methods that maintain valid mined patterns or models in the presence of user interaction and database updates. The framework uses mining summary structures that are maintained across updates or changes in user specifications. InterAct also allows effective client-server data and computation sharing. Active mining results were presented on a number of methods like discretization, associations, sequences, and similarity search.

4.2   Association Rules and Sequences

Joshi et al. open this section with a survey chapter on parallel mining of association rules and sequences. They discuss the many extant parallel solutions, and give an account of the challenges and issues for effective formulations of discovering frequent itemsets and sequences.

Morishita and Nakaya describe a novel parallel algorithm for mining correlated association rules. They mine rules based on the chi-squared metric that optimizes the statistical significance or correlation between the rule antecedent and consequent. A parallel branch-and-bound algorithm was proposed that uses a term rewriting technique to avoid explicitly maintaining lists of open and closed nodes on each processor. Experiments on SMP platforms (with up to 128 processors) show very good speedups.

Shintani and Kitsuregawa propose new load balancing strategies for generalized association rule mining using a gigabyte-sized database on a cluster of 100 PCs connected with an ATM network. In generalized associations the items are at the leaf levels in a hierarchy or taxonomy of items, and the goal is to discover rules involving concepts at multiple (and mixed) levels. They show that load balancing is crucial for performance on such large-scale clusters.

Zaki presents pSPADE, a parallel algorithm for sequence mining. pSPADE divides the pattern search space into disjoint, independent sub-problems based on suffix-classes, each of which can be solved in parallel in an asynchronous manner. Task parallelism and dynamic inter- and intra-class load balancing is used for good performance. Results on a 12 processor SMP using up to a 1 GB dataset show good speedup and scaleup.

4.3   Classification

Skillicorn presents parallel techniques for generating predictors for classification and regression models. A recent trend in learning is to build multiple prediction models on different samples from the training set, and combine them, allowing faster induction and lower error rates. This framework is highly amenable to parallelism and forms the focus of this paper.

Goil and Choudhary implemented a parallel decision tree classifier using the aggregates computed in multidimensional analysis or OLAP. They compute aggregates/counts per class along various dimensions, which can then be used for computing the attribute split-points. Communication is minimized by coalescing messages and is done once per tree level. Experiments on a 16 node IBM SP2 were presented.

Hall et al. describe distributed rule induction for learning a single model from disjoint datasets. They first learn local rules from a single site; these are merged to form a global rule set. They show that while this approach promises fast induction, accuracy tapers off (as compared to directly mining the whole database) as the number of sites increases. They suggested some heuristics to minimize this loss in accuracy.

4.4   Clustering

Johnson and Kargupta present the Collective Hierarchical Clustering algorithm for clustering over distributed, heterogeneous databases. Rather than gathering the data at a central site, they generate local cluster models, which are subsequently combined to obtain the global clustering.

Dhillon and Modha parallelized the K-means clustering algorithm on a 16 node IBM SP2 distributed-memory system. They exploit the inherent data parallelism of the K-means algorithm, by performing the point-to-centroid distance calculations in parallel. They demonstrated linear speedup on a 2GB dataset.

5   Conclusion

We conclude by observing that the need for large-scale data mining algorithms and systems is real and immediate. Parallel and distributed computing is essential for providing scalable, incremental and interactive mining solutions. The field is in its infancy, and offers many interesting research directions to pursue. We hope that this volume, representing the state-of-the-art in parallel and distributed mining methods, will be successful in bringing to surface the requirement and challenges in large-scale parallel KDD systems.

References

1. Fayyad, U., Piatetsky-Shapiro, G., Smyth, P.: From data mining to knowledge discovery: An overview. [86]
2. Fayyad, U., Piatetsky-Shapiro, G., Smyth, P.: The KDD process for extracting useful knowledge from volumes of data. Communications of the ACM **39** (1996)
3. Simoudis, E.: Reality check for data mining. IEEE Expert: Intelligent Systems and Their Applications **11** (1996) 26–33
4. DeWitt, D., Gray, J.: Parallel database systems: The future of high-performance database systems. Communications of the ACM **35** (1992) 85–98
5. Valduriez, P.: Parallel database systems: Open problems and new issues. Distributed and Parallel Databases **1** (1993) 137–165
6. Agrawal, R., Mannila, H., Srikant, R., Toivonen, H., Verkamo, A.I.: Fast discovery of association rules. In Fayyad, U., et al, eds.: Advances in Knowledge Discovery and Data Mining, AAAI Press, Menlo Park, CA (1996) 307–328
7. Park, J.S., Chen, M., Yu, P.S.: An effective hash based algorithm for mining association rules. In: ACM SIGMOD Intl. Conf. Management of Data. (1995)
8. Savasere, A., Omiecinski, E., Navathe, S.: An efficient algorithm for mining association rules in large databases. In: 21st VLDB Conf. (1995)
9. Brin, S., Motwani, R., Ullman, J., Tsur, S.: Dynamic itemset counting and implication rules for market basket data. In: ACM SIGMOD Conf. Management of Data. (1997)
10. Zaki, M.J., Parthasarathy, S., Ogihara, M., Li, W.: New algorithms for fast discovery of association rules. In: 3rd Intl. Conf. on Knowledge Discovery and Data Mining. (1997)

11. Mueller, A.: Fast sequential and parallel algorithms for association rule mining: A comparison. Technical Report CS-TR-3515, University of Maryland, College Park (1995)

12. Park, J.S., Chen, M., Yu, P.S.: Efficient parallel data mining for association rules. In: ACM Intl. Conf. Information and Knowledge Management. (1995)

13. Agrawal, R., Shafer, J.: Parallel mining of association rules. IEEE Trans. on Knowledge and Data Engg. **8** (1996) 962–969

14. Cheung, D., Han, J., Ng, V., Fu, A., Fu, Y.: A fast distributed algorithm for mining association rules. In: 4th Intl. Conf. Parallel and Distributed Info. Systems. (1996)

15. Shintani, T., Kitsuregawa, M.: Hash based parallel algorithms for mining association rules. In: 4th Intl. Conf. Parallel and Distributed Info. Systems. (1996)

16. Zaki, M.J., Ogihara, M., Parthasarathy, S., Li, W.: Parallel data mining for association rules on shared-memory multi-processors. In: Supercomputing'96. (1996)

17. Cheung, D., Hu, K., Xia, S.: Asynchronous parallel algorithm for mining association rules on shared-memory multi-processors. In: 10th ACM Symp. Parallel Algorithms and Architectures. (1998)

18. Han, E.H., Karypis, G., Kumar, V.: Scalable parallel data mining for association rules. In: ACM SIGMOD Conf. Management of Data. (1997)

19. Zaki, M.J., Parthasarathy, S., Ogihara, M., Li, W.: Parallel algorithms for fast discovery of association rules. Data Mining and Knowledge Discovery: An International Journal **1(4):343-373** (1997)

20. Tamura, M., Kitsuregawa, M.: Dynamic load balancing for parallel association rule mining on heterogeneous PC cluster systems. In: 25th Intl Conf. on Very Large Data Bases. (1999)

21. Zaki, M.J.: Parallel and distributed association mining: A survey. IEEE Concurrency **7** (1999) 14–25

22. Agrawal, R., Srikant, R.: Mining sequential patterns. In: 11th Intl. Conf. on Data Engg. (1995)

23. Srikant, R., Agrawal, R.: Mining sequential patterns: Generalizations and performance improvements. In: 5th Intl. Conf. Extending Database Technology. (1996)

24. Oates, T., Schmill, M.D., Jensen, D., Cohen, P.R.: A family of algorithms for finding temporal structure in data. In: 6th Intl. Workshop on AI and Statistics. (1997)

25. Zaki, M.J.: Efficient enumeration of frequent sequences. In: 7th Intl. Conf. on Information and Knowledge Management. (1998)

26. Shintani, T., Kitsuregawa, M.: Mining algorithms for sequential patterns in parallel: Hash based approach. In: 2nd Pacific-Asia Conf. on Knowledge Discovery and Data Mining. (1998)

27. Oates, T., Schmill, M.D., Cohen, P.R.: Parallel and distributed search for structure in multivariate time series. In: 9th European Conference on Machine Learning. (1997)

28. Weiss, S.M., Kulikowski, C.A.: Computer Systems that Learn: Classification and Prediction Methods from Statistics, Neural Nets, Machine Learning, and Expert Systems. Morgan Kaufman (1991)

29. Michie, D., Spiegelhalter, D.J., Taylor, C.C.: Machine Learning, Neural and Statistical Classification. Ellis Horwood (1994)

30. Lippmann, R.: An introduction to computing with neural nets. IEEE ASSP Magazine **4** (1987)

31. Goldberg, D.E.: Genetic Algorithms in Search, Optimization and Machine Learning. Morgan Kaufmann (1989)

32. Breiman, L., Friedman, J.H., Olshen, R.A., Stone, C.J.: Classification and Regression Trees. Wadsworth, Belmont (1984)
33. Quinlan, J.R.: C4.5: Programs for Machine Learning. Morgan Kaufman (1993)
34. Provost, F., Aronis, J.: Scaling up inductive learning with massive parallelism. Machine Learning **23** (1996)
35. Provost, F., Kolluri, V.: A survey of methods for scaling up inductive algorithms. Data Mining and Knowledge Discovery: An International Journal **3** (1999) 131–169
36. Mehta, M., Agrawal, R., Rissanen, J.: SLIQ: A fast scalable classifier for data mining. In: Proc. of the Fifth Intl Conference on Extending Database Technology (EDBT), Avignon, France (1996)
37. Shafer, J., Agrawal, R., Mehta, M.: Sprint: A scalable parallel classifier for data mining. In: 22nd VLDB Conference. (1996)
38. Joshi, M., Karypis, G., Kumar, V.: ScalParC: A scalable and parallel classification algorithm for mining large datasets. In: Intl. Parallel Processing Symposium. (1998)
39. Chattratichat, J., Darlington, J., Ghanem, M., Guo, Y., Huning, H., Kohler, M., Sutiwaraphun, J., To, H.W., Dan, Y.: Large scale data mining: Challenges and responses. In: 3rd Intl. Conf. on Knowledge Discovery and Data Mining. (1997)
40. Kufrin, R.: Decision trees on parallel processors. In Geller, J., Kitano, H., Suttner, C., eds.: Parallel Processing for Artificial Intelligence 3, Elsevier-Science (1997)
41. Zaki, M.J., Ho, C.T., Agrawal, R.: Parallel classification for data mining on shared-memory multiprocessors. In: 15th IEEE Intl. Conf. on Data Engineering. (1999)
42. Srivastava, A., Han, E.H., Kumar, V., Singh, V.: Parallel formulations of decision-tree classification algorithms. Data Mining and Knowledge Discovery: An International Journal **3** (1999) 237–261
43. Sreenivas, M., Alsabti, K., Ranka, S.: Parallel out-of-core divide and conquer techniques with application to classification trees. In: 13th International Parallel Processing Symposium. (1999)
44. Alsabti, K., Ranka, S., Singh, V.: Clouds: A decision tree classifier for large datasets. In: 4th Intl Conference on Knowledge Discovery and Data Mining. (1998)
45. Jain, A.K., Dubes, R.C.: Algorithms for Clustering Data. Prentice Hall (1988)
46. Cheeseman, P., Kelly, J., Self, M., et al.: AutoClass: A Bayesian classification system. In: 5th Intl Conference on Machine Learning, Morgan Kaufman (1988)
47. Fisher, D.H.: Knowledge acquisition via incremental conceptual clustering. Machine Learning **2** (1987)
48. Michalski, R.S., Stepp, R.E.: Learning from observation: Conceptual clustering. In Michalski, R.S., Carbonell, J.G., Mitchell, T.M., eds.: Machine Learning: An Artificial Intelligence Approach. Volume I. Morgan Kaufmann (1983) 331–363
49. Li, X., Fang, Z.: Parallel clustering algorithms. Parallel Computing **11** (1989) 270–290
50. Rivera, F., Ismail, M., Zapata, E.: Parallel squared error clustering on hypercube arrays. Journal of Parallel and Distributed Computing **8** (1990) 292–299
51. Ranka, S., Sahni, S.: Clustering on a hypercube multicomputer. IEEE Trans. on Parallel and Distributed Systems **2(2)** (1991) 129–137
52. Rudolph, G.: Parallel clustering on a unidirectional ring. In et al., R.G., ed.: Transputer Applications and Systems '93: Volume 1. IOS Press, Amsterdam (1993) 487–493
53. Olson, C.: Parallel algorithms for hierarchical clustering. Parallel Computing **21** (1995) 1313–1325
54. Judd, D., McKinley, P., Jain, A.: Large-scale parallel data clustering. In: Intl Conf. Pattern Recognition. (1996)

55. S. Goil, H.N., Choudhary, A.: MAFIA: Efficient and scalable subspace clustering for very large data sets. Technical Report 9906-010, Center for Parallel and Distributed Computing, Northwestern University (1999)
56. Stolfo, S., Prodromidis, A., Tselepis, S., Lee, W., Fan, W., Chan, P.: Jam: Java agents for meta-learning over distributed databases. In: 3rd Intl. Conf. on Knowledge Discovery and Data Mining. (1997)
57. Prodromidis, A., Stolfo, S., Chan, P.: Meta-learning in distributed data mining systems: Issues and approaches. [67]
58. Guo, Y., Sutiwaraphun, J.: Knowledge probing in distributed data mining. In: 3rd Pacific-Asia Conference on Knowledge Discovery and Data Mining. (1999)
59. Kargupta, H., Hamzaoglu, I., Stafford, B.: Scalable, distributed data mining using an agent based architecture. In: 3rd Intl. Conf. on Knowledge Discovery and Data Mining. (1997)
60. Kargupta, H., Park, B.H., Hershberger, D., Johnson, E.: Collective data mining: A new perspective toward distributed data mining. [67]
61. Parthasarathy, S., Subramonian, R.: Facilitating data mining on a network of workstations. [67]
62. Grossman, R.L., Bailey, S.M., Sivakumar, H., Turinsky, A.L.: Papyrus: A system for data mining over local and wide area clusters and super-clusters. In: Supercomputing'99. (1999)
63. Chattratichat, J., Darlington, J., Guo, Y., Hedvall, S., Kohler, M., Syed, J.: An architecture for distributed enterprise data mining. In: 7th Intl. Conf. High-Performance Computing and Networking. (1999)
64. Bhatnagar, R., Srinivasan, S.: Pattern discovery in distributed databases. In: AAAI National Conference on Artificial Intelligence. (1997)
65. Aronis, J., Kolluri, V., Provost, F., Buchanan, B.: The WoRLD: Knowledge discovery from multiple distributed databases. In: Florida Artificial Intelligence Research Symposium. (1997)
66. Freitas, A., Lavington, S.: Mining very large databases with parallel processing. Kluwer Academic Pub., Boston, MA (1998)
67. Kargupta, H., Chan, P., eds.: Advances in Distributed Data Mining. AAAI Press, Menlo Park, CA (2000)
68. Skillicorn, D.: Strategies for parallel data mining. IEEE Concurrency 7 (1999) 26–35
69. Toivonen, H.: Sampling large databases for association rules. In: 22nd VLDB Conf. (1996)
70. Zaki, M.J., Parthasarathy, S., Li, W., Ogihara, M.: Evaluation of sampling for data mining of association rules. In: 7th Intl. Wkshp. Research Issues in Data Engg. (1997)
71. Shafer, J., Agrawal, R., Mehta, M.: SPRINT: A scalable parallel classifier for data mining. In: Proc. of the 22nd Intl Conference on Very Large Databases, Bombay, India (1996)
72. Cheung, D., Xiao, Y.: Effect of data distribution in parallel mining of associations. Data Mining and Knowledge Discovery: An International Journal 3 (1999) 291–314
73. Agrawal, R., Shim, K.: Developing tightly-coupled data mining applications on a relational database system. In: 2nd Intl. Conf. on Knowledge Discovery in Databases and Data Mining. (1996)
74. Meo, R., Psaila, G., Ceri, S.: A new SQL-like operator for mining association rules. In: 22nd Intl. Conf. Very Large Databases. (1996)
75. Meo, R., Psaila, G., Ceri, S.: A tightly-coupled architecture for data mining. In: Intl. Conf. on Data Engineering. (1998)

76. Sarawagi, S., Thomas, S., Agrawal, R.: Integrating association rule mining with databases: alternatives and implications. In: ACM SIGMOD Intl. Conf. Management of Data. (1998)
77. Holsheimer, M., Kersten, M.L., Siebes, A.: Data surveyor: Searching the nuggets in parallel. [86]
78. Lavington, S., Dewhurst, N., Wilkins, E., Freitas, A.: Interfacing knowledge discovery algorithms to large databases management systems. Information and Software Technology **41** (1999) 605–617
79. Kamber, M., Han, J., Chiang, J.Y.: Metarule-guided mining of multi-dimensional association rules using data cubes. In: 3rd Intl. Conf. on Knowledge Discovery and Data Mining. (1997)
80. Klemettinen, M., Mannila, H., Ronkainen, P., Toivonen, H., Verkamo, A.I.: Finding interesting rules from large sets of discovered association rules. In: 3rd Intl. Conf. Information and Knowledge Management. (1994) 401–407
81. Shen, W.M., Ong, K.L., Mitbander, B., Zaniolo, C.: Metaqueries for data mining. [86]
82. Ng, R.T., Lakshmanan, L., Jan, J., Pang, A.: Exploratory mining and pruning optimizations of constrained association rules. In: ACM SIGMOD Intl. Conf. Management of Data. (1998)
83. Srikant, R., Vu, Q., Agrawal, R.: Mining Association Rules with Item Constraints. In: 3rd Intl. Conf. on Knowledge Discovery and Data Mining. (1997)
84. Matheus, C., Piatetsky-Shapiro, G., McNeill, D.: Selecting and reporting what is interesting. In Fayyad, U.M., Piatetsky-Shapiro, G., Smyth, P., Uthurusamy, R., eds.: Advances in Knowledge Discovery and Data Mining. AAAI/MIT Press (1996)
85. Toivonen, H., Klemettinen, M., Ronkainen, P., Hätönen, K., Mannila, H.: Pruning and grouping discovered association rules. In: MLnet Wkshp. on Statistics, Machine Learning, and Discovery in Databases. (1995)
86. Fayyad, U., Piatetsky-Shapiro, G., Smyth, P., Uthurusamy, R., eds.: Advances in Knowledge Discovery and Data Mining. AAAI Press, Menlo Park, CA (1996)

The Integrated Delivery of
Large-Scale Data Mining:
The ACSys Data Mining Project

Graham Williams[1], Irfan Altas[2], Sergey Bakin[3], Peter Christen[4],
Markus Hegland[4], Alonso Marquez[5], Peter Milne[1],
Rajehndra Nagappan[5], and Stephen Roberts[4]

[1] Cooperative Research Centre for Advanced Computational Systems
CSIRO Mathematical and Information Sciences
GPO Box 664, Canberra, ACT 2601, Australia
First.Last@cmis.csiro.au
http://www.cmis.csiro.au/ALCD
[2] School of Information Studies, Charles Sturt University
Wagga Wagga, NSW 2678, Australia
ialtas@csu.edu.au
[3] Department of Mathematics, The University of Queensland
Brisbane, Qld 4072, Australia
sergey@maths.uq.edu.au
[4] Computer Sciences Laboratory, Australian National University
Canberra, ACT 0200, Australia
First.Last@anu.edu.au
[5] Department of Computer Science, Australian National University
Canberra, ACT 0200, Australia
First.Last@anu.edu.au

Abstract. Data Mining draws on many technologies to deliver novel
and actionable discoveries from very large collections of data. The Australian Government's Cooperative Research Centre for Advanced Computational Systems (ACSys) is a link between industry and research focusing on the deployment of high performance computers for data mining. We present an overview of the work of the ACSys Data Mining
projects where the use of large-scale, high performance computers plays
a key role. We highlight the use of large-scale computing within three
complimentary areas: the development of parallel algorithms for data
analysis, the deployment of virtual environments for data mining, and
issues in data management for data mining. We also introduce the Data
Miner's Arcade which provides simple abstractions to integrate these
components providing high performance data access for a variety of data
mining tools communicating through XML.

1   Introduction

High performance computers and parallel algorithms provide the necessary platform for the delivery of novel and actionable discoveries from extremely large

M.J. Zaki, C.-T. Ho (Eds.): Large-Scale Parallel Data Mining, LNAI 1759, pp. 24–54, 2002.

collections of data. The Australian Government's Cooperative Research Centre for Advanced Computational Systems (ACSys) investigates industrial problems to direct research on the deployment of high performance computers for data mining. The multidisciplinary ACSys team draws together researchers in Statistics, Machine Learning, and Numerical Algorithms from The Australian National University and the Australian Government's research organisation CSIRO Australia. Commercial projects are drawn from the banking, insurance, and health sectors.

There are many components that contribute to the successful deployment of data mining solutions. Parallel algorithms exploit the processing capabilities of multi-processor environments to deliver models in a timely fashion. Visualisation and Virtual Environments provide useful insights into relationships in the data. And underlying all of these activities is the data itself, and in particular, the mechanisms for accessing the data. Finally, we need to provide a standard, integrated environment that can be easily tuned for particular applications, and that can facilitate the communication of data mining outcomes. In this paper we describe these components as have and are being developed collaboratively by ANU and CSIRO researchers through ACSys in partnership with Australian Industry.

We begin with a review of two algorithms developed for data mining: TPS-FEM and BMARS. Predictive model building is a core component of data mining—whether it is modelling response to marketing campaigns, modelling patterns of health care, or modelling fraudulent behaviours. Gigabytes of data collected over decades are available. And yet, it is often groups that occur infrequently that are important to our business (whether it is identifying the 5% who will respond to a mail campaign, or the less than 1% who will commit insurance fraud). Sampling is generally not an appropriate action, but instead we wish to analyse all of the data.

Given the large amount of data as well as the large number of attributes involved in data mining problems, two core challenges need to be faced. The first concerns the computational feasibility of the techniques used to build the predictive models used in data mining. This translates into the requirement that data mining techniques scale to large data sets. The second challenge is the interpretability of the resulting models. Specifically, one often has not only to be able to build a predictive model but also to obtain insight from the structure exhibited by the model. Distributing and sharing models, and combining models built from different runs over possibly different data, can benefit from addressing the interpretability question.

Exploring very large datasets with high dimensionality requires considerable support to provide the Data Miner with insights that aid in their understanding of the data. Virtual environments (VEs) for data mining are being explored towards a number of ends. The high dimensionality of the data often presented to the Data Miner leads to considerable complexity in coming to understand the interplay of the many features. Exploring this interplay more effectively can assist in the identification and selection of important features to be used for later predictive modelling and other data mining tasks. Also, as model builders are applied to ever larger datasets, the complexity of the resulting models increases correspondingly. Virtual environments can also effectively provide insights into the modelling process, and the resulting models themselves.

All aspects of data mining revolve around the data. Data is stored in a variety of formats and within a variety of database systems. Data needs to be accessed in a timely manner and potentially multiple times. Managing, transforming, and efficiently accessing the data is a crucial issue. The Semantic Extension Framework provides an environment for seamlessly extending the semantics of Java objects, allowing those objects to be instantiated in different ways and from different sources. We are beginning to explore the benefits of such a framework for ongoing data mining activities. The potential of this approach lies in all stages of the data mining process [1], from data management and data versioning, through to access mechanisms highly tuned to suit the behaviour of access of the particular predictive modelling tool being employed.

Finally, we need to bring these tools together to deliver highly configurable, and often pre-packaged or 'canned' solutions for particular applications. The Data Miner's Arcade provides simple abstractions to integrate these components providing high performance data access for a variety of data mining tools communicating through standard interfaces, and building on the developing XML standards for data mining [2].

2   Parallel Algorithms

Careful, detailed examination of each and every customer, patient, or claimant that exists in a very large dataset made available for data mining might well lead to a better understanding of the data and of underlying processes. Given the sheer size of data we are talking about in data mining, this is, of course not generally feasible, and probably not desirable. Yet, with the desire to analyse *all* the data, rather than statistical samples of the data, a data mining exercise is often required to apply computationally complex analysis tools to extremely large datasets.

Often, we characterise the task as being one of building an indicator function as a predictor of fraud, of propensity to purchase, or of improved health outcomes. We can view the function as

$$y = f(x)$$

where y is the real valued response, indicating the likelihood of the outcome, and x is the array of predictor variables (attributes or features) which encode the information thought to be relevant to the outcome. The function f can be trained on the collected data by, for example, (logistic) regression. We have been developing new computational techniques to identify such predictive models from large data sets.

Applications for such model building abound. Another example is in insurance where a significant problem is to determine optimal premium levels. When a new insurance policy is being underwritten it is important for an insurance company to estimate the risk (based on the information provided by the policy holder) or the likelihood of a claim being made against the policy. With this knowledge the insurance companies would be able to set the 'correct' premium levels and avoid undercharging as well as overcharging their customers (although competitive factors must also come into play). To estimate the risk one has to produce two models: one to predict if a policy holder is likely to make a claim; and one to predict the amount of the claim.

Algorithms commonly used in such data mining projects include generalised additive models [3], thin plate splines [4], decision tree and rule induction [5], multivariate adaptive regression splines [6], patient rule induction methods [7], evolutionary rule induction [8] and the combination of simple rules [9]. For data mining, the issue of scalability must be addressed. We illustrate this with two developments in parallel algorithms: thin plate spline finite element methods; and Multivariate Adaptive Regression Splines using B-splines.

3   Predictive Modelling with Thin Plate Splines

A first computational challenge faced in generating a predictive model originates from the large number of attributes or predictor variables. This challenge is often referred to as the *curse of dimensionality* [10]. An effective way to deal with this curse is provided by additive models of the form [11]

$$f(x) = f_0 + \sum_{i=1}^{d} f_i(x_i).$$

Similar models are used in ANOVA, where all the variables x_i are categorical. The effects of the predictor variables are added up. Thus, the effect of the value of a variable x_i is independent of the effect of a different variable x_j. We have suggested and discussed a new scalable and parallel algorithm for the determination of a (generalised) additive model in [3].

A better model includes interactions between the variables. For example, it could be the case that for different incomes the effect of the level of deductions from taxable income on the likelihood of fraud varies. Interaction models are of the form:

$$f(x) = f_0 + \sum_{i=1}^{d} f_i(x_i) + \sum_{i,j=1}^{d} f_{i,j}(x_i, x_j).$$

This model is made identifiable by additional constraints and the components f_i and $f_{i,j}$ are determined by the *backfitting algorithm* [11] which consists of repeated estimation of the components. Thus only methods for the estimation of one- and two-dimensional models are required.

The form of the models depends on the type of predictor variables. In the following we will only discuss the case of real predictor variables. In order not to exclude important functions we choose a nonparametric approach and find predictors f which are smooth and fit the data. thin plate splines [12] are an established smooth model. They are designed to have small curvature. The one-dimensional components $f_i(x_i)$ turn out to be cubic splines which are computationally very tractable using a B-spline basis. The form of the interaction terms is also known:

$$f_{x_i,x_j}(x_i,x_j) = c_0 + c_1 x_i + c_2 x_j + \sum_{k=1}^{n} b_k \, \phi\left((x_i - x_i^{(k)})^2 + (x_j - x_j^{(k)})^2\right)$$

where $\phi(r^2) = r^2 \log(r^2)$ [12]. The coefficients of the thin plate splines are determined by the linear system of the form

$$\begin{bmatrix} \Phi + \alpha I & X \\ X^T & 0 \end{bmatrix} \begin{bmatrix} b \\ c \end{bmatrix} = \begin{bmatrix} y \\ 0 \end{bmatrix}$$

where Φ is an n by n matrix with matrix elements $\Phi_{i,j} = \phi(\|x^{(j)} - x^{(i)}\|^2)$, I is the identity, X a n by 3 matrix, where the i-th row is $\left[1, \, x_1^{(i)}, \, x_2^{(i)}\right]$, b is the vector with k-th component b_k and $c = (c_0, c_1, c_2)^T$. Computationally, these equations are intractable for large data sizes n by standard direct or iterative methods, as even the formation of the matrix Φ requires $O(n^2)$ operations since it is dense. The standard techniques thus give examples of algorithms which are *not scalable* with respect to the data size. Only a few years ago it was thought that the feasibility of thin plate splines (and similar radial-basis function approaches) was limited to the case of a few hundred to thousand observations. However, new techniques have been developed since then to push these limits. One school of thought uses the locality of the problem, i.e., the fact that the value $f(x)$ only depends on observations $x^{(k)}$ which are near x [13,14]. The algorithms developed are mainly for interpolation, i.e., the case $\alpha = 0$.

We have developed a different approach which is provably scalable and may be extended to higher order interactions. We use the fact that the thin plate spline interpolant minimises the functional

$$J_1(f) = \sum_{k=1}^{n} (f(x^{(k)}) - y^{(k)})^2$$

$$+ \alpha \int \left(\left(\frac{\partial^2 f}{\partial x_1^2}\right)^2 + 2 \left(\frac{\partial^2 f}{\partial x_1 \partial x_2}\right)^2 + \left(\frac{\partial^2 f}{\partial x_2^2}\right)^2 \right) dx_1 dx_2. \tag{1}$$

The minimiser of this functional can be approximated in a finite-element space. For the solution of this problem we suggest a non-conforming method based on piecewise bilinear functions such that on the rectangular elements the function is of the form $a + b x_1 + c x_2 + d x_1 x_2$. The method finds an approximation $u = (u_1, u_2)$ of the gradient of f as a piecewise bilinear function. Instead of J_1, the following function is minimised (obtained by inserting the gradient in J_1):

$$J_2(f) = \sum_{k=1}^{n} (f(x^{(k)}) - y^{(k)})^2$$

$$+ \alpha \int \left(\left(\frac{\partial u_1}{\partial x_1} \right)^2 + \left(\frac{\partial u_1}{\partial x_2} \right)^2 + \left(\frac{\partial u_2}{\partial x_1} \right)^2 + \left(\frac{\partial u_2}{\partial x_2} \right)^2 \right) dx_1 dx_2. \tag{2}$$

It can be seen that if one chooses u with $\operatorname{curl} u = 0$ such that

$$\Delta f(x) = \operatorname{div} u(x), \quad x \in G$$

and

$$\frac{\partial f}{\partial n}(x) = u_n(x), \quad x \in \partial G$$

then the same solution as above is obtained. However, practical tests show that the curl condition is not important in achieving a good approximation [4].

The finite element solution of the optimisation problem proceeds in two stages:

1. The matrix and right-hand side of the linear system of equations is assembled. The matrix of this linear system is the sum of low rank matrices, one for each data point $x^{(i)}$.
2. The linear system of equations is solved.

The time for the first (assembly) stage depends linearly on the data size n and the time for the second (solution) stage is independent of n. Thus the overall algorithm scales with the number of data points. The data points only need to be visited once, thus there is no need to either store the entire data set in memory nor revisit the data points several times. The basis functions are piecewise bilinear and require a small number of operations for their evaluation. With this technique the smoothing of millions of data points becomes feasible.

The parallel algorithm exploits different aspects of the problem for the assembly and the solution stage. The time required for the assembly stage grows linearly as a function of data size. For simplicity we assume that the data is initially equally distributed between the local disks of the processors. (If this is not the case initial distribution costs would have to be included in the analysis.) In a first step of the assembly stage a local matrix is assembled for each processor based on the data available on its local disk. The matrix of the full problem is then the sum of the local matrices and can thus be obtained through a reduction step. This algorithm was developed and tested on a cluster of 10 Sun Sparc-5 workstations networked with a 10 Mbit/s twisted pair Ethernet using MPI [15]. The total time spent in this assembly phase is of the order

$$T_p = O(n/p) + O(m \log_2(p))$$

where m characterises the size of the assembled matrix. Thus, if the number n of the data points grows like $O(p \log_2(p))$ for fixed matrix size m the parallel efficiency is

$$E_p = \frac{T_1}{pT_p} = O\left(\frac{n}{n + mp\log_2(p)}\right) = O(1)$$

and thus there is no drop in parallel efficiency for larger numbers of processors. This basic trend is confirmed by practical experiments [15].

In the solution stage the spatial parallelism of the problem is exploited. Assume for simplicity that the domain is rectangular. If the domain was split into strips of equal size the values on the boundaries between the strips depends on the data in the neighbouring strips. However, as this dependency is local, only a fixed number of points in the neighbouring strip really have an influence on the function values $f(x)$ in the strip. A good approximation is obtained for the values on the strip by solving the smoothing problem for an expanded region containing the original strip and a sufficient number of neighbouring points. Note that by introducing redundant computations in this way, communication can be avoided. The size of the original strip is proportional to m/p and, in order to add the extra k neighbouring points, it has to be expanded by a factor kp/n. Thus the size of the expanded strip is of the order of

$$s = (m/p)(1 + kp/n).$$

As we assumed $n = O(p\log_2(p))$ to get isoefficiency [16] of the assembly phase the size of the strips is proportional to m/p asymptotically in p which shows isoefficiency for the solution stage.

This approach thus ensures a fast and efficient path to the development of predictive models.

4   Predictive Modelling with Multivariate Regression Splines

The popular Multivariate Adaptive Regression Splines (MARS) algorithm by Friedman [6] is able to produce continuous as well as easily interpretable regression models. The regression models are the special class of predictive models intended to model numeric response variables as opposed to the generalised regression models used in situations where the response is discrete. Here we give an overview of the original MARS algorithm followed by a discussion of its parallel version based on B-splines (BMARS).

MARS constructs a linear combination of basis functions which are products of one-dimensional basis functions (indicator functions in the case of categorical variables and truncated power functions in the case of numeric variables). The key to the method is that the basis functions are generated recursively and depend on the data. The important implication of the approach is that models produced by MARS involve only variables and their interactions relevant to the problem at hand. This property is especially useful in the data mining context.

BMARS [17] improves upon MARS by: using compactly supported B-spline basis functions; utilising a new scale-by-scale model building strategy; and introducing a parallel implementation. These modifications allow the stable and *fast* (compared to MARS) analysis of very large datasets.

4.1 Multivariate Adaptive Regression Splines

For the sake of simplicity, we confine ourselves to the case of purely numeric data though it should be remembered that the (appropriately modified) algorithm is able to deal with data of mixed type. The required modification will be discussed briefly, below.

In a nutshell, the original MARS is an efficient technique designed to select a (relatively high quality) model from the space of multivariate piecewise linear functions[1]. Any such function can be represented as a linear combination of the tensor product basis functions $T_{k_1...k_d}(\mathbf{x})$:

$$f(\mathbf{x}) = \sum_{k_1=0}^{K_1} \cdots \sum_{k_d=1}^{K_d} a_{k_1...k_d}, T_{k_1...k_d}(\mathbf{x}), \quad T_{k_1...k_d}(\mathbf{x}) = \prod_{j=1}^{d} b_{k_j,j}(x_j) \quad (3)$$

where $b_{0,j}(x_j) = 1$ and $\{b_{k_j,j}(x_j)\}_{k_j=1}^{K_j}$ are univariate piecewise linear basis functions of the variable x_j, $j = 1, ..., d$. The original MARS is based on the univariate truncated power basis functions:

$$b_{k_j,j}(x_j) = [x_j - t_{k_j}]_+, \quad k_j = 1, ..., K_j,$$

where t_{k_j} $k_j = 1, ..., K_j$ are certain prespecified knot locations on the variable x_j taken to be, for example, quantiles of the corresponding marginal distribution of the data points. The coefficients $a_{k_1...k_d}$ can be determined based the least squares fit of the general model (3) to the data at hand.

As can be seen, there are $\prod_{j=1}^{d}(K_j + 1)$ basis functions in the expansion (3). Therefore, the application of this approach would be feasible only in the situation where one has to deal with a moderate number of variables as well as knot locations. Also, it appears difficult to make any conclusion concerning the structure of the regression function (3): all variables as well as a large number of basis functions would generally be involved. These observations lead to the conclusion that the approach is less appropriate in the data mining context.

The MARS algorithm aims to overcome the above problems. It traverses the space of piecewise linear multivariate functions in a stepwise manner and eventually arrives at a function which, on one hand, has much simpler structure compared to the general function (3) and, on the other hand, is an adequate model for the data. The models produced by MARS have the following structure

$$f(\mathbf{x}) = \sum_{m=0}^{J} a_m T_m(\mathbf{x})$$

---

[1] Here a piecewise linear multivariate function is one which is piecewise linear with respect to any of its numeric variables.

where the basis functions $\{T_m(\mathbf{x})\}_{m=0}^{J}$ have the form

$$T_m(\mathbf{x}) = \prod_{j=1}^{d_m} [x_{v(j,m)} - t_{jm}]_+.$$

As can be seen, this model is similar to the general model (3) in that both belong to the same function space. However, the distinct feature of MARS models is that they are normally based on only a very small subset of the complete set of tensor product basis functions. The pseudo-code of the procedure which builds the subset of functions is shown below.

Algorithm 1 MARS algorithm

model $\leftarrow \{T_0(\mathbf{x}) = 1\}$
for $m = 1$ to $J_{\max}$ **do**
  $T_m(\mathbf{x}) \leftarrow 0$
  for $s = 0$ to $m - 1$ **do**
    for $j = 1$ to d **do**
      if x_j involved in $T_s(\mathbf{x})$ **then**
        continue
      else
        for $k_j = 1$ to K_j **do**
          Form $T_m^c(\mathbf{x}) = T_s(\mathbf{x}) b_{k_j,j}(x_j)$
          if $T_m^c(\mathbf{x})$ better than $T_m(\mathbf{x})$ **then**
            $T_m(\mathbf{x}) \leftarrow T_m^c(\mathbf{x})$
          end if
        end for
      end if
    end for
  end for
  model $\leftarrow$ model $\bigcup T_m(\mathbf{x})$
end for

The algorithm starts with the model containing only the constant function. All subsequent functions are produced one at a time. At each step the algorithm enumerates all possible candidate basis functions $T_m^c(\mathbf{x})$ and selects the one whose inclusion in the model results in the largest improvement of the least squares fit of the model to the data. The three nested internal loops (corresponding to the s, j, k_j loop variables) implement this selection process. The selected basis function is added to the model.

The set of candidate basis functions is seen to be comprised of all basis functions which can be derived from the ones contained in the model via multiplication by a univariate basis function. Due to the utilisation of this definition of the set of candidates, the MARS algorithm allows for a considerable reduction in the computational cost compared with another popular technique (forward subset selection procedure [18]). The number of basis functions $J_{\max}$ produced by MARS has to be specified by a user. It turns out that the quality of the model can even further be improved via removal of the less optimal tensor product basis functions from the model. This can be accomplished by means of the backward elimination procedure (see [6] for details).

As mentioned, this approach can be modified to data of mixed types. Univariate indicator functions $I[x \in A]$ can be used instead of the truncated powers whenever a categorical variable x is encountered in the Algorithm (1). Thus, the typical tensor product basis function would have the form:

$$T_m(\mathbf{x}) = \prod_{j=1}^{d_m^{num}} [x_{v(j,m)} - t_{jm}]_+ \prod_{j=1}^{d_m^{cat}} I[x_{v(j,m)} \in A_{jm}].$$

The algorithm for finding the appropriate subsets A_{jm} is very similar to the ordinary forward stepwise regression procedure [18]. The detailed discussion of the algorithm is given in [19].

4.2   Refinement of MARS via B-splines

MARS is thus based on truncated power basis functions which are used to form tensor product basis functions. However, truncated powers are known to have poor numerical properties. In our work we sought to develop a MARS-like algorithm based on B-splines which form a basis with better numerical properties. In our algorithm, called BMARS, we use B-splines of the second order (piecewise linear B-splines) to form tensor product basis functions $\prod_{j=1}^{d} B_{k_j,j}(x_j)$. Thus, the models produced by MARS and BMARS belong to the space of piecewise linear multivariate functions. In common with MARS, BMARS traverses the space of piecewise linear multivariate functions until it arrives at the model which provides an adequate fit. However, the way in which the traversal occurs is somewhat different. Apart from being a more stable basis, B-splines possess a compact support property which allows us to build models in the scale-by-scale way. The pseudo-code (Algorithm 2) illustrates the strategy.

To implement the scale-by-scale strategy, one needs B-splines of different scales. The scale is the size of the support interval of a B-spline. Given a set $\mathcal{K}$ of $K = 2^{l_0} + 1$ knots on a variable x one can construct B-splines of $l_0 + 1$ different scales based on $l_0 + 1$ nested subsets $\mathcal{K}_l$ of $K^l = (K - 1)/2^{l-1} + 1$ knots, $l = 1, ..., l_0 + 1$ respectively. The lth subset is obtained from the full set by retaining each 2^{l-1}st knot and disposing of the rest. Thus, the B-splines constructed using the lth subset of knots have on average twice as long support intervals as the B-splines constructed using the $(l - 1)$st subset.

At the start of the algorithm, the scale parameter l is set to the largest possible value l_0. Subsequently, B-splines of the largest scale only are used to form new tensor product basis functions. Upon the formation of each new tensor product basis function, the algorithm checks if the improvement of the fit due to the inclusion of the new basis function is appreciable. We use the Generalised Cross-Validation score [6] to decide if the inclusion of a new basis function improves the fit. If this is not the case, the algorithm switches over to using B-splines of the second largest scale.

Thus, new tensor product basis functions continue to be generated using B-splines of the second largest scale. Again, as soon as the algorithm detects that the inclusion of new basis functions fails to improve the fit, it switches over to using B-splines of the third largest scale. This procedure is repeated until the $J\text{max}$ number of tensor product basis functions is produced.

Algorithm 2 BMARS algorithm

---

model $\leftarrow \{T_0(\mathbf{x}) = 1\}$
$l \leftarrow l_0$ {set current scale to largest scale}
for $m = 1$ to $J\text{max}$ **do**
$\quad T_m(\mathbf{x}) \leftarrow 0$
$\quad$**for** $s = 0$ to $m - 1$ **do**
$\quad\quad$**for** $j = 1$ to d **do**
$\quad\quad\quad$**if** x_j involved in $T_s(\mathbf{x})$ **then**
$\quad\quad\quad\quad$continue
$\quad\quad\quad$**else**
$\quad\quad\quad\quad$**for** $k_j = 1$ to K_j^l **do**
$\quad\quad\quad\quad\quad$Form $T_m^c(\mathbf{x}) = T_s(\mathbf{x})B_{k_j,j}^l(x_j)$
$\quad\quad\quad\quad\quad$**if** $T_m^c(\mathbf{x})$ better than $T_m(\mathbf{x})$ **then**
$\quad\quad\quad\quad\quad\quad T_m(\mathbf{x}) \leftarrow T_m^c(\mathbf{x})$
$\quad\quad\quad\quad\quad$**end if**
$\quad\quad\quad\quad$**end for**
$\quad\quad\quad$**end if**
$\quad\quad$**end for**
$\quad$**end for**
$\quad$model $\leftarrow$ model $\bigcup T_m(\mathbf{x})$
$\quad$**if** no significant improvement of fit **then**
$\quad\quad l \leftarrow l - 1$ {decrease current scale}
$\quad$**end if**
end for

The advantage of this strategy over that of MARS is that it results in a considerable reduction of the number of candidate basis functions to be tested at each step of the algorithm. This is due to the fact that the number K_j^l of B-splines of a particular scale l is less than the total number of knots K_j: $K_j/K_j^l = 2^{l-1}$. This ratio is seen to be greater than one for all scales but the smallest ($l = 1$) one. This results in a fewer number of iterations carried out by the inner-most loop of Algorithm 2 compared to the similar loop of Algorithm 1. The results of experiments suggest that this reduction in the computational complexity comes at no cost in terms of the quality of the resulting models [20].

4.3   Parallel Implementation of BMARS

It can be shown that the computational complexity of both MARS and BMARS algorithms is linear in the number of data points as well as the number of attributes. However, when large amounts of data are to be processed, the computational time still can be prohibitively large. In order to reduce the cost of running BMARS we have developed a parallel version of the algorithm based on the Parallel Virtual Machine (PVM) system [21]. An advantage of PVM is its wide availability on a number of platforms, so that software based on it is very portable.

The idea of the parallel BMARS is very simple. Following from the structure of the Algorithm (2), each new tensor product basis function is the best function selected from the pool of candidates. The goodness of each candidate is determined via least squares fit. It turns out that these least squares fits account for the bulk of the computational cost of running BMARS. Thus, an efficient parallelisation of BMARS can be achieved via parallelisation of the least squares procedure. We use the Gram-Schmidt algorithm [22] to perform the least squares fit. It amounts to the computation of a number of scalar products and, therefore, can be efficiently parallelised using the data-partitioning approach (see, for example [21]).

Parallel BMARS was tested on a multiprocessor system having 10 SPARC processors. It was applied to the analysis of a large motor vehicle insurance data set ($\sim 1,000,000$ data records) [20] as well as taxation data [17]. The results of the experiments show that the efficiency of the algorithm is close to that of an ideal algorithm [20].

Once again, by focusing on issues relating to the performance of the algorithms on extremely large datasets from real world applications, significant improvements can be made in the "responsiveness" of the algorithms. The result is that these tools can be significantly more effectively employed in data mining.

5   Virtual Environments for Data Mining

All stages of a data mining project require considerable understanding of multidimensional data. Visualisation tools, both for exploratory data analysis and for exploring the models produced by the data analysis algorithms, can play a significant role, particularly in the context of complex models generated through data mining [23,8]. Traditional approaches tend to be limited by the mouse-keyboard-monitor interface. Virtual environments (VEs) dramatically increase the "canvas" on which to render graphic representations of the data that scale to large numbers of dimensions through an interactive, immersive, environment.

An approach being explored for this task is a technique for partitioning a 3D VE into smaller working regions, each of which is capable of holding a subspace of the original multidimensional data space [24]. The algorithm distributes a set of partitioning axes in a radial arrangement from a single common origin, with one axis for each dimension in the data set. The ends of the axes thus lie on the surface of a sphere. A convex hull is generated to connect the ends of the axes together. The axes and the space that they form can be used for a number of visualisation strategies, including rectangular prism and the use of density functions.

5.1 Multidimensional Data Sets

Representing data of high dimensionality in a form that humans can both see and understand is a considerable challenge. Understanding a large, multidimensional data set is not a trivial task. A number of methods have been developed to try to visualise multidimensional data, including parallel coordinates [25] , the hyperbox [26], pixel colouration techniques [27], worlds within worlds [28], virtual towns [29], the grand tour [30] and Chernoff faces [31].

However, to deal with the complexity and size of contemporary data sets we are investigating new approaches to the problem using Virtual Environment (VE) technology. The Multidimensional Data Orb (mdOrb) [32] has a number of properties that differentiate it from those above. Firstly, it exploits the geometric and perceptual properties of a VE to enable the presentation of more complex data. Secondly, it is a framework on which a family of distinct visualisation strategies can be carried out, rather than being a single fixed implementation. Finally, it is a highly interactive framework in which the user actively explores the data.

The mdOrb is a technique for partitioning a 3D VE into smaller working regions, each of which is capable of holding a subspace of the original multi-dimensional data space (see Figure 1). The algorithm first distributes a set of partitioning axes in a radial arrangement from a single common origin, with one axis for each dimension in the data set. The ends of the axes thus lie on the surface of a sphere. A convex hull is generated to connect the ends of the axes together using a Delaunay triangulation. The shape thus formed is a convex polygonal mesh with every vertex of the mesh being linked to the centre of the figure by an axis. Hence for a data set with N dimensions the mesh will consist of N vertices. Each triangle in the surface mesh has three vertices, and each vertex has its own axis that links it to the centre of the figure. The triad of axes forms the corner of a skewed rectangular prism - the axes and the space that they form can be used for a number of visualisation strategies.

The first strategy is to use each rectangular prism formed by a triad of axes as a skewed Cartesian three-space for a scatter plot of points (see Figure 2). The points in each three-space are given by the values of each point from the N dimensional data space in the dimensions specified by the bounding axes. Hence a single data point is represented by a mark in every three-space, where each mark is composed of the vector sum of three vectors. Each vector's direction is that of one of the axes that define the three-space. Each vector's magnitude is the value of that point in the dimension in the data space that corresponds to the given axis.

The second method calculates polygons for each data point in the N dimen-sional data space. For a given data point, the corresponding polygons' vertices lie

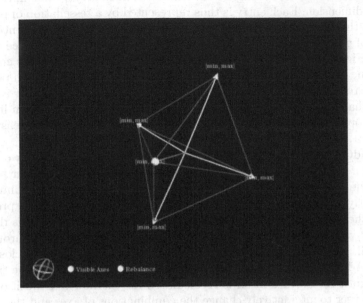

Fig. 1. Composition of projection spaces in the Orb.

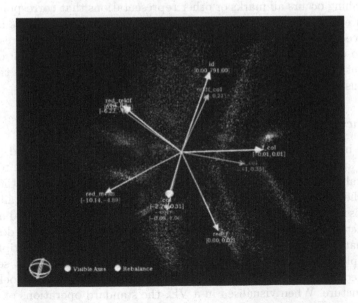

Fig. 2. Orb visualisation of multidimensional data.

on each of the orb's axes at lengths determined by the entry's value in the corresponding dimension. Each entry is thus represented by a tessellation of polygons similar to the triangles that define the three-spaces of the orb. The entry's tessellation of polygons is identical to the triangles forming the orb surface mesh as shown in Figure 1, but the length of each vertex from the origin varies according to the value of the data point in the given dimension. Due to occlusion problems we do not render each individual polygon opaquely. Instead we render a density function that illustrates how many polygons pass through each region in space. Densely populated areas appear opaque whilst sparsely populated areas appear transparent.

The mdOrb is not a static visualisation, but rather a framework on which dynamic interactive investigations can be carried out. Unlike a scatter plot matrix [33] the mdOrb does not display every possible combination of dimensions concurrently. Rather the only combinations shown are those in close proximity to each other as determined by the current tessellation. However, this does not mean that visible relationships are limited. Each axis can be moved around the orb at will, thus allowing the user to pry apart certain regions or close them together. Additionally, if the user moves an axis past the bounds of the triangles that it forms, the surface mesh is recalculated for the new axis position. This allows the user to interactively change the combinations of axes and their neighbours. For example, if a user wishes to plot two dimensions against each other they simply move the relevant axes until they are adjacent, a visual guide of the current tessellation like that shown in Figure 1 aids them in this task.

A user may wish to "brush" (or highlight) a region of interest in the orb. When brushing occurs all marks or other representations that correspond to the same data entries can be highlighted. For example, if a user brushes a cluster in one three-space, then the marks in all other three-spaces that correspond to those same entries will also be highlighted. In this way the user can correlate the different properties of individual entries or groups of entries across the entire multidimensional space.

5.2   Structural Data Models

Structural information, such as decision trees, network diagrams and program structures are often large, heavily connected and difficult to describe textually. A structural diagram such as a graph can often convey the layout of the overall data but their size often means that they are difficult to study in detail.

One possibility is to use a VE for visualising such a graph, and to alter the graph structure such that close inspection is possible [34]. The graph describing the information is first broken into multiple sections, forming a Multiple Layer and Multiple Relationship (MLMR) graph [35]. The MLMR graph separates nodes and edges into coherent groups that form modules or building blocks of the overall structure. When visualised in a VE, the standard operations of altering the viewpoint and moving and rotating the graph are supported. Additionally, the user can interactively turn on and off individual groups of nodes and edges. This allows them to interactively switch between visualising the entire graph from a global viewpoint and drilling down into a particular group of nodes and edges with irrelevant sections of the graph removed for clarity.

Figure 3 shows a visualisation of a program written in the Java language. The view shows the entire Java API with edges representing inheritance links, the program itself is shown by the grey group of nodes. The navigation icons in the lower left corner allow the user to interactively control which groups are visible. Each group of nodes is represented by a node icon and each group of edges by an edge icon, by selecting and deselecting the icons the groups of elements in the graph are turned on and off. In Figure 4 many of the groups of nodes and edges have been turned off, the only ones remaining in view are the nodes of the program and the Java packages that it inherits from. The viewpoint has been rotated and zoomed into the visible part of the graph to examine it in greater detail.

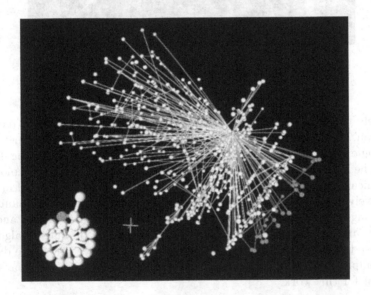

Fig. 3. Overview visualisation of structural data.

While still in its early stages, the deployment of virtual environments in data mining has much unexplored potential. Providing insights into the data through visual and immersive means allows the user to more quickly understand relationships in the data and assists in the selection of appropriate features for data mining. Further explorations are underway to use VE in the actual model building process as well as in the visualisation of the resulting models themselves.

6   Data Management

Data is stored in a variety of formats and within a variety of database systems and data warehouses, across multiple platforms. The data needs to be accessed

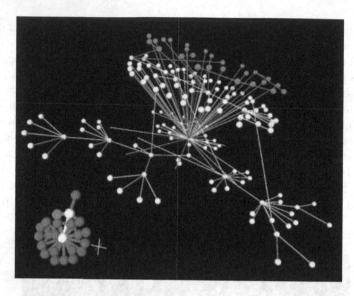

Fig. 4. In depth visualisation of portion of structural data.

in a timely manner, often after it has been pre-processed to suit the particular application. And the data will often need to be accessed multiple times for use in the single application. Efforts in this direction, including the ongoing development of the The Data Space Transfer Protocol [36], have begun to demonstrate the significance of the data access issue. Here, we describe an initial approach to effectively and seamlessly providing sophisticated data access mechanisms for data mining. A particular focus of this research is on smart caching and other optimisations which may be tuned for particular classes of analysis algorithms to improve the run time performance for data mining over very large datasets. We are employing the semantic extension framework (SEF) for Java as the environment for this work.

The semantic extension framework (SEF) for Java and the High Performance Orthogonal Persistent Java (HPOPJ) built on top of SEF [37] are abstraction tools which provide orthogonality of algorithms with respect to the data sources. This approach allows datasets to be transparently accessed and efficiently managed from many and any source. Algorithms accessing the data simply view the data as Java data structures which are intended to be efficiently instantiated as required and as determined by the semantic extensions provide for the relevant objects. We are now exploring the use of the SEF and HPOPJ to provide orthogonality and optimised access to large scale datasets.

An important problem encountered when designing data mining applications is that the programming language and the database system are different environments. Moreover, most databases do not support the same data model as the programming language. This quite common phenomenon, called the impedance mismatch, means that the programmer has to map persistent variables onto the database environment. Solving such mapping problems and keeping explicit track of persistent information wastes a significant portion of development time (sometimes more than 30%) and accounts for many programming errors. The use of the SEF for data mining enables a prototype oriented development where complex algorithms are implemented and tested quickly.

6.1 Separation of Concerns and Orthogonal Persistent Java

Separation of concerns is a new subfield of software engineering [38]. Its goal is to enable the encapsulation of all kinds of concerns in a software system such as persistence, versioning, configuration, etc. An outstanding example of separation of concerns with respect to the persistence operations is orthogonal persistence. Orthogonal persistence provides programmers with an elegant abstraction over the persistence of data. Programmers are freed from the burden of having to explicitly program the movement of data between persistent and transient stores. Orthogonally persistent Java (OPJ) refers to the application of the principles of orthogonal persistence to the Java programming language. The separation of concern with respect to the persistence operations need to be complemented with a similar separation with respect to the storage medium. For this purpose a standard interface to the underlying storage medium is necessary. The PSI interface [39] has been defined in order to address this issue. In designing PSI, we sought to balance a number of objectives: to flexibly support the needs of persistent programming languages such as OPJ; and to admit small and fast implementations.

The ACSys UPSIDE project is concerned with taking the ideals of OPJ towards industrial relevance through performance and functionality. For this reason, performance issues being addressed by the project include high efficiency storage, byte code optimisations and Java Virtual Machine (JVM) optimisations. Key functionality issues include the efficient integration of powerful transaction models into the OPJ VM (long and short transactions), and support for object instance and class versioning.

6.2 The Semantic Extension Framework

There are a number of ways in which standard Java semantics can be transparently extended, including:

1. Modifying the virtual machine to directly implement the semantic extensions either through the existing byte-code set [40,41], or via additional byte-codes [42].
2. Modifying the virtual machine to implement extended reflection capabilities through which semantic extensions can be implemented [42].
3. Preprocessing source code [43].
4. Modifying the compiler [44,45].
5. Preprocessing byte-codes (statically) [46].
6. Transforming byte-codes at class load time [47,44].

The first two approaches clearly violate the goal of portability as they depend on a modified virtual machine. The next three approaches produce portable byte-codes but require each producer of semantically extended code to have access to a modified compiler or preprocessor. Moreover, the compilation approach precludes the dynamic composition of semantic extensions. Only the last method is compatible with our goals of dynamic composition and portability. Consequently, we have adopted the last approach to semantic extensions as the basis for our semantic extension framework and our OPJ implementation (a semi-dynamic approach).

Byte-code transformations are notoriously error prone. A simple mistake during the transformation process can destroy type safety or the semantics of the program, and may lead to the byte-code modified class being rejected at class load time. A type-safe and declarative way to specify program transformations is essential to the practical application of byte-code transformations. To this end, we have defined the Semantic Extension Framework. Our framework allows for both the semantic extension of methods and the inclusion of special 'triggers' (similar in concept to database triggers) that are activated on the occurrence of particular events such as the execution of `getfield` or `putfield` Java byte-codes. The semantic extension framework is invoked when a user class is loaded. This action triggers a special semantic extension class loader to search for and load any semantic extension classes that are applicable to the user class being loaded.

A first prototype of the framework has been implemented. It has been applied to the implementation of a portable OPJ and a portable object versioning framework. We have implemented the framework using the 'PoorMan' library that provides facilities for class file parsing and basic class transformations [47].

6.3   Orthogonally Persistent Systems

Orthogonally persistent systems are distinguished from other persistent systems such as object databases by an orthogonality between data use and data persistence. This orthogonality comes as the product of the application of the following principles of persistence [48]:

Persistence Independence
> The form of a program is independent of the longevity of the data which it manipulates.

Data Type Orthogonality
> All data types should be allowed the full range of persistence, irrespective of their type.

Persistence Identification
> The choice of how to identify and provide persistent objects is orthogonal to the universe of discourse of the system.

These principles impart a transparency of persistence from the perspective of the programming language which obviates the need for programmers to maintain mappings between persistent and transient data. The same code will thus operate over persistent and transient data without distinction.

While the value of orthogonal persistence as a technology for managing complex persistent data has long been acknowledged, difficulties in efficiently implementing orthogonally persistent systems seem to have retarded its uptake in the commercial setting. Of the various challenges associated with implementing orthogonal persistence, one of the most important is that of transparently and efficiently introducing persistence semantics into the programming language runtime system.

There have been a number of efforts to extend Java with orthogonal persistence [40,49,42,41]. Most prominent among these are PJama [40] and Gem-Stone/J^{TM} [41]. In both cases orthogonal persistence is achieved by replacing the standard JVM with one that extends standard byte-code semantics to include persistence. In both cases, the virtual machine, although enhanced, remains Java compliant, allowing non persistent Java programs to execute normally.

Another common approach is the use of program transformations at the source code level. Examples of this approach include JSPIN [50] and POET [51] that replace the standard `javac` compiler. Each user class that directly extends `java.lang.Object` is modified to extend a `PersistentObject` class. Additionally, the user classes are modified to incorporate read and write barriers.

We have implemented two complete prototypes of our orthogonally persistent Java (OPJ) environment, and a third is nearing completion. All OPJ prototypes are built over the PSI interface, support an advanced transactional model, and implement orthogonal persistence through transparent semantic extensions to Java. While the first two prototypes semantically extended Java through ad-hoc bytecode modifications, the third prototype utilises the semantic extension framework described above. As a consequence, the third implementation is far less complex. A number of PSI implementations have been developed, including: a store based on the SHORE storage manager [52], a store based on Oracle RDBMS [53], a lightweight implementation using filesystems and a purpose-built high performance object store.

6.4 Orthogonal Object Versioning (OOV) Framework

Another example of the concept of the separation of concerns is Orthogonal Versioning. The general idea of Orthogonal Versioning is to extend the principles of Persistence Independence and Data Type Orthogonality to the problem of multiple versions of the same object. The versioning system is independent of the object type. All object types can have multiple versions except immutable objects such as Strings. Any object version that could be reached from any version of any persistent root is made persistent. The form of a program is the same whether it manipulates the last version or any previous version of an object. However, it is also possible to access and manipulate multiple object versions at the same time using new methods which provide explicit access to any version of an object.

We have built a first prototype of an object versioning framework based on Orthogonal Object Versioning on top of OPJ prototypes.

The advantage of such transparent versioning to data mining becomes apparent when dealing with the many transformations that are performed on the datasets used for data mining during the life time of a data mining exercise. Datasets on which the data mining tools are to be applied need to be developed from multiple source tables. The raw data needs to be transformed into features. Refinements will need to be made (and usually many times refined) to the features. As new snapshots of the dataset become available, new analyses need to be performed. Comparing the results of these new analyses to the analyses on previous versions of the datasets may shed light on changing dynamics represented in the dataset. All of these activities can be seamlessly supported using the Orthogonal Object Versioning Framework.

In summary, the separation of concerns provided by the PSI interface and HPOPJ allows a data mining tool developer to take advantage of a widely available, comprehensive information-processing infrastructure. The storage medium can be scaled from a non-transactional file system to a Relational or Object Oriented Database Management System effortlessly. Moreover, high performance storage systems such as SHORE and ANU-Store can provide access to data tuned to the particular analyses to be performed. Finally, other aspects of the semantic extension framework, including versioning, will play a significant role in simplifying the data management aspects of data mining.

7   Pulling It Together

Now consider the task of a data mining team interested in building models and exploring alternative approaches with customer data. Some basic tools might include, for example, C4.5 [5], BMARS, and TPSFEM. All are performing similar and related tasks, yet the results need to be carefully understood in the context of the tool used to generate the results. Tuning them requires different interactions with (sometimes very) different interfaces, and simply getting the data into a form that the tool can process requires many careful transformations. While sometimes seeming trivial, these are at best annoyances, and at worst they significantly inhibit the data mining process.

The first task in a data mining project, once the data is made available in some format, is to transform that data into a format suitable for each of the data mining tools to be used. Storing the data in a relational database and accessing it via ODBC or JDBC is a help, but not the whole solution. Generally, a suite of powerful tools (as might be provided to some extent by statistical packages such as SAS and Splus) is required to transform the data into the suitable format. The semantic extension framework we have introduced above will begin to play the role of a fully integrated, tunable, and very powerful base for data management on which the rest of the data mining suite sits.

To complicate the situation further, though, a data mining exercise will often combine multiple approaches to obtain discoveries that otherwise would not be possible. For example, in the Hot Spots methodology for data mining [23] clustering is used in conjunction with rule induction and domain post-processing to identify areas in the data that are of significant importance to the domain problem (the "hot spots"). The task of feeding the output of one analysis tool into others, allowing smooth interoperability throughout the process, has not been a particular focus of the data mining research community. Providing standard application programmer interfaces (APIs) to support the integration of multiple tools into a single environment has similarly received little attention. Some vendors have provided limited support in this area but the solutions tend to remain incompatible.

7.1   The Data Miner's Arcade

The Data Miner's Arcade (Figure 5) [54] provides an object-oriented framework through a collection of APIs for data access, for plug-n-play type tool integration with graphical user interfaces, and for the communication of results. A single, common, and easy to user user interface is provided to support all stages of a data mining project.

Fig. 5. The Data Miner's Arcade splash screen, showing the dynamically created toolbar reflecting just the tools available for this current invocation of the Arcade.

Access is provided to analysis tools without requiring the user to become proficient in the widely varying user interfaces. Each tool need only provide a specification of the names and types of tuning parameters supported and a suitable user interface, as in Figure 6, can be generated using a standard API (research is under way to automate this process through the use of XML-type specifications of the interface). Whilst deep expertise will still, at times, be required for the subtleties of particular tools, general straight-forward tasks can now be completed easily by end users. The more mundane Data Mining activities can thus be performed by the data owners with further support from the limited resources available from the data mining consultants as required.

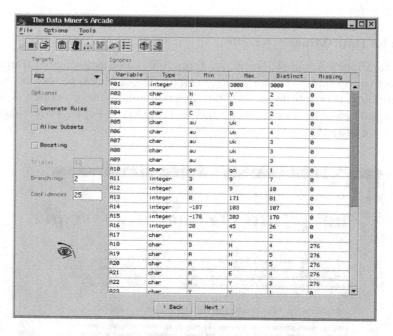

Fig. 6. The Data Miner's Arcade C5.0 interface. This has been generated for C5.0 (the commercially available and enhanced version of C4.5) providing the common advantages of GUI interfaces, including reduced effort expended on learning to drive this otherwise command-line driven application.

The general architecture of the Data Miner's Arcade is illustrated in Figure 7. Currently, access to data is provided through JDBC but is being migrated to the use of the Java semantic extension framework and OPJ, with minimal (and ideally no) change to the actual API used by the data mining tools to access the data. The data mining tools are "plugged in" to the Arcade as required. Results from the tools are then supplied to visualisation components, or to utilities that can apply the model to other datasets. The models can also be supplied to other model builders to be integrated (for ensemble type learning systems) or otherwise used in the ongoing data mining process.

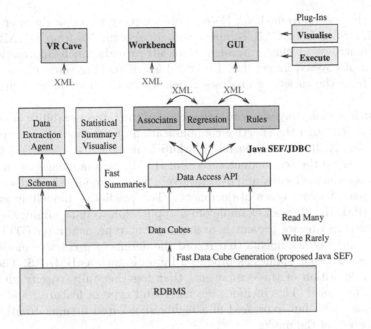

Fig. 7. A schematic of the architecture of the Data Miner's Arcade. Three APIs are identified, providing access to the data, the GUI interfaces, and output of the models.

Whilst there are a number of systems that have provided such a unified interface to a variety of tools, the architecture of The Data Miner's Arcade has a number of distinct advantages and features. These make it a unique environment for the development and integration of data mining tools. Standards are used where possible to facilitate the immediate integration of new tools as they become available. Using Java's internet oriented features, networked integration and delivery of tools allows up-to-date developments in the analysis tools to be immediately available within the Arcade. The standard API for data management (possibly coupled with the data space transfer protocol mentioned above) alleviates the need to develop data access methods for each of the tools. Data management issues are abstracted, currently through JDBC, but soon through the semantic extension framework, to dedicated components that deal with the efficient delivery of the data.

We explore the issue of the delivery of the results of the analysis tools in the next section.

7.2   XML for Communicating Models

A considerable amount of effort is required to communicate the results of current data mining tools to both other analysis tools and to end users. After struggling with the variety of analysis tools the remaining task for the data miner is to interpret the results from them. Deceptively simple yet complexly inter-related conjunctive rules from C4.5, complex numerical formulas from BMARS, and complex centroids in clustering algorithms all provide much information and nuggets of discovered knowledge. But the task of making sense of the results obtained from the variety of analyses is one which the tools provide little help with.

Research is underway to address this issue of the interoperability of the data mining tools through the effective communication of the models they generate. In particular, XML (the eXtensible Markup Language) is being used for this task. Building on the tremendous success of HTML as a language for the interchange of documents locally and over the Web, XML provides the framework for the exchange of many types of documents. The predictive modelling mark-up language (PMML) [2] is an example of its application to data mining.

To illustrate this we present here a document type definition (DTD) that describes a class of documents that record the details of predictive models represented as regression splines as produced by tools such as BMARS. The DTD contains a definition of the components that together fully specify all details of a BMARS model. This includes the name and type of features, and the actual formula itself, but expressed in a highly structured manner to allow easy communication of the model.

A snapshot of the DTD for expressing the types of models produced by BMARS is:

```
<!ELEMENT pmml          (header, model)>
<!ELEMENT header        (data-schema)>

...

<!ELEMENT model (bmars-model)>
<!ATTLIST model
  name                  CDATA          #IMPLIED
  type                  (bmars|mars)   #REQUIRED
  training-set-name     CDATA          #IMPLIED
  training-set-size     CDATA          #IMPLIED>

<!ELEMENT bmars-model (response-variable,
                       intercept,
                       tensor-product-basis-function*)>

<!ATTLIST bmars-model
  lsf-level-of-interactions   CDATA      #IMPLIED
  small-scale-features        (yes|no)   #IMPLIED

  ...
>

<!ELEMENT response-variable   (#PCDATA)>
<!ELEMENT intercept           (#PCDATA)>
```

```
<!ELEMENT tensor-product-basis-function
  (coefficient, (bspline-basis-function
                 |indicator-basis-function)+)>
```

. . .

Thus, BMARS generates a model that is expressed as a document conforming to this specification. For example, the model that partially consists of

$$x_{17} = 9170 + 1270 f_1(x_8) + \ldots + 1510 f_i(x_5) \ldots$$

will be represented as:

```
<?xml version="1.0"?>
<!DOCTYPE pmml SYSTEM "mars.dtd">
<pmml>
<header>
<data-schema>
  ...
</data-schema>
</header>

<model
  name="cc_a_model"
  type="bmars"
  training-set-name="claim_data"
  training-set-size="2131231">

  <bmars-model
    level-of-interaction="1"
    small-scale-features="no"
    ...>

    <response-variable>x17</response-variable>
    <intercept>+0.917E+04</intercept>

    <tensor-product-basis-function>
      <coefficient>-0.127E+04</coefficient>
      <bspline-basis-function>
        <variable>x8</variable>
        <knots>
          +0.000E+00  +0.000E+00  +0.600E+02
        </knots>
      </bspline-basis-function>
    </tensor-product-basis-function>

    ...

    <tensor-product-basis-function>
```

```
<coefficient>-0.151E+04</coefficient>
<indicator-basis-function>
  <variable>x5</variable>
  <map-function>
        1      1.00000000              0
        2      2.00000000              0
        3      3.00000000              1
        4      4.00000000              0
  </map-function>
</indicator-basis-function>
</tensor-product-basis-function>

  . . .


  </bmars-model>
</model>
</pmml>
```

We now have a model of our dataset expressed in a form that can easily be distributed and communicated to other tools that may provide various visualisations of the model, combine this particular model with similar models generated from BMARS (or other tools) on different versions of the dataset, or to run the model against other, previously unseen, data. Figure 8 shows a typical output from Arcade where a plugin has been used to take the XML generated by BMARS to generate MATLAB instructions to produce the resulting graph of the interactions between two of the variables in the model.

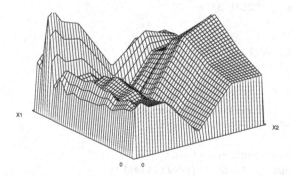

Fig. 8. Sample output from an Arcade plug-in which can generate a MatLab script for the graphing of the interaction between two variables represented in a model generated by BMARS. The BMARS model is stored as an XML document.

The Data Miner's Arcade, then, provides an environment for the development for packaged solutions for data mining. It aims to take advantage of and to develop standards to allow tools to interoperate. Rapid integration of new algorithms has been a central focus, as well as the ease in tuning it for particular tasks.

8 Summary

We have presented in this paper a snapshot of ongoing research being performed within ACSys by CSIRO Australia and the Australian National University in data mining. The research is guided by tackling real world data mining projects. Much of the research addresses the need to employ high performance and parallel computers for large scale data mining. To this end, efficient and parallel algorithms for data mining are being developed, including TPSFEM and BMARS. High powered visualisation techniques are being researched for data mining. The seamless management of data in ways that provide fast access from the data mining tools is the third area we focussed on in this paper. Research is under way to explore the benefits of using a semantic extension framework for Java for this task. Finally, the Data Miner's Arcade is being developed as a framework for the integration of these many streams in our research, introducing XML as an effective means for effecting the communications.

Acknowledgements

The authors acknowledge the support provided by the Cooperative Research Centre for Advanced Computational Systems (ACSys) established under the Australian Government's Cooperative Research Centres Program. The work reported on here has been performed by the ACSys Data Mining Project. Contributions from both the Australian National University and CSIRO Australia staff are acknowledged. Peter Christen is supported by the Swiss National Science Foundation

References

1. Fayyad, U.M., Piatetsky-Shapiro, G., Smyth, P.: From data mining to knowledge discovery: An overview. In Fayyad, U.M., Piatetsky-Shapiro, G., Smyth, P., Uthurusamy, R., eds.: Advances in Knowledge Discovery and Data Mining. AAAI Press (1996) 26
2. Grossman, R., Bailey, S., Ramu, A., Malhi, B., Hallstrom, P., Pulleyn, I., Qin, X.: The management and mining of multiple predictive models using the predictive modelling markup language. Information and Software Technology **41** (1999) 26, 48
3. Hegland, M., McIntosh, I., Turlach, B.: A parallel solver for generalised additive models. submitted (1999) 27, 27
4. Hegland, M., Roberts, S., Altas, I.: Finite element thin plate splines for surface fitting. In Noye, B., Teubner, M., Gill, A., eds.: Computational Techniques and Applications: CTAC97, World Scientific (1997) 289–296 27, 29
5. Quinlan, J.R.: C4.5: Programs for Machine Learning. Morgan Kaufmann, San Mateo, CA (1993) 27, 44
6. Friedman, J.: Multivariate adaptive regression splines. The Annals of Statistics **19** (1991) 1–141 27, 30, 33, 33
7. Friedman, J.H., Fisher, N.I.: Bump hunting in high dimensional data. http://www-stat.stanford.edu/~jhf/ftp/prim.ps.Z (1997) 27

8. Williams, G.J.: Evolutionary hot spots data mining. In: Advances in Data Mining (PAKDD99). Lecture Notes in Computer Science. Springer-Verlag (1999) 27, 35
9. Mason, L., Bartlett, P.L., Baxter, J.: Direct optimization of margins improves generalization in combined classifiers. http://wwwsyseng.anu.edu.au/~lmason/nips98.ps (1998) 27
10. Bellman, R.: Adaptive Control Processes: A Guided Tour. Princeton University Press, Princeton (1961) 27
11. Hastie, T., Tibshirani, R.: Generalized Additive Models. Volume 43 of Monographs on Statistics and Applied Probability. Chapman and Hall, London (1990) 27, 27
12. Wahba, G.: Spline models for observational data. In: CBMS-NSF Regional Conference Series in Applied Mathematics. Volume 59., SIAM (1990) 28, 28
13. Beatson, R., Light, W.: Fast evaluation of radial basis functions: methods for two-dimensional polyharmonic splines. IMA J. Numer. Anal. **17** (1997) 343–372 28
14. Beatson, R., Powell, M.: An iterative method for thin plate spline interpolation that employs approximations to lagrange functions. In: Numerical analysis 1993 (Dundee 1993). Volume 303 of Pitman Res. Notes Math. Ser., Longman Sci. Tech., Harlow (1994) 17–39 28
15. Christen, P., Altas, I., Hegland, M., Roberts, S., Burrage, K., Sidje, R.: A Parallel Finite Element Surface Fitting Algorithm for Data Mining. submitted to IC Press (1999) 29, 30
16. Grama, A.Y., Gupta, A., Kumar, V.: Isoefficiency: measuring the scalability of parallel algorithms and architectures. IEEE parallel and distributed technology: systems and applications **1** (1993) 12–21 30
17. Bakin, S., Hegland, M., Williams, G.: Mining taxation data with parallel BMARS. Submitted for publication, Parallel Algorithms and Applications (1999) 30, 35
18. Miller, A.J.: Subset Selection in Regression. Chapman and Hall (1990) 32, 33
19. Friedman, J.H.: Estimating functions of mixed ordinal and categorical variables. Technical Report 108, Stanford University (1991) 33
20. Bakin, S.: Adaptive Regression and Model Selection in Data Mining Problems. PhD thesis, Australian National University (1999) 34, 35, 35
21. Geist, A., Beguelin, A., Dongarra, J., Jiang, W., Manchek, R.: PVM: Parallel Virtual Machine. MIT Press (1994) 35, 35
22. Golub, G.H., Van Loan, C.F.: Matrix Computations. The Johns Hopkins University Press, Baltimore (1983) 35
23. Williams, G.J., Huang, Z.: Mining the knowledge mine: The Hot Spots methodology for mining large, real world databases. In Sattar, A., ed.: Advanced Topics in Artificial Intelligence (AI97). Volume 1342 of Lecture Notes in Computer Science. Springer-Verlag (1997) 340–348 35, 45
24. Nagappan, R.: Visualising multidimensional non-geometric data sets. Submitted for publication (1999) 35
25. A. Inselberg, B.D.: Parallel coordinates: A tool for visualising multi-dimensional geometry. In: Proceedings of IEEE Visualisation '90. (1990) 36
26. Alpern, B., Carter, L.: The hyperbox. In: Proceedings of IEEE Visualisation '91. (1991) 36
27. Keim, D.A., Kriegel, H.P.: Visdb: Database exploration using multidimensional visualization. Computer Graphics and Applications (1994) 40–49 36
28. Beshers, C., Feiner, S.: Worlds within worlds: Metaphors for exploring n-dimensional virtual worlds. In: ACM Symposium on User Interface Software and Technology. (1990) 36

29. Leonard, R.: Information visualization of the federal budget. In: Data Visualization Conference. (1997) 36
30. Asimov, D.: A tool for viewing multidimensional data. SIAM Journal of Scientific and Statisical Computing (1985) 36
31. Chernoff, H.: The use of faces to represent points in k-dimensional space graphically. Journal of the American Statistical Association **68** (1973) 361–368 36
32. Nagappan, R.: Visualising multidimensional nongeometric data sets. In: SPIE Visual Data Exploration and Analysis VII, San Jose, CA (2000) 36
33. Cleveland, W.S.: Visualising Data. Hobart Press, Summit NJ (1993) 38
34. Nagappan, R., Lin, T.: A virtual environment for exploring relational information. In: Proceedings of SimTecT '99. (1999) 38
35. Lin, T., Cheung, R., He, Z., K, K.S.: Exploration of data from modelling and simulation through visualisation. In: Proceedings of the Third International SimTecT Conference, Adelaide, Australia (1998) 38
36. Bailey, S., Creel, E., Grossman, R.L., Gutti, S., Sivakumar, H.: A high performace implementation of the data space transfer protocol. In: Proceedings of the KDD99 Workshop on Large-Scale Parallel Data Mining, ACM SIGKDD (1999) 40
37. Marquez, A., Zigman, J., Blackburn, S.: Fast, portable orthogonally persistent java using semi dynamic semantic extensions. Submitted for publication (1999) 40
38. Harold Ossher and Peri Tarr: Multi-dimensional separation of concerns in Hyperspace. Research report, IBM (1999) 41
39. Blackburn, S.M., Stanton, R.B.: The transactional object cache: A foundation for high performance persistent system construction. In Morrison, R., Jordan, M., Atkinson, M., eds.: Advances in Persistent Object Systems: Proceedings of the Eighth International Workshop on Persistent Object Systems, August 30–September 1, 1998, Tiburon, CA, U.S.A., San Francisco, Morgan Kaufmann (1999) 37–50 41
40. Atkinson, M.P., Jordan, M.J., Daynès, L., Spence, S.: Design issues for Persistent Java: A type-safe, object-oriented, orthogonally persistent system. In Connor, R., Nettles, S., eds.: Seventh International Workshop on Persistent Object Systems, Cape May, NJ, U.S.A, Morgan Kaufmann (1996) 33–47 41, 43, 43
41. GemStone Systems: GemStone/J. http://www.gemstone.com/ (1999) 41, 43, 43
42. Kutlu, G., Moss, J.E.B.: Exploiting reflection to add persistence and query optimization to a statically typed object-oriented language. In Morrison, R., Atkinson, M., eds.: Advances in Persistent Object Systems: Proceedings of the Eighth International Workshop on Persistent Object Systems, Tiburon, CA, U.S.A., Morgan Kaufmann (1998) 123–135 41, 41, 43
43. Boyland, J., Catsagna, G.: Parasitic methods: An implementation of multimethods for Java. In: Proceedings of the 1997 ACM SIGPLAN Conference on Object-Oriented Programming Systems, Languages & Applications (OOPSLA '97), Atlanta, Georgia, October 5-9, 199. Volume 32 of SIGPLAN Notices., ACM Press (1997) 66–76 41
44. Agesen, O., Freund, S.N., Mitchell, J.C.: Adding type parameterization to the Java language. In: OOPSLA'97, Proceedings on the 1997 Conference on Object-Oriented Programming Systems, Languages, and Applications. Volume 32 of SIGPLAN Notices., Atlanta, GA, U.S.A., ACM (1997) 49–65 41, 41
45. Thorup, K.K.: Genericity in Java with virtual types. In Aksit, M., Matsuoka, S., eds.: ECCOP'97 - Object-Oriented Programming, 11th European Conference, Jyväskylä, Finland, June 9–13, 1997. Number 1241 in Lecture Notes in Computer Science (LNCS), Springer-Verlag (1997) 444–471 41

46. Hosking, A., Nystrom, N., Cutts, Q., Brahnmath, K.: Optimizing the read and write barriers for orthogonal persistence. In Morrison, R., Jordan, M., Atkinson, M., eds.: Advances in Persistent Object Systems: Proceedings of the Eighth International Workshop on Persistent Object Systems, Tiburon, CA, U.S.A., August 30–September 1, 1998, San Francisco, Morgan Kaufmann (1998) 37–50   41

47. Bokowski, B., Dahm, M.: Poor man's genericity for Java. In: Proceedings of JIT'98, Frankfurt am Main Germany, Springer Verlag (1998)   41, 42

48. Atkinson, M.P., Morrison, R.: Orthogonally persistent systems. The VLDB Journal **4** (1995) 319–402   42

49. Tjasink, S.J., Berman, S.: Providing persistence on small machines. In Morrison, R., Atkinson, M., eds.: Eighth International Workshop on Persistent Object Systems, Tiburon, CA, U.S.A. (1998)   43

50. John V. E. Ridgway, C.T., Wileden, J.C.: Toward assessing approaches to persistence for java. In Jordan, M., Atkinson, M., eds.: Advances in Persistent Object Systems: Proceedings of the Eighth International Workshop on Persistent Object Systems, August 13–15, 1998, San Francisco, CA, U.S.A., San Francisco, Morgan Kaufmann (1998)   43

51. POET: POET Programmer's Guide, SDK Java Edition. Product documentation, POET Software Corporation (1998)   43

52. Carey, M.J., DeWitt, D.J., an d Nancy E. Hall, M.J.F., McAuliffe, M.L., Naughton, J.F., Schuh, D.T., Solomon, M.H., Tan, C.K., Tsatalos, O.G., th J. White, S.: Shoring up persistent applications. In Snodgrass, R.T., Winslett, M., eds.: Proceedings on the 1994 ACM-SIGMOD Conference on the Management of Data. Volume 23 of SIGMOD Record., Minneapolis, MN, U.S.A., ACM (1994) 383–394   43

53. Oracle Corporation: Oracle 8.1. http://www.oracle.com/ (1999)   43

54. Williams, G.: The Data Miner's Arcade: A standards-based platform for the delivery of data mining.
http://www.cmis.csiro.au/Graham.Williams/dataminer/Arcade.html   (1998)   45

A High Performance Implementation of the Data Space Transfer Protocol (DSTP)

Stuart Bailey, Emory Creel, Robert Grossman[1,2],
Srinath Gutti, and Harinath Sivakumar

[1] National Center for Data Mining, University of Illinois at Chicago
Chicago IL 60607, USA
grossman@uic.edu,
WWW home page: http://www.ncdm.uic.edu
[2] Magnify, Inc.,
100 South Wacker Drive, Suite 1130
Chicago, IL 60606, USA

Abstract. With the emergence of high performance networks, clusters of workstations can now be connected by commodity networks (meta-clusters) or high speed networks (super-clusters) such as the very high speed Backbone Network Service (vBNS) or Internet2's Abilene. Distributed clusters are enabling a new class of data mining applications in which large amounts of data can be transferred using high performance networks and statistically and numerically intensive computations can be done using clusters of workstations.

In this paper, we briefly describe a protocol called the Data Space Transfer Protocol (DSTP) for distributed data mining. With high performance networks, it becomes possible to move large amounts of data for certain queries when necessary. This paper describes the design of a high performance DSTP data server called Osiris which is designed to efficiently satisfy data requests for distributed data mining queries. In particular, we describe 1) Osiris's ability to lay out data by row or by column, 2) a scheduler intended to handle requests using standard network links and requests using network links enjoying some type of premium service, and 3) a mechanism designed to hide latency.

1 Introduction

In this paper we consider some of the issues that arise in distributed data mining when large amounts of data are moved between sites. One of the fundamental trade-offs in distributed data mining is between the cost of computation and the accuracy of results. We assume: 1) that there is a cost for moving data between sites, and 2) that the most accurate model is obtained by moving all the data to a single site. Leaving some or all of the data in place, building local models, and merging the resulting models, produces a model which is less accurate, but which, in general, is also less expensive to compute.

The cost of moving data to a central location with the commodity Internet has tended to produce either distributed data mining systems which build local classifiers and then combine them or data mining systems that use standard

M.J. Zaki, C.-T. Ho (Eds.): Large-Scale Parallel Data Mining, LNAI 1759, pp. 55–64, 2000.
© Springer-Verlag Berlin Heidelberg 2000

interfaces such as ODBC or JDBC. These protocols work best when moving relatively small amounts of data to a central location. Examples of the former include JAM [18] and BODHI [15]; examples of the latter include Kensington [11].

In a previous paper [22], we have pointed out that there are many intermediate cases in which building classifiers that are close to the optimal one results in moving some of the data, leaving some of the data in place, building local classifiers, and combining them. In this paper, we are concerned with the design of network protocols and middle-ware for distributed data mining systems which have the ability to move some data and to leave other data in place. For example, Papyrus [7] is a distributed data mining system of this type.

Three fundamental challenges faced by distributed data mining systems are:

Problem A. How can the analysis of distributed data be simplified?
Problem B. How can the amount of data per site be scaled?
Problem C. How can the number of sites be scaled?

To address Problem A, we introduced a protocol called the Data Space Transfer Protocol (DSTP) [1]. In this paper, we are concerned with how we can design DSTP data servers for distributed data mining which scale up as the amount of data per site increases (Problem B). We describe a high performance DSTP server we are designing called Osiris, which is a component of a distributed and high performance data mining system we are building called Papyrus [7].

One method of satisfying the computing and i/o requirements for high performance data mining is to use clusters of workstations [7] [16] [19] — *compute clusters* to satisfy the CPU requirements and *data clusters* to satisfy the i/o requirements. With the recent advances in high performance networks, geographically distributed clusters of workstations can be connected not only with commodity networks but also with high performance networks such as the NSF vBNS Network supported by MCI and the Internet2 Abilene Network supported by Qwest. For example, for the distributed data mining tests reported below, we used a data cluster in Chicago connected to a compute cluster in Washington, D.C. over a DS-3 link running at 45 Mb/s. Our first DSTP implementation provided approximately 3 Mb/s of throughput, while our current implementation provides approximately 30 Mb/s of throughput, a 10x improvement. See Table 1.

Based upon our previous experience analyzing the performance of another distributed data mining system we built [10], we decided to focus on three questions:

What do we store? More precisely, how should we physically layout the data on the server? By row or by column? Can we precompute intermediate quantities to speed up queries?

What do we move? More precisely, to what extent should data or meta-data be moved from node to node? There are several possibilities: we can move data, we can move predictive models, or we can move the results of computations. If we decide to move data, we can move data by table, by row, or by column.

How do we move it? What application protocol should be used for moving data in data space? How can data be moved in parallel between nodes? How can QoS be exploited to improve data transport? What is the effect of latency on data mining queries? What transport protocol should we use? Given multiple requests to a data server, how should the requests be scheduled?

The 10x performance gain we mentioned above resulted from careful understanding of these issues. Section 2 describes related work and background material. Section 3 describes data space and the data space transfer protocol. Section 4 describes the DSTP server and three experimental studies. Section 5 is the conclusion and summary.

2 Background and Related Work

In this section, we provide some background material and discuss some of the related work in this area. With the exception of [19] and [16], the work we know of in this area is limited to data mining over commodity networks. This section is adapted from [8].

Several systems have been developed for distributed data mining. Perhaps the most mature are: the JAM system developed by Stolfo et al. [18], the Kensington system developed by Guo et al. [11], and BODHI developed by Kargupta et al. [15]. These systems differ in several ways:

Data strategy. Distributed data mining can choose to move data, to move intermediate results, to move predictive models, or to move the final results of a data mining algorithm. Distributed data mining systems which employ *local learning* build models at each site and move the models to a central location. Systems which employ *centralized learning* move the data to a central location for model building. Systems can also employ *hybrid learning*, that is, strategies which combine local and centralized learning. JAM and BODHI both employ local learning while Kensington implements a centralized approach using standard protocols such as JDBC to move data over the commodity Internet.

Task strategy. Distributed data mining systems can choose to coordinate a data mining algorithm over several sites or to apply data mining algorithms independently at each site. With *independent learning*, data mining algorithms are applied to each site independently. With *coordinated learning,* one (or more) sites coordinate the tasks within a data mining algorithm across several sites.

Model Strategy. Several different methods have been employed for combining predictive models built at different sites. The simplest, most common method is to use *voting* and combine the outputs of the various models with a majority vote [4]. *Meta-learning* combines several models by building a separate meta-model whose inputs are the outputs of the various models and whose output is the desired outcome [18]. *Knowledge probing* considers learning from a black box viewpoint and creates an overall model by examining the input and the outputs to the various models, as well as the desired output [11]. Multiple models, or what are often called ensembles or committees of models, have been used for quite a while in (centralized) data mining. A variety of methods have been studied for combining models in an ensemble, including Bayesian model averaging and model selection [17], partition learning [6], and other statistical methods, such as mixture of experts [23]. JAM employs meta-learning, while Kensington employs knowledge probing.

Papyrus is designed to support different data, task and model strategies. For example, in contrast to JAM, Papyrus can not only move models from node to node, but can also move data from node to node, when that strategy is desired. In contrast to BODHI, Papyrus is built over a data warehousing layer which can move data over both commodity and high performance networks. Also, Papyrus is a specialized system which is designed for clusters, meta-clusters, and super-clusters, while JAM, Kensington and BODHI are designed for mining data distributed over the Internet.

Moore [16] stresses the importance of developing an appropriate storage and archival infrastructure for high performance data mining and discusses work in this area. The distributed data mining system developed by Subramonian and Parthasarathy [19] is designed to work with clusters of SMP workstations and like Papyrus is designed to exploit clusters of workstations. Both this system and Papyrus are designed around data clusters and compute clusters. Papyrus also explicitly supports clusters of clusters and clusters connected with different types of networks.

3   Data Space and the Data Space Transfer Protocol

We begin by describing some of the key concepts following [1].

Data Space. We assume that data is distributed over nodes in a global network, which we call a *data space.*

Rows and Columns. Although the data may be more complicated, we assume that the data is organized into tables, and that each table is organized into rows (records) and columns (observations). Records may contain missing values.

Catalog Files. Each DSTP server has a special file called the *catalog file* containing meta-data about the data sets on the server.

DSTP. We assume that there is a server on each node which can move data to other nodes using a protocol called the *data space transfer protocol (DSTP).* Depending upon the request, DSTP servers may return one or more columns, one or more rows, or entire tables. DSTP servers can also return meta-data about tables and the data they contain.

Universal Correlation Keys. A row may have one or more keys. Certain keys called *Universal Correlation Keys* (UCK) are used for relating data on two different DSTP servers. For example, key-value pairs (k_i, x_i) on DSTP Server 1 can be combined with key-value pairs (k_j, y_j) on DSTP Server 2 to produce a table (x_k, y_k) in a DSTP client. The DSTP client can then find a function $y = f(x)$ relating x and y.

Horizontal Store: Store Size = 4.4 GB			
NC	ADR in Mb/s	TDT in Giga bytes	TTT in seconds	EPR in Events/second
1	3.06	4.4	11777.5	64
2	6.07	4.4	5926.59	253
4	10.05	4.4	3590.40	655
8	16.92	4.4	2132.05	2811
16	23.32	4.4	1550.91	7731
32	34.93	4.4	1032.24	23245

Vertical Store: Store Size = 4.0 GB			
NC	ADR in Mb/s	TDT in Mega bytes	TTT in seconds	EPR in Events/second
1	1.39	269.5	1549.05	400
2	2.75	269.5	797.00	1554
4	3.81	269.5	566.42	4377
8	6.75	269.5	320.45	15482
16	9.74	269.5	223.05	44590
32	13.96	269.5	152.52	126918

Table 1. Performance analysis of horizontal vs. vertical stores.
NC - Number of clients requesting data
ADR - Aggregate Data Rate
TDT - Total Data Transferred
TTT - Total Time Taken for completion of application
EPR - Events Processing Rate

Since DSTP client applications need only collect meta-data from the catalog files and need only move the relevant columns, these type of applications tend to scale better as the number of sites increases (Problem C) than distributed data mining applications which must move entire files. Recall that we are interested in the case in which some data is moved. Of course, if sufficient accuracy can be obtained by local analysis followed by combining models, this is usually less expensive than strategies which require that data be moved.

Notice that from this perspective, distributed databases are concerned with the efficient *updates* of distributed *rows*, while distributed data mining applications are concerned with the efficient *reading* and analysis of distributed *columns*.

In the next section, we describe our efforts to produce DSTP servers which can efficiently manage large data sets.

4   The Osiris DSTP Server

Osiris is a high performance DSTP Server which is designed to provide efficient read access to data. In our design, efficient read access is delivered by implementing high performance storage support, high performance network transfer support, and differentiated service support.

In this section we discuss our implementations of these support mechanisms and some preliminary experimental results which attempt to quantify the relative performance gains for each technique. All three mechanisms are implemented in process space and do not require any special tuning of the underlying hardware or operating systems. We felt it was important to provide performance improvements that were independent of the underlying system in order to increase portability.

4.1 Rows and Columns

Tabular data may be laid out on disk by row or by column. Since data from disk is transfered by block, certain queries will be more efficient when the data is laid out by row (*horizontally*) and other queries will be more efficient when the data is laid out by column (*vertically*).

DSTP client applications accessing data may request either rows of data or columns of data. If a column of data is requested and the underlying storage layout is *horizontal*, then each block will contain quite a bit of unwanted data. The same is true if a row of data is requested and underlying layout is *vertical*.

Since horizontal layouts speed up certain distributed data mining queries and vertical layouts speed up others, Osiris stores data in both formats. Although this doubles the amount of space required, the I/O traffic is reduced significantly. Since Osiris is a distributed system, the I/O traffic ultimately passes through a network communication link. Since network bandwidth is sufficiently more expensive than disk capacity, we feel the 2X increase in required storage is more than compensated for.

The following results are from a proof of concept DSTP data server located at the University of Illinois at Chicago being accessed by multiple clients located at an Internet2 member facility in Washington, D.C. called Highway One. The two sites are connected by the NSF/MCI vBNS Network. Even though vBNS is an OC-3 network offering maximum bandwidth of 155 Mb/s, the end nodes at Highway One were connected via a DS-3 link, which limited the maximum bandwidth of the testbed to 45 Mb/s.

For this test, we used an application benchmark we developed called the *Event Benchmark*, which is broadly derived from high energy physics. The data consists of a large collection of *events*, with each event containing several hundred attributes. An energy like function is computed from the attributes of an event and the energies of the event are histogrammed.

To better understand quantitative effects of the Horizontal/Vertical Layout strategy, we first laid out the data *horizontally* and ran the application, and then we laid out the data *vertically* and ran the application.

In the first case, all the event data was stored as rows (i.e., each event was a row). In the second case, the event data was stored attribute by attribute as columns. The *Event Benchmark* specifies that event level summary data is to be stored separately and analyzed at run-time to find out which attributes are to be requested and processed. In other words, this particular application requests columns of data based on some criteria. Therefore, we expected that a *vertical* layout should provide better performance.

Table 1 shows the performance results. The Event Processing Rate (EPR) is an an application benchmark of efficiency. Aggregate Data Rate (ADR) and Total Data Transferred (TDT) are system performance measures. The desired result is to maximize application efficiency with the least load on the system. Clearly, the *vertical* layout provided better performance, as expected.

NC	ART-P in seconds	ART-PS in seconds	ART-C in seconds	ART-CS in seconds
1	606.3	570.4	422.1	447.4
2	577.5	557.5	445	463.5
3	574.4	558.5	568.5	581.3
4	566.6	566.5	715	740
5	565.9	562.16	880.9	892.7

Table 2. Performance of Diff-Serv scheduler
NC - Number of clients requesting data per service type
ART-P - Average run-time for premium clients (no scheduling)
ART-PS - Average run-time for premium clients (with Diff-Serv scheduling)
ART-C - Average run-time for commodity clients (no scheduling)
ART-CS - Average run-time for commodity clients (with Diff-Serv scheduling)

This experiment demonstrates the effect that layout has on application performance. Because we cannot predict whether applications will request rows or columns, storing the data both *horizontally* and *vertically* will guarantee performance gain.

4.2   Differentiated Service Support with Diff-Serv Scheduler

Osiris is being developed to simultaneously serve clients on both commodity and high performance networks. Because of the *premium* nature of high performance networks, it is desirable that clients on these networks have some precedence over clients on commodity networks. Treating *premium clients* and *commodity clients* differently constitutes a type of Quality of Service(QoS) called *differentiated services* [20].

Differentiated service support in Osiris is another mechanism that attempts to contribute to the requirement of efficient read access. In this context, efficiency refers to system wide resource utilization as opposed to per process performance.

Because the currently popular Internet protocol suite (IP) does not support any kind of QoS mechanism, we chose to implement differentiated service support as a characteristic of the scheduling mechanism for client requests to Osiris. We refer to this scheduler as the Diff-Serv Scheduler.

When a client attaches to Osiris, it informs the server whether it is a *premium client* or a *commodity client*. Data block requests are then scheduled for service as

TM	TT in seconds	AATR in Mbps
traditional single socket	96	8.3
PSocket size 2	57	14.0
PSocket size 3	34	23.5
PSocket size 4	30	26.7
PSocket size 5	26	30.8
PSocket size 6	26	30.8
PSocket size 7	26	30.8

Table 3. Performance of Transport Layer Multiplexing with PSocket. (Note: The practical limit of the 45 Mb/s DS-3 appears to be about 35 Mb/s.)
TM - Transport Mechanism
TT - Transfer Time for 100 MBytes
AATR - Application Apparent Transfer Rate

they arrive with *premium client* requests getting preferential treatment. Please see [12] for full design and implementation details of the Diff-Serv Scheduler.

For our experimental study, a single server was run on a machine connected to the network through Switched Fast Ethernet (100 Mbps). An equal number of clients connected to both Switched Fast Ethernet (*premium clients*) and Switched Ethernet (*commodity clients*) were launched and connected to the server.

The *premium clients* each made 10,000 random block requests, and the *commodity clients* each made 5,000 random block requests. The default block size for Osiris is 16KB. Every client waited for an exponentially distributed random delay between block requests. This delay was introduced to cause a Poisson distribution of request arrivals to the server and was an attempt to simulate real application behavior.

Experiments were conducted which compare system performance with Diff-Serv scheduling turned on against system performance with Diff-Serv scheduling turned off. Measurements were made with a total of two to ten clients. The results are presented in Table 2. Please note that when Diff-Server scheduling is turned off, the system defaults to FIFO scheduling.

The desired results were achieved. In all cases, *premium client* response time improved while *commodity client* response time diminished when our implementation of Diff-Serv scheduling was turned-on.

4.3   High Performance Network Transfer Support with PSocket

It has been well documented that latency characteristics of TCP over wide area networks, or more precisely networks with large "bandwidth · delay" products, have a significant negative impact on per process communication performance [13]. Various protocol and implementation level solutions have been suggested [14] [5]. One technique is for the sender to send multiple messages to the receiver in parallel [21].

In order to provide high performance network transfer support, we allow a single process to break up a message and then send the pieces in parallel over multiple communication links (e.g., TCP sockets) to the receiver who then rebuilds the entire message. We refer to this technique as Transport Layer Multiplexing and have implemented a simple-to-use interface for application integration called PSocket (as in Parallel Socket). For full details please refer to [2].

Osiris will use PSockets to increase the data transfer rate on a per client process basis. The results in Table 3 are from a single, non-threaded sender process using PSocket, located at the University of Illinois at Chicago, sending data to a single non-threaded receiver process using PSocket located at Highway One. The two sites are connected by the NSF/MCI vBNS Network. Highway One connects to vBNS via a DS-3 link, which limited the maximum theoretical bandwidth of the testbed to 45 Mb/s.

The experiment measured the wall clock transfer time of a 100 MByte buffer. Results show that with a PSocket of size 5, a large portion of the practical transfer rate of the DS-3 was consumed by the transfer. As a reference, the transfer rate using traditional, single socket programming was given.

5 Conclusion

In general, the less data which distributed data mining systems move, the less expensive the computation. However, due to the level of accuracy required or to the nature of the data, it is sometimes necessary to move large amounts of data between sites. With the emergence of high performance networks this becomes practical in many circumstances in which it would have previously been impractical.

In this paper, we have described some of the design considerations for a high performance data server called Osiris which is part of the Papyrus distributed data mining infrastructure and presented some experimental results describing its use on an application benchmark requiring the computation of histograms.

In particular, we describe a design which supports high performance storage, high performance network transfer, and differentiated network services, such as commodity links and high performance links. This design provides at least a 10x improvement over a more naive design. We expect this to grow to 100x for certain applications and network configurations.

References

1. S. Bailey, E. Creel, and R. L. Grossman, DataSpace: Protocols and Languages for Distributed Data Mining, National Center for Data Mining/Laboratory for Advanced Computing Technical Report, http://www.ncdm.uic.edu, 1999.
2. S. Bailey, R. L. Grossman, Transport Layer Multiplexing with PSocket, National Center for Data Mining Technical Report, 1999.
3. P. Chan and H. Kargupta, editors, Proceedings of the Workshop on Distributed Data Mining, The Fourth International Conference on Knowledge Discovery and Data Mining New York City, 1999, to appear.

4. T. G. Dietterich, Machine Learning Research: Four Current Directions, AI Magazine Volume 18, pages 97-136, 1997.
5. D. J. Farber, J. D. Touch, An Experiment in Latency Reduction, IEEE Infocom, Toronto, June 1994, pp. 175-181.
6. R. L. Grossman, H. Bodek, D. Northcutt, and H. V. Poor, Data Mining and Tree-based Optimization, Proceedings of the Second International Conference on Knowledge Discovery and Data Mining, E. Simoudis, J. Han and U. Fayyad, editors, AAAI Press, Menlo Park, California, 1996, pp 323-326.
7. R. L. Grossman, S. Bailey, S. Kasif, D. Mon, A. Ramu and B. Malhi, The Preliminary Design of Papyrus: A System for High Performance, Distributed Data Mining over Clusters, Meta-Clusters and Super-Clusters, Proceedings of the Workshop on Distributed Data Mining, The Fourth International Conference on Knowledge Discovery and Data Mining New York City, August 27-31, 1998, to appear.
8. R. L. Grossman and Y. Guo, An Overview of High Performance and Distributed Data Mining, submitted for publication.
9. R. L. Grossman, S. Bailey, A. Ramu and B. Malhi, P. Hallstrom, I. Pulleyn and X. Qin, The Management and Mining of Multiple Predictive Models Using the Predictive Modeling Markup Language (PMML), Information and Software Technology, 1999.
10. The Terabyte Challenge: An Open, Distributed Testbed for Managing and Mining Massive Data Sets, Proceedings of the 1998 Conference on Supercomputing, IEEE.
11. Y. Guo, S. M. Rueger, J. Sutiwaraphun, and J. Forbes-Millott, Meta-Learnig for Parallel Data Mining, in Proceedings of the Seventh Parallel Computing Workshop, pages 1-2, 1997.
12. S. Gutti, A Differentiated Services Scheduler for Papyrus DSTP Servers, Master's Thesis, University of Illinois at Chicago, 1999.
13. V. Jacobson, Congestion Avoidance and Control, SIGCOMM '88, Stanford, CA., August 1988.
14. V. Jacobson, and R. Braden, TCP Extensions for Long-Delay Paths, RFC-1072, LBL and USC/Information Sciences Institute, October 1988.
15. H. Kargupta, I. Hamzaoglu and B. Stafford, Scalable, Distributed Data Mining Using an Agent Based Architecture, in D. Heckerman, H. Mannila, D. Pregibon, and R. Uthurusamy, editors, Proceedings the Third International Conference on the Knowledge Discovery and Data Mining, AAAI Press, Menlo Park, California, pages 211-214, 1997.
16. R. W. Moore, C. Baru, R. Marciano, A. Rajasekar, and M. Wan, Data-Intensive Computing, Ian Foster and C. Kesselman, editors, The Grid: Blueprint for a New Computing Infrastructure, Morgan Kaufmann, San Francisco, 1999, pages 105-129.
17. A. E. Raftery, D. Madigan, and J. A. Hoeting, 1996. Bayesian Model Averaging for Linear Regression Models. Journal of the American Statistical Association 92:179-191.
18. S. Stolfo, A. L. Prodromidis, and P. K. Chan, JAM: Java Agents for Meta-Learning over Distributed Databases, Proceedings of the Third International Conference on Knowledge Discovery and Data Mining, AAAI Press, Menlo Park, California, 1997.
19. R. Subramonian and S. Parthasarathy, An Architecture for Distributed Data Mining, to appear.
20. B. Teitelbaum and J. Sikora (1998), Differentiated Services for Internet2, Draft Proposal, http://www.internet2.edu/qos/may98Workshop/html/diffserv.html
21. J. D. Touch, Parallel Communication, the proceedings of Infocomm 1993, San Francisco CA. March 28-April 1, 1993.
22. R. L. Grossman and A. Turinsky, Optimal Strategies for Distributed Data Mining using Data and Model Partitions, submitted for publication.
23. Xu, L.; and M.I. Jordan, M. I. 1993. EM Learning on A Generalised Finite Mixture Model for Combining Multiple Classifiers. In Proceedings of World Congress on Neural Networks. Hillsdale, NJ: Erlbaum

Active Mining in a Distributed Setting

Srinivasan Parthasarathy, Sandhya Dwarkadas, and Mitsunori Ogihara

Department of Computer Science
University of Rochester
Rochester, NY 14627–0226
{srini,sandhya,ogihara}@cs.rochester.edu

Abstract. Most current work in data mining assumes that the data is static, and a database update requires re-mining both the old and new data. In this article, we propose an alternative approach. We outline a general strategy by which data mining algorithms can be made *active* — i.e., maintain valid mined information in the presence of user interaction and database updates. We describe a runtime framework that allows efficient caching and sharing of data among clients and servers. We then demonstrate how existing algorithms for four key mining tasks: Discretization, Association Mining, Sequence Mining, and Similarity Discovery, can be re-architected so that they maintain valid mined information across i) database updates, and ii) user interactions in a client-server setting, while minimizing the amount of data re-accessed.

1 Introduction

As we enter the digital information era, one of the greatest challenges facing organizations and individuals is how to turn their rapidly expanding data stores into accessible knowledge. Digital data sources are ubiquitous and encompass all spheres of human endeavor: from a supermarket's electronic scanner to a world wide web server, from a credit card reader to satellite data transmissions. Organizations and individuals are increasingly turning to the extraction of useful information, referred to as data mining, from such databases. Such high-level patterns, or inferences, extracted from the data may provide information on customer buying patterns, on-line access patterns, fraud detection, weather trends, etc.

A typical data mining technique can be thought of as an exploration over a huge user-defined pattern space, with the role of the data being to select patterns with a desired degree of confidence. The set of accepted patterns is a function of both the data and the user-defined pattern space (controlled by the input parameters). The data mining process tends to be interactive and iterative in nature, i.e., after observing the results from the first round of mining, the user may choose to repeatedly modify the input parameters, thereby affecting the set of accepted patterns. Also, since businesses are constantly collecting data, the data is also subject to change, again affecting the set of accepted patterns.

M.J. Zaki, C.-T. Ho (Eds.): Large-Scale Parallel Data Mining, LNAI 1759, pp. 65–82, 2000.

Most current techniques, which tend to be static in nature, simply re-execute the algorithm in the case of data updates or user interaction. There are several limitations to this approach. First, although many of these techniques have parallel solutions [20,28,4] that are efficient in storage, access, and scale, they are still computationally expensive. Second, re-executing the algorithm requires re-examining both the old and new data, and hence I/O continues to be a bottleneck. These problems are further exacerbated in applications such as electronic commerce and stock sequence analysis, where it is important to execute the query in real or near-real time, in order to meet the demands of on-line transactions. Also, more and more such applications are being deployed as client-server applications where the server is physically separate from the client machine. Such a setup is also common within an organization's intra-net when there may be several groups mining, perhaps with separate agendas, from a common dataset. Ensuring reasonable response times in such applications is made more difficult due to the network latency and server load overheads. This leads to the following challenge:

In order to meet the demands of such interactive applications, can existing algorithms be re-architected, making them efficient in the presence of user interactions and data updates, in a distributed client-server setting?

1.1   Proposed Solution

We refer to algorithms that maintain valid mined information in the presence of user interaction and database updates as *active* algorithms. The main challenge is to perform the active mining in a storage and time efficient manner. This paper describes a general strategy by which data mining tasks can be re-architected to work efficiently with the constraints outlined above.

We accomplish our objective by maintaining a *mining summary structure* across database updates and user interactions. On a database update, the revamped algorithm replaces accesses to the old data with accesses to the mining summary structure whenever possible. This ensures that information that is previously mined can be re-used when the database is updated. On a user interaction, the hope is that the mining summary structure can answer the query without accessing the original data.

The design criteria for such a summary structure are: i) it should allow for incremental maintenance as far as possible, i.e., the mining summary structure from the old data along with the data update should ideally be sufficient to produce the new summary structure, avoiding accesses to the old data as far as possible, ii) it should store sufficient information to address a wide range of useful user interactions, and iii) it should be small enough to fit in memory so that accessing it rather than the old data provides a significant performance gain.

While the above solution can potentially solve the active mining problem, deploying these algorithms efficiently in a distributed setting is non-trivial. In typical client-server applications, the client makes a request to the server, the server computes the result, and then sends the result back to the client. The query execution time is significantly influenced by the speed of the client-server link as well as the server load. Since the interactions in our applications are often iterative in nature, caching the aforementioned summary structure on the client side so that repeated accesses may be performed locally eliminates overhead and delays due to network latency and server load. In order for this to be an effective solution, the summary structure should not be very large (re-emphasizing point iii) above), and an efficient mechanism for communicating updates is required.

Such summary structure sharing requires efficient caching support. We have built a general-purpose framework called InterAct that facilitates the development of interactive applications. InterAct supports sharing among interactive client-server applications. The key to the framework is an efficient mechanism to facilitate client-controlled consistency and sharing of objects among clients and servers (this allows applications that can tolerate some information loss to take advantage of this to increase efficiency by reducing communication). Advantages within the scope of our work include: the ability to cache relevant data on the client to support interactivity, the ability to update cached data (when the data changes on the server) according to application or user preferences while minimizing communication overhead, and the ability to extend the computation boundary to the client to reduce the load on the server. We use this framework to develop our applications.

1.2   Contributions

In this paper:

1. We describe a general methodology for creating *active* mining solutions for existing applications.
2. We present active mining solutions for discretization, association mining, sequence mining, and similarity discovery in a distributed setting.
3. We describe the InterAct framework, which, along with the changes to the algorithms for active mining, allows effective client-server distribution of the computation.

The next section presents the InterAct framework on top of which we implement our active mining algorithms. We also outline our general approach to the problem of making algorithms *active*. Sections 3 (Discretization),4 (Association/Sequence Mining), and 5 (Similarity Discovery) describe the applications we look at and our specific approach to make each of them *active*. We present and evaluate our experimental results in Section 6. Section 8 details our conclusions.

2   InterAct Framework

InterAct is a runtime framework that presents the user with a transparent and efficient data sharing mechanism across disparate processes. The goal is to combine efficiency and ease-of-use. InterAct allows clients to cache relevant shared data locally, enabling faster response times to interactive queries. Further, InterAct provides flexible client-controlled mechanisms to map and specify consistency requirements for shared data.

In order to accomplish its goal of transparently supporting interactive applications, InterAct:

- Defines a data (structure) format for shared objects that is address space and architecture independent. Our implementation relies on the use of C++ and some programmer annotation to identify the relevant information about shared data to the runtime framework.
- Identifies, defines, and supports the different types of consistency required by such applications (described in [16]). In many domains (electronic commerce, credit card transactions), the data that is being queried is constantly being modified. The rate at which these modifications are required to be updated in the client's cached copy may vary on the basis of the domain, application, or specific user. This rate can be controlled by exploiting the appropriate consistency model to enhance application performance.
- Provides an underlying mechanism to transparently handle the consistency demands as well as complex object transfer requirements. The goal here is to reduce programming complexity by hiding as much of the underlying communication from the application developer as possible.

For more framework details and the consistency types supported, see [16].

2.1   Active Mining and InterAct

Since mining applications typically operate on large data sets that reside on a data server, communicating these datasets to the client would be infeasible. However, in this paper we show that it is possible to design useful summary structures for a range of mining applications, so that subsequent queries can operate on these summary structures. This summary data structure can be generated by the data distiller (server), and subsequently operated on by the client. Hence, the applications can be structured as shown in Figure 1, so that the data server is responsible for creating the data structure(s), mapping them onto a *virtual shared dataspace*, and subsequently keeping them up-to-date. The client can then map the data structure(s) from the *virtual shared dataspace* under a desired consistency model, thus enabling the client to respond to interactive queries without having to go to the data server.

In order for the above setup to be effective the summary data structure should satisfy three key properties. First, it should be able to directly answer a range of interactive queries without requiring access to the data as far as possible. This criterion minimizes the client-server communication, as well as server load. Second, the summary structure should be incrementally maintainable. This criterion ensures that changes to the data can be rapidly reflected in the summary structure. Third, the summary structure should not be very large as otherwise communicating it to the client may be very expensive. In the ensuing sections, we describe how such summary structures can be designed for Discretization, Association and Sequence Mining, and Similarity Discovery.

Interactive Client-Server Mining

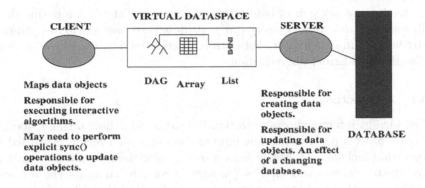

Fig. 1. Client-Server Mining using InterAct

3   2-D Discretization

Discretization is the process by which the range of a given *base* attribute (or independent variable) is partitioned into mutually exclusive and exhaustive intervals based on the value of a related *goal* attribute (or dependent variable), whose behavior we would like to predict or understand. Discretization has primarily been used for summarization [8], as well as for growing a decision tree [19].

Typically, a single attribute is used as the decision variable. However, one can also consider extensions to more than one base attribute (e.g., $X > 5 \wedge Y < 6$) as long as the decisions remain simple. The need for this is often encountered where repetitive applications of the single-attribute discretization do not provide optimal results, while a single, integrated two-dimensional approach does.

In [17], the partitioning of a two dimensional base attribute space is defined in terms of *control points*. A single control point partitions the base attribute space into 4 rectangular regions. The rectangular regions are induced by drawing lines through the control point that are perpendicular to the two axes. Two control points partition the base attribute into up to 9 regions. The effect of discretization is to approximate the behavior of the goal attribute as the same for all points in a region. The purpose of the algorithm is to find the position of the control point(s) that optimizes a given objective function.

The input to a discretization algorithm could be either the raw data or a joint probability density function (pdf) of the base and goal attributes derived from the data. Using the data directly eliminates errors associated with pdf estimation. However, using a pdf enables one to use more meaningful error metrics such as Entropy [9]. Second, it permits users to encode domain knowledge by altering the shape and type of kernel (normal, poisson, binomial, etc.) used for density estimation. Further, it lends itself to a client-server architecture where density estimation could be done on the server and a compact representation shipped to the client.

Evaluating any pair of base attributes involves 2 steps: computing the three dimensional probability density (pdf) estimate (two base attributes and the goal attribute), and searching for the optimal (determined by the objective function: Classification Error) discretization.

3.1   Interactivity

The idea in interactive discretization is that an end user ought to be able to modify process parameters. The interactive features currently supported in our algorithm include: i) choosing from a set of algorithms (brute force search, approximate search), and metrics (entropy, error), to compute the optimal discretization, ii) changing the number of control points (1, or 2), iii) changing the position of control points, and iv) changing the parameters for pdf estimation.

Ideally, all these features need to be supported efficiently without excessive I/O or computation.

3.2   Summary Structure

As mentioned earlier, the summary structure required to support such interactions efficiently is the joint pdf $p(base_1, base_2, goal)$. This pdf is estimated at discrete locations. While several techniques exist to estimate the density of an unknown pdf, the most popular ones are histogram, moving window, and kernel estimates [7]. We use the histogram estimate described in [7]. The advantage of this estimate is that it can be incrementally maintained in a trivial manner (a histogram estimate is essentially the frequency distribution normalized to one). Moreover, the more complicated kernel estimates can easily be derived from this basic estimate [7].

With a few modifications, the histogram pdf estimate can handle each of the interactions described above. If there are n points in the estimate, computing the objective function for a given control point takes $O(n)$ time. Since the objective of discretization is to find the control point(s) that optimizes the given objective function, a brute force search will take $O(n^2)$ ($O(n^4)$ for two control points) time. Recently, we have shown that smarter methods can reduce this time complexity to $O(n)$ ($O(n^2)$ for two control points) with additional memory ($O(n)$). Alternatively, fast approximate searches like simulated annealing can be used to generate good discretizations quickly [17].

Changing the control point in small incremental ways (moving the control point along one of the two axes in unit steps), enables one to compute the new objective functions (entropy or error) in unit time at the cost of additional storage ($O(n)$). Changing the parameters for pdf estimation can also be done quickly using the histogram estimate [7].

In order for the summary structure to be cost effective, the size of the structure (n, the number of points in the estimate) must be small enough so that i) it can be cached easily on remote clients, and ii) it can allow for faster interactions. In the next section, we describe an experiment that explores the tradeoff between the size of the summary structure and the accuracy of the discretization obtained.

Accuracy vs. Summary Size. We evaluate the premise that it is possible to create a condensed representation of the data (probability density function) without serious degradation in the quality of discretizations obtained. This enables efficient client-server partitioning, and allows off-loading parts of the computation to another machine, thereby reducing the load on the server, and potentially improving interaction efficiency.

Experimentally, we have found that the number of points at which the pdf needs to be evaluated (determined by grid size) without significant quality degradation is not large. Our results are summarized in Figure 2. The results reported are for two synthetic data sets, XOR and LL. These are described in [17] [1]. Both have 100,000 instances and 2 base attributes. It is easy to see that the quality (error minimization) of discretization does not improve much beyond a grid size of 64^2.

Data Set	Grid Size	Error
XOR	16^2	18.87%
XOR	32^2	18.13%
XOR	64^2	17.90%
XOR	128^2	17.86%
LL	16^2	12.47%
LL	32^2	12.2%
LL	64^2	12.2%
LL	128^2	12.3%

Fig. 2. Effect of grid size for pdf evaluation on quality of results

The resulting summary structure for discretization satisfies all the properties for efficient active mining: it is bounded and small, it can be used to handle a wide range of client queries without going back to the original database, and it can be incrementally maintained.

---

[1] Available via anonymous ftp from `ftp.cs.rochester.edu/pub/u/srini`

4   Association/Sequence Mining

In this section, we consider two of the central data-mining tasks, i.e., the discovery of association rules and the discovery of sequences. The discussion below follows [28] (associations) and [27] (sequences).

The problem of mining association rules over *basket* data was introduced in [2,3]. It can be formally stated as: Let $\mathcal{I} = \{i_1, i_2, \cdots, i_m\}$ be a set of m distinct attributes, also called *items*. Each transaction T in the database $\mathcal{D}$ of transactions, has a unique identifier, and *contains* a set of items, such that $T \subseteq \mathcal{I}$. An *association rule* is an expression $A \Rightarrow B$, where $A, B \subset \mathcal{I}$, are sets of items called *itemsets*, and $A \cap B = \emptyset$. Each itemset is said to have a *support S* if $S\%$ of the transactions in $\mathcal{D}$ contain the itemset. The association rule is said to have *confidence C* if $C\%$ of the transactions that contain A also contain B, i.e., $C = S(A \cup B)/S(A)$, i.e., the conditional probability that transactions contain the itemset B, given that they contain itemset A.

Sequence Mining can be thought of as association mining over temporal datasets. A *sequence* is an ordered (over time) list of nonempty itemsets. A sequence of itemsets $\alpha_1, \ldots, \alpha_n$ is denoted by $(\alpha_1 \mapsto \cdots \mapsto \alpha_n)$. The *length* of a sequence is the sum of the sizes of each of its itemsets. The database is divided into a collection of customer sets where each customer set contains the set of transactions that customer is involved in in order of occurrence. For a database D and a sequence α, the *support* or *frequency* of α in D, is the number of customers in D whose sequences contain α as a subsequence. A rule $A => B$ involving sequence A and sequence B is said to have *confidence c* if $c\%$ of the customers that contain A also contain B.

The basic approach to mining associations and sequences is a two step iterative approach. First, identify the set of candidate associations/sequences for a given number of items. Second, compute the set of associations/sequences from the candidate set that meet the user-specified criteria, forming the basis for the candidates in the next iteration (adding one to the number of items considered). We use the ECLAT [28] (associations) and SPADE [27] (sequences) algorithms as the basis for our work.

4.1   Interactivity

The idea in interactive association mining (or interactive sequence mining) is that an end user be allowed to query the database for association rules at differing values of support and confidence. The goal is to allow such interaction without excessive I/O or computation. Interactive usage of the system normally involves a lot of manual tuning of parameters and re-submission of queries that may be very demanding on the memory subsystem of the server. In most current algorithms, multiple passes have to be made over the database for each $< support, confidence >$ pair. This leads to unacceptable response times for online queries. Our approach to the problem of supporting such queries efficiently is to create pre-processed summaries that can quickly respond to such online queries.

A typical set of queries that such a system could support include: i) **Simple Queries:** identify the rules for support x%, confidence y%, ii) **Refined queries:** where the support value is modified ($x + y$ or $x - y$) involves the same procedure, iii) **Quantified Queries:** identify the k most important rules in terms of support, confidence pairs or find out for what support/confidence values can we generate exactly k rules, iv) **Including Queries:** find the rules including itemsets $i_1, \ldots, i_n$, v) **Excluding Queries:** compute the rules excluding itemsets $i_1, \ldots, i_n$, and vi) **Hierarchical Queries:** treat items $i_1, \ldots, i_n$, as one item and return the new rules.

4.2 Summary Structure

In [1], the concept of an Association Lattice L is defined. An association X is said to be adjacent to an association Y if one of them can be obtained from the other by adding a single item. Specifically, an association X is a parent of Y if Y can be obtained by adding one item to X. We allow directed edges from parents to children. It is then easy to see that if a directed path exists from a vertex V to a vertex U then $V \subset U$. Further, each node in the lattice is weighted by the support S of the given association it represents. The sequence lattice is obtained in a similar manner.

The preprocessing step of the algorithm involves computing such a lattice for a small enough support S_{min}, such that all future queries will involve a support S larger than S_{min}. If the above holds, and given such a lattice, we can produce answers to all but one (**Hierarchical queries**) [2] of the queries described in the previous section at interactive speeds without going back to the original database. This is easy to see as all of the queries will basically involve a form of pruning over the lattice. A lattice, as opposed to a flat file containing the relevant associations/sequences, is an important data structure as it permits rapid querying for associations [1] and sequences [18]. This lattice can also be incrementally maintained for associations [25] and sequences [18]. Due to limited space, we do not describe it here.

Accuracy vs. Summary Size. Unlike in discretization, the size of the summary structure is not bounded for a choice of S_{min}. It depends on the data and the choice of S_{min}. For small enough S_{min} the lattice can be very large (larger than the original data itself in some cases!). However, for most practical cases (e.g., $S_{min} = 0.05\%$, dataset = 170MB) the resulting lattice (4MB) is manageable and the applications can benefit from client side caching of the data structure.

The summary structure satisfies the three properties for efficient active mining: it can be used to handle a wide range of client queries without going back to the original database, it can be incrementally maintained, and for most practical instances, the size of the lattice is not too large.

---

[2] These queries require recomputation on the server. However, because of the way we access the data, and the way it is stored we limit accesses to the old data.

5 Similarity Discovery

Similarity is a central concept in data mining. Discovering the similarity among attributes enables reduction in dimensions of object profiles as well as provides useful structural information on the hierarchy of attributes. Das et al [6] proposed a novel measure for attribute similarity in transaction databases. The similarity measure proposed compares the attributes in terms of how they are individually correlated with other attributes in the database. The choice of the other attributes (called the probe set) reflects the examiner's viewpoint of relevant attributes to the two. Das et al show that the choice of the probe set strongly affects the measurement.

There are some limitations to this basic approach. First, when the examiner does not know what the relevant attributes are, their approach offers no solutions. A brute force search would be impractical. Second, the approach limits the probe elements to singleton attributes and does not allow boolean attribute formulae.

If one is not interested in probe attributes of small frequency, an alternative approach can be to use the associations generated by an algorithm such as ECLAT [28] as the probe set. The similarity metric between attributes "a" and "b" can be defined in terms of association sets (A, the set of all associations involving "a" but excluding "a". For instance if "adl" were a valid association, then "dl" would belong to the set A. Similarly, B, the set of all associations involving "b" but excluding "b".) and their associated supports (sup):

$$Sim(A, B) = \frac{\sum_{x \in A \cap B} \max\{0, 1 - \alpha | \sup_{\mathcal{A}}(x) - \sup_{\mathcal{B}}(x)|\}}{\|A \cup B\|},$$

where α is a user-defined normalizing variable that defaults to one. This approach is fast and scales well in practice. It also permits boolean attribute formulae(a limitation of the Das et al [6] approach) as part of the probe set. Since we use associations as the probe set, this approach can also be used to measure the similarity between different homogeneous datasets and is not limited to measuring attribute similarity.

5.1 Interactive Similarity

In our approach the following interactions are currently supported: i)**Boolean Pruning:** Prune the probe space (association sets) to only those parts of the association sets that satisfy a given boolean formula, ii) **Identifying influential attributes:** Identify the (set of) probe attribute(s) that contribute most to the similarity/dissimilarity metric, and iii) **Changing the minimum support**.

5.2 Summary Structure

In this application, the summary structure required is the association lattice described in Section 4.2. For dataset similarity, the association lattices of both datasets are required.

Once the association lattices are obtained, the basic algorithm computes the similarity measure. The different interactions are supported as follows.

For Boolean Pruning, the algorithm basically prunes both lattices according to the boolean formula, yielding sets A^1 and B^1. The similarity metric is then recomputed by replacing A with A^1 and B with B^1. For Identifying Influential Attributes, for a singleton attribute "1", the algorithm prunes out all elements in the association lattice that do not contain "1". It then computes the similarity between the two datasets. This step is repeated for all singleton attributes and the resulting similarities are sorted. The higher ranked attributes influence similarity while the lower ranked attributes influence dis-similarity.

Accuracy vs. Summary Size. Like association mining, the size of the summary structure is not bounded for a choice of S_{min}. However, unlike association mining, similarity discovery is less attuned to this choice. Fixing an S_{min} apriori is an acceptable solution for the purpose of computing similarities. This limits the size of the data structure, ensuring that the three properties for active mining are satisfied for this application.

6 Experimental Evaluation

In order to completely evaluate all aspects of our work, we evaluate the impact of our summary structure with respect to three qualities; its interactive performance, its incremental performance, and the efficacy of client-server work distribution by caching the summary structure and executing queries locally. We first describe in detail the queries we evaluated on each of the applications, and their associated datasets.

6.1 Application Properties

We executed a series of queries for each application. For association mining, we executed a simple query (find rules with support x%) followed by a quantified query (find the 400 most important associations). For sequence mining, we executed a combination of including (all sequences including item x) and excluding sequences (all sequences excluding item y). For discretization, we executed the base algorithm (find the optimal discretization) and then asked the system to move the control points to a new location and compute the new error. In similarity discovery, we asked the system to compute the pair-wise similarities for four datasets and then asked it to recompute the similarities under boolean pruning, as well as identify the most influential attributes.

Each of the queries was executed on an appropriate dataset. For association mining, we executed our queries using a synthetic dataset generated adopting the methodology described in [3]. The dataset we used (T10.I6.D3200) contained on average 10 items per transaction, and 3,200,000 transactions. The size of the resulting dataset is 140MB.

For sequence mining, we executed our queries using a synthetic dataset generated by a similar procedure [27]. The dataset we used (C250.I6.T10) contained on average 10 transactions per customer, and 250,000 customers, where each transaction is variable in length. The size of the resulting dataset is 55MB.

For discretization, we used the XOR dataset [17]. The dataset has 100,000 instances and 3 attributes (two base,one goal) per instance. There are 2 categories for the goal attribute, C0 and C1. The size of the resulting dataset is 4MB.

For similarity discovery, we executed our queries against a real dataset, the Reuters dataset [3]. The data set consists of 21578 articles from the Reuters newswire in 1987. Each article has been tagged with keywords. The size of the dataset is 27MB. For our evaluation, we represented each news article as a transaction with each keyword being an item.

For each of the applications considered: Associations, Sequences, Discretization and Similarity, the size of the summary structures were 3.3MB, 1.0MB, 0.5MB, and 2.0MB, respectively. It is easy to see that in all of the cases the summary structure is a significant reduction from the original dataset and is small enough to enable effective *active* mining.

6.2   *Active* Mining Performance

Application	Client (143Mhz)	Client (270Mhz)	Recompute	IS (*incr* 5%)
Association Mining	2.4	1.5	540.7	10
Sequence Mining	0.58	0.35	150	7
Discretization	0.87	0.55	505.8	18
Similarity	0.35	0.11	10	10

Table 1. Active Mining Performance: Execution Times in seconds

We summarize the results on interactive and incremental mining performance here. In this paper, we have described a methodology for off-loading the interactive querying feature onto client machines as opposed to executing on the server, and shipping the results to the data mining client. In order to clearly demonstrate the effectiveness of this approach, we wanted to compare executing queries on slower clients (143Mhz and 270Mhz UltraSparcs) using the designed summary structure versus recomputing the result on the fastest server we have available (600MHz Alpha Station 4100s).

The results of the experiment are shown in Table 1. The first column corresponds to the application we evaluated, the second column contains the execution time of the query on a 143Mhz client using the appropriate summary structure, the third column similarly contains the execution time on a 270Mhz client, and the fourth column represents the execution time of running the query

---
[3]   www.research.att.com/~lewis/reuters21578.html

from scratch on the 600 MHz Alpha, without the use of the summary structure. For all of the applications, the execution time with the summary structure is orders of magnitude faster than re-executing the query from scratch. This is despite the fact that the results obtained for re-executing the query without the summary structure is on a much faster server.

The fifth column of our table, **Incremental Speedup (IS)**, represents the speedup obtained from maintaining the structure incrementally, rather than re-creating it on a database update. This part of the experiment was also performed on the 600MHz Alpha Station 4100. The (*incr* 5%) in the column header corresponds to the increment size. The datasets described in the previous sections are divided into two partitions, one containing 95% of the transactions (or instances) and the other containing the remaining 5%. The first partition we assume is the original dataset, while the second partition is treated as the increment dataset. The speedup numbers in this column compare the speedup of using an incremental algorithm as opposed to re-executing the algorithm on the entire (original + increment) data (column 4). The performance gains from the incremental approach ranges from good (speedup of 7) to excellent (speedup of 18). As expected, incrementally maintaining the summary structure for the discretization application results in the best speedup since it is the easiest to maintain.

6.3   Distributed Performance

Application	Client(143)					Client(270)				
	CSC	SSRC		L-SSRC		CSC	SSRC		L-SSRC	
Ethernet (Mbps)		10	100	10	100		10	100	10	100
Association	2.4	4.05	1.6	7.2	2.5	1.5	2.5	1.4	5.1	2.3
Sequence	0.58	0.85	0.55	1.35	0.86	0.35	0.63	0.5	1.18	0.73
Discretization	0.87	1.35	0.67	2.75	1.08	0.55	0.94	0.6	1.6	0.98
Similarity	0.35	1.5	0.55	2.7	0.98	0.11	0.9	0.37	2.4	0.94

Table 2. Time (in seconds) to Execute Query in a Distributed Environment

In typical client-server applications, the client makes a request to the server, the server computes the result, and then sends the result back to the client. Since the interactions in our applications are often iterative in nature, caching the summary data structure on the client side so that repeated accesses may be performed locally can potentially improve query execution times.

We present results on the efficacy of caching the summary structure in a distributed environment consisting of SUN workstations connected by 10 or 100 Mbps switched Ethernet. The clients in each application interact with the server by sharing the summary data structures with the server. The server creates the summary data structure and updates it corresponding to changes in the database (which we simulate). The potential gain from client-side caching depends on a number of factors: the size of the shared data, the speed of the client, the network latency, the server load, and the frequency of data modification. We evaluate the effect of each of these factors.

We ran each of our applications under the following scenarios:

1. Client-Side Caching (CSC): the client caches the summary structure and executes the query on the local copy (the execution times reported here do not reflect the time to communicate the summary structure, which gets amortized over several queries).
2. Server Ships Results to Client (SSRC): the client queries the server and the server ships the results back to the client. This scenario is similar to the use of an RPC mechanism. In order to better understand the impact of server load, we varied the number of clients serviced by the server from one (SSRC) to eight (Loaded-SSRC).

We measured the time to execute each query under both scenarios. We evaluated each scenario on a range of client machines, from an UltraSparc (143Mhz) machine to an UltraSparc IIi (270Mhz). In each case, our server was an 8-processor 336 MHz UltraSparc II machine. Results are presented in Table 2 for these scenarios under two different network configurations. We varied the network configuration by choosing clients that are connected to the server via a 10 Mbps or a 100 Mbps Ethernet network. For each of the applications considered: Associations, Sequences, Discretization, and Similarity, the size of the results shipped by the server (total data communicated) were 1.5MB, 0.25MB, 0.5MB and 0.75MB respectively.

The results in Table 2 show that client-side caching is beneficial for all but a few of the cases. In particular, the following trends are observed. Client-side caching is more beneficial under the following scenarios: the network bandwidth is low (speedups from client-side caching under the 10Mbps configuration are larger (1.5 to 23) than the 100Mbps numbers (0.6 to 9)), the server is loaded (comparing the L-SSRC column (speedups of 1.1 to 9) with the SSRC column(speedups of 0.6 to 3.5) with a 100 Mbps network), the client is a fast machine (comparing the columns involving the 270Mhz clients versus the 143Mhz clients), or the time to execute the query is low (comparing the row involving the similarity discovery with the row involving association mining). In other words, the benefits from client-side caching are a function of the computation/communication ratio. The lower the ratio, the greater the gain from client-side caching. The fact that InterAct enables such caching is very useful for such applications especially when deployed on the Internet.

In addition, the client maps the shared summary data structures using one of the set of consistency models provided by InterAct. Choosing the right consistency model for a given application depends on its tolerance for stale data. Updates are then transmitted to the client according to the consistency model chosen. Results obtained show that the average update times are several orders of magnitude faster than existing approaches such as RPC. For a detailed analysis of our update protocol and results pertaining to these applications, see [16].

7   Related Work

7.1   Distributed Data Mining Systems

Several systems have been developed for distributed data mining. The JAM [22] (Java Agents for Meta-learning) and the BODHI [13] system assume that the data is distributed. They employ local learning techniques to build models at each distributed site, and then move these models to a centralized location. The models are then combined to build a meta-model whose inputs are the outputs of the various models and whose output is the desired outcome. The Kensington [12] architecture treats the entire distributed data as one logical entity and computes an overall model from this single logical entity. The architecture relies on standard protocols such as JDBC to move the data. The Id-Vis [23] architecture is a general-purpose architecture designed with data mining applications in mind to work with clusters of SMP workstations. Both this system and the Papyrus system [11] are designed around data servers, compute servers, and clients. The Id-Vis architecture explicitly supports interactivity through the interactive features of the Distributed Doall programming primitive. However, the interactions supported are limited to partial result reporting and bare-bones computational steering.

Our work is complementary to the above distributed data mining systems. Their focus is on how to build data mining systems or specific data mining applications when the data and processing capacity is distributed. Our focus is on making existing algorithms *active*.

7.2   Incremental Mining

In [5], an incremental algorithm for maintaining association rules is presented. A major limitation of this algorithm is that it may require $O(k)$ database (original plus increment) scans, where k is the size of the largest frequent itemset. In [10], two incremental algorithms were presented – the *Pairs* approach stores the set of frequent 2-sequences, while the *Borders* algorithm keeps track of the frequent set and the negative border. An approach very similar to the Borders algorithm was also proposed in [25].

There has been almost no work addressing the incremental mining of sequences. One related proposal in [26] uses a dynamic suffix tree based approach to incremental mining in a single long sequence. However, we are dealing with sequences across different customers, i.e., multiple sequences of sets of items as opposed to a single long sequence of items. To the best of our knowledge there has been no work to date on the incremental mining of discretization and similarity discovery.

7.3   Interactive Mining

A mine-and-examine paradigm for interactive exploration of associations was presented in [14]. The idea is to mine and produce a large collection of frequent patterns. The user can then explore this collection by the use of *templates* specifying what's interesting and what's not. They only consider inclusive and exclusive templates (corresponding to our **Including** and **Excluding** queries), whereas our approach handles a wider range of queries, in an efficient manner.

A second approach to exploratory analysis is to integrate the constraint checking inside the mining algorithm. One such approach was presented in [21]. Recently, [15] presented the CAP algorithm for extracting all frequent associations matching a rich class of constraints. Our approach relies on constraining the final results rather than integrating it inside the mining algorithm.

An online algorithm for mining associations at different values of support and confidence, was presented in [1]. Like their approach, we rely on a lattice framework to produce results at interactive speeds. Our approach relies on a different base algorithm [28] for generating associations and this allows us to compute a wider range of queries, as well as, compute such queries faster.

An interactive approach to discretization was presented in [24] for traditional one-dimensional discretization. They also use a probability density estimate of the base attribute to allow for certain user interactions in a manner similar to ours. However, their problem domain is much simpler then ours and therefore the interactive queries supported are relatively easier to compute. We are not aware of any such work on interactive mining, within the domain of sequence and similarity discovery.

Most of the incremental and interactive mining approaches tend to focus on isolated applications leading to a proliferation of solutions with little or no inter-operability. Our approach is the first that tries to integrate the incremental and interactive components in a distributed setting. Furthermore, we outline a general strategy for making mining algorithms *active* in such a setting.

8   Conclusions

In this paper, we described our approach to active data mining in a client-server setting. We presented a general method for creating efficient interactive mining algorithms, and in addition, demonstrated its efficacy in a distributed setting using the InterAct framework. We applied this general methodology to several data mining tasks: discretization, association mining, sequence mining, and similarity discovery.

To summarize our method, we maintain a *mining summary structure* that is valid across database updates and user interactions. On a user interaction, the mining summary structure can answer the query without re-accessing the actual data. On a database update, the amount of the original database that needs to be re-examined is minimized. Lastly, by caching the summary structure on the client using InterAct, we can eliminate overheads due to network latency and server loads.

Experimental results show that executing queries using the appropriate summary structure can improve performance by several orders of magnitude. Furthermore, for all the applications considered, the summary structures can be incrementally maintained with up to an 18-fold improvement over re-creating the summary structures on a database update. Finally, up to a 23-fold improvement in query execution times was observed when the clients cache the summary structure and execute the query locally.

References

1. C. Aggarwal and P. Yu. Online generation of association rules. In *IEEE International Conference on Data Engineering*, February 1998.
2. R. Agrawal, T. Imielinski, and A. Swami. Mining association rules between sets of items in large databases. In *ACM SIGMOD Conf. Management of Data*, May 1993.
3. R. Agrawal, H. Mannila, R. Srikant, H. Toivonen, and A. Inkeri Verkamo. Fast discovery of association rules. In U. Fayyad and et al, editors, *Advances in Knowledge Discovery and Data Mining*, pages 307–328. AAAI Press, Menlo Park, CA, 1996.
4. D. Cheung, J. Han, V. Ng, A. Fu, and Y. Fu. A fast distributed algorithm for mining association rules. In *4th Intl. Conf. Parallel and Distributed Info. Systems*, December 1996.
5. D. Cheung, J. Han, V. Ng, and C. Wong. Maintenance of discovered association rules in large databases: an incremental updating technique. In *12th IEEE Intl. Conf. on Data Engineering*, February 1996.
6. G. Das, H. Mannila, and P. Ronkainen. Similarity of attributes by external probes. In *Proceedings of the 4th Symposium on Knowledge Discovery and Data-Mining*, 1998.
7. L. Devroye. A course in density estimation. In *Birkhauser:Boston MA*, 1987.
8. J. Dougherty, R. Kohavi, and M. Sahami. Supervised and unsupervised discretization of continuous features. *12th ICML*, 1995.
9. U. Fayyad and K. Irani. Multi-interval discretization of continuous-valued attributes for classification learning. *14th IJCAI*, 1993.
10. R. Feldman, Y. Aumann, A. Amir, and H. Mannila. Efficient algorithms for discovering frequent sets in incremental databases. In *2rd ACM SIGMOD Workshop on Research Issues in Data Mining and Knowledge Discovery*, May 1997.
11. R. Grossman, S. Bailey, S. Kasif, D. Mon, A. Ramu, and B. Malhi. Design of papyrus: A system for high performance, distributed data mining over clusters, meta-clusters and super-clusters. In *Proceedings of Workshop on Distributed Data Mining, alongwith KDD98*, Aug 1998.
12. Y. Guo, S. Rueger, J. Sutiwaraphun, and J. Forbes-Millot. Meta-learning for parallel data mining. In *Proceedings of the Seventh Parallel Computing Workshop*, 1997.
13. H. Kargupta, I. Hamzaoglu, and B. Stafford. Scalable, distributed data mining using an agent based architecture. In *KDD*, Aug 1997.
14. M. Klemettinen, H. Mannila, P. Ronkainen, H. Toivonen, and A. I. Verkamo. Finding interesting rules from large sets of discovered association rules. In *3rd Intl. Conf. Information and Knowledge Management*, pages 401–407, November 1994.
15. R. T. Ng, L. Lakshmanan, J. Jan, and A. Pang. Exploratory mining and pruning optimizations of constrained association rules. In *ACM SIGMOD Intl. Conf. Management of Data*, June 1998.
16. S. Parthasarathy and S.Dwarkadas. Shared state for client server applications. TR716, Department of Computers Science, University of Rochester, June 1999.

17. S. Parthasarathy, R. Subramonian, and R. Venkata. Generalized discretization for summarization and classification. In *PADD98*, January 1998.
18. S. Parthasarathy, M. Zaki, M. Ogihara, and S. Dwarkadas. Incremental and interactive sequence mining. TR715, Department of Computers Science, University of Rochester, June 1999.
19. J. R. Quinlan. *C4.5: Programs for Machine Learning.* Morgan Kaufmann, Los Altos CA, 1993.
20. J. Shafer, R. Agrawal, and M. Mehta. Sprint: A scalable parallel classifier for data mining. In *22nd VLDB Conference*, March 1996.
21. R. Srikant, Q. Vu, and R. Agrawal. Mining Association Rules with Item Constraints. In *3rd Intl. Conf. on Knowledge Discovery and Data Mining*, August 1997.
22. S. Stolfo, A. Prodromidis, and P. Chan. Jam:java agents for meta-learning over distributed databases. In *KDD*, Aug 1997.
23. R. Subramonian and S. Parthasarathy. A framework for distributed data mining. In *Proceedings of Workshop on Distributed Data Mining, alongwith KDD98*, Aug 1998.
24. R. Subramonian, R. Venkata, and J. Chen. A visual interactive framework for attribute discretization. In *Third International Conference on Knowledge Discovery and Data Mining*, pages 82–88, 1997.
25. S. Thomas, S. Bodagala, K. Alsabti, and S. Ranka. Incremental updation of association rules. In *KDD97*, Aug 1997.
26. K. Wang. Discovering patterns from large and dynamic sequential data. *J. Intelligent Information Systems*, 9(1), August 1997.
27. M. J. Zaki. Efficient enumeration of frequent sequences. In *7th Intl. Conf. on Information and Knowledge Management*, November 1998.
28. M. J. Zaki, S. Parthasarathy, M. Ogihara, and W. Li. New parallel algorithms for fast discovery of association rules. *Data Mining and Knowledge Discovery: An International Journal*, 1(4):343-373, December 1997.

Efficient Parallel Algorithms for Mining Associations*

Mahesh V. Joshi, Eui-Hong (Sam) Han, George Karypis, and Vipin Kumar

Department of Computer Science, University of Minnesota
Minneapolis, MN 55455, USA
{mjoshi,han,karypis,kumar}@cs.umn.edu

Abstract. The problem of mining hidden associations present in the large amounts of data has seen widespread applications in many practical domains such as customer-oriented planning and marketing, telecommunication network monitoring, and analyzing data from scientific experiments. The combinatorial complexity of the problem and phenomenal growth in the sizes of available datasets motivate the need for efficient and scalable parallel algorithms. The design of such algorithms is challenging. This chapter presents an evolutionary and comparative review of many existing representative serial and parallel algorithms for discovering two kinds of associations. The first part of the chapter is devoted to the non-sequential associations, which utilize the relationships between events that happen together. The second part is devoted to the more general and potentially more useful sequential associations, which utilize the temporal or sequential relationships between events. It is shown that many existing algorithms actually belong to a few categories which are decided by the broader design strategies. Overall the aim of the chapter is to provide a comprehensive account of the challenges and issues involved in effective parallel formulations of algorithms for discovering associations, and how various existing algorithms try to handle them.

1 Introduction

One of the important problems in data mining [1] is discovering associations present in the data. Such problems arise in the data collected from scientific experiments, or monitoring of physical systems such as telecommunications networks, or from transactions at a supermarket. The problem was formulated originally in the context of the transaction data at supermarket. This *market basket* data, as it is popularly known, consists of transactions made by each customer.

---

* This work was supported by NSF grant ACI-9982274, by Army High Performance Computing Research Center cooperative agreement number DAAH04-95-2-0003/contract number DAAH04-95-C-0008, the content of which does not necessarily reflect the position or the policy of the government, and no official endorsement should be inferred. Access to computing facilities was provided by AHPCRC, Minnesota Supercomputer Institute. Related papers are available via WWW at URL: http://www.cs.umn.edu/~kumar.

M.J. Zaki, C.-T. Ho (Eds.): Large-Scale Parallel Data Mining, LNAI 1759, pp. 83–126, 2002.
© Springer-Verlag Berlin Heidelberg 2002

Each transaction contains items bought by the customer. The goal is to see if occurrence of certain items in a transaction can be used to deduce occurrence of other items, or in other words, to find associative relationships between items. If indeed such interesting relationships are found, then they can be put to various profitable uses such as shelf management, inventory management, etc. Thus, *association rules* were born [2]. Simply put, given a set of items, association rules predict the occurrence of some other set of items with certain degree of confidence. The goal is to discover *all* such *interesting* rules. This problem is far from trivial because of the exponential number of ways in which items can be grouped together and different ways in which one can define interestingness of a rule. Hence, much research effort has been put into formulating efficient solutions to the problem.

It is commonly agreed upon that the number of occurrences of a set of items in a given transaction database, called *support,* can be used to formulate the interestingness of association rules derived from it. A more formal definition of association rules will follow later in the chapter, but informally, the association rule discovery problem usually translates into finding all sets of items that satisfy a pre-specified minimum threshold on support, and then postprocessing them to find the interesting rules. Such itemsets are called *frequent.* In this chapter, we concentrate on the most time consuming operation in this discovery process, which is the discovery of frequent itemsets. Since usually the number of distinct items is large in transaction-based databases, the total number of potential itemsets satisfying the support threshold can be prohibitively large. The first algorithm that handled this problem of exponential explosion elegantly was the Apriori algorithm [3] . This algorithm used a very fundamental property of the support of itemsets: an itemset of size k can meet the minimum level of support only if all of its subsets also meet the minimum level of support. This property is used to systematically prune the search space of desired itemsets, by progressively increasing the length of the itemsets being discovered. Briefly, in an iteration k, all *candidate* k-itemsets (of length k) are formed such that all its $(k-1)$-subsets are frequent. The number of occurrences of these candidates are then counted in the transaction database. Efficient data structures are used to perform fast counting. Overall, the algorithm has been successful on a wide variety of transaction databases. Since its conception, many other algorithms [4,5,6,7,8,9,10,11,12,13] have emerged that improve upon the runtime, I/O, and scalability performance of the Apriori algorithm by various efficient means of pruning the itemset search space and counting the candidate occurrences in large databases. In this chapter, we describe serial Apriori algorithm in detail, and give a comparative review of many other representative serial algorithms.

Many practical applications of association rules involve huge transaction databases which contain a large number of distinct items. In such situations, the serial algorithms like Apriori running on single-processor machines may take unacceptably large times. This is despite of the algorithmic improvements proposed in many serial algorithms. The primary reasons are the memory, CPU speed, and I/O bandwidth limitations faced by single-processor machines. As an example, in the Apriori algorithm, if the number of candidate itemsets becomes too large, then they might not all fit in the main memory, and multiple database passes would be required within each iteration, incurring expensive I/O cost. This implies that, even with the highly effective pruning method of Apriori, the task of finding all association rules can require a lot of computational and memory resources, especially when the data is enormous and high-dimensional (large number of distinct items). This is true of most of the other serial algorithms as well, and it motivates the development of parallel formulations.

Computational work in association rule discovery consists of candidate generation and counting their occurrences. The memory requirements come from storing the candidates generated. In order to extract concurrency, the computational work and the memory requirements need to be distributed among all the available processors. In this chapter, we discuss the pros and cons of different work and memory distribution approaches by studying various parallel formulations of the Apriori-like algorithms in an evolutionary manner. Most existing parallel algorithms can be classified based on how the candidates are distributed among processors. We give details of the representative algorithms [14,15,5,16,17,11,6], and briefly review few other parallelization strategies [18,19,20,21].

The concept of association rules can be generalized and made more useful by observing another fact about transactions. All transactions have a timestamp associated with them; i.e. the time at which the transaction occurred. If this information can be put to use, one can find relationships such as if an item A was bought by a customer, then he/she is likely to buy an item B in a few days time. The usefulness of this kind of rules gave birth to the problem of discovering *sequential patterns* or *sequential associations*.

In general, the data can be characterized in terms of objects and events happening on these objects. The supermarket transaction data that we have discussed so far, is just one special case of this general characterization, where a customer is an object and items bought by him/her are the events. It is, however, applicable to many other application domains. For example, in experiments from molecular biology, an organism or its chromosome can be an object and its behavior observed under various conditions can form events. In a telecommunication network, switches can be objects and alarms happening on them can be events. The events happening in such data are related to each other via the temporal relationships of *together* and *before* (or *after*). The *association rules* utilize only the *together* part of the relationship. The concept is extended to the *sequential patterns* [22] or *episodes* [23], which take into account the sequential (*before/after*) relationship as well. The formulation in [22] is motivated by the supermarket transaction data, and the one in [23] is motivated by the telecommunication alarm data. A unified and generalized formulation of sequential associations is proposed in [24].

These formulations of sequential associations are not only important because they represent more powerful and predictive relationships, but they are also important from the algorithmic point of view because bringing in the sequential relationships increases the combinatorial complexity of the problem enormously.

The total number of possible sequential associations is much larger than that of non-sequential associations. Various algorithms proposed so far [22,23,25,26,24], try to contain the complexity by imposing various temporal constraints, and by using the anti-monotonicity of the support criterion. However, as the data becomes enormous and high-dimensional, single-processor algorithms become computationally very expensive, especially because of the more complex nature of sequential associations; and hence, the need for efficient parallel algorithms is even more as compared to non-sequential associations. In many situations, the techniques used in parallel algorithms for discovering standard non-sequential associations can be extended easily to discover sequential associations. However, different issues and challenges arise specifically due to the sequential nature and various ways in which interesting associations can be defined. In the final part of this chapter, we discuss all these issues and challenges, and a few parallel formulations for resolving them.

The rest of this chapter is organized as follows. Section 3 provides an overview of the serial algorithms for mining association rules. Section 4 describes parallel algorithms for finding association rules. Section 5 contains a description of a generalized formulation of sequential associations and parallel algorithms to discover them. Section 6 summarizes the chapter.

2   Association Rule Discovery: Problem Definition

Let T be the set of transactions where each transaction is a subset of the itemset I. Let C be a subset of I, then we define the *support count* of C with respect to T to be:

$$\sigma(C) = |\{t | t \in T, C \subseteq t\}|.$$

Thus $\sigma(C)$ is the number of transactions that contain C. For example, consider a set of transactions from supermarket as shown in Table 1. The items set I for these transactions is {Bread, Beer, Coke, Diaper, Milk}. The support count of

Table 1. Transactions from supermarket.

TID	Items
1	Bread, Coke, Milk
2	Beer, Bread
3	Beer, Coke, Diaper, Milk
4	Beer, Bread, Diaper, Milk
5	Coke, Diaper, Milk

{Diaper, Milk} is $\sigma(Diaper, Milk) = 3$, whereas $\sigma(Diaper, Milk, Beer) = 2$.

An *association rule* is an expression of the form $X \xrightarrow{s,\alpha} Y$, where $X \subseteq I$ and $Y \subseteq I$. The *support* s of the rule $X \xrightarrow{s,\alpha} Y$ is defined as $\sigma(X \cup Y)/|T|$, and the confidence α is defined as $\sigma(X \cup Y)/\sigma(X)$. For example, consider a

rule {Diaper, Milk} $\Longrightarrow$ {Beer}, i.e. presence of diaper and milk in a transaction tends to indicate the presence of beer in the transaction. The support
of this rule is $\sigma(Diaper, Milk, Beer)/5 = 40\%$. The confidence of this rule is
$\sigma(Diaper, Milk, Beer)/\sigma(Diaper, Milk) = 66\%$. A rule that has a very high
confidence (i.e., close to 1.0) is often very important, because it provides an accurate prediction on the association of the items in the rule. The support of a
rule is also important, since it indicates how frequent the rule is in the transactions. Rules that have very small support are often uninteresting, since they do
not describe significantly large populations. This is one of the reasons why most
algorithms [3,27,5] disregard any rules that do not satisfy the minimum support condition specified by the user. This filtering due to the minimum required
support is also critical in reducing the number of derived association rules to
a manageable size. Note that the total number of possible rules is proportional
to the number of subsets of the itemset I, which is $2^{|I|}$. Hence the filtering is
absolutely necessary in most practical settings.

The task of discovering an association rule is to find all rules $X \overset{s,\alpha}{\Longrightarrow} Y$, such
that s is greater than or equal to a given minimum support threshold and α is
greater than or equal to a given minimum confidence threshold. The association
rule discovery is composed of two steps. The first step is to discover all the
frequent itemsets (candidate sets that have more support than the minimum
support threshold specified). The second step is to generate association rules
from these frequent itemsets. The computation of finding the frequent itemsets
is much more expensive than finding the rules from these frequent itemsets.
Hence in this chapter, we only focus on the first step.

3 Serial Algorithms for Frequent Itemset Discovery

A number of serial algorithms have been developed for discovering frequent itemsets. There are two broad commonalities among all the algorithms. First, they all
use the anti-monotone property of the itemset support criterion. This property
states that as the length of the itemset increases, its support either decreases
or stays the same; or in other words, a k-itemset is frequent only if all of its
$(k-1)$-subitemsets are frequent. *Apriori* algorithm [3] was one of the first algorithms, which pioneered the use of this property. *Apriori* used it systematically
to control the exponential growth in the number of possible itemsets that need
to be searched to get the desired frequent itemsets. The second commonality
among the algorithms is that they all need to search through a common itemset
lattice. Briefly, given an itemset I, a *lattice* is a systematic enumeration of all
the subsets of I, starting with an empty set at the bottom, all the singleton
itemsets at the first level, all 2-itemsets at second level, and so on. A k-itemset
that has k items in it and appears at the kth level of the lattice, is linked to all
its $(k-1)$-subitemsets appearing at level $k-1$. The manner in which the algorithms decide to traverse this lattice, and the way they use the anti-monotone
property of support, are two of the crucial factors that determine their perfor-
mances. In this section, we first give a brief description of the *Apriori* algorithm,

not only because of its historical importance but also because the primary parallel algorithms discussed in this chapter are based on *Apriori*. Later, we give a comparative summary of many other serial algorithms.

3.1 Apriori Algorithm

The high level structure of the *Apriori* algorithm is given in Figure 1. The *Apriori* algorithm consists of a number of passes. Initially F_1 contains all the items (i.e., itemset of size one) that satisfy the minimum support requirement. During pass k, the algorithm finds the set of frequent itemsets F_k of size k that satisfy the minimum support requirement. The algorithm terminates when F_k is empty. In each pass, the algorithm first generates C_k, the candidate itemsets of size k. Function *apriori_gen*(F_{k-1}) constructs C_k by extending frequent itemsets of size $k - 1$. This ensures that all the subsets of size $k - 1$ of a new candidate itemset are in F_{k-1}. Once the candidate itemsets are found, their frequencies are computed by counting how many transactions contain these candidate itemsets. Finally, F_k is generated by pruning C_k to eliminate itemsets with frequencies smaller than the minimum support. The union of the frequent itemsets, $\bigcup F_k$, is the frequent itemsets from which we generate association rules.

```
1. F₁ = { frequent 1-itemsets} ;
2. for ( k = 2; F_{k-1} ≠ φ; k++ ) {
3.       C_k = apriori_gen(F_{k-1})
4.       for all transactions t ∈ T {
5.            subset(C_k, t)
6.       }
7.       F_k = {c ∈ C_k | c.count ≥ minsup}
8. }
9. Answer = ∪ F_k
```

Fig. 1. Apriori Algorithm

Computing the counts of the candidate itemsets is the most computationally expensive step of the algorithm. One naive way to compute these counts is to perform string-matching of each transaction against each candidate itemset. A faster way of performing this operation is to use a candidate hash tree in which the candidate itemsets are hashed [3]. The key idea behind a hash tree is that all the candidates in a given transaction can be found relatively quickly by hashing on the items of the transaction. Here we explain this via an example.

Figure 2 shows one example of the candidate hash tree with candidates of size 3. The internal nodes of the hash tree have hash tables that contain links to child nodes. The leaf nodes contain the candidate itemsets. First, let us see

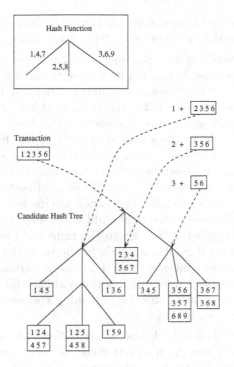

Fig. 2. Subset operation on the root of a candidate hash tree.

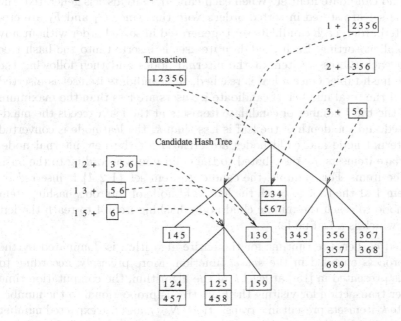

Fig. 3. Subset operation on the left most subtree of the root of a candidate hash tree.

how this hash tree is used to search for the candidate itemsets present in a given transaction; i.e., how the *subset* function (step 5 in Figure 1) works.

The *subset* function traverses the hash tree from the root with every item in a transaction as a possible starting item of a candidate. In the next level of the tree, all the items of the transaction following the starting item are hashed. This is done recursively until a leaf is reached. At this time, all the candidates at the leaf are checked against the transaction and their counts are updated accordingly. Figure 2 shows the subset operation at the first level of the tree with transaction $\{1\ 2\ 3\ 5\ 6\}$. The item 1 is hashed to the left child node of the root and the following transaction $\{2\ 3\ 5\ 6\}$ is applied recursively to the left child node. The item 2 is hashed to the middle child node of the root and the whole transaction is checked against two candidate itemsets in the middle child node. Then item 3 is hashed to the right child node of the root and the following transaction $\{5\ 6\}$ is applied recursively to the right child node. Figure 3 shows the subset operation on the left child node of the root. Here the items 2 and 5 are hashed to the middle child node and the following transactions $\{3\ 5\ 6\}$ and $\{6\}$ respectively are applied recursively to the middle child node. The item 3 is hashed to the right child node and the remaining transaction $\{5\ 6\}$ is applied recursively to the right child node.

We just described how a hash tree is used. Now, let us see how it is constructed. Note that, a new hash tree is constructed in every iteration of the algorithm. Initially, the hash tree contains only a root node, which is a leaf node containing no candidate itemset. When each candidate itemset is generated, the items in the set are stored in sorted order. Note that since C_1 and F_1 are created in sorted order, each candidate set is generated in sorted order without any need for explicit sorting. Each candidate itemset is inserted into the hash tree by hashing each successive item at the internal nodes and then following the links in the hash table. Once a leaf is reached, the candidate itemset is inserted at the leaf if the total number of candidate itemsets are less than the maximum allowed. If the total number of candidate itemsets at the leaf exceeds the maximum allowed and the depth of the leaf is less than k, the leaf node is converted into an internal node and child nodes are created for the new internal node. The candidate itemsets are distributed to the child nodes according to the hash values of the items. For example, the candidate item set $\{1\ 2\ 4\}$ is inserted by hashing item 1 at the root to reach the left child node of the root, hashing item 2 at that node to reach the middle child node, hashing item 4 to reach the left child node which is a leaf node.

As stated earlier, the runtime for the entire algorithm is dominated by the counting process encoded in the *subset* function. More precisely, according to the analysis presented in [15], at level k of the algorithm, the computation time required per transaction for visiting the hash tree is proportional to the number of candidate k-itemsets present in a transaction (N_{C_k}), and the expected number of distinct leaf nodes visited by the transaction. It is shown that as the number of leaf nodes in hash tree grows larger, the runtime gets dominated more by N_{C_k}.

3.2   Other Serial Algorithms

In the previous subsection, we described *Apriori*, one of the first and most popular algorithms for generating frequent itemsets. There are many other algorithms proposed after the conception of *Apriori*. We will briefly describe some representative algorithms, namely DHP [4], Tree Projection algorithms [11,12], PARTITION [5], the sampling-based algorithms [7], a set of algorithms proposed in [6], a family of algorithms proposed in [9], the DIC algorithm [10], the FP-tree based algorithm [13], and a trie-based algorithm [8].

As stated earlier, these algorithms differ in their ways of traversing the itemset lattice, and the ways in which they use the anti-monotone property of itemset support. In the following, we classify the algorithms primarily based on their lattice traversal strategies. Another dimension where the algorithms differ is the way they handle the transaction database; i.e. how many passes they make over the entire database and how they reduce the size of the processed database in each pass. With these points in mind, we present a comparative summary of all the algorithms.

Level-Wise Algorithms: A class of algorithms generates candidate k-itemsets from frequent $(k - 1)$-itemsets. These are called level-wise algorithms. We have already described *Apriori*, one of the first level-wise algorithms. Here we describe some more. Like *Apriori*, DHP and breadth-first Tree Projection algorithms make a pass over the entire database at every level of the algorithm. They differ in the ways they optimize on the number of candidates generated, and the ways that make the counting phase efficient.

DHP [4] (direct hashing and pruning) algorithm improves upon the *Apriori* algorithm in two ways. First, it reduces the candidate space by looking ahead in the transactions for potentially frequent $(k+1)$-itemsets while counting candidate k-itemsets. This is achieved by hashing all potentially frequent $(k + 1)$-subsets of each transaction to a common hash table, and using this hash table to prune some $(k + 1)$-candidates without counting them. The algorithm, however, must balance the trade-off between the size of the hash table and its effectiveness in aggressive pruning. The second factor which allows DHP to improve upon *Apriori*, is its idea of *transaction trimming*. While counting at level k, each item in a transaction is checked for whether it appears in at least k different candidate k-itemsets. If it does not, then it will not be present in any subsequent candidate j-itemsets ($j > k$), and hence it can be removed from the transaction. Similarly, while preparing the hash table at level k, if an item does not appear in any of the $(k + 1)$-itemsets being hashed, then it can be removed from the transaction. If the hashing scheme is effective in pruning many candidates at an early level, then this transaction trimming scheme reduces the active transaction database size substantially, which in turn can reduce the computation time spent per transaction.

Tree Projection algorithms [11,12] achieve candidate space pruning as well as counting efficiency by combining a novel idea of representing the candidates in a lexicographic tree structure with a way of reducing the transaction database size in every pass by *projecting* the transactions onto this lexicographic tree. In a lexicographic tree, each node is associated with a k-itemset. A node can be extended into multiple children nodes via items that are lexicographically larger than all the items in its itemset. The new children represent $(k + 1)$-itemsets. Tree Projection algorithms grow the lexicographic tree progressively such that only the nodes corresponding to frequent itemsets are generated. The level-wise version of the algorithm grows the tree in a breadth-first manner. In iteration k, it extends all the nodes at level $k - 1$. The candidate extensions of a given node are formed by using only the frequent extensions at its parent. One of the key features of the algorithm is that the counts for the itemsets represented by the candidate extensions are gathered by using the set of *projected* transactions at the parent. The concept of projection is involved. Briefly, the algorithm maintains a list of *active items* and *active extensions* for each node. When a transaction is projected at a node, only the items that occur in the active item list are kept. The transaction gets recursively projected along the paths determined by active extensions. The idea is, only those items in a transaction percolate down the tree that can potentially be useful in extending the tree by one more level. With every pass of the algorithm, many extensions become progressively inactive, which in turn results in the reduction of active item list sizes at all nodes. Thus, the size of the projected transaction set reduces progressively. This yields the algorithm its efficiency in the counting phase. Use of sophisticated counting techniques such as cache-blocking on the candidate count matrix at each node, further add to the efficiency of the algorithm. The concept of projection can be thought of as a more generalized form of transaction trimming used in DHP. Also, the concept of active items and active extensions effectively render the lexicographic tree as a precise, dynamic version of the hash-tree structures used in *Apriori*.

The PARTITION [5] and sampling-based algorithms [7] are level-wise, but only on a small portion of the entire database. In fact, use of smaller subsets of database allows them to optimize the database performance by making at most two passes over the entire database.

PARTITION algorithm takes the idea of support monotonicity further. It partitions the database into multiple parts, and observes that if an itemset is frequent in the entire database then it is frequent in at least one of the partitions, when the frequency is computed relative to the partition size. This observation is used to prune the potential frequent itemsets by counting the candidates in smaller local partitions. A level-wise algorithm is employed to generate all *locally frequent* itemsets. All such itemsets are gathered and their global counts are collected in a second pass over the database. Thus, only two database passes are needed. In order to achieve true gain in performance, the algorithm has to minimize the effect of data skew across partitions by randomizing the partitioning scheme. It also has to take care of the trade-off between the partition size and number of partitions. Finding locally large itemsets in smaller partitions is quick, but the lower amount of information available in smaller partitions also tends to give rise to many false positives because the support is counted with respect to their small size. The PARTITION algorithm has one more novel feature as compared to *Apriori*, which can potentially accelerate the counting phase. It uses *vertical data layout* in which the transaction-id list (*tid-list*) is stored for each item. This is an inverted version of the horizontal layout used in *Apriori*, where a list of items is stored for each transaction. It is made sure that the size of each partition is such that all the required tid-lists in a partition fit in the main memory. This allows the itemset support counting to be performed efficiently by intersecting the tid-lists of its individual items.

The SPTID and SPEAR algorithms, proposed by [6] and summarized in [28], are identical in spirit to PARTITION. SPTID uses the vertical layout whereas SPEAR uses the horizontal layout of database. Their optimization over PARTI-TION comes from the use of *prefix tree* as an efficient substitute for hash tree in the counting phase. Prefix tree can avoid counting of unnecessary candidates, and allows efficient search for subsets because many subsets are compressed into a single path of the tree. This tree is similar in structure to the lexicographic tree of Tree Projection algorithms. However, the lexicographic tree is used in a much more sophisticated and effective manner by the Tree Projection algorithms.

The sampling-based algorithms proposed in [7] use a randomly sampled partition of the database to find locally frequent itemsets in that partition. The gain in performance is possible due to the less amount of data that the algorithms work on, making it attractive for large databases. However, in order to ensure the completeness of the frequent itemsets discovered, the algorithm has to do several things. First, it has to reduce the support threshold used for discovering frequent sets in the sampled data. This is done with the hope of capturing most of the actual frequent itemsets. Despite of this reduction in support threshold (which cannot be reduced below certain level), some itemsets will be missing. The algorithm has a novel systematic strategy of checking for all the missing itemsets. It introduces a concept of *negative border* of the locally frequent item-sets. This border is formed by all minimal small itemsets; i.e., the sets which are infrequent but all their subsets are frequent. Locally frequent sets and the sets in their negative border are counted in the entire database, and these global counts are used to see if any true frequent itemsets are lost by sampling. Since the algorithm is based on a random sample, the authors present a probabilistic analysis that relates the sample size, the limit on lowering support threshold, and accuracy that can be achieved.

Non-level-wise Algorithms: The class of non-level-wise algorithms consists of the hybrid lattice traversal technique proposed in [9], the DIC algorithm [10], the SEAR and SPINC algorithms of [6], and the depth-first version of the tree projection algorithm [12]. Like PARTITION and sampling-based algorithms, the design goal for these algorithms is reduction in the number of passes made over the entire database. However, the major point of difference is their itemset lat-tice traversal technique. Instead of a level-wise (or breadth-first) traversal, they interleave the depth-first and breadth-first searches with the database passes. In other words, the candidate generation and candidate counting phases are interleaved.

The lattice traversal algorithms proposed in [9] use a vertical layout (similar to PARTITION). One pass is made over the database to generate the item tid-lists. After that, no more passes are required over the database. Only the tid-lists need to be scanned. A novel feature of all their algorithms is that they are seeded by an itemset clustering method. The clustering allows them to identify close approximations to the potentially maximal itemsets. This may substantially prune the candidate search space by dividing the original itemset lattice into smaller sub-lattices formed only by items belonging to same cluster. They propose three different approaches to traverse these smaller itemset sub-lattices. The bottom-up approach does a breadth-first traversal of the lattice starting with the 2-itemsets. This is similar to the level-wise algorithms. But it faces a problem of generating all the subsets of frequent itemsets, especially when the goal is to find only the maximal frequent sets. The top-down approach caters specifically to that need, and starts with potentially maximal itemsets given by the clustering, and goes down the lattice until all the maximal frequent itemsets are found. This approach faces the problem of costly multi-way intersections of tid-lists as well as it suffers from the approximate nature of clusters. A hybrid approach combines the good features of both approaches, and is shown to be better than the two. Although it is true that the entire database is scanned once, there are several passes made over the individual tid-lists. The main performance gain achieved may be attributed to their clustering scheme to prune the search space clubbed with an underlying assumption that the tid-lists for individual items or 2-itemsets are not very large.

The DIC algorithm [10] is a recent non-level-wise algorithm which is actually closer to the sampling-based algorithms. Instead of using a random sample of the database and potentially losing some frequent item-sets, it proposes a systematic search of the database that reduces the number of database passes to some number between 1 and the total number of passes that would be made by a level-wise algorithm. Unlike level-wise algorithms which count only k-itemsets in one pass of the algorithm, DIC starts counting longer itemsets after some fixed intervals during a given database pass. For example, in a database of 10000 transactions, it starts computing 1-itemsets at first transaction, then some 2-itemsets start getting counted after M=1000 transactions, some 3-itemsets start getting counted after 2*M=2000 transactions, and so on. The value of M can be changed. Each itemset that the algorithm decides to count, gets counted in each transaction. The algorithm keeps track of potential frequent itemsets and potential minimal small itemsets. The counting starts only for those itemsets whose subsets have been found frequent in the data visited so far. Essentially the amount of lattice traversed by the algorithm is same as that by a level-wise algorithm, but the dynamic nature of counting the itemsets gives the algorithm a flexibility to reduce database passes. The crucial factor for its performance is the ability to identify frequent subsets of a given itemset early enough so that the itemset starts getting counted early. Ideally if the probability of seeing a given itemset in any fraction of transactions is the same, then DIC performs very well. However, if the dataset is not *homogeneous*, then the performance would suffer.

The authors of DIC identify this problem and propose some remedies such as randomization and relaxing the support threshold.

The SEAR algorithm of [6] uses the same prefix tree that is used in level-wise SPTID and SPEAR algorithms by the same author. Its key feature is the concept of *pass bundling*, which makes it a non-level-wise algorithm and allows it to save on the number of database passes. In pass bundling, instead of generating only k-candidates in a pass, candidates of length $k + 1$, $k + 2$ are also generated. Generation stops when the candidates don't fit in the memory. Then a single database scan counts all these candidates. Of course, pass bundling can help only in the lower levels of the tree, where the number of candidates is small, because of the trade-off between the reduced I/O passes and increase in computation due to lack of candidate pruning. Another algorithm, SPINC, given in [6] is an optimization of the PARTITION-based algorithm SPEAR. Making use of the sequential processing nature of partitions, SPINC starts gathering partial global counts for the locally frequent candidates of a given partition in all the subsequent partitions. Contrast this with PARTITION which waits until second pass to gather global counts for all locally frequent itemsets. For large partition sizes, SPINC can significantly reduce the counting workload in second database pass. The early counting of some global candidates yields SPINC a non-level-wise flavor in counting phase, although the local candidate generation is still level-wise in each partition[1]. Refer to [6] for an empirical comparison between SEAR, SPINC, SPTID, and SPEAR algorithms. It presents interesting results as to the effectiveness of vertical versus horizontal layouts, and pros and cons of using partitioning mechanisms.

The depth-first version of the tree projection algorithm [12] generates the lexicographic tree in a depth-first manner, making it a non-level-wise algorithm. The crucial factor for its performance is that the entire transaction database needs to fit in the memory, which is not very practical for many transaction databases. Hence, we will not review it in detail here.

Algorithms that Do not Generate Candidates: Finally, we briefly review a class of algorithms [8,13] that choose a radically different approach to discover frequent itemsets. These algorithms do not subscribe to the generate-and-count paradigm of previously described algorithms. They infer frequent itemsets directly from the transaction database without candidate generation. The algorithm based on *FP-trees* [13] uses a compact trie-like representation of the transaction database that is used to directly infer the frequent itemsets involving a given frequent item. This compact representation is achieved using the data structure called frequent pattern tree (FP-tree), which is a data structure based on set-enumeration tree formed using frequency-ordered 1-itemsets. It is constrained using the given transaction database in the following manner. Each

---

[1] Although SPINC was proposed much earlier, its concept of starting counting earlier is similar to that of DIC. Of course, the two differ substantially in how candidates are generated, which eventually affects the number of I/O passes and number of false positives generated by each.

transaction is transformed to a frequency-ordered set of items and is mapped to the set-enumeration tree. The counts of items on the path it gets mapped to are incremented by one. All the occurrences of a given item are linked across the tree. Once FP-tree is constructed, for each item, the algorithm finds all the frequent itemsets having that item as the last item (in frequency-order). This is achieved by using the prefix paths to all the occurrences of that item in the tree. A systematic recursive decomposition of the prefix paths yields all the desired frequent itemsets. If this process is mapped to a lattice traversal process, then the algorithm essentially traverses the lattice in a top-down fashion (i.e. going from longer itemsets down to smaller itemsets), starting with the itemset formed by all the frequent items in the union of the items occurring in the prefix paths. However, its recursion process breaks the lattice down into only the interesting sub-lattices driven by the increasingly smaller FP-trees. The authors show their algorithm to be an order of magnitude faster than the *Apriori* algorithm and considerably faster than the Tree Projection algorithm.

A related algorithm proposed in [8], also uses the compact trie [29] representation of the transaction database, to directly infer the frequent associations. However, unlike FP-tree, which encodes the entire transaction database into a trie-like structure, their algorithm constructs a trie only out of those subsets of a transaction that contains less than a pre-specified number of items. This was motivated by their observation that the largest frequent itemsets do not generally contain more than 8-10 items. Once the trie is constructed, they use all the subsets present in the trie as potential frequent sets. However, unlike FP-tree based algorithm, they do not give a systematic algorithm for inferring actual frequent itemsets based on support.

This concludes our survey of the representative serial algorithms for computing frequent itemsets.

4   Parallel Formulations for Frequent Itemset Discovery

The enormity and high dimensionality of datasets typically available as input to the problem of association rule discovery, makes it an ideal problem for solving on multiple processors in parallel. The primary reasons are the memory and CPU speed limitations faced by single processors. Despite of many improved serial algorithms, the sheer amount of required computational work may result in prohibitively large runtimes on single processors. Thus, it is critical to design efficient parallel algorithms to do the task. Another reason for designing parallel algorithms comes from the fact that many transaction databases are already available in parallel databases or they are distributed at multiple sites to begin with. The cost of of bringing them all to one site or one computer for serial discovery of association rules can be prohibitively expensive.

We reviewed many different serial algorithms in previous subsection. Except for a few, most of these algorithms involve generation of candidate itemsets and counting them in the transaction database. This is especially true of the level-wise algorithms such as Apriori. First, we present possible parallel formulations of such algorithms and map the existing parallel algorithms to these formulations. In the end, we review parallel formulations of some non-level-wise algorithms.

Before proceeding further, we would like to comment on the platforms of applicability of the algorithms. The focus of this chapter is on algorithms that are primarily designed for distributed memory parallel architectures, which use message-passing as the primary means of inter-processor communications. Some of the algorithms can be modified to work on shared memory architectures with some effort, but design issues for such architectures are quite different from those discussed here. As a matter of fact, the programming model for shared memory architectures is simpler compared to that for the distributed memory architectures. Moreover, shared memory architectures do not scale well to handle large databases. Very little work has been done on parallel algorithms for shared memory machines. A review of them can be found in [28].

The distributed shared memory (DSM) architectures are becoming more popular nowadays, which allow a physically distributed memory to belong to a globally shared logical address space. The algorithms designed for distributed memory machines can be readily adapted to such architectures by relying on the communication subsystem's implementation of message passing via logical shared memory. But, the performance of the algorithms can be certainly tuned to the DSM architecture by re-designing some serial tasks to get them executed by multiple symmetric multiprocessors (SMP) in a shared-memory fashion. Some algorithms that we review in the last part of this section have been tuned in this way [18,28].

4.1   Parallel Formulations of Level-Wise Algorithms

The computational work in level-wise algorithms can be viewed to consist of two parts: the effort spent in generating the candidates and the effort spent in counting them. In order to distribute this work among processors, multiple possibilities emerge depending on how the transactions and candidate itemsets are assigned to processors. The need for parallel algorithms comes from the transaction database being too large (enormity of the database), or possible number of frequent itemsets being too large (because of high dimensionality of the database), or both. Correspondingly, in order to achieve concurrency, either the candidates need to be counted in parallel, or they need to be generated in parallel, or both these phases need to be done in parallel.

We assume that the transaction database is too large to be replicated among all processors. For most practical problems in data mining, this is a fair or rather necessary assumption. Usually, the transactions are distributed among processors equally. Given this, the issue becomes how to distribute the candidates among processors such that their counting and generation is effectively parallelized. There are three possibilities. One is to replicate the candidates on all processors, the other is to avoid replication, and the third is to allow partial replication. In the following we review in detail various algorithms based on these possibilities. The discussion takes into account the issues of minimizing parallelization overheads, extracting concurrency, and utilizing the total available memory effectively.

Replicating Candidate Itemsets

One possible way to parallelize is to simply replicate the candidate generation process on all the processors, and parallelize the counting process. Here are a few representative algorithms that take this approach.

- **Count Distribution (CD):** In this parallel formulation of Apriori algorithm, proposed in [30], each processor computes how many times all the candidates appear in the locally stored transactions. This is done by building the entire hash tree that corresponds to all the candidates and then performing a single pass over the locally stored transactions to collect the counts. The global counts of the candidates are computed by summing these individual counts using a global reduction operation [31]. This algorithm is illustrated in Figure 4. Note that since each processor needs to build a hash tree for all the candidates, these hash trees are identical at each processor. Thus, excluding the global reduction, each processor in the *CD* algorithm executes the serial *Apriori* algorithm on the locally stored transactions.
  This algorithm has been empirically shown to scale linearly with the number of transactions [30]. A detailed scalability analysis is presented by [15]. Given N number of transactions and P number of processors, if M is the total number of candidates that get generated, then they show that the parallel runtime of the algorithm is $T_s/P + O(M)$, where T_s is the serial runtime of the algorithm. The $O(M)$ term comes from the hash tree construction and global reduction of counts. This indicates that the algorithm is scalable in number of transactions, however it does not parallelize the computation of building the candidate hash tree. This step becomes a bottleneck with large number of processors. Furthermore, if the number of candidates is large, then the hash tree does not fit into the main memory. In this case, this algorithm has to partition the hash tree and compute the counts by scanning the database multiple times, once for each partition of the hash tree. The cost of extra database scanning can be expensive on machines with slow I/O system. Note that the number of candidates increases if either the number of distinct items in the database increases or if the minimum support level of the association rules decreases. Thus the *CD* algorithm is effective for small number of distinct items and a high minimum support level.

- **Parallel PARTITION Algorithm:** The parallel formulation of the serial PARTITION algorithm has been given in [5]. The serial algorithm has inherent parallelism in it as far as processing of each partition is concerned. The algorithm is very similar to the count distribution algorithm, in that the data is distributed and the candidate set is replicated among processors. The difference is that the frequent itemsets are counted in four stages. In the first stage, each processor discovers *locally frequent* itemsets assuming

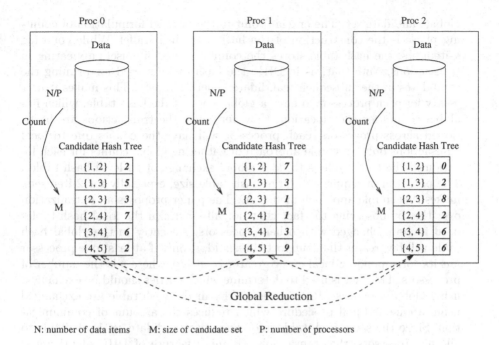

N: number of data items   M: size of candidate set   P: number of processors

Fig. 4. Count Distribution (CD) Algorithm

that its local data is the entire database. Next, these itemsets are exchanged among processors, forming the global candidate set. In the third stage, local counts for these candidates are computed by scanning the local data again. Finally, a communication operation is performed to add up the local counts to get the global counts for the candidates, from which globally frequent itemsets can be determined. As in the serial case, the vertical data layout used in parallel PARTITION can make the counting phase efficient, and allows it to avoid multiple scans of the local database. In this algorithm, the size of the candidate set generated in second stage is dependent on the size of local datasets and skew in the data. It could potentially be bigger than the candidate set in CD because of false positives, and hence can cause the algorithm to lose its main purpose of achieving efficiency by pruning based on local counts.

– **PDM Algorithm:** Another parallel algorithm which is based on the serial Apriori-like algorithm is PDM [16], which is a parallel formulation of the DHP [4] algorithm. The approach to parallelization is very much similar to the CD algorithm. The difference is in the fact that DHP differs from Apriori in its use of hash tables to look ahead into the potential candidates of next phase. The phase of candidate generation is parallelized using a parallel nested loop join algorithm. Each processor generates a small disjoint subset of entire candidate set. These sets are exchanged by all nodes to generate global candidate set. The crucial point in the parallel formulation of counting phase is the construction of the hash table in parallel. While counting k-itemsets, the hash table stores the counts of $k + 1$-itemsets appearing in transactions. Note that, as in DHP, the hash table is used for pruning the candidates in the subsequent candidate generation pass. This makes it necessary for each processor to have a global copy of the hash table, which has global counts for each location. However, since the transactions are partitioned across processors, each processor will have the counts due to local transactions only. A simple approach of gathering global counts for each location in the hash table is to do a global exchange of all local hash tables. The potential of requiring a large hash table size, especially for 2-itemsets, makes this simple approach inefficient. The paper proposes an optimization over this by observing the fact that not all entries in the local hash tables need to be exchanged with other processors. An entry in the global hash table will be greater than support threshold, s, only if at least one processor has its corresponding local entry greater than s/p, where p is the number of processors. This fact is used to determine which entries should be exchanged using global broadcast. Rest of the entries in the hash table are exchanged using a clue-and-poll procedure which reduces the amount of communication. Since the same hash table and the entire candidate set is available to all the processors, the transaction trimming feature of DHP algorithm is easily maintained in PDM as well. Each processor tries to reduce the size of transactions in its local partition. Overall, PDM is similar to CD. But, effective parallelization of hash table construction, the possible advantages gained by a good hashing function, and the transaction trimming might give PDM an edge over CD.

– **Count Distributed Tree Projection Algorithm:** This formulation proposed in [11] is based on the CD algorithm described above. Identical lexicographic tree, upon which the tree projection algorithms are based, is built on each processor and counts are communicated at every level. As with CD, this parallel formulation works well only if the lexicographic tree fits in memory, and its scalability with number of candidates is poor.

– **Some Other Replication Based Algorithms:** The NPA (Non-Partitioned Apriori) algorithm, proposed in [17] is identical to CD algorithm. The PEAR algorithm given in [6], is also identical in spirit to the CD algorithm; the only difference being that it uses SEAR algorithm instead of Apriori for the candidate generation and local support counting phases within each processor. Finally, the PPAR algorithm of [6] is identical to the parallel PARTITION algorithm. It is a parallel formulation of the SPEAR algorithm discussed in section 3.2.

Partitioning Candidate Itemsets

Given the problems possibly encountered because of the replication of candidates, an alternative approach would be to partition the candidates among processors. However, many issues arise regarding how to partition them and how to effectively parallelize counting for a given partitioning. Following algorithms handle these issues. DD algorithm discussed first makes a simple yet weak effort to parallelize. The next algorithm, IDD, improves upon it greatly. A few other algorithms are also described in the end.

- **Data Distribution (DD):** This algorithm [30] addresses the memory problem of the *CD* algorithm by partitioning the candidate item-sets among the processors. This partitioning is done in a round robin fashion. Each processor is responsible for computing the counts of its locally stored subset of the candidate item-sets for all the transactions in the database. In order to do that, each processor needs to scan the portions of the transactions assigned to the other processors as well as its locally stored portion of the transactions. In the *DD* algorithm, this is done by having each processor receive the portions of the transactions stored in the other processors as follows. Each processor allocates P buffers (each one page long and one for each processor). At processor P_i, the ith buffer is used to store transactions from the locally stored database and the remaining buffers are used to store transactions from the other processors. Now each processor P_i checks the P buffers to see which one contains data. Let l be this buffer (ties are broken in favor of buffers of other processors and ties among buffers of other processors are broken arbitrarily). The processor processes the transactions in this buffer and updates the counts of its own candidate subset. If this buffer corresponds to the buffer that stores local transactions (i.e., $l = i$), then it is sent to all the other processors (via asynchronous sends), and a new page is read from the local database. If this buffer corresponds to a buffer that stores transactions from another processor (i.e., $l \neq i$), then it is cleared and this buffer is marked available for next asynchronous receive from any other processors. This continues until every processor has processed all the transactions. Having computed the counts of its candidate item-sets, each processor finds the frequent item-sets from its candidate item-set and these frequent item-sets are sent to every other processor using an all-to-all broadcast operation [31]. Figure 5 shows the high level operations of the algorithm. Note that each processor has a different set of candidates in the candidate hash tree. The SPA (Simply Partitioned Apriori) algorithm, proposed in [17], is identical to DD. It partitions the candidates among processors in a round robin manner. Each transaction is broadcast to all the processors so as to generate a global count for *all* the candidates. The DD algorithm exploits the total available memory better than *CD*, as it partitions the candidate set among processors. As the number of processors increases, the number of candidates that the algorithm can handle also increases. However, as reported in [30], the performance of this algorithm is

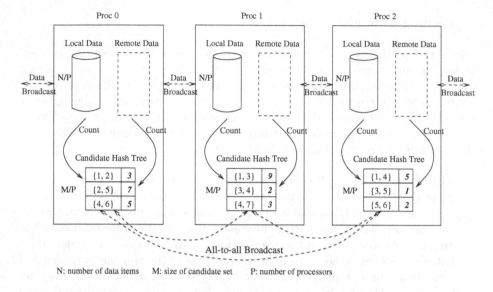

N: number of data items   M: size of candidate set   P: number of processors

Fig. 5. Data Distribution (DD) Algorithm

significantly worse than the *CD* algorithm. The run time of this algorithm is 10 to 20 times more than that of the *CD* algorithm on 16 processors [30]. The problem lies with the communication pattern of the algorithm and the redundant work that is performed in processing all the transactions.

The communication pattern of this algorithm causes three problems. First, during each pass of the algorithm each processor sends to all the other processors the portion of the database that resides locally. In particular, each processor reads the locally stored portion of the database one page at a time and sends it to all the other processors by issuing $P - 1$ send operations. Similarly, each processor issues a receive operation from each other processor in order to receive these pages. If the interconnection network of the underlying parallel computer is fully connected (i.e., there is a direct link between all pairs of processors) and each processor can receive data on all incoming links simultaneously, then this communication pattern will lead to a very good performance. In particular, if $O(N/P)$ is the size of the database assigned locally to each processor, the amount of time spent in the communication will be $O(N/P)$. However, even on the parallel computer with fully connected network, if each processor can receive data from (or send data to) only one other processor at a time, then the communication will be $O(N)$. On all realistic parallel computers, the processors are connected via a sparser networks (such as 2D, 3D or hypercube) and a processor can receive data from (or send data to) only one other processor at a time. On such machines, this communication pattern will take significantly more than $O(N)$ time because of contention within the network.

Second, in architectures without asynchronous communication support and with finite number of communication buffers in each processor, the proposed all-to-all communication scheme causes processors to idle. For instance, consider the case when one processor finishes its operation on local data and sends the buffer to all other processors. Now if the communication buffer of any receiving processors is full and the outgoing communication buffers are full, then the send operation is blocked.

Third, if we look at the size of the candidate sets as a function of the number of passes of the algorithm, we see that in the first few passes, the size of the candidate sets increases and after that it decreases. In particular, during the last several passes of the algorithm, there are only a small number of items in the candidate sets. However, each processor in the DD algorithm still sends the locally stored portions of the database to all the other processors. Thus, even though the computation decreases, the amount of communication remains the same.

The redundant work is introduced due to the fact that every processor has to process every single transaction in the database. In CD (see Figure 4), only N/P transactions go through each hash tree of M candidates, whereas in DD (see Figure 5), all N transactions have to go through each hash tree of M/P candidates. Although, the number of candidates stored at each processor has been reduced by a factor of P, the amount of computation performed for each transaction has not been proportionally reduced. According to the analysis presented in [15], in general, the amount of work per transaction will go down by a factor much smaller than P.

The detailed analysis of parallel runtime is given in [15], according to which the algorithm is not scalable with respect to number of transactions, but it scales well with respect to number of candidates.

- **Intelligent Data Distribution (IDD):** This algorithm was proposed in [32]. It solves the problems of the DD algorithm. First, in IDD, the locally stored portions of the database are sent to all the other processors by using a ring-based all-to-all broadcast described in [31]. Compared to DD, where all the processors send data to all other processors, IDD performs only a point-to-point communication between neighbors, thus eliminating any communication contention that DD algorithm faces. Thus, the all-to-all broadcast operation takes $O(N)$ time on *any* parallel architecture that can be embedded in a ring. Furthermore, if the time to process a buffer does not vary much, then there is little time lost in idling. Also, when it is implemented using asynchronous communication operations, the computation and communication operations can be overlapped.

  Second problem of DD that IDD improves upon is that of redundant work. In order to eliminate the redundant work due to the partitioning of the candidate item-sets, IDD finds a fast way to check whether a given transaction can potentially contain any of the candidates stored at each processor. This cannot be done by partitioning C_k in a round-robin fashion. However, if C_k is partitioned among processors in such a way that each processor gets item-sets that begin only with a subset of all possible items, then the items of a transaction can be checked against this subset to determine if the hash tree contains candidates starting with these items. The hash tree is traversed with only the items in the transaction that belong to this subset. Thus, the redundant work problem of *DD* is solved by the intelligent partitioning of C_k.

These points can be understood better by looking at Figure 6, which shows the high level picture of the algorithm. In this example, Processor 0 has all

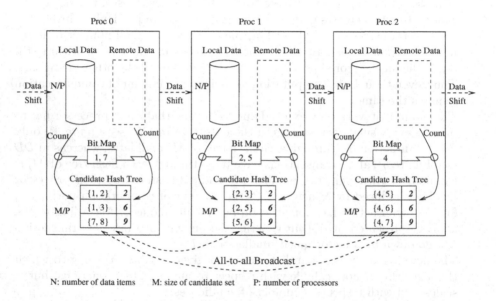

Fig. 6. Intelligent Data Distribution (IDD) Algorithm

the candidates starting with items 1 and 7, Processor 1 has all the candidates starting with 2 and 5, and so on. Each processor keeps the first items of the candidates it has in a bit-map. In the *Apriori* algorithm, at the root level of hash tree, every item in a transaction is hashed and checked against the hash tree. However, in IDD, at the root level, each processor filters every item of the transaction by checking against the bit-map to see if the processor contains candidates starting with that item of the transaction. If the processor does not contain the candidates starting with that item, the processing steps involved with that item as the first item in the candidate can be skipped. This reduces the amount of transaction data that has to go through the hash tree; thus, reducing the computation. For example, let {1 2 3 4 5 6 7 8} be a transaction that processor 0 is processing in the *subset* function discussed in Section 3.1. At the top level of the hash tree, processor 0 will only proceed with items 1 and 7 (i.e., 1 + 2 3 4 5 6 7 8 and 7 + 8). When the page containing this transaction is shifted to processor 1, this processor will only process items starting with 2 and 5 (i.e., 2 + 3 4 5 6 7

8 and 5 + 6 7 8). Figure 7 shows how this scheme works when a processor contains only those candidate item-sets that start with 1, 3 and 5.

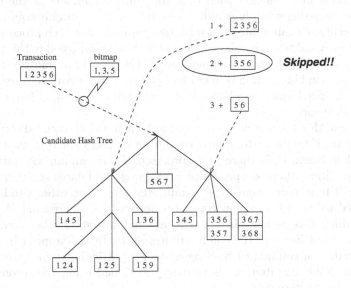

Fig. 7. Subset operation on the root of a candidate hash tree in IDD.

Thus for each transaction in the database, IDD partitions the amount of work to be performed among processors, thus eliminating most of the redundant work of *DD*. Note that both the judicious partitioning of the hash tree (indirectly caused by the partitioning of candidate item-set) and the filtering step are required to eliminate this redundant work.

The intelligent partitioning of the candidate set used in *IDD* brings up the issue of load balancing. One of the criteria of a good partitioning involved here is to have an equal number of candidates in all the processors. This gives about the same size hash tree in all the processors and thus provides good load balancing among processors. Note that in the *DD* algorithm, this was accomplished by distributing candidates in a round robin fashion. This does not give any guarantees of load balance. Even in IDD, a naive method for assigning candidates to processors can lead to a significant load imbalance. For instance, consider a database with 100 distinct items numbered from 1 to 100 and that the database transactions have more data items numbered with 1 to 50. Let the candidates be partitioned between two processors. If all the candidates starting with items 1 to 50 are assigned to processor P_0 and all candidates starting with items 51 to 100 to processor P_1, then there would be more work for processor P_0.

To achieve an equal distribution of the candidate item-sets, the authors of IDD use a partitioning algorithm that is based on bin-packing [33]. For each item, they first compute the number of candidate item-sets starting with this particular item. Note that at this time they do not actually store the candidate item-sets, but they just store the number of candidate item-sets starting with each item. Then a bin-packing algorithm is used to partition these items in P buckets such that the sum of numbers of the candidate item-sets starting with these items in each bucket are roughly equal. Once the location of each candidate item-set is determined, then each processor locally regenerates and stores candidate item-sets that are assigned to this processor. Note that bin-packing is used per pass of the algorithm and the amount of time spent on bin-packing is minor compared to the overall runtime. Figure 6 shows the partitioned candidate hash tree and its corresponding bitmaps in each processor.

Note that this scheme will not be able to achieve an equal distribution of candidates if there are too many candidate itemsets starting with the same item. For example, if there are more than M/P candidates starting with the same item, then one processor containing candidates starting with this item will have more than M/P candidates even if no other candidates are assigned to it. This problem gets more serious with increasing P. One way of handling this problem is to partition candidate item sets based on more than the first items of the candidate item sets. In this approach, whenever the number of candidates starting with one particular item is greater than the threshold, this item set is further partitioned using the second item of the candidate item sets.

Note that the equal assignment of candidates to the processors does not guarantee the perfect load balance among processors. This is because the cost of traversal and checking at the leaf node are determined not only by the size and shape of the candidate hash tree, but also by the actual items in the transactions. However, in the experiments, authors [32] have observed a reasonably good correlation between the size of candidate sets and the amount of work done by each processor. For example, with 4 processors, the load imbalance was 1.3% in terms of the number of candidate sets, which translated into 5.4% load imbalance in the actual computation time. With 8 processors, load imbalance was 2.3% in the number of candidate sets, and this resulted in 9.4% load imbalance in the computation time. Since the effect of transactions on the work load cannot be easily estimated in advance, IDD scheme only ensures that each processor has roughly equal number of candidate itemsets in the local hash tree.

A detailed analysis of the load balancing issues and scalability of IDD is given in [15]. In summary, IDD has the flexibility of minimizing the data movement cost by overlapping the counting computation with data communication. Moreover, it does not perform any redundant computation as in DD, which makes it more scalable than DD with respect to number of transactions, and it is scalable with respect to the number of candidates.

– **HPA Algorithm:** The HPA (Hash Partitioned Apriori) algorithm, given in [17], is similar in spirit to the IDD algorithm. It tries to reduce the communication overhead of sending each transaction to every processor. It assigns the candidates to processors using a hash function, which determines the processor a candidate gets assigned to. In the counting phase, if candidate k-itemsets are being counted, then each transaction in local database is first processed to find all the k-itemsets present in it. Each such itemset is hashed using the same hash function as used for partitioning the candidates to derive the destination processor, and is sent to that processor. This partitioning due to hashing function can be considered similar to the mechanism of partitioning candidates in IDD. The hashing-based candidate distribution of HPA may lead to load imbalances.

- **Intelligent Data Distributed Tree Projection Algorithm:** This formulation proposed in [11] is based on the IDD algorithm. The lexicographic tree, upon which the tree projection algorithms are based, is distributed among different processors based on the first item in the tree. Using the active item lists at the root of each of the processor's lexicographic tree, only relevant transactions can be communicated to a given processor. This can save on the communication overhead.

Hybrid Approach: Partial Replication of Candidate Itemsets

We saw two approaches: pure replication of candidates and pure partitioning with no replication. However, according to analyses of these approaches, especially for CD and IDD, it can be seen that each approach has some issues regarding scalability. In particular, CD is scalable with respect to number of transaction because of replicated candidate sets, whereas IDD is scalable with respect to number of candidates. This hybrid approach is essentially an attempt to see if two approaches can be combined via partial replication of candidates, to achieve better scalability than both. In the following, we discuss some algorithms that have been able to do this successfully.

- **HD (Hybrid Distribution) Algorithm:** The *IDD* algorithm exploits the total system memory by partitioning the candidate set among all processors. The average number of candidates assigned to each processor is M/P, where M is the number of total candidates. As more processors are used, the number of candidates assigned to each processor decreases. This has two implications. First, with fewer number of candidates per processor, it is much more difficult to balance the work. Second, the smaller number of candidates gives a smaller hash tree and less computation work per transaction. Eventually the amount of computation may become less than the communication involved. This would be more evident in the later passes of the algorithm as the hash tree size further decreases dramatically. This reduces overall efficiency of the parallel algorithm. This will be an even more serious problem in a system that cannot perform asynchronous communication.

  The *Hybrid Distribution* (*HD*) algorithm addresses the above problem by combining the *CD* and the *IDD* algorithms in the following way. Consider a P-processor system in which the processors are split into G equal size groups, each containing P/G processors. In the *HD* algorithm, we execute the *CD* algorithm as if there were only P/G processors. That is, we partition the transactions of the database into P/G parts each of size $N/(P/G)$, and assign the task of computing the counts of the candidate set C_k for each subset of the transactions to each one of these groups of processors. Within each group, these counts are computed using the *IDD* algorithm. That is, the transactions and the candidate set C_k are partitioned among the processors of each group, so that each processor gets roughly $|C_k|/G$ candidate item-sets and N/P transactions. Now, each group of processors computes the counts using the *IDD* algorithm, and the overall counts are computing by performing a reduction operation among the P/G groups of processors.

The *HD* algorithm can be better visualized if we think of the processors as being arranged in a two dimensional grid of G rows and P/G columns. The transactions are partitioned equally among the P processors. The candidate set C_k is partitioned among the processors of each column of this grid. This partitioning of C_k is identical for each column of processors; i.e., the processors along each row of the grid get the same subset of C_k. Figure 8 illustrates the *HD* algorithm for a 3×4 grid of processors. In this example, the *HD* algorithm executes the *CD* algorithm as if there were only 4 processors, where the 4 processors correspond to the 4 processor columns. That is, the database transactions are partitioned in 4 parts, and each one of these 4 hypothetical processors computes the local counts of all the candidate item-sets. Then the global counts can be computed by performing the global reduction operation. However, since each one of these hypothetical processors is made up of 3 processors, the computation of local counts of the candidate item-sets in a hypothetical processor requires the computation of the counts of the candidate item-sets on the database transactions sitting on the 3 processors. This operation is performed by executing the *IDD* algorithm within each of 4 hypothetical processors. This is shown in the step 1 of Figure 8. Note that processors in the same row have exactly the same candidates, and candidate sets along the each column partition the total candidate set. At the end of this operation, each processor has complete count of its local candidates for all the transactions located in the processors of the same column (i.e., of a hypothetical processor). Now a reduction operation is performed along the rows such that all processors in each row have the sum of the counts for the candidates in the same row. At this point, the count associated with each candidate item-set corresponds to the entire database of transactions. Now each processor finds frequent item-sets by dropping all those candidate item-sets whose frequency is less than the threshold for minimum support. These candidate item-sets are shown as shaded in Figure 8(b). In the next step, each processor performs all-to-all broadcast operation along the columns of the processor mesh. At this point, all the processors have the frequent sets and are ready to proceed to the next pass.

The *HD* algorithm determines the configuration of the processor grid dynamically. In particular, the *HD* algorithm partitions the candidate set into a big enough section and assign a group of processors to each partition. Let m be a user specified threshold. If the total number of candidates M is less

Step 1: Partitioning of Candidate Sets and Data Movement Along the Columns

Step 2: Reduction Operation Along the Rows

Step 3: All-to-all Broadcast Operation Along the Columns

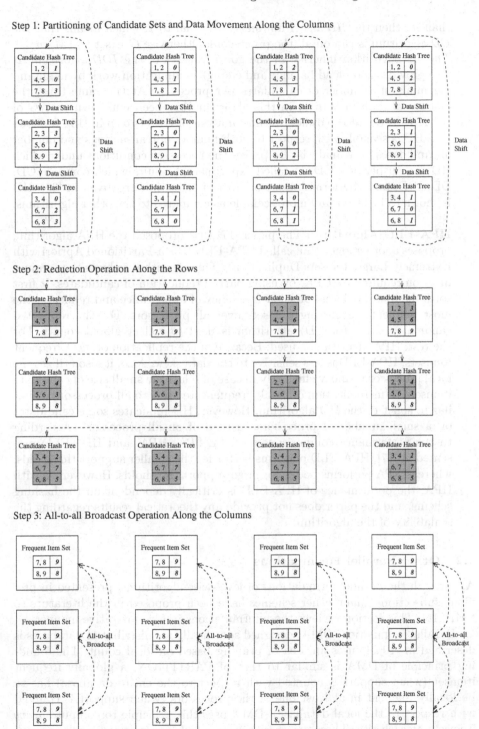

Fig. 8. Hybrid Distribution (HD) Algorithm in 3×4 Processor Mesh ($G = 3, P = 12$)

than m, then the *HD* algorithm makes G equal to 1, which means that the *CD* algorithm is run on all the processors. Otherwise G is set to $\lceil M/m \rceil$. The *HD* algorithm inherits all the good features of the *IDD* algorithm. It also provides good load balance and enough computation work by maintaining minimum number of candidates per processor. At the same time, the amount of data movement in this algorithm has been cut down to $1/G$ of the *IDD*. A detailed parallel runtime analysis of HD is given in [15]. It shows that HD is scalable with respect to both number of transactions and number of candidates. The analysis also proves the necessary conditions under which HD can outperform CD. Detailed experimental results which compare CD, DD, IDD, and HD formulations of Apriori algorithm are given in [32]. HD is shown to be faster and more scalable as compared to the other algorithms.

- **HPA-ELD Algorithm:** The paper [17] that proposed the HPA algorithm, proposes another algorithm called HPA-ELD (Hash-Partitioned Apriori with Extremely Large Itemsets Duplication). This algorithm reduces the communication required by HPA, by using partial replication of candidates. It first sorts the itemsets based on their frequency of appearance and replicates the most frequently occurring itemsets over all processors. For the replicated candidates, NPA (or CD) algorithm is used to collect global counts. For the rest, HPA algorithm is used. Because of the replication of most frequent itemsets, HPA-ELD is less sensitive to the data skew. Also, it also utilizes the local processor memory efficiently in case of relatively small size of candidate itemsets. This replication of highly frequent itemsets to all processors is similar in spirit to the HD algorithm. However, HD replicates some candidates on a small number of processors, instead of on all processors. According to the performance comparisons of NPA, SPA, HPA, and HPA-ELD presented in [17], HPA-ELD performs better for the smaller support thresholds, whereas NPA performs better for large support thresholds. However, as with HPA, the performance of HPA-ELD is critically dependent on the hashing scheme, and the paper does not provide any theoretical results regarding the scalability of the algorithm.

4.2   Other Parallel Formulations

Along with the parallel formulations of level-wise algorithms, presented in previous subsections, many other schemes have been proposed in the literature so far[19,18]. This section reviews these formulations in a comparative manner.

Parallel formulation, DMA, designed specifically for distributed databases is described in [19]. It uses an idea of pruning based on local count. The founding principle of DMA is similar to that of PARTITION: a globally frequent itemset (when support is counted with respect to the entire database) has to be locally frequent in at least one of the processors (when support is counted with respect to the local database). DMA uses this principle to compute *heavy* itemsets at each site. These are the itemsets which are frequent locally as well as globally. The $k + 1$-candidates are locally generated using the local heavy

k-itemsets instead of using the globally frequent k-itemsets. Use of heavy itemsets can generate much smaller number of candidates overall, when compared to the CD algorithm which uses globally frequent k-itemsets. Local counts for these candidates are collected by scanning the database once. The candidates which are not locally frequent are pruned away and the remaining candidates are communicated to all other processors. Each processor measures the local count for each candidate received from remote processors, and sends it back to the processor who requested it. Adding up local and remote counts, each processor determines which of the candidates are globally frequent and forms the local heavy set. Local heavy sets are exchanged by a broadcast operation to find global frequent sets, and the algorithm continues to the next iteration. Note that DMA uses horizontal data layout similar to CD and DD, unlike the vertical data layout used in PARTITION. There are several optimizations possible in this main DMA algorithm, especially for reducing the communication overheads and the number of database passes. Following two paragraphs give their brief description.

DMA is designed for distributed environments characterized by low bandwidth interconnection network; hence, it has mechanisms to optimize the communication overheads. It assigns each candidate a host site, and uses a count polling procedure to gather the global count for it by systematic coordination of the requests for local counts from remote sites. In this form, DMA is similar in nature to the DD algorithm where candidates as well as the data are distributed across processors. This DMA algorithm is identical to the FDM algorithm with local pruning given in [20]. A global pruning strategy is also described in [20], which may reduce the number of candidate itemsets. It makes the local counts of each $(k - 1)$-candidate available at all sites and uses them to prune some k-candidates. The idea is that a k-candidate's global count is bounded from above by the sum of the upper bound on its local count at all the processors, which is in turn determined by the minimum support of its $(k - 1)$-subsets at each processor.

If DMA is implemented naively, in each iteration, each processor would need to make two passes over its local database; one for counting the candidates generated from local heavy itemsets, and second for candidates received from remote processors. The paper identifies this and proposes an optimization for making only a single scan by generating all the candidates that would be generated at all remote sites, and collecting counts for these along with the locally generated candidates. This optimization brings the algorithm closer to the CD algorithm, except that the candidate set generated in DMA could be potentially much smaller than the one in CD (because of the use of heavy itemsets). In the performance results shown in the paper, DMA performs better than CD, mainly because of the reduction in the number of candidates generated. It should be noted that although DMA uses the same principle as PARTITION, its sensitivity to the problems of small partition size and data skew is less than PARTITION. This is because PARTITION, in an effort of reducing the database scans, generates *all* locally frequent itemsets in its first scan of the database. It does not have the flexibility of interleaving the global information with local information in every iteration over k. This causes it to generate many false positives which need to be counted in the second pass over the database.

As noted earlier, DMA is designed for distributed environment. A version of it, called FPM (Fast Parallel Mining), suitable for parallel environment (faster interconnection network) is given in [21] and summarized in [28]. It simply replaces the count polling mechanism of DMA with an all-to-all broadcast of local supports to all the processors. The authors also provide an entropy-based measure to analyze data-skew among the processors by computing probabilities of itemsets at each processors. Similar to DMA, FPM also outperforms CD algorithm.

The last set of algorithms that we will discuss here is the parallel formulations of the itemset-clustering based lattice traversal algorithms given in [9]. As described in section 3.2, these algorithms try to find potential maximal frequent itemsets by pruning the search space of itemsets. This pruning is achieved by finding clusters of related items, using either the equivalence class method or the hypergraph clique method. Each cluster corresponds to a potential maximal itemset. Such itemsets form disjoint sub-lattices of the entire itemset lattice. The idea behind the parallel formulations given in [18] is essentially to identify such sub-lattices and assign them to different processors so that the processing of each sub-lattice can be done entirely independently. The algorithms try to achieve load balance by estimating the work needed for each sub-lattice and determining the number of sub-lattices to be assigned to each processor. In order to achieve independent processing of each sub-lattice, the algorithms bring all the transaction data (tid-lists) required for that sub-lattice to the processor assigned to process the sub-lattice. These algorithms offer ideal opportunity to be designed for DSM parallel architectures. Once the sub-lattices are assigned to multi-processor nodes, the frequent itemset generation within each sub-lattice can be performed by running a shared memory parallel algorithm on multiple SMP processors available within the node.

These parallel algorithms have the same advantages that are enjoyed by their serial counterparts, specifically those of doing at most two database scans and performing efficient counting by simple tid-list intersection. Along with these, the parallel formulations have the advantage of reducing communication overhead involved in communicating candidates or counts. But, these algorithms have limitations also. First, they have to pay the cost of replicating parts of the database across multiple processors. Second, the amount of concurrency that the algorithm can achieve depends entirely on the quality of clusters it can find, and on the transaction dataset. If the number of clusters is very few, then the algorithm may not fully utilize the total number of processors available, thus making it unscalable to larger number of processors. In the worst case, the algorithm may reduce to serial algorithm with a single processor working on the entire problem because of lack of multiple maximal potential itemsets. The hypergraph clique based clustering can be used avoid such worst case scenarios. But, clique based techniques tend to become expensive based on how dense the hypergraph gets, which in turn depends on the nature of transactions and the support threshold level. Another possibility where these algorithms can become expensive is when the number of clusters is such that the items appearing in different clusters have a large overlap. In such cases, the algorithm may end up replicating a large part of the database to all the processors. As an aside, the idea of itemset clustering using equivalence classes used in these algorithms is similar to the Candidate Distribution algorithm of[14], which assigns candidates to processors based on their equivalence classes.

5   Bringing in the Sequential Relationships

The data collected from scientific experiments, or monitoring of physical systems such as telecommunications networks, or from transactions at a supermarket, have inherent sequential nature to them. Sequential nature means that the events occurring in such data are related to each other by relationships of the form *before* (or *after*) and *together*. The concept of item-sets and association rules discussed so far takes into account only the *together* part of the relationship, the information provided by the *before/after* relationships is ignored. This information could be very valuable in finding more interesting patterns hidden in the data, which could be useful for many purposes such as prediction of events or identification of better sequential rules that characterize different parts of the data.

In this section, we discuss the concept of *sequential associations*, more commonly known as *sequential patterns*, and algorithms to discover them.

5.1   Universal Sequential Associations: Definition

Sequential associations are defined in the context of an input sequence data characterized by three columns: *object, timestamp*, and *events*. Each row records occurrences of events on an object at a particular time. An example is shown in Figure 9(a). Alternative way to look at the input data is in terms of the time-line representations of all objects as illustrated in Figure 9(b). Note that the term *timestamp* is used here as a generic term to denote a measure of sequential (or temporal) dimension.

Various definitions of *object* and *events* can be used, depending on what kind of information one is looking for. For example, in one formulation, object can be a telecommunication switch, and event can be an alarm type occurring on the switch. With this, the sequences discovered will indicate interesting patterns of occurrences of alarm types occurring at a switch. In another formulation, object can be a *day*, and event can be a switch or a pair of switch and type of the alarm occurring on it. This will give interesting sequential relations between different switches or switch-alarm type pairs over a day. In another example, if an object is a customer and events are the items bought by the customer, then the discovered sequential patterns will throw insight into the relationships between items bought by customers.

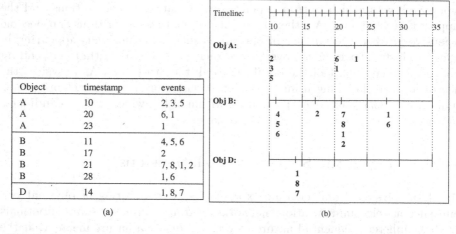

Object	timestamp	events
A	10	2, 3, 5
A	20	6, 1
A	23	1
B	11	4, 5, 6
B	17	2
B	21	7, 8, 1, 2
B	28	1, 6
D	14	1, 8, 7

(a)   (b)

Fig. 9. Example Input Data: (a) Flat representation, (b) Timeline Representation

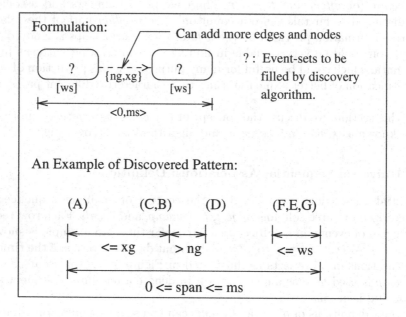

Fig. 10. Simplified Universal Formulation of Sequential Patterns

Given this input data, the goal is to discover universal sequential associations or patterns. A universal pattern is defined as a relationship between sets of events, which conforms to the given event constraints, structural constraints, and timing constraints. Detailed description can be found in [24]. For the purpose of discussion in this chapter, we will assume a simplified representation given in Figure 10. Although simplified, this representation still preserves the key generalization capabilities of universal formulation. The simplified universal sequential pattern is essentially a sequence of sets of events, which conform to the given timing constraints. As an example, the sequential pattern (A) (C,B) (D), encodes a relationship that event D occurs after an event-set (C,B), which in turn occurs after event A. However, this pattern may not be useful by itself. For example, if events are alarms, then D could be occurring hours after event A, which may not be useful in predicting dependence of D on A. Similarly, if alarms B and C occur just a few milliseconds apart, then putting a strict order on their occurrences may not be very useful; i.e. events within a event-set should be allowed to happen independent of their order but within a short time duration. These issues motivate a need to incorporate timing constraints in the sequential pattern definition. In particular, the occurrences of events in a sequential pattern are governed by the following timing constraints:

- **Maximum Span**(ms): The maximum allowed time difference between the latest and earliest occurrences of events in the *entire* sequence.
- **Event-set Window Size**(ws): The maximum allowed time difference between the latest and earliest occurrences of events in any *event-set*.
- **Maximum Gap**(xg): The maximum allowed time difference between the latest occurrence of an event in an event-set and the earliest occurrence of an event in its immediately preceding event-set.
- **Minimum Gap**(ng): The minimum required time difference between the earliest occurrence of an event in an event-set and the latest occurrence of an event in its immediately preceding event-set.

The constraints and structure described above form just one part of the definition. The other important part is to define what is an *interesting* sequence. We assume that the interestingness of a sequence to be defined based on how many times it occurs in the input data; i.e. its support. If the support is greater than a user-specified *support threshold*, then the sequence is called *frequent* or *interesting*. The number of occurrences of a sequence can be computed in many ways. Five different methods of counting are described in [24], out of which four are described below.

The method COBJ (Count Objects) counts at most one occurrence of a sequence for every object. In the example shown in Figure 11, (1)(2) has two occurrences, one for object A and one for object B, assuming $ms > 2$. This method may not capture the sequences which are exhibited many times within a single object, which could really determine its interestingness. In the second method CWIN (Count Windows), the support of a sequence is equal to the number of span-size windows it appears in. Each span-size window has a duration of ms, and consecutive windows have an overlap of $ms - 1$ units. Windows can span across a single object; i.e., no window can span across multiple objects. The support is added over all objects to get final support for a sequence. As shown in Figure 11(a), with $ms = 4$, sequence (1)(2) has support of 3 for Object A, because it occurs in windows starting at time-points 0, 1, and 2. For object B, it occurs in 5 windows, hence the total support is 8. In other counting methods, instead of counting the span-windows, actual occurrences of a sequence are counted. Two options, CDIST (Count Distinct Occurrences with No Overlap)

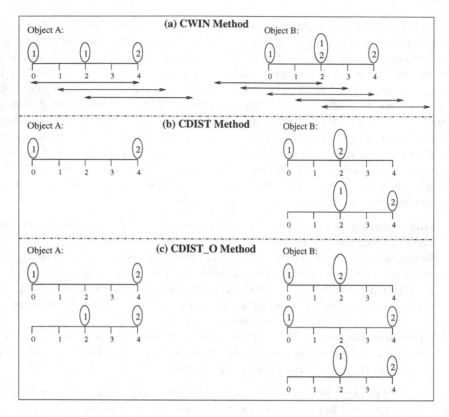

Fig. 11. Illustration of Methods of Counting Support

and CDIST_O (Count Distinct Occurrences with Overlap), are illustrated in Figure 11(b) and Figure 11(c), respectively. In CDIST, an event-timestamp pair is considered at most once in counting occurrences of a given sequence. So, there is only 1 occurrence of (1)(2) for Object A in the example, because there is no corresponding event 2's occurrence for event 1@2, 2@4 was used up in first occurrence. In CDIST_O, the occurrences are counted such that each new occurrence found has at least one different event-timestamp pair than previously found occurrences. So, (1)(2) has 3 occurrences for object B, and total of 5 occurrences, using this method.

The choice of which counting method to use is dependent on the problem and the judgment of the person using the discovery tool. For the purpose of our discussion in this paper, we will assume the CWIN method, because it is fairly general as compared to COBJ method in the way it counts multiple occurrences within an object.

As stated earlier, the definition of universal sequential patterns presented above is a simplified version of a more sophisticated representation given in [24], which allows specification of more constraints on the pattern. Among the prominent ones are the structural constraints in the form of a directed acyclic graph (dag), and the event constraints. As a matter of fact, the simplified version described here represents a most general version of a single path of the dag-based representation. In the remainder of this chapter, unless otherwise stated, whenever we refer to universal sequential patterns, the reader should assume the simplified form of Figure 10.

The universal sequential patterns actually unify and generalize the notions of generalized sequential patterns (GSP) proposed in [25] and episodes proposed in [34], both of which can be shown to be the special cases of the universal formulation. If the maximum span constraint is considered ineffective ($ms \to \infty$) and COBJ method is used for counting, then the formulation is identical to GSP. If constraint $xg \geq ms$ and the CWIN counting method are used, then the formulation is equivalent to the *episodes* of [34]. In fact, for algorithmic convenience, the generic notion of episodes is broken down into two special kinds of episodes: serial and parallel. In addition to $xg \geq ms$ constraint and CWIN counting method, if we impose $ng = 0$ and set ws such that each event-set is restricted to have only one event, then the universal formulation becomes equivalent to serial episodes. On the other hand, if additional constraints are set to $ws = ms$ and $ng \geq ms$, then the formulation is equivalent to the parallel episodes.

There are a few other formulations of sequential patterns proposed in the literature [26,35]. In terms of representation capability, they can be shown to be the special cases of the sophisticated version of universal sequential patterns given in [24]. The formulation of [26] is equivalent to a dag that has a rigid structure, only the ng and xg timing constraints, and stricter event constraints. The formulation given in [35] is based on regular expressions (RE). The deterministic finite automaton representation of their formulation can be shown to be a special case of the universal sequential patterns of [24]. Also, each of the paths of this automaton can be represented by the simplified universal sequential associations of Figure 10.

In summary, the formulation of universal sequential associations, with its representational capabilities and versatility of counting methods, is fairly general for a wide variety of sequential data.

5.2   Serial Algorithms for Sequential Associations

The complexity of discovering frequent sequences is much more than the complexity of mining non-sequential associations. The reason is that, the maximum number of sequences having k events is $O(m^k 2^{k-1})$, where m is the total number of distinct events in the input data. In contrast, there are only $\binom{m}{k}$ possible item-sets of size k, given m distinct items. Using the definition of interestingness of a sequence, and the timing constraints imposed on the events occurring in a sequence, many of these sequences can be pruned. But in order to contain the computational complexity, the search space needs to be traversed in a manner that searches only those sequences that would potentially satisfy both the support and timing constraints. The GSP algorithm given in [25] addresses this issue by building frequent sequences level-wise. Like Apriori, it makes use of the anti-monotonicity property of the support. The frequent sequences having $k - 1$ events can be used to build a *candidate* sequence having k events, such that all its $(k - 1)$-subsequences are frequent. The algorithm also takes into account the timing constraints relevant to the formulation of [25]. This algorithm has been modified in [24] to handle the universal sequential patterns. The main modifications are done in order to take into account the multiple counting strategies and to account for the maximum span (ms) constraint. Especially when the counting strategies other than COBJ are used, entire timeline of each object needs to be scanned to count all occurrences of every candidate. Data structures such as hash tree can be used to quickly find the candidates that may exist in a given timeline, but such structures will be helpful only for the *first* occurrence of a candidate. The rest of the occurrences need to be found by scanning the entire remaining timeline. A detailed description of how the algorithm works using hash tree structures is given in [24].

A few other algorithms also exist for discovering sequential patterns, but they cater to formulations of sequential patterns that are less general than the universal sequential associations. In particular, the algorithm SPADE proposed in [36], assumes the formulation of [22] with no timing constraints. The SPIRIT algorithms of [35] cater to their formulation based on regular expressions.

5.3   Parallel Formulation: Issues, Challenges, and Some Solutions

If the input sequence data has following features, then serial[2] algorithms briefly described in the previous subsection face severe limitations.

- Enormity; i.e., large number of objects and/or large time-lines for many objects. Serial algorithms would take a very long time to in the counting phase for such datasets.
- High dimensionality; i.e., large number of events. The number of candidates generated for such datasets will be very large; hence, either they may not fit in the memory available for a single processor, or they would make the hash tree data structures act counter-productively if their size and structure is not optimally managed.

This motivates the need for parallel formulations. The design strategies used for parallel algorithms in the context non-sequential associations can be used as a starting point for parallelization in the context of sequential patterns. However, specific design issues arise because of the different ways in which universal sequential patterns generalize over standard associations. The crucial factors are the lengths of the object time-lines defined in terms of the number of events happening on them, the value of maximum-span timing constraint (ms), and the

---

[2] The terms serial and sequential should not be confused. Traditionally, sequential and serial are both used to describe algorithms that would run on single processor machines. Here, we use the term serial to represent such algorithms, and reserve the term sequential to indicate the temporal or sequential nature of the input data

total number of objects. In this section, we briefly discuss the issues and research challenges involved in developing effective parallel formulations. In particular, we describe two parallel formulations, EVE (event distribution) and EVECAN (event and candidate distribution) [37].

EVE-S: Simple Event Distribution Algorithm. This algorithm is essentially an extension of the CD algorithm for discovering non-sequential associations, except that the transactions are replaced with more generic objects. For shorter time-lines (less number of events happening on the object) and relatively large number of objects, the input data is distributed such that the total number of events is as evenly distributed as possible within the constraint that a processor gets the entire timeline of every object allocated to it. The assumption here is that the computational work associated with an object is proportional to the number of events happening on it. The counting phase is performed in an embarrassingly parallel way, except for the final communication operation required to accumulate the candidate counts. EVE-S is illustrated in Figure 12. A similar algorithm called NPSPM (non-partitioned sequential pattern mining) is proposed by [17]. They assume the restricted GSP[25] formulation of sequential patterns. Also, they cater only to the supermarket transaction scenario, which indeed is fitting for the EVE-S algorithm also, because usually object (customer) time-lines contain small number of transactions, each in turn consisting of small number of events (items).

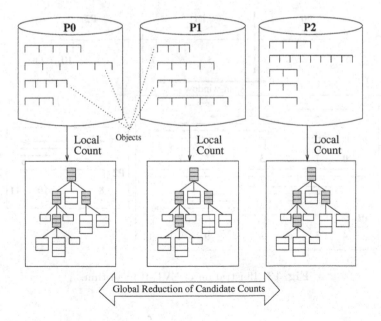

Fig. 12. Illustration of EVE-S algorithm.

EVE-R: Event Distribution with Partial Data Replication. This formulation is designed for the scenario in which there are relatively small number of objects (less than the number of processors), each object has a long timeline (in terms of duration as well as number of events), and the span value (ms) is relatively small. The input data is distributed as follows. The timeline for each object is split across different processors such that the total number of events assigned to different processors is similar. Note that the sequence occurrences are computed in span-size windows. We assume that the span value is small such that no span window spans across more than two processors. But, still each processor will have some span-windows that do not have sufficient data to declare the occurrence of an sequence in them. This is resolved in EVE-R by gathering such missing data from neighboring processors. Each processor gathers data that is required to process the last span-window beginning on that processor. This is illustrated in Figure 13. Since we assume that span-windows do not straddle more than two processors, just the neighbor-to-neighbor communication is sufficient. Once every span-window is complete on all processors, each processor processes only those span-windows which begin at the events originally assigned to it. For example, processor P0 processes windows that begin at time instances 0, 1, 2, and 3, whereas processor P1 will process windows that begin at 4, 5, 6, and 7. By distributing the events equitably, load balance can be achieved. As in EVE-S algorithm, the occurrences are collected by a global communication (reduction) operation, in the end.

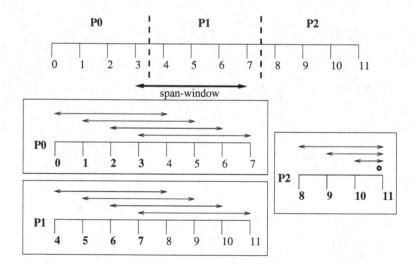

Fig. 13. Illustration of EVE-R algorithm.

EVE-C: Complex Event Distribution Algorithm. This formulation depicts the most complex scenario as far as distribution of the counting workload is concerned. This happens when there are small number of objects, each object has a long timeline (in terms of duration as well as number of events), and the span value is large such that after splitting the object time-lines across processors, the span-windows straddle more than two processors. There are two ways to handle this.

One way is to replicate the data across processors such that no processor has any incomplete or partial span-window. This is the same idea used in EVE-R. What makes it different is the fact that the amount of replication can become very large in this case. So, if processors do not have enough disk space to hold the entire replicated information, this approach may not be feasible. Even when there is enough disk space available on each processor, the replication of data may result in a lot of replication of work. The details are given in [37], but to summarize, when data is replicated, there is trade-off between the approach of replicating the work with no communication cost (except for the data replication cost), and the approach of avoiding work replication by paying the extra cost of communicating the candidate occurrences.

The second way to handle this is not to replicate the data. Now, two kinds of situations need to be handled. In the first situation, those occurrences that are found completely on a single processor might contribute to span-windows that begin on other processors. Care should be taken to avoid the double counting which, as shown in [37], requires communication of ranges of occurrences of candidates between processors. Second situation occurs when some candidates cannot be declared to occur in some span-windows because there of the insufficiency of the data available on a single processor. This scenario actually gives rise to the most complex method of parallelizing the counting process. The details are given in [37], but the key idea is that only partial occurrences of candidates can be found by each processor. This partial work needs to be communicated to other processors to complete the search. First issue is amount of concurrency that can be achieved in this process, which can be increased by breaking down the granularity of computation and doing asynchronous communications. The second and more serious issue comes from the nature sequential association discovery problem, in which each span-size window has a potential to support exponential number of sequences. Hence, the amount of partial work that needs to be transferred can quickly become large. In summary, avoiding replication of data can make the algorithm very expensive.

Thus depending on the scenario, there is a trade-off between the cost of replicating and storing the data versus the cost of communicating large amount partial work among processors. A detailed discussion is given in [37].

Event and Candidate Distribution (EVECAN) Algorithm. In the set of EVE algorithms described above, it is assumed that the candidates are replicated over all the processors. This may not be desirable when the number of candidates is very large, and given the complexity of sequential patterns, such scenarios are not uncommon. EVE algorithms face two inefficiencies when the number of candidates is large. First, the set of candidates may not fit in the memory of a processor, in which case they need to be counted in parts. This involves multiple I/O passes over the disk for counting the candidates. Secondly, EVE algorithms builds candidates serially on all processors, thus losing out on extracting the possible concurrency. The amount of time spent in generating the large number of candidates can be significantly large.

These issues are addressed in the second formulation, called EVECAN (event and candidate distribution) [37]. In this algorithm, the input data is partitioned similar to EVE. But, now the candidates are also distributed. They are stored in a distributed hash table. The hashing criterion is designed to maintain equal number of candidates on all processors. One simple hash function can be based on the lexicographical ordering of candidates and splitting them among processors such that all candidates assigned to one processor have a common prefix sequence. The non-local candidates required for the candidate generation phase are obtained using the scalable communication structure of the parallel hashing paradigm introduced in [38]. In the counting phase, all the processors must count all the candidates. There are two options. In the first option, the candidates are kept stationary at processors and the input data is circulated among processors in a fashion similar to that of the round-robin scheme proposed for IDD algorithm of [32]. But this option may work only when the span value is small, in which case the granularity of communication could be the span-size windows. However, for large values of span, it could become very expensive to send all the span-windows to all the processors. In such cases, the second option can be used, which is to circulate the candidates in a round-robin fashion. In both the options, a hash function is used to do a relatively quick search of whether a span-window can contain the local or the remotely received candidates. Figure 14 pictorially depicts the EVECAN algorithm.

Another set of parallel algorithms are given in [39]. These are also based on distribution of objects as well as candidates. However, these algorithms assume the restricted sequential pattern format given in [25]; hence, there is no notion of span (ms), and they count only one occurrence of a sequence in a given object's timeline (COBJ counting method). Also they assume market basket type of data, in which the object time-lines are usually very short. SPSPM (Simple Partitioned Sequential Pattern Mining) algorithm distributes the candidates in a simple round-robin manner, whereas HPSPM (Hash Partitioned Sequential Pattern Mining) distributes candidates in a more intelligent manner using hash functions. These are straight-forward extensions of the SPA and HPA algorithms [17] designed for the parallel discovery of non-sequential associations. The counting in SPSPM is performed in a way similar to the DD algorithm for non-sequential associations, where every object's timeline is sent to every processor. HPSPM, in k^{th} iteration, generates all the k-sequences (sequences with k events) present in each object's timeline and hashes them using the same hash function as was used for hashing the candidates to distribute them among processors. Each k-sequence is sent to the processor it hashes to, and is searched for in the list of candidates stored there. The HPSPM algorithm has been shown to perform better than NPSPM and SPSPM [39].

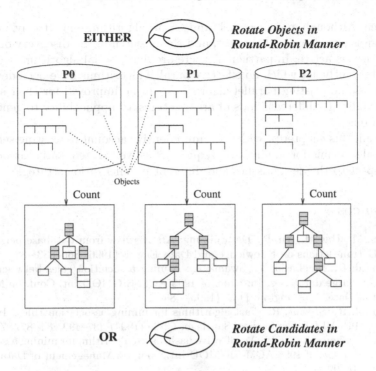

Fig. 14. Illustration of EVECAN algorithm for parallel discovery of universal sequential associations.

If HPSPM is to be extended to discover universal sequential patterns, then it faces precisely the same issues which motivate the EVECAN design discussed above. In its current formulation, HPSPM will face huge amount of communication overhead in the presence of large object timelines and large span constraint. EVECAN suggests systematic way to handle this by using the communication mechanisms similar to that of IDD. Also, EVECAN suggests an alternative possibility of reducing the overhead by communicating the candidates instead of object subsequences.

6 Summary

In this chapter, we presented an evolutionary and comparative review of many existing algorithms for solving a very popular and important problem of mining associations from data. We considered the traditional non-sequential associations which originated from the transaction or market basket kind of data as well as the more generalized sequential association formulation which is useful to wider variety of datasets in real world. The chapter mainly elaborates on various design issues involved in parallel formulations of association discovery algorithms, and how existing parallel algorithms map to only a few categories of formulations. In the process, a comprehensive survey of many existing serial algorithms is also given. Although many parallel (and serial) algorithms exist today, no single algorithm is superior to all the rest, and the research in the discovery of associations remains active. In particular, there are many serial algorithms that have emerged recently, for which no effective parallel algorithms have been developed yet. Even some existing parallel algorithms can be improved for their scalability, portability to different kinds of architectures, or applicability to generalized formulations.

Overall, this chapter provides a comprehensive account of existing serial and parallel algorithms for mining non-sequential as well as sequential associations with respect to the design issues and different parallelization strategies.

References

1. Chen, M., Han, J., Yu, P.: Data mining: An overview from database perspective. IEEE Transactions on Knowledge and Data Eng. **8** (1996) 866–883   83
2. Agrawal, R., Imielinski, T., Swami, A.: Mining association rules between sets of items in large databases. In: Proc. of 1993 ACM-SIGMOD Int. Conf. on Management of Data, Washington, D.C. (1993)   84
3. Agrawal, R., Srikant, R.: Fast algorithms for mining association rules. In: Proc. of the 20th VLDB Conference, Santiago, Chile (1994) 487–499   84, 87, 87, 88
4. Park, J., Chen, M., Yu, P.: An effective hash-based algorithm for mining association rules. In: Proc. of 1995 ACM-SIGMOD Int. Conf. on Management of Data. (1995) 84, 91, 91, 99
5. Savasere, A., Omiecinski, E., Navathe, S.: An efficient algorithm for mining association rules in large databases. In: Proc. of the 21st VLDB Conference, Zurich, Switzerland (1995) 432–443   84, 85, 87, 91, 92, 98
6. Mueller, A.: Fast sequential and parallel algorithms for association rule mining: A comparison. Technical Report CS-TR-3515, Dept. of Computing Science, University of Maryland, College Park, MD (1995)   84, 85, 91, 93, 93, 95, 95, 95, 100, 100
7. Toivonen, H.: Sampling large databases for association rules. In: Proc. of the 22nd VLDB Conference. (1996)   84, 91, 92, 93
8. Amir, A., Feldman, R., Kashi, R.: A new and versatile method for association generation. In Komorowski, H.J., Zytkow, J.M., eds.: Proceedings of Principles of Data Mining and Knowledge Discovery, First European Symposium (PKDD'97). Lecture Notes in Computer Science. Volume 1263. Springer, Trondheim, Norway (1997) 221–231   84, 91, 95, 96
9. Zaki, M.J., Parthasarathy, S., Ogihara, M., Li, W.: New algorithms for fast discovery of association rules. In: Proc. of the Third Intl Conference on Knowledge Discovery and Data Mining. (1997)   84, 91, 93, 94, 112
10. Brin, S., Motwani, R., Ullman, J.D., Tsur, S.: Dynamic itemset counting and implication rules for market basket data. In: Proc. of 1997 ACM-SIGMOD Int. Conf. on Management of Data, Tucson, Arizona (1997) 255–264   84, 91, 93, 94
11. Agarwal, R.C., Aggarwal, C., Prasad, V.V.V.: A tree projection algorithm for generation of frequent itemsets. Journal of Parallel and Distributed Computing (Special Issue on High Performance Data Mining) (2000)   84, 85, 91, 91, 100, 107
12. Agarwal, R.C., Aggarwal, C., Prasad, V.V.V.: Depth-first generation of large itemsets for association rules. Technical Report RC-21538, IBM Research Division (1999)   84, 91, 91, 93, 95

13. Han, J., Pei, J., Yin, Y.: Mining frequent patterns without candidate genera-
    tion. Technical Report CMPT99-12, School of Computing Science, Simon Fraser
    University (1999) 84, 91, 95, 95
14. Agrawal, R., Shafer, J.: Parallel mining of association rules: Design, implementa-
    tion and experience. Technical Report RJ10004, IBM Research Division, Almaden
    Research Center (1996) 85, 113
15. Han, E., Karypis, G., Kumar, V.: Scalable parallel data mining for association
    rules. IEEE Transactions on Knowledge and Data Eng. (1999)   85, 90, 98, 103,
    103, 106, 110
16. Park, J., Chen, M., Yu, P.: Efficient parallel data mining for association rules.
    In: Proceedings of the 4th Intl Conf. on Information and Knowledge Management.
    (1995) 85, 99
17. Shintani, T., Kitsuregawa, M.: Hash based parallel algorithms for mining associ-
    ation rules. In: Proc. of the Conference on Parallel and Distributed Information
    Systems. (1996) 85, 100, 101, 106, 110, 110, 119, 122
18. Zaki, M.J., Parthasarathy, S., Ogihara, M., Li, W.: New parallel algorithms for
    fast discovery of association rules. Data Mining and Knowledge Discovery: An
    International Journal 1 (1997) 85, 97, 110, 112
19. Cheung, D., Ng, V., Fu, A., Fu, Y.: Efficient mining of association rules in dis-
    tributed databases. IEEE Transactions on Knowledge and Data Eng. 8 (1996)
    911–922 85, 110, 110
20. Cheung, D., Han, J., Ng, V.T., nd Y. Fu, A.W.F.: A fast distributed algorithm
    for mining association rules. In: Proc. of 1996 International Conference on Parallel
    and Distributed Information Systems (PDIS'96), Miami Beach (1996) 85, 111,
    111
21. Cheung, D., Xiao, Y.: Effect of data skewness in parallel mining of association
    rules. In: Research and Development in Knowledge Discovery and Data Mining:
    Second Pacific-Asia Conference (PAKDD'98), Melbourne, Australia (1998) 85,
    112
22. Agrawal, R., Srikant, R.: Mining sequential patterns. In: Proc. of the Intl Confer-
    ence on Data Engineering (ICDE), Taipei, Taiwan (1996) 85, 85, 86, 118
23. Mannila, H., Toivonen, H., Verkamo, A.I.: Discovering frequent episodes in se-
    quences. In: Proc. of the First Intl Conference on Knowledge Discovery and Data
    Mining, Montreal, Quebec (1995) 210–215 85, 85, 86
24. Joshi, M.V., Karypis, G., Kumar, V.: Universal formulation of sequential pat-
    terns. Technical Report TR 99-021, Department of Computer Science, University
    of Minnesota, Minneapolis (1999) 85, 86, 114, 115, 116, 117, 117, 118, 118
25. Srikant, R., Agrawal, R.: Mining sequential patterns: Generalizations and perfor-
    mance improvements. In: Proc. of the Fifth Intl Conference on Extending Database
    Technology, Avignon, France (1996) 86, 117, 117, 118, 119, 122
26. Bettini, C., Wang, X.S., Jajodia, S.: Testing complex temporal relationships in-
    volving multiple granularities and its application to data mining. In: Proc. of ACM
    PODS'96, Montreal (1996) 68–78 86, 117, 117
27. Houtsma, M.A.W., Swami, A.N.: Set-oriented mining for association rules in re-
    lational databases. In: Proc. of the 11th Intl Conf. on Data Eng., Taipei, Taiwan
    (1995) 25–33 87
28. Zaki, M.J.: Parallel and distributed association mining: A survey. IEEE Concur-
    rency (Special Issue on Data Mining) (1999) 93, 97, 97, 112
29. Sedgewick, R.: Algorithms. Second edn. Addison-Wesley (1988) 96
30. Agrawal, R., Shafer, J.: Parallel mining of association rules. IEEE Transactions
    on Knowledge and Data Eng. 8 (1996) 962–969 98, 98, 101, 101, 102

31. Kumar, V., Grama, A., Gupta, A., Karypis, G.: Introduction to Parallel Computing: Algorithm Design and Analysis. Benjamin Cummings/ Addison Wesley, Redwod City (1994) 98, 101, 103
32. Han, E., Karypis, G., Kumar, V.: Scalable parallel data mining for association rules. In: Proc. of 1997 ACM-SIGMOD Int. Conf. on Management of Data, Tucson, Arizona (1997) 103, 106, 110, 122
33. Papadimitriou, C.H., Steiglitz, K.: Combinatorial Optimization: Algorithms and Complexity. Prentice-Hall, Englewood Cliffs, NJ (1982) 105
34. Mannila, H., Toivonen, H., Verkamo, A.I.: Discovery of frequent episodes in event sequences. Technical Report C-1997-15, Department of Computer Science, University of Helsinki, Finland (1997) 117, 117
35. Garofalakis, M.N., Rastogi, R., Shim, K.: SPIRIT: Sequential pattern mining with regular expression constraints. In: Proc. of the 25th VLDB Conference, Edinburgh, Scotland (1999) 223–234 117, 117, 118
36. Zaki, M.J.: Efficient enumeration of frequent sequences. In: Proc. of 7th International Conference on Information and Knowledge Management (CIKM'98), Washington DC (1998) 68–75 118
37. Joshi, M.V., Karypis, G., Kumar, V.: Parallel algorithms for mining sequential associations: Issues and challenges. Technical Report under preparation, Department of Computer Science, University of Minnesota, Minneapolis (1999) 119, 121, 121, 121, 121, 122
38. Joshi, M.V., Karypis, G., Kumar, V.: ScalParC: A new scalable and efficient parallel classification algorithm for mining large datasets. In: Proc. of the 12th International Parallel Processing Symposium, Orlando, Florida (1998) 122
39. Shintani, T., Kitsuregawa, M.: Mining algorithms for sequential patterns in parallel: Hash based approach. In: Research and Development in Knowledge Discovery and Data Mining: Second Pacific-Asia Conference (PAKDD'98), Melbourne, Australia (1998) 283–294 122, 122

Parallel Branch-and-Bound Graph Search for Correlated Association Rules

Shinichi Morishita[1] and Akihiro Nakaya[2]

[1] Department of Information Science
Office 301, 7th Building
Faculty of Science, University of Tokyo
7-3-1 Hongo, Bunkyo-ku, Tokyo 113-0033, Japan
moris@is.s.u-tokyo.ac.jp
[2] Department of Genome Knowledge Discovery System (Hitachi)
Institute of Medical Science, University of Tokyo
4-6-1, Shirokane-dai, Minato Ward, Tokyo 108-8639, Japan
nakaya@ims.u-tokyo.ac.jp

Abstract. There have been proposed efficient ways of enumerating all the association rules that are interesting with respect to support, confidence, or other measures. In contrast, we examine the optimization problem of computing the optimal association rule that maximizes the significance of the correlation between the assumption and the conclusion of the rule. We propose a parallel branch-and-bound graph search algorithm tailored to this problem. The key features of the design are (1) novel branch-and-bound heuristics, and (2) a rule of rewriting conjunctions that avoids maintaining the list of visited nodes. Experiments on two different types of large-scale shared-memory multi-processors confirm that the speed-up of the computation time scales almost linearly with the number of processors, and the size of search space could be dramatically reduced by the branch-and-bound heuristics.

1 Introduction

Many organizations are seeking strategies for processing or interpreting massive amounts of data that will inspire new marketing strategies or lead to the next generation of scientific discoveries. In response to those demands, in recent years, decision support systems and data mining systems have rapidly attracted strong interests, and numerous optimization techniques for computing decision trees, clusters, and association rules have been proposed. Among those techniques, the development of efficient ways of computing association rules has attracted considerable attention.

Association Rules. Given a set of records, an association rule is an expression of the form $X \Rightarrow Y$, where X and Y are tests on records, and X and Y are called the *assumption* and the *conclusion*, respectively. Consider the market basket analysis problem [1]. An example of an association rule is: "50% of customers

M.J. Zaki, C.-T. Ho (Eds.): Large-Scale Parallel Data Mining, LNAI 1759, pp. 127–144, 2000.

who purchase bread also buy butter; 20% of customers purchase both bread and butter." We will describe the rule by

$$(Bread = 1) \Rightarrow (Butter = 1).$$

We call 50% the *confidence* of the rule and 20% the *support* of the rule.

The significance of an association rule has been evaluated by support and confidence [1,2]. Higher support implies that the coverage of the rule is sufficiently large, while higher confidence shows that the prediction accuracy of using the assumption X as a test for inferring the conclusion Y is sufficient. In their pioneering work, Agrawal et al. [1,2] define that an association rule is interesting if its support and confidence are no less than given thresholds, and they propose *Apriori* algorithm that enumerates all the interesting association rules. The idea of Apriori algorithm has been explored by many researchers [2,8,9,10,11,12].

Motivating Example. Higher support and higher confidence, however, are not necessarily sufficient for evaluating the correlation between the assumption and the conclusion of an association rule. Brin et al. [5] address this problem, and the following example illustrates this issue.

Example 1. Consider the super market basket analysis problem [1]. Let *Bread*, *Butter* and *Battery* be Boolean attributes. Suppose that the support and the confidence of the following rule are 29% and 48.3%, respectively:

$$(Bread = 1) \wedge (Butter = 1) \Rightarrow (Battery = 1),$$

which means that customers who purchase both bread and butter may also buy batteries. This implication differs from our common sense, but the support and the confidence are fairly high, and hence one may conclude that the rule presents some unknown behavior of the customers. From a statistical viewpoint, however, we also ought to look at the negative implication that when customers who do not purchase both bread and butter may also buy batteries. In Table 1, which is called a contingency table, the row $(Bread = 1) \wedge (Butter = 1)$ and the row $not((Bread = 1) \wedge (Butter = 1))$ show the number of customers who do and do not meet $(Bread = 1) \wedge (Butter = 1)$, while the column $(Battery = 1)$ and the column $not(Battery = 1)$ shows their corresponding numbers, similarly.

	$(Battery = 1)$	$not(Battery = 1)$	Sum
$(Bread = 1) \wedge (Butter = 1)$	29	31	60
$not((Bread = 1) \wedge (Butter = 1))$	21	19	40
Sum	50	50	100

Table 1. Contingency Table

Note that $Battery = 1$ holds for 50% of all the customers, which is higher than 48.3%, and hence customers satisfying $(Bread = 1) \wedge (Butter = 1)$ are less likely to meet $Battery = 1$. Thus there is a slight negative correlation between $(Bread = 1) \wedge (Butter = 1)$ and $Battery = 1$, though it is not significant. ∎

The above example suggests that we should measure the statistical significance of the correlation between the assumption and the conclusion. To measure the significance of correlation, the χ^2 value has usually been applied to the contingency table associated with the rule. The benefit of using the χ^2 value is that we can evaluate the significance of an association rule by a single value rather than multiple values such as support and confidence. All association rules can be ordered by their χ^2 values. We are then interested in finding the optimal association rule that maximizes the χ^2 value. Or we want to list the best n association rules in descending order of χ^2 value. We can also provide a cutoff value — say, at the 95% significance level — for χ^2, and then we can enumerate all the association rules whose χ^2 values are no less than that threshold. We will consider those problems, and we call an association rule *correlated* if its χ^2 value is optimal, sub-optimal or no less than a given threshold value.

Related Work. Brin et al.[5] have studied this problem from a slightly different aspect. Instead of finding correlated association rules, they focus on the computation of a set of primitive tests that are not independent by the chi-squared test. Using the strategy of Apriori algorithm [2], they present an algorithm for enumerating all the sets of primitive tests that are not independent, but the algorithm is not intended to compute correlated association rules.

Example 2. Let us consider the market basket analysis problem again. Suppose that $(Spaghetti = 1)$, $(Tabasco = 1)$, and $(Battery = 1)$ are not independent, because $(Spaghetti = 1)$ and $(Tabasco = 1)$ are correlated. We however cannot conclude that $(Spaghetti = 1) \wedge (Tabasco = 1) \Rightarrow (Battery = 1)$ is a correlated association rule, since the assumption and the conclusion may not be correlated at all. ∎

One may try to use Brin et al.'s algorithm to enumerate instances of $X \cup Y$ that are not independent and then try to derive correlated association rules. But there could be numerous instances of $X \cup Y$ from which no correlated association rules could be created, because even if primitive tests in X are correlated, X and Y are not correlated at all.

To keep the computation efficient, Brin et al. use a minimum support threshold as a pruning criteria. In practice, selecting a minimum support threshold requires some considerations, because using a higher threshold often results in pruning important patterns with lower support, while using a lower threshold might produce a huge amount of patterns, which is computationally costly. From the viewpoint of statistics, only the χ^2 value is essential, and hence Brin et al. discuss the possibility of avoiding the heuristics of using the minimum support threshold. We will work in this direction.

Overview. We define our problem more formally. Given a set of Boolean attributes, we select B as a special attribute and call it an *objective* attribute, while we call all the other attributes *conditional*. We use conditional attributes in the assumption of a rule. Consider all the association rules of the form

$$(A_1 = v_1) \wedge \ldots \wedge (A_k = v_k) \Rightarrow (B = 1),$$

where $v_i = 0$ or 1. We first remark that it is NP-hard to compute the optimal conjunction in the assumption that maximizes the χ^2 value. One may try to modify Apriori algorithm to compute the optimal conjunction, but this approach may not be promising, because Apriori algorithm is designed to enumerate all the possible association rules of interest, while our optimization problem targets the optimal conjunction or sub-optimal ones.

To cope with such optimization problems, one common approach is an iterative improvement graph search algorithm that initially selects a candidate conjunction by using a greedy algorithm and then tries to improve the ensemble of candidate conjunctions by a local search heuristic; that is, from a conjunction we generate a *neighboring* conjunction that is obtained by replacing one primitive test with another, by deleting a test, or by inserting a new test. Figure 1(a) represents the search space of all conjunctions by an undirected graph in which a pair of neighboring conjunctions is connected by an edge. Starting from the initial conjunction represented by the square dot, we want to search the graph without visiting the same node more than once. Figure 1(b) illustrates such an example.

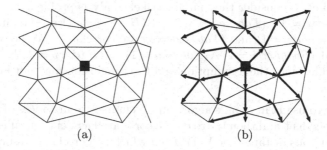

(a)   (b)

Fig. 1. The figure (a) shows the search space of conjunctions. The figure (b) shows the distributed search tree rooted at the square black dot.

To accelerate the performance of graph search, parallelizing the search has been studied for various discrete optimization problems [3,6]. We will exploit this approach for searching the optimal conjunction. To avoid the repetition of visiting the same node, conventional graph search algorithms maintain the list of visited nodes [3,6], which however could be a severe bottleneck of parallel search. We instead propose a rule of rewriting a conjunction to others. We first apply the rewriting rule to the initial conjunction to obtain child conjunctions, and then we repeat application of the rule to descendant conjunctions so that we can visit every conjunction just once without maintaining the list of visited conjunctions. Moreover, each application of the rewriting rule can be well parallelized.

If the initial conjunction is empty, it is rather trivial to build such a search tree. For instance, we can create one child of a conjunction by inserting one primitive test. In general, however, an arbitrary conjunction could be selected as the initial conjunction, and we need to create a neighboring conjunction by using one of replacement, deletion, or insertion, which makes the extraction of a search tree non-trivial.

To reduce the size of the search tree, we develop a branch-and-bound heuristics appropriate for the significance of correlation. We also develop implementation techniques such as materialization of projections and maintenance of distributed priority queues.

2 Preliminaries

Attributes, Records, and Primitive Tests. The domain of a Boolean attribute is $\{0,1\}$, where 0 and 1 represent true and false, respectively. Let B be a Boolean attribute, let t denote a record (tuple), and let $t[B]$ be the value for attribute B. A *primitive* test has the form $B = v$ where v is either 0 or 1. A record t meets $B = v$ if $t[B] = v$. A conjunction of primitive tests $t_1, t_2, \ldots, t_k$ is of the form $t_1 \wedge t_2 \wedge \ldots \wedge t_k$. A record t meets a conjunction of primitive tests if t satisfies all the primitive tests. We simply call primitive tests and conjunctions *tests*.

Association Rules. From a given set of Boolean attributes, we select one as a special attribute and call it the *objective* attribute. We call all the other attributes *conditional*. Let B be the objective attribute. An *association rule* has the form:

$$(A_1 = v_1) \wedge \ldots \wedge (A_k = v_k) \Rightarrow (B = v),$$

where $A_i (i = 1, \ldots, k)$ is an conditional attribute, and each of v_i and v is either 0 or 1. For instance, $(Bread = 1) \wedge (Butter = 1) \Rightarrow (Battery = 1)$ is an association rule.

	Y is true.	Y is false	Sum of Row
X is true.	$|R_1^t|(= y)$	$|R_1^f|(= x - y)$	$|R_1|(= x)$
X is false.	$|R_2^t|(= m - y)$	$|R_2^f|(= n - x - (m - y))$	$|R_2|(= n - x)$
Sum of Column	$|R^t|(= m)$	$|R^f|(= n - m)$	$|R|(= n)$

Table 2. Contingency Table

Consider association rule $X \Rightarrow Y$. Let R be a set of records over $\mathcal{R}$, and let $|R|$ denote the number of records in R. Let R_1 be the set of records that meet the assumption X, and let R_2 denote $R - R_1$. We call a record t *positive* (*negative*, resp.) if t satisfies (does not meet) the conclusion Y. Let R^t and R^f denote the set of positive and negative records in R, respectively. Table 2 summarizes numbers of records that meet each condition. Since R is given and fixed, we assume that $|R|$, $|R^t|$, and $|R^f|$ are constants, but $|R_1^t|$, $|R_2^t|$, $|R_2^f|$, and $|R_2^f|$ may vary according to the choice of the assumption X. Let n and m denote $|R|$ and $|R^t|$ respectively, then $|R^f| = n - m$. Let x and y denote $|R_1|$ and $|R_1^t|$ respectively. Observe that if we specify the values of x and y, the values of all the other variables are determined.

Chi-Squared Value. The chi-squared value is a normalized deviation of observation from expectation. Table 2 presents observed numbers of records. Expected numbers are calculated as follows: In the entire relation, the probability that a positive record occurs is $\frac{|R^t|}{|R|} = \frac{m}{n}$. Since the observed number of records satisfying X is $|R_1|$, the expected number of records meeting both X and Y is $|R_1|$ times $\frac{m}{n}$. Table 3 presents expected numbers of records. The chi-squared value

	Y is true.	Y is false
X is true.	$\|R_1\|\frac{m}{n}$	$\|R_1\|\frac{n-m}{n}$
X is false.	$\|R_2\|\frac{m}{n}$	$\|R_2\|\frac{n-m}{n}$

Table 3. Expected Numbers of Records

is defined as the total of the squared difference between the observed number and the expected number divided by the expected number for each cell; that is,

$$\frac{(|R_1^t|-|R_1|\frac{m}{n})^2}{|R_1|\frac{m}{n}} + \frac{(|R_1^f|-|R_1|\frac{n-m}{n})^2}{|R_1|\frac{n-m}{n}} + \frac{(|R_2^t|-|R_2|\frac{m}{n})^2}{|R_2|\frac{m}{n}} + \frac{(|R_2^f|-|R_2|\frac{n-m}{n})^2}{|R_2|\frac{n-m}{n}}.$$

Since all the variables are determined by x and y, we will refer the above formula by $\chi^2(x, y)$. If X and Y are independent, the observed number is equal to the expected number (in this case, $\frac{y}{x} = \frac{m}{n}$), and therefore $\chi^2(x, y)$ is equal to 0. In the chi-squared test, if $\chi^2(x, y)$ is greater than a cutoff value – say, at the 95% significance level —, we reject the independence assumption.

Convexity of Function. Let $\phi(x, y)$ be a function that is defined on $(x, y) \in D$. $\phi(x, y)$ is a *convex* function on D if for any (x_1, y_1) and (x_2, y_2) in D and any $0 \le \lambda \le 1$,

$$\phi(\lambda(x_1, y_1) + (1 - \lambda)(x_2, y_2)) \le \lambda\phi(x_1, y_1) + (1 - \lambda)\phi(x_2, y_2).$$

Let $(x_3, y_3) = \lambda(x_1, y_1) + (1-\lambda)(x_2, y_2)$, then $\phi(x_3, y_3) \le \max(\phi(x_1, y_1), \phi(x_2, y_2))$.

Proposition 2.1. $\chi^2(x, y)$ is a convex function defined on $0 \le y \le x$.

Proof. For any δ_1 and δ_2, define $V = \delta_1 x + \delta_2 y$. Prove $\partial^2 \chi^2(x,y)/\partial V^2 \geq 0$.

The convexity of $\chi^2(x,y)$ is crucial to prove the intractability of computing the optimal conjunction. We also use the convexity to derive an effective branch-and-bound heuristics.

Theorem 1. Let S denote a set of conjunctions that use conditional attributes, and Y be the objective conclusion. It is NP-hard to find the optimal conjunction $X \in S$ such that the chi-squared value of $X \Rightarrow Y$ is maximum.

Proof. The case for the entropy value is proved in [7]. In the proof, the convexity of the entropy function is essentially used. The argument carries over to the case for the chi-squared value, because the chi-squared function is also convex.

3   Parallel Branch-and-Bound Graph Search

Search Space as an Undirected Graph. Let V denote the set of all conjunctions that use conditional attributes. A conjunction C_1 is *adjacent to* another conjunction C_2 if C_1 is obtained by replacing a primitive test in C_2 with another, by deleting a primitive test in C_2, or inserting a new one to C_2.

Example 3. Let C be the conjunction $(A_1 = 1) \wedge (A_2 = 0) \wedge (A_3 = 1)$. C is adjacent to $(A_1 = 1) \wedge (A_2 = 0) \wedge (A_4 = 0)$, because $(A_3 = 1)$ in C is replaced by $(A_4 = 0)$. Also, C is adjacent to $(A_1 = 1) \wedge (A_3 = 1)$ and $(A_1 = 1) \wedge (A_2 = 0) \wedge (A_3 = 1) \wedge (A_5 = 1)$. ∎

Let E denote the set of undirected edges between pairs of adjacent nodes in V; that is, $E = \{(C_1, C_2) \mid C_1 \text{ is adjacent to } C_2\}$. The undirected graph (V, E) represents the search space of all conjunctions. We call (V, E) the *undirected graph* of *adjacency*. Figure 1(a) in Section 1 presents an example. We define the *distance* between nodes v and u by the length of the shortest path between v and u. Put another way, the distance shows the minimum number of operations on primitive tests to generate u from v.

Requirements on Search Tree. Suppose that we are given an arbitrary node $t_1 \wedge \ldots \wedge t_k$ in the search space (V, E) as the initial conjunction. To realize the local search strategy starting from $t_1 \wedge \ldots \wedge t_k$, we need to generate a search tree rooted at $t_1 \wedge \ldots \wedge t_k$ such that (1) the depth from $t_1 \wedge \ldots \wedge t_k$ to any node v in the tree is equal to the distance between $t_1 \wedge \ldots \wedge t_k$ and v in (V, E), and (2) each conjunction is enumerated to appear just once in the tree. For instance, Figure 1(b) illustrates such a search tree rooted at the square black dot.

To build a search tree, we first present a way of creating a unique path from the root of the initial conjunction to the node of any conjunction. We then show how to assemble all the paths into a search tree.

Creating a Unique Path from the Initial Conjunction to Any Conjunction. We introduce a way of representing a conjunction uniquely with respect to the initial conjunction. We develop this idea motivated by techniques for enumerating geometric objects [4]. We assume that all the primitive tests are sorted in a total order, and we denote the order by $x_1 < x_2$. For simplicity of presentation, we introduce a dummy test $\perp$ that is strictly smaller than any test t; that is, $\perp < t$. Let S denote the set of all the primitive tests. Let $t_1 \wedge \ldots \wedge t_k$ be the the initial conjunction given. Let C denote an arbitrary conjunction of primitive tests in S. We represent C by a list of primitive tests according to the following steps:

1. If $t_i (1 \leq i \leq k)$ appears in C, place t_i at the i-th position in the list. Otherwise, leave the i-th position open.
2. Sort all the primitive tests that appear in C but are not in $\{t_1, \ldots, t_k\}$, in the ascending order. Let SL denote the sorted list. Select and remove the first primitive test in SL, and assign it to the leftmost open position. Repeat this process until SL becomes to be empty.

Observe that any conjunction can be represented by the unique list of primitive tests, and hence we call it the *canonical* list.

Example 4. Let $t_1 \wedge t_2 \wedge t_3 \wedge t_4 \wedge t_5$ be the initial conjunction. Its canonical list is $[t_1, t_2, t_3, t_4, t_5]$. Let $\bigcirc$ denote an open position. The canonical list of $t_4 \wedge a_1 \wedge t_2 \wedge a_2 \wedge t_5 \wedge a_3$, where $a_1 < a_2 < a_3$, is obtained as follows: We first create $[\bigcirc, t_2, \bigcirc, t_4, t_5]$ by placing each t_i of $t_4 \wedge a_1 \wedge t_2 \wedge a_2 \wedge t_5 \wedge a_3$ at the i-th position. We then assign a_1 and a_2 respectively to the first and the third positions, which are open, and we append a_3 at the end of the list. Consequently we have $[a_1, t_2, a_2, t_4, t_5, a_3]$.

The canonical list of $t_4 \wedge a_1 \wedge a_2$, where $a_1 < a_2$, is obtained similarly. We first create $[\bigcirc, \bigcirc, \bigcirc, t_4, \bigcirc]$, and then assign a_1 and a_2 into the first and the second positions, respectively. Thus we obtain $[a_1, a_2, \bigcirc, t_4, \bigcirc]$. ∎

We show how to rewrite the canonical list of the initial conjunction to that of an arbitrary target conjunction, which creates a unique path from the root to any node. Intuitively, we scan two lists together from left to right, and when we find different primitive tests at the same position, we perform one of replacement, deletion, or insertion so that the initial conjunction is transformed into the target conjunction after the scan.

Example 5. Consider canonical lists $[t_1, t_2, t_3, t_4, t_5]$ and $[a_1, t_2, a_2, t_4, t_5, a_3]$. Since the two primitive tests at the first position are different, we replace t_1 by a_1. We then see the difference at the third position, and we replace t_3 by a_2. Finally, a_3 at the sixth position of $[a_1, t_2, a_2, t_4, t_5, a_3]$ does not appear in $[t_1, t_2, t_3, t_4, t_5]$, and hence we insert a_3. Consequently we have rewritten $[t_1, t_2, t_3, t_4, t_5]$ to $[a_1, t_2, a_2, t_4, t_5, a_3]$ by the following sequence of operations:

$$[t_1, t_2, t_3, t_4, t_5] \overset{\text{replacement}}{\to} [a_1, t_2, t_3, t_4, t_5] \overset{\text{replacement}}{\to}$$
$$[a_1, t_2, a_2, t_4, t_5] \overset{\text{insertion}}{\to} [a_1, t_2, a_2, t_4, t_5, a_3]$$

We have applied three operations, and the distance between $t_1 \wedge t_2 \wedge t_3 \wedge t_4 \wedge t_5$ and $a_1 \wedge t_2 \wedge a_2 \wedge t_4 \wedge t_5 \wedge a_3$ in the graph of conjunctions is also 3. ∎

There are some issues on sequences that use deletion.

Example 6. Consider the following two sequences

- $[t_1, t_2, t_3, t_4, t_5] \overset{\text{deletion}}{\to} [\bigcirc, t_2, t_3, t_4, t_5] \overset{\text{insertion}}{\to} [a_1, t_2, t_3, t_4, t_5]$
- $[t_1, t_2, t_3, t_4, t_5] \overset{\text{replacement}}{\to} [a_1, t_2, t_3, t_4, t_5]$

The second sequence gives the minimum length path in the undirected graph of adjacency. The following two sequences show another issue:

- $[a_1, t_2, t_3, t_4, t_5, t_6] \overset{\text{deletion}}{\to} [a_1, \bigcirc, t_3, t_4, t_5, t_6] \overset{\text{replacement}}{\to} [a_1, \bigcirc, a_2, t_4, t_5, t_6]$
- $[a_1, t_2, t_3, t_4, t_5, t_6] \overset{\text{replacement}}{\to} [a_1, a_2, t_3, t_4, t_5, t_6] \overset{\text{deletion}}{\to} [a_1, t_2, \bigcirc, t_4, t_5, t_6]$

$[a_1, \bigcirc, a_2, t_4, t_5, t_6]$ is not a canonical list, because $\bigcirc$ appears before a_2. ∎

In each case of the above example, we want to derive the second sequence only. We can solve this problem by using the rule that we do not allow replacement nor insertion once deletion is used. We will prove that this restriction does not overlook the canonical list of any conjunction.

Making Canonical Lists Distributable to Arbitrary Multiple Processes.
We present a way of distributing the canonical lists of conjunctions to arbitrary multiple processes so that each process can continue to rewrite independently. Consider the following sequence again:

$$[t_1, t_2, t_3, t_4, t_5] \overset{\text{replacement}}{\to} [a_1, t_2, t_3, t_4, t_5] \overset{\text{replacement}}{\to}$$
$$[a_1, t_2, a_2, t_4, t_5] \overset{\text{insertion}}{\to} [a_1, t_2, a_2, t_4, t_5, a_3]$$

Suppose that we assign the third canonical list $[a_1, t_2, a_3, t_4, t_5]$ to one process. We want to avoid giving to the process the history of creating the previous two canonical lists, because in general the history could be lengthy. We rather provide minimum information to the process so that the process can continue to rewrite the canonical list. For instance, it is enough to provide the information that primitive tests up to the third position have been updated, a_2 is the largest primitive test that has been most recently added, and no primitive test has been deleted. With this information, we can then append a_3, which is greater than a_2, at the end of $[a_1, t_2, a_2, t_4, t_5]$.

In general, we add the following auxiliary information to a canonical list $[x_1, \ldots, x_n]$, and we represent the extension by $\langle [x_1, \ldots, x_n], n, i, max, dmode \rangle$, which we also call a *canonical* list.

- n: The number of primitive tests in the canonical list.
- i: Let j be an index such that $i \le j$. We can update the primitive test at the j-th position in the next step.

- max: max denotes the largest primitive test among all the primitive tests that have been added. In the next step, we need to add a new primitive test that is greater than max when we perform replacement or insertion. For the initial conjunction we set max to $\perp$, where $\perp$ is the dummy test smaller than any primitive test.
- $dmode$: For the initial conjunction, $dmode = 0$. Once deletion is applied, $dmode$ is set to 1. When $dmode = 1$, only deletion is applicable.

Application of replacement, insertion or deletion to is defined as follows:

- **Replacement**: When $i \leq n$ and $dmode = 0$, we can replace the j-th ($j \geq i$) primitive test with x such that $max < x$ and $x \notin \{t_1, \ldots, t_k\}$.
$$\langle [x_1, \ldots, x_n], n, i, max, 0 \rangle \overset{\text{replacement}}{\rightarrow}$$
$$\langle [x_1, \ldots, x_{j-1}, x, x_{j+1}, \ldots, x_n], n, j+1, x, 0 \rangle.$$
- **Insertion**: When $dmode = 0$, we can insert x such that $max < x$ and $x \notin \{t_1, \ldots, t_k\}$ at the end of the list.
$$\langle [x_1, \ldots, x_n], n, i, max, 0 \rangle \overset{\text{insertion}}{\rightarrow}$$
$$\langle [x_1, \ldots, x_n, x], n+1, n+2, x, 0 \rangle.$$
- **Deletion**: When $i \leq n$, we can delete the j-th ($j \geq i$) primitive test, and we set $dmode$ to 1.
$$\langle [x_1, \ldots, x_n], n, i, max, dmode \rangle \overset{\text{deletion}}{\rightarrow}$$
$$\langle [x_1, \ldots, x_{j-1}, \bigcirc, x_{j+1}, \ldots, x_n], n-1, j+1, max, 1 \rangle$$

Table 4 presents two examples of such sequences.

	$\langle [t_1, t_2, t_3, t_4, t_5], 5, 1, \perp, 0 \rangle$			$\langle [t_1, t_2, t_3, t_4, t_5, t_6], 6, 1, \perp, 0 \rangle$
$\overset{\text{replacement}}{\rightarrow}$	$\langle [a_1, t_2, t_3, t_4, t_5], 5, 2, a_1, 0 \rangle$		$\overset{\text{replacement}}{\rightarrow}$	$\langle [a_1, t_2, t_3, t_4, t_5, t_6], 6, 2, a_1, 0 \rangle$
$\overset{\text{replacement}}{\rightarrow}$	$\langle [a_1, t_2, a_2, t_4, t_5], 5, 4, a_2, 0 \rangle$		$\overset{\text{replacement}}{\rightarrow}$	$\langle [a_1, a_2, t_3, t_4, t_5, t_6], 6, 3, a_2, 0 \rangle$
$\overset{\text{insertion}}{\rightarrow}$	$\langle [a_1, t_2, a_2, t_4, t_5, a_3], 6, 7, a_3, 0 \rangle$		$\overset{\text{deletion}}{\rightarrow}$	$\langle [a_1, a_2, \bigcirc, t_4, t_5, t_6], 5, 4, a_2, 1 \rangle$
			$\overset{\text{deletion}}{\rightarrow}$	$\langle [a_1, a_2, \bigcirc, t_4, \bigcirc, t_6], 4, 6, a_2, 1 \rangle$

Table 4. Examples of Distributable Sequences

Theorem 2. Let A and B denote a given initial conjunction and an arbitrary conjunction. There exists a unique sequence of application of replacement, insertion or deletion that rewrites the canonical list of A to that of B. Furthermore, the number of instances of application is equal to the distance between A and B in the undirected graph of adjacency. ■

Proof. The proof is an induction on the number of positions where the two primitive tests disagree in A and B, and let d denote the number. Observe that d is equal to the distance between A and B in the undirected graph of adjacency. We construct a unique sequence of rewriting A into B by applying one of the three operations d times.

Suppose that the initial conjunction A contains n primitive tests in it, and its canonical form is $[t_1, \ldots, t_n]$. Let n_B denote the number of primitive tests in B. In what follows, for simplicity and readability, we assume that A and B denote their canonical forms.

We first consider the base case when $d = 1$. Since $d = 1$, the number of primitive conjunctions n_B is either $n - 1$, n or $n + 1$. In each case, we can generate B from A by the application of deletion, replacement, or insertion.

- When $n_B = n - 1$, B must contain an open position $\bigcirc$, and suppose that $\bigcirc$ is located at the j-th position. Deleting the j-th primitive test in A yields B.
- When $n_B = n$, suppose that A and B disagree at the j-th position. B can be generated by replacing the primitive test at the j-th position in A with that at the j-th position in B.
- When $n_B = n + 1$, A and B are equal except that B has an extra primitive test at the $(n + 1)$-th position, and hence B can be created by inserting the last primitive test of B into A.

When $d > 1$, we consider the three cases below:

- When $n_B < n$, B must contain some open positions, and let j denote the last position where $\bigcirc$ is located. Replace $\bigcirc$ at j-th open position in B with the primitive test at the j-th position in A, and let B' denote the result. By the inductive hypothesis, there exists a unique sequence of $(d-1)$ operations that rewrite A into B'. Note that B can be rewritten from B' by one operation of deletion.
- When $n_B = n$, A and B disagree at d positions, and let j denote the last position of disagreement. Let B' denote the result of replacing the primitive test at the j-th position in B with that at the j-th position in A. B' can be obtained from A by $(d - 1)$ operations by the inductive hypothesis, and B can be generated from A by one operation of replacement.
- When $n_B > n$, B has extra $(n_B - n)$ primitive tests at the end. Let B' denote the result of deleting the last primitive test from B. By the inductive hypothesis, there is a unique sequence of $(d-1)$ operations to rewrite A into B'. We can obtain B by the application of insertion to B'.

Distributable Search Tree. The *distributable search tree* is a binary tree that displays all the sequences from the initial canonical list to the canonical list of any conjunction. Figure 2 illustrates such an example. Theorem 2 implies that any distributable search tree meets the two requirements on search trees; that is, (1) the depth from the root to any node v in the tree is equal to the distance between the root and v in the graph of adjacency, and (2) each conjunction is enumerated to appear just once in the tree.

Furthermore any node in a distributable search tree can be assigned to any process in a flexible manner.

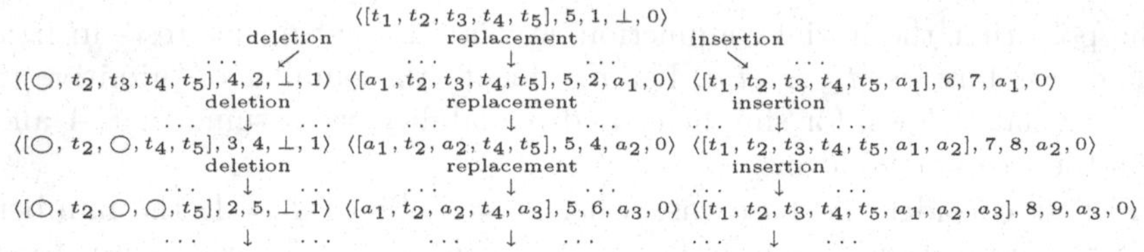

$$\langle [t_1, t_2, t_3, t_4, t_5], 5, 1, \perp, 0 \rangle$$

deletion $\qquad$ replacement $\qquad$ insertion

$\cdots \swarrow \qquad \cdots \downarrow \cdots \qquad \searrow \cdots$

$\langle [\bigcirc, t_2, t_3, t_4, t_5], 4, 2, \perp, 1 \rangle \quad \langle [a_1, t_2, t_3, t_4, t_5], 5, 2, a_1, 0 \rangle \quad \langle [t_1, t_2, t_3, t_4, t_5, a_1], 6, 7, a_1, 0 \rangle$

deletion $\qquad$ replacement $\qquad$ insertion

$\cdots \downarrow \cdots \qquad \cdots \downarrow \cdots \qquad \cdots \downarrow \cdots$

$\langle [\bigcirc, t_2, \bigcirc, t_4, t_5], 3, 4, \perp, 1 \rangle \quad \langle [a_1, t_2, a_2, t_4, t_5], 5, 4, a_2, 0 \rangle \quad \langle [t_1, t_2, t_3, t_4, t_5, a_1, a_2], 7, 8, a_2, 0 \rangle$

deletion $\qquad$ replacement $\qquad$ insertion

$\cdots \downarrow \cdots \qquad \cdots \downarrow \cdots \qquad \cdots \downarrow \cdots$

$\langle [\bigcirc, t_2, \bigcirc, \bigcirc, t_5], 2, 5, \perp, 1 \rangle \quad \langle [a_1, t_2, a_2, t_4, a_3], 5, 6, a_3, 0 \rangle \quad \langle [t_1, t_2, t_3, t_4, t_5, a_1, a_2, a_3], 8, 9, a_3, 0 \rangle$

$\cdots \downarrow \cdots \qquad \cdots \downarrow \cdots \qquad \cdots \downarrow \cdots$

Fig. 2. Example of Distributable Search Tree

Best-First Search. Next we discuss how to traverse the distributed search tree. Suppose that we compute an initial conjunction by a greedy algorithm that always makes the choice that looks best at the moment. Next we need to consider how to scan the distributed search tree rooted at the initial conjunction. One may try the depth-first search or the breadth-first search, but when we look for the conjunction that maximizes the chi-squared value, we should make a locally optimal choice in hope that this choice will lead to the global optimal solution. We therefore select the best-first search strategy that expands a node whose chi-squared value is maximum at the moment.

We implement the best-first search by using a priority queue. First we insert the initial conjunction into the empty queue. We repeat the process that we remove the first node v from the queue, compute the chi-squared value of v, update the best chi-squared value if necessary, use the chi-squared value of v to prioritize each child of v, and insert all the chide nodes of v into the queue.

Later in this section we show how to distribute the queue to multiple processes, but before that we show two techniques to improve the performance of the best-first search.

Branch-and-Bound Heuristics. Suppose that we examine a node v in a distributable search tree. The following theorem shows how to compute an upper bound of the best chi-squared value that could be obtained by scanning all the nodes in the subtree rooted at v. If the upper bound is smaller than the optimum chi-squared value at the moment, we can ignore and prune the subtree.

Theorem 3. Let v be a node in a distributed tree. Suppose that

$$v = \langle [x_1, \ldots, x_i, x_{i+1}, \ldots, x_k], k, i+1, -, - \rangle.$$

Let a (b, resp.) denote the number of (positive) records that meet $x_1 \wedge \ldots \wedge x_i$. Let w be an arbitrary descendant of v. Note that the conjunction of w contains $x_1 \wedge \ldots \wedge x_i$. Let p (q, resp.) denote the number of (positive) records that meet the conjunction of w. Recall that $\chi^2(p, q)$ is the chi-squared value of w, and we have:

$$\chi^2(p, q) \leq \max\{\chi^2(b, b), \chi^2(a - b, 0)\}.$$

Proof. Let n and m denote respectively the number of records and the number of positive records in the entire relation. Consider the points (a, b) and (p, q) in the two-dimensional Euclidean plane. It is easy to see that (p, q) falls in the convex region whose vertexes are $(0, 0)$, (b, b), (a, b), and $(a - b, 0)$. To be more precise, we have $0 \leq p \leq a \leq n$, $0 \leq q \leq b \leq m$, $q \leq p$, $b \leq a$, and $(p - q) \leq (a - b)$. When $y/x = m/n$, $\chi^2(x, y)$ is zero and minimum. Because of the convexity of $\chi^2(x, y)$, it follows that $\chi^2(p, q) \leq \max\{\chi^2(b, b), \chi^2(a - b, 0)\}$.

Materialized Projections. Let $v = \langle [x_1, \ldots, x_i, x_{i+1}, \ldots, x_{n_1}], n_1, i+1, -, -\rangle$ be an arbitrary node in a distributed tree. Note that any node in the subtree rooted at v must contain all the primitive tests in $\{x_1, \ldots, x_i\}$, because none of $\{x_1, \ldots, x_i\}$ is updated in the subtree. We call the set of records that meet $x_1 \wedge \ldots \wedge x_i$ the *materialized projection* for v.

A materilized projection could be very large in practice. To utilize the main memory efficiently, we implemented a materialized projection by creating a bit array of indexes to records in the materialized projection. If the bit of an index is on, the record of the corresponding index belongs to the materialized projection. For instance, the size of a bit array for a large database containing ten million records is $1.25MB$. Such bit arrays may still require large memory space during the execution, especially when the queue becomes to be long during the computation and cannot fit in the main memory. In this case, we put aside nodes with lower priorities, which might not be processed for a while, to the secondary disk at the moment, and later we restore them back to the main memory.

We now discuss the benefit of associating the materialized projection with each node. Let $w = \langle [x_1, \ldots, x_i, y_{i+1}, \ldots, y_{n_2}], n_2, j+1, -, -\rangle$ be a descendant of v. When we compute the chi-squared value of w, we need to count the number of records that satisfy the conjunction of w. It suffices to check if each record in the materialized projection for v also satisfies $y_{i+1} \wedge \ldots \wedge y_{n_2}$. The materialized projection could be much smaller than the entire relation. Since counting the number of records that satisfy a conjunction is the crucial step of the whole computation, the use of materialized projections could reduce the computation time substantially. The materialized projection of each node can be computed in an incremental manner; that is, the materialized projection for a child node is a subset of that for its parent.

Distributing Priority Queue to Multiple Processes. It remains to parallelize the single process version of the best-first search. The key extension is to divide the single queue into multiple disjoint queues and to distribute them to multiple processes. Balancing sizes of queues among multiple processes at run time is rather straightforward, because any node can be processed by any process. Each process maintains its own queue and broadcasts the locally best chi-squared value to the others when the value is updated.

There are a couple of concerns that do not arise previously. The first issue is that broadcasting the update of the locally best chi-squared value may increase the communication overhead between the processes. Another concern is that short delay of the broadcast may slightly deteriorate the overall performance, because the branch-and-bound heuristics uses the best chi-squared value at the moment. Tests however show that updates do not occur so often, and therefore those concerns are not serious in practice.

Listing Best n Conjunctions. We have so far presented an algorithm for computing the optimal conjunction, but it is easy to modify the algorithm to list the best n conjunctions. To this end, we can change to maintain the list of the best n conjunctions instead of the best conjunction. After this modification, the branch-and-bound heuristics still works, because we can use the n-th node instead of the best node to prune the search space according to Theorem 3.

4   Experimental Results

Implementation. We implemented our algorithm by using C++ and POSIX thread library. Experiments were performed on two different types of large scaled shared-memory multi-processors. One is Sun Microsystems Ultra Enterprise 10000 with 64 UltraSPARC processors running at 250MHz, 16GB of main memory, and 1MB of L2 cache for each processor, working under Solaris 2.5.1. Another is SGI Origin 2000 with 128 R10000 processors running at 195MHz, 24GB main memory, and 4MB L2 cache for each processor, running under IRIX 6.5SE. We limit the size of main memory to 2GB in order to verify that our implementation uses at most 2GB of main memory. In the case of SGI Origin 2000, since the time to access the remote memory is almost three times larger than the time to access the local memory, we had to implement each thread to keep a local copy of the entire relation to accelerate the overall performance.

Test Data. We randomly generated such a relation that the relation contains one hundred thousand records and the value of an attribute in a record is equal to 1 with a probability of p. We show the experimental results when $p = 0.3$, because in this case, the execution time was at most several hours, and therefore we can measure the speed-up and the effect of the branch-and-bound heuristics in a reasonable amount of time. The relation contains one hundred conditional attributes and one objective attribute. We used one hundred primitive tests of the form $(A = 1)$, where A is a conditional attribute. As the conclusion, we used $(B = 1)$, where B is the objective attribute. We selected the initial conjunction in a greedy manner. We applied our implementation to the test data until the algorithm terminates; that is, all the queues become to be empty, and the optimal conjunction is identified.

Effect of Branch-and-Bound Heuristics. Since there are one hundred primitive tests, the algorithm could generate 2^{100} conjunctions in the worst case. As a result of the branch-and-bound heuristics, however, the algorithm generates much less conjunctions. We have performed the cases when numbers of threads are 1, 2, 4, 8, 16, 32, 64, and 128. The total number of conjunctions inserted into the distributed queues ranges from 24194 to 24463. We have observed that every conjunction examined during the search contains at most four primitive tests. Note that the number of all conjunctions with at most four primitive tests is about 4.3×10^6. This figure again indicates that the branch-and-bound heuristics can drastically reduce the search space.

Effect of Maintaining Distributed Queues. In order to analyze the effect of maintaining distributed queues assigned to multiple processes, Table 5 shows the statistics of the number of conjunctions inserted into each queue. Consider the set of the numbers of conjunctions inserted into all distributed queues. For each number of threads, Table 5 presents the minimum number, the maximum number, the average number, and the standard deviation of the set of those numbers. Observe that the standard deviation of each case is fairly small, which implies that distributing conjunctions to multiple threads works well.

#(threads)	Enterprise 10000				Origin 2000			
	min	max	avg	s.d.	min	max	avg	s.d.
2	12106	12176	12141	35	11431	12852	12141.5	710.5
4	5544	6473	6070.5	335.7	5843	6382	6093.8	201.3
8	2734	3411	3035.3	226.4	2814	3223	3057.9	128.6
16	884	2085	1523.4	309.7	1364	2106	1528.9	166.8
32	453	1189	764.5	150.3	551	1169	746.0	142.1
64	244	632	383.6	101.0	201	765	382.2	103.0
128	N/A	N/A	N/A	N/A	85	413	191.1	67.9

Table 5. Statistics of Numbers of Conjunctions Inserted into Distributed Queues

Speed-Up. The *speed-up ratio* of n threads is defined as the ratio of the execution time of one thread to the execution time of n threads. Figure 3 (a) and (b) present that the speed-up scales almost linearly with the number of threads on both Sun Microsystems Ultra Enterprise 10000 and SGI Origin 2000. Table 6 shows the execution time in seconds.

#(threads)	Enterprise 10000		Origin 2000	
	Execution Time	Speed-up Ratio	Execution Time	Speed-up Ratio
1	6,760	1.00	6,503	1.00
64	202	33.47	219	31.30
128	N/A	N/A	135	48.17

Table 6. Execution Time in Seconds and Speed-up Ratio

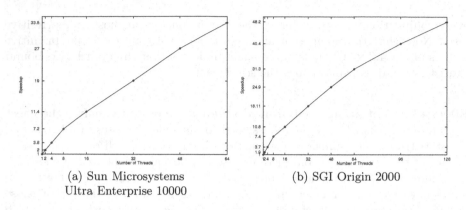

(a) Sun Microsystems
Ultra Enterprise 10000

(b) SGI Origin 2000

Fig. 3. Speed-up Ratio

Optimizing the Objective Criteria. Until the system finds the optimal conjunction, it outputs the optimal conjunction at the moment. Let X and Y denote the assumption and the conclusion of an association rule. Table 7 presents candidates of the optimal conjunction that the system output during the computation when the system was executed as 64 threads on Sun Enterprise 10000.

	X is true.		X is false.		
Assumption X	Y is true.	Y is false.	Y is true.	Y is false.	χ^2
$[t_1, t_2]$	9807	4240	20575	65378	12014.836
$[a_{10}, t_2]$	5962	411	24420	69207	12841.383
$[a_{15}, a_{23}, a_{90}]$	5810	161	24572	69457	13445.606
$[t_1, a_{39}, a_{90}]$	5833	148	24549	69470	13559.018

Table 7. Candidates of Optimal Conjunctions Calculated During the Computation ($[t_1, t_2]$ is the initial conjunction, and $[t_1, a_{39}, a_{90}]$ is the optimal one.)

Relationship between Execution Time and Size of Search Space. We have so far presented the performance of our system applied to the set of one hundred thousand records such that the value of each attribute in a record is equal to 1 with a probability of $p = 0.3$. If we use higher values for the probability p, the number of conjunctions examined increases, and therefore the total execution time also grows. Table 8 summarizes the performance results of executing our algorithm as 32 threads on SUN Ultra Enterprise 10000. The execution time does not always scale to the number of conjunctions examined, since time to handle a longer conjunction with more primitive tests decreases because of the effect of using materialized projections. The execution time also depends on the structure of the search tree. But in general, the growth of the number of conjunctions raises the execution time.

p	Execution Time in Seconds	Number of Conjunctions
0.3	354	24,463
0.4	1,396	74,169
0.5	2,525	233,148
0.6	8,261	803,280

Table 8. Relationship between the Performance and the Size of Search Space

5 Conclusion

We have examined the optimization problem of computing the optimal conjunction maximizing the chi-squared value that indicates the significance of the correlation between the assumption and the conclusion of the rule. Although this optimization problem is NP-hard, we have introduced a novel data structure called the distributable search tree, and we have presented how to construct this tree and how to speed up the performance of searching the distributable search tree on multiple processes. Our technique carries over to the general cases when we use the entropy function, the gini index, or the correlation coefficient as evaluation criteria.

In Section 4, we use a synthesis data to evaluate the performance of our system. In practice, we have been applying our system to the analysis of multiple factors leading to a common disease such as diabetes, or high blood sugar level. This case poses another problem of finding a conjunction to split data into two classes so that the average of the objective numeric attribute values in one class is substantially higher than that in the other class. It is however NP-hard to find the optimal conjunction that maximizes the interclass variance [7]. Developing an effective branch-and-bound heuristics for this case is an interesting problem.

Acknowledgements

All experimental results are done by using parallel machines at Human Genome Center, Institute of Medical Science, University of Tokyo. This research is partly supported by Grant-in-Aid for Scientific Research on Priority Areas "Discovery Science" from the Ministry of Education, Science and Culture, Japan.

References

1. R. Agrawal, T. Imielinski, and A. Swami. Mining association rules between sets of items in large databases. In *Proceedings of ACM SIGMOD*, pages 207–216, May 1993.
2. R. Agrawal and R. Srikant. Fast algorithms for mining association rules. In *Proceedings of VLDB Conference*, pages 487–499, 1994.
3. G. Y. Ananth, V. Kumar, and P. Pardalos. Parallel processing of discrete optimization problems. 1993.
4. D. Avis and K. Fukuda. A basis enumeration algorithm for linear systems with geometric applications. *Applied Mathematics Letters*, 5:39–42, 1991.
5. S. Brin, R. Motwani, and C. Silverstein. Beyond market baskets: Generalizing association rules tocorrelations. In *Proceedings of ACM SIGMOD*, pages 265–276. *SIGMOD Record* 26(2), June 1997.
6. V. Kumar, A. Grama, and G. Karypis. *Introduction to Parallel Computing: Design and Analysis of Algorithms*. Benjamin Cummings, Nov. 1993.
7. S. Morishita. On classification and regression. In *Proceedings of Discovery Science, DS'98, Lecture Notes in Artificial Intelligence*, volume 1532, pages 40–57, Dec. 1998.
8. R. T. Ng, L. V. Lakshmanan, J. Han, and A. Pang. Exploratory mining and pruning optimizations of constrained association rules. In *Proceedings of ACM SIGMOD*, pages 13–24, June 1998.
9. J. S. Park, M.-S. Chen, and P. S. Yu. An effective hash-based algorithm for mining association rules. In *Proceedings of ACM SIGMOD*, pages 175–186, May 1995.
10. R. J. Bayardo Jr. Efficiently Mining Long Patterns from Databases. In *Proceedings of ACM SIGMOD*, pages 85–93, June 1998.
11. R. J. Bayardo Jr., R. Agrawal, D. Gunopulos. Constraint-Based Rule Mining in Large, Dense Databases. In *Proceedings of ICDE*, pages 188-197, March 1999.
12. R. Srikant and R. Agrawal. Mining quantitative association rules in large relational tables. In *Proceedings of ACM SIGMOD*, June 1996.

Parallel Generalized Association Rule Mining on Large Scale PC Cluster

Takahiko Shintani and Masaru Kitsuregawa

Institute of Industrial Science, The University of Tokyo
{shintani,kitsure}@tkl.iis.u-tokyo.ac.jp
http://www.tkl.iis.u-tokyo.ac.jp/

Abstract. One of the most important problems in data mining is discovery of association rules in large database. In our previous study, we proposed parallel algorithms and candidate duplication based load balancing strategies for mining generalized association rules and showed our algorithms could attain good performance on 16 nodes parallel computer system. However, as the number of nodes increase, it would be difficult to achieve flat workload distribution.

In this paper, we present the candidate partition based load balancing strategy for parallel algorithm of generalized association rule mining. This strategy partitions the candidate itemsets so that the number of candidate probes for each node is equalized each other with estimated support count by the information of previous pass. Moreover, we implement the parallel algorithms and load balancing strategies for mining generalized association rules on a cluster of 100 PCs interconnected with an ATM network, and analyze the performance using a large amount of transaction dataset. Through the several experiments, we showed the load balancing strategy, which partition the candidate itemsets with considering the distribution of candidate probes and duplicate the frequently occurring candidate itemsets, can attain high performance and achieve good workload distribution on one hundred PC cluster system.

1 Introduction

Recently, PC (Personal computer) clusters have become a hot research topic in the field of parallel and distributed computing. Today's parallel computer systems are moving away from proprietary hardware components to commodity parts for CPUs, disks and memories. While an interconnection network has not yet been commoditized, ATM technology becomes the standard for high speed communication. Moreover, PC performance is increasing incredibly rapidly these days and the price of PCs remains inexpensive compared with that of workstation. Thus looking over recent technology trends, ATM connected PC clusters are very promising platform for massively parallel processing. We developed a PC cluster system consisting of 100 PCs for parallel processing[1]. We believe that data intensive applications such as data mining are very important applications for parallel processing.

Data mining has attracted a lot of attention for discovering useful information such as rules and previously unknown patterns existing between data items

M.J. Zaki, C.-T. Ho (Eds.): Large-Scale Parallel Data Mining, LNAI 1759, pp. 145–160, 2000.
© Springer-Verlag Berlin Heidelberg 2000

embedded in large databases, which allows effective utilization of large amount of accumulated transaction log. Association rule mining is one of the most important problems in data mining. Association rule is the rule about what items are bought together within the transaction, such as "70% of the customers who buy A and B also buy C". Usually, the classification hierarchy over the data items is available. Users are interested in generalized association rules that span different levels of the hierarchy, since sometimes more interesting rules can be derived by taking the hierarchy into account[2,3]. In our previous study, we proposed parallel algorithms and the candidate duplication based load balancing strategies for mining generalized association rules, and evaluated their performance on 16-node shared-nothing parallel machine[4]. In [4], we showed that our algorithms could attain good performance on 16 nodes system. However, as the number of processor increase, it would be difficult to achieve flat workload distribution.

In this paper, we present the candidate partition based load balancing strategy for parallel algorithms of generalized association rule mining. This strategy partitions the candidate itemsets so that the number of candidate probes for each node is equalized each other with estimated support count by the information of previous pass. In our previous study, we proposed the candidate duplication based load balancing strategies, in which the workload is not considered at candidate partitioning. Moreover, we implement the parallel algorithms and the load balancing strategies for mining generalized association rules on a cluster of 100 PCs interconnected with an ATM network, and analyze the performance of our algorithms using a large amount of transaction dataset. In [5], the parallel algorithms for mining flat association rules are experimented on 128 processor system. However, the transaction data is not read from actual disk in the experiments. In that experiments, the small transactions are kept in the buffer, and the transactions are read from the buffer instead of the actual disks. The size of transaction data does not exceed 50MBytes. On the other hand, the transactions are read from the actual disk and used a large amount of transactions (1GBytes) in our experiments.

This paper is organized as follows. In next section, we explain the parallel algorithms for mining generalized association rules. In section 3, we present load balancing strategies for parallel generalized association rule mining. In section 4, we show our large scale PC cluster system. Performance evaluations are given in section 5. Section 6 concludes the paper.

2 Parallel Generalized Association Rule Mining

First we introduce some basic concepts of generalized association rules presented in [2]. Let $\mathcal{I} = \{i_1, i_2, \ldots, i_m\}$ be a set of items. Let $\mathcal{T}$ be a classification hierarchy on the items, which organize relationships of items in a tree form, shown in Figure 1. An edge in $\mathcal{T}$ represents an *is-a* relationship. Let $\mathcal{D} = \{t_1, t_2, \ldots, t_n\}(t_i \subseteq \mathcal{I})$ be a set of transactions, where each transaction t has an associated unique identifier called TID. We say a transaction t *contains* a set of items X, if X

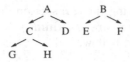

Fig. 1. The classification hierarchy

is a subset of t and the ancestor of items in t. The itemset X has *support* s in the transaction set $\mathcal{D}$, if $s\%$ of transactions in $\mathcal{D}$ contain X, here we denotes $s = supp(X)$. An *generalized association rules with classification hierarchy* is an implication of the form $X \Rightarrow Y$, where $X, Y \subset \mathcal{I}$, $X \cap Y = \phi$ and no item in Y is an ancestor of any item in X. Each rule has two measures of value, *support* and *confidence*. The *support* of the rule $X \Rightarrow Y$ is $supp(X \cup Y)$. The *confidence* c of the rule $X \Rightarrow Y$ in the transaction set $\mathcal{D}$ means $c\%$ of transactions in $\mathcal{D}$ that contain X also contain Y, which can be written as the ratio $supp(X \cup Y)/supp(X)$. Here a rule $x \Rightarrow ancestor(x)$ is redundant, since its confidence is always 100%.

The problem of mining generalized association rules is to find all the rules that satisfy a user-specified minimum support(min_supp) and minimum confidence (min_conf) on the assumption that we are given a set of transactions $\mathcal{D}$ and a classification hierarchy over the items. This problem can be decomposed into two subproblems:

1. Find all itemsets that have support above the user-specified minimum support. These itemsets are called the *large itemsets* and the other itemsets are called *small itemsets*.
2. For each large itemset, derive all rules that have more than user-specified minimum confidence as follows: for large itemset X and any Y ($Y \subset X$), if $supp(X)/supp(X - Y) \geq min\_conf$, then the rule $(X - Y) \Rightarrow Y$ is derived.

The second subproblem, which derive the association rules, is processed in a straightforward manner. However, because of the large size of transaction data sets used in data mining, the first subproblem, which requires scanning the database, is a nontrivial problem. Most of association rule mining research focus this first subproblem.

Here we explain the Cumulate algorithm for finding all large itemsets, proposed in [2]. Our parallel algorithms are based on this algorithm. First, the Cumulate algorithm generates candidate itemsets, then scans the transition database to determine whether the candidate itemsets satisfy the user specified minimum support. In the first pass (pass 1), support count for each item is counted by scanning the transaction database. All the items which satisfy the minimum support are picked out. These items are called large item (L_1). Hereafter k-itemset is defines a set of k items. The second pass (pass 2), the 2-itemsets are generated using L_1 which is called the candidate 2-itemsets (C_2), and delete any candidate in C_2 that consists of an item and its ancestor. Note that we need not count any itemset which contains both an item and its ancestor. Then the support count of C_2 is counted by scanning the transaction database. At the end of scanning the transaction data, the large 2-itemsets (L_2) which satisfy minimum support are determined. The following pass to find the large k-itemset is as described bellow.

1. Generate candidate itemsets:
   The candidate k-itemsets (C_k) are generated using large $(k-1)$-itemsets (L_{k-1}) as follows: join L_{k-1} with L_{k-1} and delete all the k-itemsets whose some of the $(k-1)$-itemsets are not in L_{k-1}. If k is 2, delete any candidates in C_2 that consists of an item and its ancestor.
2. Count support:
   Read the transaction database, add all ancestors of the items in a transaction t that are present in C_k. Increment the support count of the candidates in C_k that are contained in t.
3. Determine large itemsets:
   The candidate itemsets in C_k are checked for whether they satisfy the minimum support or not, then the large k-itemsets (L_k) are determined.

This procedure terminates when the large itemset becomes empty.

2.1   Parallel Algorithms

In this section, we describe parallel algorithms on shared-nothing parallel machines, NPGM(Non Partitioned Generalized association rule Mining) and H-HPGM (hash) (Hierarchical Hash Partitioned Generalized Association Rule Mining), proposed in [4].

2.2   Non Partitioned Generalized Association Rule Mining: NPGM

If the size of all the candidate itemsets is smaller than the size of the memory of each node, all the nodes can hold whole candidate itemsets. In such a case, parallelization is straightforward. By partitioning the transaction database over all the nodes, the transaction data can be read and candidate itemsets can be counted in parallel. In NPGM, the candidate itemsets are copied over all the nodes, each node can work independently and the final statistics are gathered into a coordinator node where minimum support conditions are examined. The procedure of pass k is as follows.

1. Generate candidate itemsets:
   Each node generates C_k using L_{k-1}. If k is 2, delete the candidates that contains an items and its ancestor.
2. Count support:
   Each node reads the transaction database from its local disk, generates extended transaction t' by adding all ancestors of the items in a transaction t that are present in C_k.
   Increment the support count of the candidates in C_k that are contained in t'.

3. Determine large itemsets:
   After reading all the transaction data, all node's support count are gathered into the coordinator node and checked to determine whether the minimum support condition is satisfied or not.

If the size of all the candidate itemsets exceeds the local memory of a single node, the candidate itemsets are partitioned into fragments, each of which can fits within the local memory of a single node, and the above process is repeated for each fragment. The disk I/O becomes prohibitively costly when the candidate itemsets becomes large.

2.3 Hierarchical Hash Partitioned Generalized Association Rule Mining: H-HPGM(Hash)

H-HPGM(hash) partitions the candidate itemsets among the nodes taking the classification hierarchy into account so that all the candidate itemsets whose root items are identical be allocated to the same node, which eliminates communication of the ancestor items. Thus the communication overhead can be kept low. The procedure of pass k is as follows.

1. Generate candidate itemsets:
   Each node generates C_k in the same way as NPGM. For each candidate, the destination node ID is determined by applying the hash function to replacing each item of the candidate itemset with their root items. If the ID is its own, insert it into the candidate table(C_k^n).
2. Count support:
   Each node reads the transaction database from its local disk and generates extended transaction t' by replacing the item in t with the large item in its ancestors which is closest to the bottom, if there are small items. For each node n, select the related items from t' and send them to n-th node. For the itemsets received from other nodes and those locally generated, generate k-itemset from the itemsets and increment the support count of this k-itemset and its all ancestor candidates.
3. Determine large itemsets:
   After reading all the transactions, each node can determine the large itemset in C_k^n. The coordinator node gather all the large k-itemset.

3 Load Balancing Strategy

In this section, we present two kinds of load balancing strategies, the candidate partition based strategy and the candidate duplication based strategy. The candidate partition based strategy equalizes the number of candidate probes with estimated support count by the statistics of data. The candidate duplication based strategy, which was proposed in our previous study[4], duplicates the frequently occurring candidate itemset among all the nodes.

3.1   Candidate Partition Based Load Balancing Strategy

In H-HPGM(hash), each node probes the itemsets generated with received itemset against its own candidate table. The number of candidate probes is associated with the support of assigned candidate itemsets. This means that the workload depends on the assigned candidate itemsets. Some itemsets have higher support value, which cause a large number of candidate probes. In our load balancing strategy, we assign the candidate itemsets so that the number of candidate probes for each nodes be equal each other. Here, we have to set the weighting factor for each itemset. Since real support value is attained after the execution, the exact weighting factor is not available before the execution. In our load balancing strategy, we set the weighting factor from the statistics of data obtained at previous pass. H-HPGM(hash) algorithm is consisted with several passes. For each pass, the transaction database is scanned and the large k-itemsets are determined. At pass k, we can utilize the support value of large $(k-1)$-itemset. Suppose X is a candidate itemset at pass k, the support count of all the size-$(k-1)$ subsets of X are available. The upper bound of the support value of X is the minimum value of the support count of all the size-$(k-1)$ subsets of X[6,7], i.e., the maximum value of support value of itemset X is defined as follows:

$$max\_supp(X) = min\{supp(Y) \mid Y \subset X, \text{ and } |Y| = k-1\} \tag{1}$$

Here, $supp(Y)$ means the support of itemset Y. Thus, we estimate the support of candidate k-itemset using the support of large $(k-1)$-itemsets and employ them to set the weighting factor.

H-HPGM with Statistics: H-HPGM(stat). H-HPGM(hash) partitions the candidate itemsets among the nodes so that all the candidate itemsets whose root items are the same be allocated to the same node. That is, H-HPGM(hash) divides the candidate itemsets into the hierarchy of the candidate itemsets and allocates such whole hierarchy to a node. Thus the granule is a hierarchies, that is, a tree.

We set the weighting factor for the granule of candidate partition, that is, the combination of trees. The weighting factor of the combination of trees X is defined by following.

$$W(X) = \sum_{y \in Y} max\_supp(y) \tag{2}$$

Here, $W(X)$ means the weighting factor of X, Y means all the descendant candidate itemsets of X. For example, we consider that the taxonomy of items at pass 2 is given in Figure 2. The weighting factor of the combination of trees $\{1, 1\}$ and $\{1, 2\}$ are calculated as follows:

$$W(\{1,1\}) = min\{supp(\{4\}), supp(\{5\})\} + min\{supp(\{5\}), supp(\{10\})\}$$

$$W(\{1,2\}) = min\{supp(\{1\}), supp(\{2\})\} + min\{supp(\{1\}), supp(\{6\})\}$$
$$+ \ldots$$
$$+ min\{supp(\{7\}), supp(\{10\})\} + min\{supp(\{10\}), supp(\{15\})\}$$

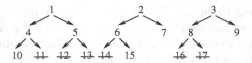

Fig. 2. Taxonomy at Pass 2

(1) **for each** size-k combination of root items x **do**
(2)   Select the minimum node n whose weight is smallest of all the nodes
(3) $C_k^n := x$ and all descendant candidates of x
         (C_k^n means the set of candidates allocated to n-th node)
(4) $CW(n) + =$ weight of x
         ($CW(n)$ means the sum of weight of allocated candidates to n-th node)
(5) **end**

Fig. 3. The procedure to allocate the size-k combination of root items

The procedure to calculate the weighting factor and to allocate the candidate itemsets among the nodes at pass k are as follows.

1. Generate the size-k combination of root items.
2. Calculate the weighting factor of the size-k combination of root items using the equation (2).
3. Sort the size-k combination of root items based on their weight.
4. The size-k combination of root items are allocated among the nodes so that the sum of weighting factor of allocated size-k combination is equalized for each node (Figure 3).

3.2 Candidate Duplication Based Load Balancing Strategy

In the case that the size of the candidate itemsets is smaller than the available system memory, H-HPGM(hash) and H-HPGM(stat) do not use the remaining free space. If the transaction data is skewed, that is, there are some itemsets which appear very frequently in the transaction data, the node which is allocated such itemsets will receive a lot of transaction data, which incurs a system bottleneck. The candidate duplication based strategies handle this problem by identifying such frequently occurring itemsets, duplicating them among all the nodes and counting the support locally. The duplicated candidates are processed in the same way as NPGM. The remaining candidates are partitioned and processed in the same way as H-HPGM(stat).

In the candidate duplication based load balancing strategy, the effect increase as the size of duplicated candidate itemsets increase. In order to attain both flat workload distribution and flat distribution of the number of candidate itemsets among the nodes, we modify the equation of setting the weighting factor as follows:

$$W(X) = \frac{\sum_{y \in Y} max\_supp(y)}{\# \ of \ transactions} + \frac{CN(X)}{CN_k - CN^D} \tag{3}$$

Here, $CN(X)$ means the number of descendant candidate itemsets of X, CN_k means the number of candidate itemsets at pass k, CN^D means the number of duplicated candidate itemsets. Y means the descendant candidate itemsets of X excluding the duplicated candidate itemsets.

We named the load balancing strategy using the equation(3), H-HPGM(stat+). The procedure to allocate the partitioning candidate itemsets among the nodes is obtained by replacing the equation (2) in step 2 with equation (3) in the procedure of H-HPGM(stat).

1. Same as H-HPGM(stat).
2. Calculate the weighting factor of the size-k combination of root items using the equation (3)
3. – 4. Same as H-HPGM(stat).

For example, we consider that the taxonomy of items at pass 2 is given in Figure 2. Assume the number of duplicated candidate itemsets is 0. The weighting factor of the combination of trees $\{1,1\}$ and $\{1,2\}$ are calculated as follows:

$$
\begin{aligned}
W(\{1,1\}) = &\ [min\{supp(\{4\}), supp(\{5\})\} + min\{supp(\{5\}), supp(\{10\})\}] \\
&\ / \{\# \ of \ transactions\} \\
&\ + \{2 \ / \ 45\}
\end{aligned}
$$

$$
\begin{aligned}
W(\{1,2\}) = &\ [min\{supp(\{1\}), supp(\{2\})\} + min\{supp(\{1\}), supp(\{6\})\} \\
&\ + \ldots + min\{supp(\{10\}), supp(\{15\})\}] \ / \ \{\# \ of \ transactons\} \\
&\ + \{16 \ / \ 45\}
\end{aligned}
$$

H-HPGM(stat+) with Tree Grain Duplicate: H-HPGM-TGD(stat+).
H-HPGM-TGD(stat+) detects the tree whose candidate itemsets contain frequently occurred items, duplicates them among the nodes and counts the support count locally for those itemsets like in NPGM. The procedure to detect the duplicated candidates in pass k is as follows.

1. Count up the number of candidates allocated for each node by generating the k-itemsets using L_{k-1} and calculate the size of free memory space.
2. Count the number of descendant candidates for each root k-items combination.
3. Generate k-items combination from root items. Here, these k-items combination contain the items consisting of the same items, such as $\{1,1\}$.
4. Sort the combination of root items based on those item's frequency of appearance.
5. Choose the most frequently occurring combination of root itemsets and duplicate them and their descendant candidate itemsets among the nodes.
6. The remaining candidate itemsets are partitioned in the same way as H-HPGM(stat+).

H-HPGM(stat+) with Path Grain Duplicate: H-HPGM-PGD(stat+).
H-HPGM-PGD(stat+) picks up the leaf large items and sorts them based on
their support value. Then it chooses the most frequently occurring itemsets and
copies them and their all ancestor itemsets over all the nodes. Since the granule
of candidate duplication employed in H-HPGM-PGD(stat+) is smaller than H-
HPGM-TGD(stat+), it can balance the load among the nodes more effectively.
The procedure to detect the duplicated candidates in pass k is as follows.

1. – 3. Same as H-HPGM-TGD(stat+).
4. Pick up the large items in L_{k-1} which is the closest to the bottom, and sort
   them based on their support value.
5. Choose the first several most frequently occurring items using the sorted list
   derived at "4", and duplicate it and its all ancestor candidates among the
   nodes.
6. Same as H-HPGM-TGD(stat+).

H-HPGM(stat+) with Fine Grain Duplicate: H-HPGM-FGD(stat+).
H-HPGM-FGD(stat+) checks the frequently occurring itemsets which consists
of the any level items. It duplicates them and their all ancestor itemsets over all
the nodes. Thus only the frequent candidate itemsets are duplicated. The granule
of candidate duplication becomes finer. The procedure to detect the duplicated
candidates in pass k is as follows.

1. – 3. Same as H-HPGM-TGD(stat+).
4. Sort the large items based on their count support value.
5. Choose the first most frequently occurring candidate itemsets, and duplicate
   them and their all ancestor candidates among the nodes.
6. Same as H-HPGM-TGD(stat+).

4   Large Scale PC Cluster System

4.1   Components of Cluster

Our PC cluster system[1] consists of one hundred 200MHz Pentium Pro PCs,
connected with an 155Mbps ATM switch as well as by 10Mbps Ethernet network.
Figure 4 shows an overview of the PC cluster. Each node consists of components
shown in Table 1. We use the RFC-1483 PVC driver for IP over ATM. TCP/IP
is used as a communication protocol. HITACHI's AN1000-20, which has 128
ports, is used as an ATM switch.

5   Performance Analysis

We implement the parallel algorithms and the load balancing strategies on the
PC cluster system. The transaction database is evenly partitioned over the local

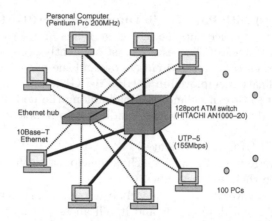

Fig. 4. An overview of the PC cluster

Table 1. Each node of PC cluster

CPU	Intel 200MHz Pentium Pro
Chipset	Intel 440FX
Main memory	64MBytes
Disk drive	For OS
	Western Digital Caviar 32500 (EIDE, 2.5GB)
	For database
	Seagate Barracuda (Ultra SCSI, 4.3GB)
OS	Solaris2.5.1 for x86
ATM NIC	Interphase 5515 PCI ATM Adapter

disk of all the nodes. Solaris socket library is used for the inter-process communication. All processes are connected with each other by socket connections, thus forming mesh topology. To evaluate the performance of the proposed parallel algorithms, synthetic dataset emulating retail transactions is used. The generation procedure is described in [2]. Table 2 shows the meaning of the various parameters and the characteristics of the dataset used in our experiment.

5.1 Execution Time

We show the number of candidate itemsets and large itemsets, and the execution time at each pass in Table 3. 64 nodes in PC cluster system are used, and the minimum support is set to 0.3% in this experiments.

NPGM can attain the best performance when the number of candidate itemsets is small, since NPGM does not require the communication of transaction data for the support count process. When the number of candidate itemsets becomes large such as pass 2, the single node's memory cannot hold the entire candidate itemsets, the performance of NPGM is degrade. H-HPGM(hash) and H-HPGM(stat) partition the candidate itemsets among the nodes. These

Table 2. Parameters of dataset

Parameter	
Number of transactions	20,000,000 (file size 1GB)
Average size of the transactions	5
Average size of the maximal potentially large itemsets	5
Number of maximal potentially large itemsets	10,000
Number of items	50,000
Number of roots	100
Number of levels	5–6
Fanout	5

Table 3. # of candidate itemsets and large itemsets, and execution time at each pass

Pass	C	L	Execution time (sec)			
			NPGM	H-HPGM (hash)	H-HPGM (stat)	H-HPGM-FGD(stat+)
1	50000	1361	3.4	3.4	3.4	3.4
2	881548	4188	592.8	272.9	178.5	153.9
3	31404	970	116.2	195.1	157.4	118.1
4	3153	176	69.3	132.6	101.1	70.9
5	927	86	52.8	89.7	82.0	53.4
6	322	5	13.6	31.1	28.5	13.7
Total			848.1	724.8	550.9	413.4

C : Number of candidate itemsets
L : Number of large itemsets

candidate partition based algorithms outperform than NPGM when the number of candidate is large. Because of the effect of the candidate partition based load balancing strategy, H-HPGM(stat) achieves better performance than H-HPGM(hash) at all the range of minimum support. When the number of candidate itemsets is small, the performance of H-HPGM(hash) and H-HPGM(stat) is worse than NPGM. H-HPGM(hash) and H-HPGM(stat) partition the candidate itemsets at all the pass. When the number of candidate becomes small compared with the number of nodes, the number of the allocated candidate itemsets for each node decrease, the most of memory space does not utilized. H-HPGM-FGD(stat+) can archive good performance at all the passes. In the case that each node's memory can hold the entire candidate itemsets, H-HPGM-FGD(stat+) behaves the same way as NPGM. Because of some overhead, the execution time of H-HPGM-FGD(stat+) is a little longer than that of NPGM when the number of candidate itemsets is small. The whole execution time of H-HPGM-FGD(stat+) is best.

In Figure 5, we show the execution time at pass 2 varying the minimum support. Hereafter, we show only the result at pass 2, since the number of candidate

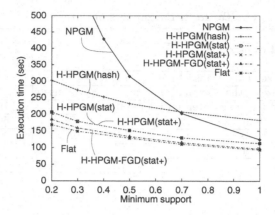

Fig. 5. Execution time

itemsets and the execution time for pass 2 is the longest. 64 nodes in PC cluster system are used in this experiment. We show the result of the best workload distribution, named Flat, as an ideal result. By using the real support count information to set the weighting factor, we can attain the most flat workload distribution.

The execution time of all the algorithms increases when the minimum support becomes small. Especially, the execution time of NPGM increases sharply. When the minimum support reduces, the number of candidate itemsets increases. On the other hand, the candidate partitioned methods can attain good performance at the small minimum support. The performance of H-HPGM(stat) and H-HPGM(stat+) is almost equal. The difference of these two algorithm is whether the weighting factor takes the distribution of candidate itemsets into account. H-HPGM-FGD(stat+) attains the best performance of all the range of minimum support.

5.2 The Distribution of Allocated Candidate Itemsets for Each Node

Figure 6 shows the distribution of allocated candidate itemsets for each node at pass 2. The vertical axis is the standard deviation of the number of candidate itemsets for each node. The minimum support is varying from 0.2% to 0.5%.

H-HPGM(stat+) attains flat candidate distribution. Since H-HPGM(stat+) sets the weighting factor considering not only the distribution of workload but also the distribution of the number of candidate itemsets among the nodes, it can attain flat distribution of candidate itemsets.

5.3 Performance with Varying the Size of Duplicated Candidates

Here, we show the performance of load balancing strategies with varying the size of duplicated candidate itemsets at pass 2. Figure 7 shows the execution time.

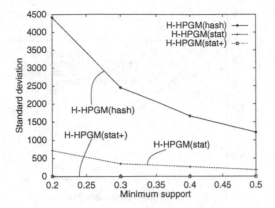

Fig. 6. The distribution of candidate itemsets at pass 2

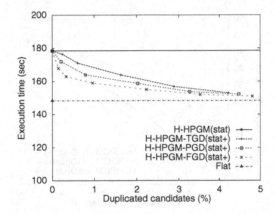

Fig. 7. Execution time with varying the size of duplicated candidates

Figure 8 is the workload distribution. Figure 9 is the percentage of candidate probes for duplicated candidate itemsets to all the candidate probes. Figure 10 is the average amount of received messages for each node. In these experiments, the minimum support is set to 0.3% and 64 nodes of PC cluster system is activated.

As the size of duplicated candidate itemsets increases, the execution time of candidate duplication based load balancing strategy is reduced and the workload distribution becomes balanced. The candidate duplication based load balancing strategies detect the frequently occurring candidate itemsets and duplicate them so that the remaining free space could be utilized as much as possible. Especially, H-HPGM-FGD(stat+) can reduce the execution time at small candidate duplication size. Since H-HPGM-FGD(stat+) employs the smallest granule duplication strategy, it can show the ability if the remaining free memory space is small. Figure 9 shows that the small size of duplicated candidates occupies the large number of candidate probes in the candidate duplication based load

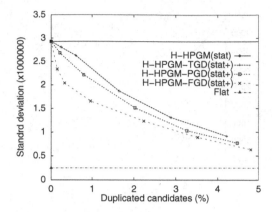

Fig. 8. The number of candidate probes at pass 2

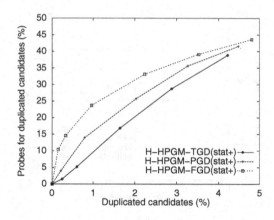

Fig. 9. Percentage of candidate probes for duplicated candidates at pass 2

balancing strategies. In these strategies, we duplicate the frequently occurring candidate itemsets. Support count process for duplicated candidate itemsets can be locally processed like as NPGM, which reduce the communication overhead and effective to attain flat workload distribution.

5.4   Speedup

Figure 11 shows the speedup ratio with varying the number of nodes used 16, 32, 64 and 100. The curves are normalized by the execution time of 16 nodes system. Here, the minimum support is set to 0.3%.

The load balancing strategies attain higher linearity than H-HPGM(hash). Since H-HPGM(hash) partitions the candidate itemsets using hash function without considering the load balancing and duplicates no candidate itemsets, the workload skew degrades the linearity. Though H-HPGM(stat) partitions

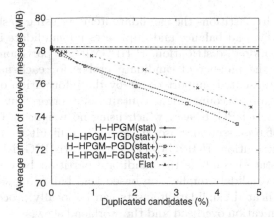

Fig. 10. Average amount of received messages at pass 2

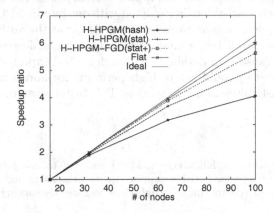

Fig. 11. Speedup ratio at pass 2

the candidate itemsets taking the load balancing into account, it cannot attain sufficient linearity. On the other hand, H-HPGM-FGD(stat+), duplicating the frequently occurring candidate itemsets and partitioning the other candidate itemsets with considering the load balance, can attain the highest linearity. In Figure 11, H-HPGM-FGD(stat+) achieves good performance on one hundred nodes system. By considering both the distribution of workload and that of the number of candidate itemsets, we can attain good performance.

6   Conclusions

In this paper, we presented the candidate partition based load balancing strategies for parallel mining algorithms of generalized association rule and evaluated their performance through the implementation on large scale PC cluster system.

H-HPGM(hash) partitions the candidate itemsets using hash function without considering the load balance and duplicates no candidate itemsets, it cannot attain flat workload distribution. H-HPGM(stat) partitions the candidate itemsets so that the number of candidate probes for each node is equalized each other with estimated support count by the information of previous pass. This estimated support count might contain some error, but it attain better performance than H-HPGM(hash) which using no weighting factor. However, as the number of processor increase, it would be difficult to achieve sufficient flat workload distribution. H-HPGM-TGD(stat+), H-HPGM-PGD(stat+) and H-HPGM-FGD(stat+) combine the candidate partition based load balancing strategy and the candidate duplication based load balancing strategy. Support counting for duplicated candidate itemsets can be locally processed, which reduce the communication overhead and the workload skew.

We examined the effectiveness of parallel algorithms and their load balancing strategies on large scale parallel computer system using the large amount of transaction dataset. Our system is consisted with one hundred PC's and 1GBytes transaction database was used for experiment. As far as the authors know, there has no research on parallel data mining over such large scale systems using such large amount of transaction database. Through several experiments, we showed H-HPGM-FGD(stat+) could attain high performance and achieve sufficiently good workload distribution on one hundred PC cluster system.

References

1. Tamura, T., Oguchi, M., Kitsuregawa, M.: Parallel database processing on a 100 node pc cluster: Cases for decision support query processing and data mining. In: Proceedings of Supercomputing 97::High Performance Networking and Computing. (1997)
2. Srikant, R., Agrawal, R.: Mining generalized association rules. In: Proceedings of 21th International Conference on Very Large Data Bases. (1995) 407–419
3. Han, J., Fu, Y.: Discovery of multiple-level association rules from large databases. In: Proceedings of 21th International Conference on Very Large Data Bases. (1995) 420–431
4. Shintani, T., Kitsuregawa, M.: Parallel algorithms for mining generalized association rules with classification hierarchy. In: Proceedings of 1998 ACM SIGMOD International Conference on Management of Data. (1998) 25–36
5. Han, E.H., Karypis, G., Kumar, V.: Scalable parallel data mining for association rules. In: Proceedings of 1997 ACM SIGMOD International Conference on Management of Data. (1997) 277–288
6. Cheung, D., Han, J., Ng, V., Fu, A., Fu, Y.: A fast distributed algorithm for mining association rules. In: Proceedings of 4th International Conference on Parallel and Distributed Information Systems. (1996) 31–42
7. Cheung, D., Ng, V., Fu, A., Fu, Y.: Efficient mining of association rules in distributed databases. In: IEEE Transactions on Knowledge and Data Engineering, Vol.8, No. 6. (1996) 911–922

Parallel Sequence Mining on
Shared-Memory Machines

Mohammed J. Zaki

Computer Science Department
Rensselaer Polytechnic Institute
Troy, NY 12180
zaki@cs.rpi.edu
http://www.cs.rpi.edu/~zaki

Abstract. We present pSPADE, a parallel algorithm for fast discovery of frequent sequences in large databases. pSPADE decomposes the original search space into smaller suffix-based classes. Each class can be solved in main-memory using efficient search techniques, and simple join operations. Further each class can be solved independently on each processor requiring no synchronization. However, dynamic inter-class and intra-class load balancing must be exploited to ensure that each processor gets an equal amount of work. Experiments on a 12 processor SGI Origin 2000 shared memory system show good speedup and excellent scaleup results.

1   Introduction

The sequence mining task is to discover a sequence of attributes, shared across time among a large number of objects in a given database. For example, consider a web access database at a popular site, where an object is a web user and an attribute is a web page. The discovered patterns are the sequences of most frequently accessed pages at that site. This kind of information can be used to restructure the web-site, or to dynamically insert relevant links in web pages based on user access patterns. There are many other domains where sequence mining has been applied, which include discovering customer buying patterns in retail stores, identifying plan failures [1], finding network alarm patterns [2], and so on.

The task of discovering all frequent sequences in large databases is quite challenging. The search space is extremely large. For example, with m attributes there are, in the worst case, $O(m^k)$ potential sequences of length at most k. Fortunately, in practice only a small fraction of all potential sequences are shared among many database objects or transactions, the so-called frequent sequences. Nevertheless, given the search complexity, serial algorithms cannot provide scalability, in terms of the data size and the performance, for large databases. Because there is always this limit to the performance of a single processor, we must rely on parallel multiprocessor systems to fill this role.

M.J. Zaki, C.-T. Ho (Eds.): Large-Scale Parallel Data Mining, LNAI 1759, pp. 161–189, 2000.

Two approaches for utilizing multiple processors have emerged: *distributed memory*, in which each processor has a private memory; and *shared memory*, in which all processors access common memory. A shared-memory architecture has many desirable properties. Each processor has direct and equal access to all the memory in the system. Parallel programs are easy to implement on such a system. A different approach to multiprocessing is to build a system from many units, each containing a processor and memory. In a distributed memory architecture, each processor has its own local memory that can only be accessed directly by that processor. For a processor to have access to data in the local memory of another processor, a copy of the desired data elements must be sent from one processor to the other, utilizing the message passing programming paradigm. Although a shared memory architecture offers programming simplicity, the finite bandwidth of a common bus can limit scalability. A distributed memory architecture cures the scalability problem by eliminating the bus, but at the cost of programming simplicity. It is possible to combine the best of both the worlds by providing a shared global address space abstraction over physically distributed memory. Such an architecture is called distributed-shared memory (DSM) system. It provides ease of programming, yet retains scalability at the same time. The shared-memory abstraction can be provided in hardware or software.

The target architecture we use in this paper is hardware distributed-shared memory (HDSM). Our HDSM platform is a 12 processor SGI Origin 2000 system, which is a cache-coherent non-uniform memory access (CC-NUMA) machine. For cache coherence the hardware ensures that locally cached data always reflects the latest modification by any processor. It is NUMA because reads/writes to local memory are cheaper than reads/writes to a remote processor's memory. The main challenge in obtaining high performance on these systems is to ensure good *data locality*, making sure that most read/writes are to local memory, and reducing/eliminating *false sharing*, which occurs when two different shared variables are (coincidentally) located in the same cache block, causing the block to be exchanged between the processors due to coherence maintenance operations, even though the processors are accessing different variables. Of course, the other factor influencing parallel performance for any system is to ensure good *load balance*, i.e., making sure that each processor gets an equal amount of work.

In this paper we present pSPADE, a parallel algorithm for discovering the set of all frequent sequences, targeting shared-memory systems. pSPADE is an asynchronous algorithm, in that it requires no synchronization among processors, except when a load imbalance is detected. For sequence mining on large databases with millions of transactions the problem of I/O minimization becomes paramount. However, most current algorithms are iterative in nature, requiring as many full database scans as the longest frequent sequence, which is clearly very expensive. Some of the methods, especially those using some form of sampling, can be sensitive to the data-skew, which can adversely effect performance. Most approaches also use very complicated internal data structures which have poor locality [3], and add additional space and computation overheads. pSPADE has been designed such that it has good locality and has little false sharing.

The key features of our approach are as follows:

1. We use a *vertical idlist* database format, where we associate with each sequence a list of objects in which it occurs, along with the time-stamps. We show that all frequent sequences can be enumerated via simple temporal idlist intersections.
2. We use a lattice-theoretic approach to decompose the original search space into smaller pieces — the suffix-based classes — which can be processed independently in main-memory. This decomposition is recursively applied within each parent class to produce even smaller classes at the next level,
3. We propose an asynchronous algorithm, where processors work on separate classes at the first level, without any need for sharing or synchronization. To ensure good load balance, we propose a dynamic load balancing scheme, where any free processors joins a busy processor in solving newly formed classes at higher levels.

pSPADE is based on SPADE [4], a sequential algorithm for efficient enumeration of frequent sequences, and thus shares many of its performance features. pSPADE not only minimizes I/O costs by reducing database scans, but also minimizes computational costs by using efficient search schemes. The vertical idlist based approach is also relatively insensitive to data-skew. In fact, idlist skew leads to faster support counting, since the result of an intersection of two lists is always bounded by the size of the *smaller* idlist. An extensive set of experiments is performed on a 12 processor SGI Origin 2000. pSPADE delivers reasonably good speedup, and scales linearly in the database size, and a number of other database parameters.

The rest of the paper is organized as follows: We describe the sequence discovery problem in Section 2 and discuss related work in Section 3. Section 4 describes the serial algorithm, while the design and implementation issues for pSPADE are presented in Section 5. An experimental study is presented in Section 6, and we conclude in Section 7.

2   Sequence Mining

The problem of mining sequential patterns can be stated as follows: Let $\mathcal{I} = \{i_1, i_2, \cdots, i_m\}$ be a set of m distinct attributes, also called *items*. An *itemset* is a non-empty unordered collection of items (without loss of generality, we assume that items of an itemset are sorted in increasing order). All items in an itemset are assumed to occur at the same time. A *sequence* is an ordered list of itemsets. The itemsets in a sequence are ordered according to their associated time-stamp. An itemset i is denoted as $(i_1 i_2 \cdots i_k)$, where i_j is an item. An itemset with k items is called a k-*itemset*. A sequence α is denoted as $(\alpha_1 \mapsto \alpha_2 \mapsto \cdots \mapsto \alpha_q)$, where the sequence *element* α_j is an itemset. A sequence with k items $(k = \sum_j |\alpha_j|)$ is called a k-*sequence*. For example, $(B \mapsto AC)$ is a 3-sequence. An item can occur only once in an itemset, but it can occur multiple times in different itemsets of a sequence.

A sequence $\alpha = (\alpha_1 \mapsto \alpha_2 \mapsto \cdots \mapsto \alpha_n)$ is a *subsequence* of another sequence $\beta = (\beta_1 \mapsto \beta_2 \mapsto \cdots \mapsto \beta_m)$, denoted as $\alpha \preceq \beta$, if there exist integers $i_1 < i_2 < \cdots < i_n$ such that $\alpha_j \subseteq \beta_{i_j}$ for all α_j. For example the sequence $(B \mapsto AC)$ is a subsequence of $(AB \mapsto E \mapsto ACD)$, since the sequence elements $B \subseteq AB$, and $AC \subseteq ACD$. On the other hand the sequence $(AB \mapsto E)$ is not a subsequence of (ABE), and vice versa. We say that α is a proper subsequence of β, denoted $\alpha \prec \beta$, if $\alpha \preceq \beta$ and $\beta \not\preceq \alpha$. A sequence is *maximal* if it is not a subsequence of any other sequence.

A *transaction* $\mathcal{T}$ has a unique identifier and *contains* a set of items, i.e., $\mathcal{T} \subseteq \mathcal{I}$. A *customer*, $\mathcal{C}$, has a unique identifier and has associated with it a list of transactions $\{\mathcal{T}_1, \mathcal{T}_2, \cdots, \mathcal{T}_n\}$. Without loss of generality, we assume that no customer has more than one transaction with the same time-stamp, so that we can use the transaction-time as the transaction identifier. We also assume that the list of customer transactions is sorted by the transaction-time. Thus the list of transactions of a customer is itself a sequence $\mathcal{T}_1 \mapsto \mathcal{T}_2 \mapsto \cdots \mapsto \mathcal{T}_n$, called the *customer-sequence*. The database, $\mathcal{D}$, consists of a number of such customer-sequences.

A customer-sequence, $\mathcal{C}$, is said to *contain* a sequence α, if $\alpha \preceq \mathcal{C}$, i.e., if α is a subsequence of the customer-sequence $\mathcal{C}$. The *support* or *frequency* of a sequence, denoted $\sigma(\alpha)$, is the the total number of customers that contain this sequence. Given a user-specified threshold called the *minimum support* (denoted *min_sup*), we say that a sequence is *frequent* if occurs more than *min_sup* times. The set of frequent k-sequences is denoted as $\mathcal{F}_k$.

Given a database $\mathcal{D}$ of customer sequences and *min_sup*, the problem of mining sequential patterns is to find all frequent sequences in the database. For example, consider the customer database shown in figure 1. The database has three items (A, B, C), four customers, and twelve transactions in all. The figure also shows all the frequent sequences with a minimum support of 75% or 3 customers.

3   Related Work

3.1   Serial Algorithms

The problem of mining sequential patterns was introduced in [5]. They also presented three algorithms for solving this problem. The *AprioriAll* algorithm was shown to perform equal to or better than the other two approaches. In subsequent work [6], the same authors proposed the GSP algorithm that outperformed *AprioriAll* by up to 20 times. They also introduced maximum gap, minimum gap, and sliding window constraints on the discovered sequences. Recently, SPADE [4] was shown to outperform GSP by a factor of two in the general case, and by a factor of ten with a pre-processing step. We therefore based pSPADE on our sequential SPADE method.

The problem of finding *frequent episodes* in a sequence of events was presented in [7]. An episode consists of a set of events and an associated partial order over the events. Our definition of a sequence can be expressed as an episode,

DATABASE		
CID	TID	Items
	10	A B
1	20	B
	30	A B
	20	A C
2	30	A B C
	50	B
	10	A
3	30	B
	40	A
	30	A B
4	40	A
	50	B

FREQUENT SET (75% Minimum Support)
{A, A->A, B->A, B, AB, A->B, B->B, AB->B}

Fig. 1. Original Database

however their work is targeted to discover the frequent episodes in a single long event sequence, while we are interested in finding frequent sequences across many different customer-sequences. They further extended their framework in [8] to discover *generalized episodes*, which allows one to express arbitrary unary conditions on individual episode events, or binary conditions on event pairs. The MEDD and MSDD algorithms [9] discover patterns in multiple event sequences; they explore the rule space directly instead of the sequence space.

The GSP Algorithm. Before we proceed further, we need to give some more details on GSP, since it is forms the core of the previous work on parallel sequence mining.

$\mathcal{F}_1 = \{$ frequent 1-sequences $\}$;
for $(k = 2; \mathcal{F}_{k-1} \neq \emptyset; k = k + 1)$ **do**
$\quad C_k =$ Set of candidate k-sequences;
$\quad$ **for** all customer-sequences $\mathcal{E}$ in the database **do**
$\quad\quad$ Increment count of all $\alpha \in C_k$ contained in $\mathcal{E}$
$\quad \mathcal{F}_k = \{\alpha \in C_k | \alpha.sup \geq min\_sup\}$;
Set of all frequent sequences $= \bigcup_k \mathcal{F}_k$;

Fig. 2. The GSP Algorithm

GSP makes multiple passes over the database. In the first pass, all single items (1-sequences) are counted. From the frequent items a set of *candidate* 2-sequences are formed. Another pass is made to gather their support. The frequent 2-sequences are used to generate the candidate 3-sequences, and this process is repeated until no more frequent sequences are found. There are two main steps in the algorithm.

1. **Candidate Generation**: Given the set of frequent $(k-1)$-sequences $\mathcal{F}_{k-1}$, the candidates for the next pass are generated by joining $\mathcal{F}_{k-1}$ with itself. A pruning phase eliminates any sequence at least one of whose subsequences is not frequent. For fast counting, the candidate sequences are stored in a *hash-tree*.
2. **Support Counting**: To find all candidates contained in a customer-sequence $\mathcal{E}$, all k-subsequences of $\mathcal{E}$ are generated. For each such subsequence a search is made in the hash-tree. If a candidate in the hash-tree matches the subsequence, its count is incremented.

The GSP algorithm is shown in Figure 2. For more details on the specific mechanisms for constructing and searching hash-trees, please refer to [6] (note: the second iteration is optimized to directly use arrays for counting the support of 2-sequences, instead of using hash trees).

3.2   Parallel Algorithms

While parallel association mining has attracted wide attention [10,11,12,13,14,15, 16] there has been relatively less work on parallel mining of sequential patterns. Three parallel algorithms based on GSP were presented in [17]. All three approaches partition the datasets into equal sized blocks among the nodes. In NPSPM, the candidate sequences are replicated on all the processors, and each processor gathers local support using its local database block. A reduction is performed after each iteration to get the global supports. Since NPSPM replicates the entire candidate set on each node, it can run into memory overflow problems for large databases. SPSPM partitions the candidate set into equal-sized blocks and assigns each block to a separate processor. While SPSPM utilizes the aggregate memory of the system, it suffers from excessive communication, since each processor's local database has to be broadcast to all other processors to get the global support. HPSPM uses a more intelligent strategy to partition the candidate sequences using a hashing mechanism. It also reduces the amount of communication needed to count the global support. Experiments were performed on an IBM SP2 distributed memory machine. HPSPM was shown to be the best approach.

The main limitation of all these parallel algorithms is that they make repeated passes over the disk-resident database partition, incurring high I/O overheads. Furthermore, the schemes involve exchanging the remote database partitions during each iteration, resulting in high communication and synchronization overhead. They also use complicated hash structures, which entail additional

overhead in maintenance and search, and typically also have poor cache locality [3]. As we shall show in the experimental section, pSPADE is successful in
overcoming all these problems.

pSPADE bears similarity to our previous parallel association mining work [16],
but it differs in three important respects. First, the itemset search space forms
a very small subset of the the sequence search space. Many of the optimizations proposed for generating clique-based partitions of the search space no
longer work. The temporal idlist intersections also differ significantly from the
non-temporal joins in associations. Second, the association work presented distributed memory algorithms, while pSPADE targets shared-memory systems,
the first such study for parallel sequence mining. Finally, pSPADE uses a recursive dynamic load balancing scheme, in contrast to the purely static load
balancing scheme used for association mining in [16].

4   The Serial SPADE Algorithm

In this section we describe SPADE [4], a serial algorithm for fast discovery of
frequent sequences, which forms the basis for the parallel pSPADE algorithm.

Sequence Lattice. SPADE uses the observation that the subsequence relation $\preceq$
defines a partial order on the set of sequences, also called a *specialization relation.*
If $\alpha \preceq \beta$, we say that α is more general than β, or β is more specific than α.
The second observation used is that the relation $\preceq$ is a *monotone specialization
relation* with respect to the frequency $\sigma(\alpha)$, i.e., if β is a frequent sequence, then
all subsequences $\alpha \preceq \beta$ are also frequent. The algorithm systematically searches
the sequence lattice spanned by the subsequence relation, from the most general
to the maximally specific frequent sequences in a breadth/depth-first manner.
For example, Figure 3 A) shows the lattice of frequent sequences for our example
database.

Support Counting. Most of the current sequence mining algorithms [6] assume a
horizontal database layout such as the one shown in Figure 1. In the horizontal
format the database consists of a set of customers (*cid's*). Each customer has a
set of transactions (*tid's*), along with the items contained in the transaction. In
contrast, we use a *vertical* database layout, where we associate with each item
X in the sequence lattice its *idlist*, denoted $\mathcal{L}(X)$, which is a list of all customer
(*cid*) and transaction identifiers (*tid*) pairs containing the atom. Figure 3 B)
shows the idlists for all the frequent items.

Given the sequence idlists, we can determine the support of any k-sequence
by simply intersecting the idlists of any two of its $(k - 1)$ length subsequences.
In particular, we use the two $(k - 1)$ length subsequences that share a common
suffix (the generating sequences) to compute the support of a new k length
sequence. A simple check on the cardinality of the resulting idlist (actually, the
number of distinct *cids*) tells us whether the new sequence is frequent or not.
Figure 3C) shows this process pictorially. It shows the initial vertical database

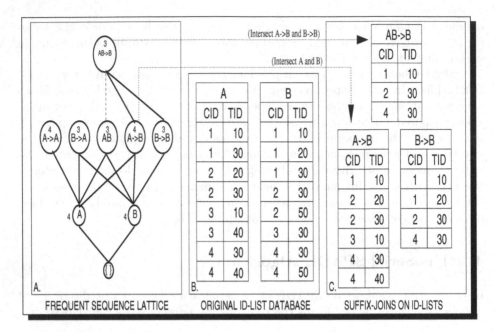

Fig. 3. A. Frequent Sequence Lattice; B. Initial Idlist Database; C. Temporal Idlist Intersections

with the idlist for each item. The intermediate idlist for $A \mapsto B$ is obtained by intersecting the lists of A and B, i.e., $\mathcal{L}(A \mapsto B) = \mathcal{L}(A) \cap \mathcal{L}(B)$. Similarly, $\mathcal{L}(AB \mapsto B) = \mathcal{L}(A \mapsto B) \cap \mathcal{L}(B \mapsto B)$. The temporal intersection is more involved; exact details will be discussed below.

Lattice Decomposition – Suffix-Based Classes. If we had enough main-memory, we could enumerate all the frequent sequences by traversing the lattice, and performing temporal intersections to obtain sequence supports. In practice, however, we only have a limited amount of main-memory, and all the intermediate idlists will not fit in memory. SPADE breaks up this large search space into small, independent, manageable chunks which can be processed in memory. This is accomplished via suffix-based equivalence classes. We say that two k length sequences are in the same class if they share a common $k - 1$ length suffix. The key observation is that each class is a sub-lattice of the original sequence lattice and can be processed independently. For example, Figure 4A) shows the effect of decomposing the frequent sequence lattice for our example database, by collapsing all sequences with the same 1-length suffix into a single class. There are two resulting suffix classes, namely, $\{[A], [B]\}$, which are referred to as *parent classes*. Each class is independent in the sense that it has complete information for generating all frequent sequences that share the same suffix. For example, if a class $[X]$ has the elements $Y \mapsto X$, and $Z \mapsto X$. The only possible frequent sequences at the next step can be $Y \mapsto Z \mapsto X$, $Z \mapsto Y \mapsto X$, and $(YZ) \mapsto X$.

It should be obvious that no other item Q can lead to a frequent sequence with the suffix X, unless (QX) or $Q \mapsto X$ is also in $[X]$.

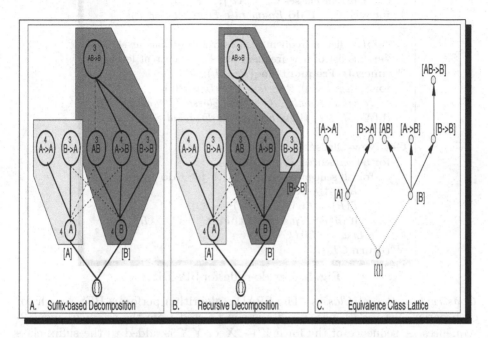

Fig. 4. A) Initial Decomposition: Suffix Length 1, B) Level 2 Decomposition: Suffix Length 2, C) Recursive Decomposition: Class Tree

SPADE recursively decomposes the sequences at each new level into even smaller independent classes. Figure 4B) shows the effect of using 2-length suffixes. If we do this at all levels we obtain a tree of independent classes as shown in Figure 4C). This computation tree is processed in a breadth-first manner, within each parent class. In other words, parent classes are processed one-by-one, but within a parent class we process the new classes in a breadth-first search (BFS). Figure 5 shows the pseudo-code for the breadth-first search in SPADE. The input to the procedure is a list of classes $PrevL$, along with the idlist for each of their elements. Frequent sequences are generated by intersecting the idlists of all pairs of sequences in each class and checking the cardinality of the resulting idlist against min_sup. The sequences found to be frequent at the current level form classes for the next level $NewL$. This level-wise process is repeated until all frequent sequences have been enumerated. In terms of memory management it is easy to see that we need memory to store intermediate idlists for at most two consecutive levels within a parent class. Once all the frequent sequences for the next level have been generated, the sequences at the current level can be deleted.

```
SPADE (min_sup, D):
    F₁ = { frequent items or 1-sequences };
    F₂ = { frequent 2-sequences };
    C = { parent classes Cᵢ = [Xᵢ]};
    for each Cᵢ ∈ C do Enumerate-Frequent-Seq(Cᵢ);

//PrevL is list of frequent classes from previous level
//NewL is list of new frequent classes for current level
Enumerate-Frequent-Seq(PrevL):
    for (; PrevL ≠ ∅; PrevL = PrevL.next())
        NewL = NewL ∪ Get-New-Classes (PrevL.item());
    if (NewL ≠ ∅) then Enumerate-Frequent-Seq(NewL);

Get-New-Classes(S):
    for all sequences Aᵢ ∈ S do
        for all sequences Aⱼ ∈ S, with j ≥ i do
            R = Aᵢ ∪ Aⱼ;
            L(R) = L(Aᵢ) ∩ L(Aⱼ);
            if (σ(R) ≥ min_sup) then Cᵢ = Cᵢ ∪ {R};
        CList = CList ∪ Cᵢ;
    return CList;
```

Fig. 5. Pseudo-code for SPADE

Constructing Parent Classes. The SPADE algorithm performs BFS search for each parent class. Each parent class is constructed from the set of frequent 2-sequences. A sequence of the form $Y \mapsto X$ or YX is added to the suffix class $[X]$. Let $N = |\mathcal{I}|$ be the number of frequent items, and A the average idlist size in bytes. A naive implementation for computing the frequent 2-sequences requires $\binom{N}{2}$ idlist intersections for all pairs of items. The amount of data read is $A \cdot N \cdot (N-1)/2$, which corresponds to around $N/2$ data scans. This is clearly inefficient. Instead of the naive method, we use a preprocessing step to gather the counts of all 2-sequences above a user specified lower bound. Since this information is invariant, it has to be computed once, and the cost can be amortized over the number of times the data is mined. For another method that doesn't require pre-processing, and for additional details on the SPADE algorithm, we refer the reader to [4].

Disk Scans. Before processing each of the parent classes from the initial decomposition, all the relevant item idlists for that class are scanned into from disk into memory. All the other frequent sequences are enumerated using temporal joins. If all the initial classes have disjoint set of items, then each item's idlist is scanned from disk only once during the entire frequent sequence enumeration process over all sub-lattices. In the general case there will be some degree of overlap of items among the different sub-lattices. However, only the database portion corresponding to the frequent items will need to be scanned, which can be a lot smaller than the entire database. Furthermore, sub-lattices sharing many common items can be processed in a batch mode to minimize disk access. Thus, our algorithms will usually requires only a few database scans, in contrast to the current approaches which require as many scans as the longest frequent sequence (this can be reduced somewhat by combining candidates of multiple lengths in later passes).

Temporal Idlist Intersection. We now describe how we perform the temporal idlist intersections for two sequences, since this forms the heart of the computation of SPADE, and is crucial in understanding the parallelization strategies.

Given a suffix equivalence class $[S]$, it can contain two kinds of elements: an itemset of the form XS or a sequence of the form $Y \mapsto S$, where X and Y are items, and S is some (suffix) sequence. Let's assume without loss of generality that the itemsets of a class always precede its sequences. To extend the class for the next level it is sufficient to intersect the idlists of all pairs of elements. However, depending on the pairs being intersected, there can be up to three possible resulting frequent sequences:

1. **Itemset vs Itemset**: If we are intersecting XS with YS, then we get a new itemset XYS.
2. **Itemset vs Sequence**: If we are intersecting XS with $Y \mapsto S$, then the only possible outcome is new sequence $Y \mapsto XS$.
3. **Sequence vs Sequence**: If we are intersecting $X \mapsto S$ with $Y \mapsto S$, then there are three possible outcomes: a new itemset $XY \mapsto S$, and two new sequences $X \mapsto Y \mapsto S$ and $Y \mapsto X \mapsto S$. A special case arises when we intersect $X \mapsto S$ with itself, which can only produce the new sequence $X \mapsto X \mapsto S$.

Consider the idlist for the items A and B shown in Figure 3 B). These are taken to be sequence elements $A \mapsto \emptyset$ and $B \mapsto \emptyset$ for the class $[\emptyset]$. To get the idlist for the resultant itemset AB, we need to check for *equality* of cid-tid pairs. In our example, $\mathcal{L}(AB) = \{(1, 10), (1, 30), (2, 20), (4, 30)\}$. It is frequent at 75% minimum support level (i.e., 3 out of 4 customers). Note that support is incremented only once per customer.

To compute the idlist for the sequence $A \mapsto B$, we need to check for a *follows* temporal relationship, i.e., for a given pair (c, t_1) in $\mathcal{L}(A)$, we check whether there exists a pair (c, t_2) in $\mathcal{L}(B)$ with the same cid c, but with $t_2 > t_1$. If this is true, it means that the item B follows the item A for customer c. The resultant idlist for $A \mapsto B$ is shown in Figure 3 C). We call $A \mapsto B$ the *forward* follows intersection. The idlist of $B \mapsto A$ is obtained by reversing the roles of A and B. We call $B \mapsto A$ the *reverse* follows intersection. As a further optimization, we generate the idlists of the (up to) three possible new sequences in just one join.

5 The Parallel pSPADE Algorithm

In this section we describe the design and implementation of the parallel pSPADE algorithm. We begin with a brief review of the SGI Origin architecture.

5.1 SGI Origin 2000

The SGI Origin 2000 machine is a hardware distributed shared memory CC-NUMA (cache-coherent, non-uniform-memory-access) machine, in which shared main memory is distributed amongst the nodes. This shared memory is accessible to every processor in the system. It is also modular and scalable; that is, the system can be increased in size (scaled) by adding node boards in a hyper-cube topology, and connected by the CrayLink interconnect. Figure 6 shows the configuration of our 12 processor Origin. It also shows what a full 16-processor system would look like. A 'P' denotes a processor; 'N' a node board, containing two processors and some amount of memory; and 'R' a router that routes data between nodes.

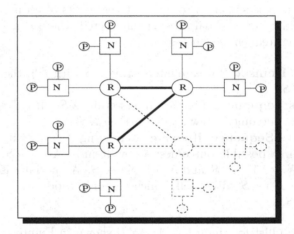

Fig. 6. 12 Processor SGI Origin 2000

5.2 pSPADE: Design and Implementation

pSPADE will be best understood when we imagine the computation as a dynamically expanding irregular tree of independent suffix-based classes, as shown in Figure 7. This example tree represents the search space for the algorithm, with a maximum of five levels. There are three independent parent suffix-based equivalence classes. These are the only classes visible at the beginning of computation. Since we have a shared-memory machine, there is only one copy on disk of the database in the vertical idlist format. It can be accessed by any processor, via a local file descriptor. Given that each class in the tree can be solved independently the crucial issue is how to achieve a good load balance, so that each processor gets an equal amount of work. We would also like to maximize locality and minimize/eliminate cache contention.

There are two main paradigms that may be utilized in the implementation of parallel sequence mining: a *data parallel* approach or a *task parallel* approach.

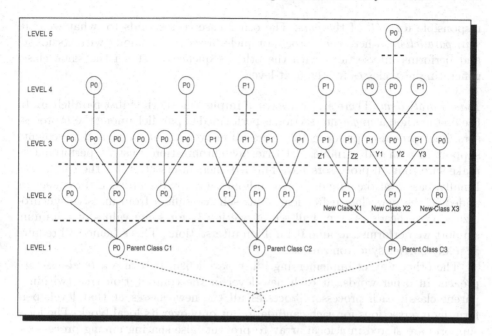

Fig. 7. Dynamic and Irregular Computation Tree of Classes

In data parallelism P processors work on distinct portions of the database, but synchronously process the global computation tree. It essentially exploits intra-class parallelism, i.e., the parallelism available within a class. In task parallelism, the processors share the database, but work on different classes in parallel, asynchronously processing the computation tree. This scheme is thus based on inter-class parallelism.

Data Parallelism. As mentioned above, in a data parallelism approach, P processors work on distinct partitions of the database (i.e., idlists), but synchronously process the global computation tree. In other words, we only need to describe how the work of a single node of the computation tree is performed in parallel among all the available processors. Each node corresponds to an equivalence class of frequent sequences, which needs to be expanded to the next level. The main computation within each class is simply the temporal idlist intersections that are performed for all pairs of elements in the class.

Data parallelism can come in two flavors, since we can partition the idlists horizontally or vertically. In horizontal partitioning we split each idlist into blocks and assign these horizontal blocks to processors, while in a vertical partitioning we assign a separate idlists to each processor. The first case corresponds to, what we call, *idlist parallelism*, in which we partition each idlist into P ranges over the customer sequence *cids* (for example, processor 0 is responsible for the *cid* range $0 \cdots l$, processor 1 for range $l + 1 \cdots 2l$, and so on). Each processor is responsible for $1/P$ of the *cids*. The other case corresponds to, what we call, *join parallelism*, where each processor picks a sequence (along with its idlist) and performs intersections with the other sequence idlists in the same class, generating new classes for the next level.

Idlist Parallelism. There are two ways of implementing the idlist parallelism. In the first method a *single* intersection is performed in parallel among the P processors. Each processor performs the intersection over its *cid* range, and increments support in a shared variable. A barrier synchronization must be performed to make sure that all processors have finished their intersection for the candidate. Finally, based on the support this candidate may be discarded if infrequent or added to the new class if frequent. This scheme suffers from massive synchronization overheads. As we shall see in Section 6, for some values of minimum support we performed around 0.4 million intersections. This scheme will require as many barrier synchronizations.

The other way of implementing idlist parallelism is to use a *level-wise* approach. In other words, at each new level of the computation tree (within a parent class), each processor processes all the new classes at that level, performing intersections for each candidate, but only over its local block. The local supports are stored in a local array to prevent false sharing among processors. After a barrier synchronization signals that all processors have finished processing the current level, a sum-reduction is performed in parallel to determine the global support of each candidate. The frequent sequences are then retained for the next level, and the same process is repeated for other levels until no more frequent sequences are found.

Figure 8 shows the pseudo-code for the single and level-wise idlist data parallelism. The single idlist data parallelism requires modification to the *Get-New-Classes* routine in the SPADE algorithm, by performing each intersection in parallel followed by a barrier (we prefix the modified routine with SID – Single IDlist). The level-wise idlist data parallelism requires modification to the *Enumerate-Frequent-Seq* routine in the SPADE algorithm, by performing local intersection for all classes at the current level, followed by a barrier before the next level can begin (we prefix the modified routine with LID – Level-wise IDlist). Figure 9 depicts the two methods pictorially. For example, in the single idlist method we perform a single intersection, say between items A and B, in parallel; processor P_0 performs intersections on the cid range 1 to 500, while P_1 performs the joins over the cid range 501-1000. Note that even though the ranges are equal, the actual cid's falling in those blocks may be skewed. Figure 9 also shows the level-wise idlist parallelism. In this approach, all processors perform the $\binom{5}{2} + 5 = 15$ possible intersections (i.e., for $AA, AB, AC, AD, AE, BB, BC, \cdots, DE$) in parallel over their cid block, which is then followed by a sum-reduction to get global support.

We implemented the level-wise idlist parallelism and found that it performed very poorly. In fact, we got a speed-down as we increased the number of processors (see Section 6). Even though we tried to minimize the synchronization as much as possible, performance was still unacceptable. Since a candidate's memory cannot be freed until the end of a level, the memory consumption of this approach is also extremely high. We need to keep the temporary idlists of all newly generated candidates (both infrequent and frequent) since we can't say if a candidate is frequent until all processors have finished the current level. We were thus unable to run this algorithm for low values of minimum support. Also, when the local memory is not sufficient the Origin allocates remote memory for the intermediate idlists, causing a performance hit due to the NUMA architecture.

SID-Get-New-Classes(S):
    for all sequences $A_i \in S$ **do**
        for all sequences $A_j \in S$, with $j > i$ **do**
        $R = A_i \cup A_j$;
        do in parallel for all processors p
            $\mathcal{L}_p(R) = \mathcal{L}_p(A_i) \cap \mathcal{L}_p(A_j)$;
        barrier;
        $\mathcal{L}(R) = \bigcup_p \mathcal{L}_p(R)$;
        if $(\sigma(R) \geq min\_sup)$ **then** $C_i = C_i \cup \{R\}$;
        $CList = CList \cup C_i$;
    return $CList$;

LID-Enumerate-Frequent-Seq($PrevL$):
    while $(PrevL \neq \emptyset)$
        do in parallel for all processors p
        $NewL_p = NewL_p \cup$
            $Get\text{-}New\text{-}Classes\,(PrevL.item())$;
        $PrevL = PrevL.next()$;
    end while
    barrier;
    $NewL = \bigcup_{p \in P} NewL_p$;
    if $(NewL \neq \emptyset)$ **then**
        $Enumerate\text{-}Frequent\text{-}Seq(NewL)$;

Fig. 8. Single vs. Level-Wise Idlist Data Parallelism

Join Parallelism. Join parallelism is based on the vertical partitioning of the idlists among processors. Each processor performs intersections for different sequences within the same class. Once the current class has been expanded by one level, the processors must synchronize, before moving on to the next class. Figure 9 shows how join parallelism works. P_0 gets the items A, C, and E, and is responsible for generating and testing all candidates which have those items as a prefix (i.e., the candidates $AA, AB, AC, AD, AE, CC, CD, CE$, and EE). P_1 on the other hand is responsible for all candidates with the prefix B or D (i.e., BB, BC, BD, BE, DD, and DE). While we have not implemented this approach, we believe that it will fare no better than idlist parallelism. The reason

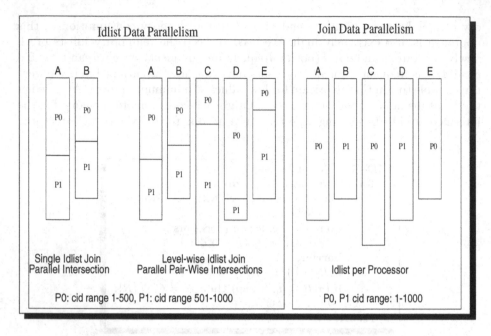

Fig. 9. Idlist (Single and Level-wise) vs. Join Data Parallelism (2 processors, cid range 1-1000)

is that it requires one synchronization per class, which is better than the single candidate idlist parallelism, but still much worse than the level-wise idlist parallelism, since there can be many classes.

Task Parallelism. In task parallelism all processors have access to one copy of the database, but they work on separate classes. We present a number of load balancing approaches starting with a static load balancing scheme and moving on to a more sophisticated dynamic load balancing strategy. It is important to note that we use a breadth first search for frequent sequence enumeration within each parent class, but the parent classes themselves are scheduled independently for good load balance.

Static Load Balancing (SLB). Let $\mathcal{C} = \{C_1, C_2, C_3\}$ represent the set of the parent classes at level 1 as shown in Figure 7. We need to schedule the parent classes among the processors in a manner minimizing load imbalance. In our approach an entire parent class is scheduled on one processor. Load balancing is achieved by assigning a weight to each parent equivalence class based on the number of elements in the class. Since we have to consider all pairs of items for the next iteration, we assign the weight $W_i^1 = \binom{|C_i|}{2}$ to the class C_i. Once the weights are assigned we generate a schedule using a greedy heuristic. We sort the classes on the weights (in decreasing order), and assign each class in turn to the least loaded processor, i.e., one having the least total weight at that point. Ties are broken by selecting the processor with the smaller identifier. These steps are done concurrently on all the processors since all of them have access to $\mathcal{C}$. We also studied the effect of other heuristics for assigning class weights, such as $W_i^2 = \sum_j |\mathcal{L}(A_j)|$ for all items A_j in the class C_i. This cost function gives each class a weight proportional to the sum of the supports of all the items. We also tried a cost function that combines the above two, i.e., $W_i^3 = \binom{|C_i|}{2} \cdot \sum_j |\mathcal{L}(A_j)|$. We did not observe any significant benefit of one weight function over the other, and decided to use W^1.

SLB $(min\_sup, \mathcal{D})$:
   $\mathcal{C} = \{$ parent classes $C_i = [X_i]\}$;
   Sort-on-Weight($\mathcal{C}$);
   for all $C_i \in \mathcal{C}$ **do** //create work Queue
      $P_j = $ *Proc-with-Min-Weight*();
      $Q_{P_j} = Q_{P_j} \cup C_i$;
   for all processors P_j
      for all classes $C_i \in Q_{P_j}$ **do** *Enumerate-Frequent-Seq*(C_i);

Fig. 10. The SLB (Static Load Balancing) Algorithm

Figure 10 shows the pseudo-code for the SLB algorithm. We schedule the parent classes on different processors based on the class weights. Once the parent classes have been scheduled, the computation proceeds in a purely asynchronous manner since there is never any need to synchronize or share information among the processors. If we apply W^1 to the class tree shown in Figure 7, we get $W_1^1 = W_2^1 = W_3^1 = 3$. Using the greedy scheduling scheme on two processors, P_0 gets the parent classes C_1 and C_3, and P_1 gets the parent class C_2. The two nodes process these classes in a BFS manner. We immediately see that SLB suffers from load imbalance, since after processing C_1, P_0 will be busy working on C_3, while after processing C_2, P_1 has no more work. The main problem with SLB is that, given the irregular nature of the computation tree there is no way of accurately determining the amount of work (i.e., the number of frequent sequences that might be generated from it) per class statically.

Inter-Class Dynamic Load Balancing (CDLB). To get better load balancing we can utilize inter-class dynamic load balancing. Instead of a static or fixed class assignment of SLB, we would like each processor to dynamically pick a new parent class to work on from the list of parent classes not yet processed.

We also make use of the class weights in the CDLB approach. First, we sort the parent classes in decreasing order of their weight. This forms a logical central task queue of independent classes. Each processor atomically grabs one class from this logical queue. It processes the class completely and then grabs the next available class. This is essentially a self-scheduling scheme [18]. Note that each class usually has a non-trivial or coarse amount of work, so we don't have to worry about contention among processors to acquire new tasks. Since classes are sorted on their weights, processors first work on large classes before tackling smaller ones, which helps to achieve a greater degree of load balance. The pseudo-code for CDLB algorithm appears in Figure 11. The *compare-and-swap* (CAS) is an atomic primitive on the Origin. It compares *classid* with i. If they are equal it replaces *classid* with $i + 1$, returning a 1, else it returns a 0. The use of CAS ensures that processors acquire separate classes to work on.

```
CDLB (min_sup, D):
    C = { parent classes C_i = [X_i]};
    Sort-on-Weight(C);
    shared int classid=0;
    for each processor P_j do in parallel
        for (i = 0; i < |C|; i + +)
            if (compare_and_swap (classid, i, i + 1))
                Enumerate-Frequent-Seq(C_i);
```

Fig. 11. The CDLB (Dynamic Load Balancing) Algorithm

If we apply CDLB to our example computation tree in Figure 7, we might expect a scenario as follows: In the beginning P_1 grabs C_1, and P_0 acquires C_2. Since C_2 has less work, P_0 will grab the next class C_3 and work on it. Then P_1 becomes free and finds that there is no more work, while P_0 is still busy. For this example, CDLB did not buy us anything over SLB. However, when we have a large number of parent classes CDLB has a clear advantage over SLB, since a processor grabs a new class only when it has processed its current class. This way only the free processors will acquire new classes, while others continue to process their current class, delivering good processor utilization. We shall see in Section 6 that CDLB can provide up to 40% improvement over SLB. We should reiterate that the processing of classes is still asynchronous. For both SLB and CDLB, false sharing doesn't arise, and all work is performed on local memory, resulting in good locality.

Recursive Dynamic Load Balancing (RDLB). While CDLB improves over SLB by exploiting dynamic load balancing, it does so only at the inter-class level, which may be too coarse-grained to achieve a good workload balance. RDLB addresses this by exploiting both inter-class and intra-class parallelism.

To see where the intra-class parallelism can be exploited, let's examine the behavior of CDLB. As long as there are more parent classes remaining, each processor acquires a new class and processes it completely using BFS search. If there are no more parent classes left, the free processors are forced to idle. The worst case happens when $P-1$ processors are free and only one is busy, especially if the last class has a deep computation tree (although we try to prevent this case from happening by sorting the classes, so that the classes predicted to be small are at the end, it can still happen). We can fix this problem if we provide a mechanism for the free processors to join the busy ones. We accomplish this by recursively applying the CDLB strategy at each new level, but only if there is some free processor waiting for more work. Since each class is independent, we can treat each class at the new level in the same way we treated the parent classes, so that different processors can work on different classes at the new level.

```
1. shared int FreeCnt = 0; //Number of free processors
2. shared int GlobalFlg = 0; //Is there more work?
3. shared list GlobalQ; //Global list of classes

pSPADE (min_sup, D):
4.    GlobalQ = C = { parent classes C_i = [X_i]};
5.    Sort-on-Weight(C);
6.    Process-GlobalQ();
7.    FreeCnt + +;
8.    while (FreeCnt ≠ P)
9.        if (GlobalFlg) then
10.           FreeCnt − −; Process-GlobalQ(); FreeCnt + +;

Process-GlobalQ():
11.    shared int classid = 0;
12.       parallel for (i = 0; i < GlobalQ.size(); i + +)
13.          if (compare_and_swap (classid, i, i + 1))
14.             RDLB-Enumerate-Frequent-Seq(C_i);
15.    GlobalFlg = 0;

RDLB-Enumerate-Frequent-Seq(PrevL):
16.    for (; PrevL ≠ ∅; PrevL = PrevL.next())
17.       if (FreeCnt > 0) then
18.          Add-to-GlobalQ(PrevL.next()); GlobalFlg = 1;
19.       NewL = NewL ∪ Get-New-Classes (PrevL.item());
20.    if (NewL ≠ ∅) then RDLB-Enumerate-Frequent-Seq(NewL);
```

Fig. 12. The pSPADE Algorithm (using RDLB)

Figure 12 shows the pseudo-code for the final pSPADE algorithm, which uses the recursive dynamic load balancing (RDLB) scheme. We start with the parent classes and insert them in the global class list, *GlobalQ*. Each processor atomically acquires classes from this list until all parent classes have been taken, similar to the CDLB approach (*Process-GlobalQ()* on line 6 is the same as the main loop in CDLB). Note that each parent class is processed in a BFS manner.

As each processor finishes its portion of the parent classes, and no more parent classes are left, it increments the shared variable *FreeCnt*, and waits for more work. When a processor is processing the classes at some level, it periodically checks if there are any free processors (line 17). If so, it keeps one class for itself, and inserts the remaining classes at that level ($PrevL$) in $GlobalQ$, emptying $PrevL$ in the process, and sets $GlobalFlg$. This processor continues working on the classes ($NewL$) generated before a free processor was detected. Note that all idlist intersections are performed in the routine $Get\text{-}New\text{-}Classes()$ (as shown in Figure 5).

When a waiting processor sees that there is more work (i.e., $GlobalFlg = 1$), it starts working on the classes in $GlobalQ$. Finally, when there is no more work in the global queue, $FreeCnt$ equals the number of processors P, and the computation stops. To reiterate, any class inserted into the global queue is treated as a parent class, and is processed in a purely breadth-first manner. If and when a free processor is detected, a busy processor adds all classes on its current level into the global queue for shared processing.

Let's illustrate the above algorithm by looking at the computation tree in Figure 7. The nodes are marked by the processors that work on them. First, at the parent class level, P_0 acquires C_1, and P_1 acquires C_2. Since C_2 is smaller, P_1 grabs class C_3, and starts processing it. It generates three new classes at the next level, $NewL = \{X_1, X_2, X_3\}$, which becomes $PrevL$ when P_1 starts the next level. Let's assume that P_1 finishes processing X_1, and inserts classes Z_1, Z_2 in the new $NewL$.

In the meantime, P_0 becomes free. Before processing X_2, P_1 notices in line 17, that there is a free processor. At this point P_1 inserts X_3 in $GlobalQ$, and empties $PrevL$. It then continues to work on X_2, inserting Y_1, Y_2, Y_3 in $NewL$. P_0 sees the new insertion in $GlobalQ$ and start working on X_3 in its entirety. P_0 meanwhile starts processing the next level classes, $\{Z_1, Z_2, Y_1, Y_2, Y_3\}$. If at any stage it detects a free processor, it will repeat the procedure described above recursively (i.e., inserting remaining classes in $GlobalQ$). Figure 7 shows a possible execution sequence for the class C_3. It can be seen that RDLB tries to achieve as good a load balance as possible by keeping all processors busy.

The RDLB scheme of pSPADE preserves the good features of CDLB, i.e., it dynamically schedules entire parent classes on separate processors, for which the work is purely local, requiring no synchronization, and exploiting only inter-class parallelism so far. Intra-class parallelism is required only for a few (hopefully) small classes towards the end of the computation. We simply treat these as new parent classes, and schedule each class on a separate processor. Again no synchronization is required except for insertions and deletions from $GlobalQ$. In summary, computation is kept local to the extent possible, and synchronization is done only if a load imbalance is detected.

6   Experimental Results

In this section we present the parallel performance of pSPADE. Experiments were performed on a 12 processor SGI Origin 2000 machine at RPI, with 195 MHz R10000 MIPS processors, 4MB of secondary cache per processor, 2GB of main memory, and running IRIX 6.5. The databases were stored on an attached 7GB disk in flat-files. Since there is only one I/O node in our setup, all disk I/O is serial.

Dataset	C	T	S	I	D	Size
C10T5S4I1.25D1M	10	5	4	1.25	1M	320MB
C10T5S4I2.5D1M	10	5	4	2.5	1M	320MB
C20T2.5S4I1.25D1M	20	2.5	4	1.25	1M	440MB
C20T2.5S4I2.5D1M	20	2.5	4	2.5	1M	440MB
C20T2.5S8I1.25D1M	20	5	8	1.25	1M	640MB
C20T5S8I2D1M	20	5	8	2	1M	640MB
C5T2.5S4I1.25DxM	5	2.5	4	1.25	1M-10M	110MB-1.1GB

Table 1. Synthetic Datasets

Dataset	MinSup	# FreqSeq	Time(P=1)	#Seq/Time
C10T5S4I1.25D1M	0.25%	96344	379.7s	254
C10T5S4I2.5D1M	0.33%	180381	625.5s	289
C20T2.5S4I1.25D1M	0.25%	67291	270.3s	249
C20T2.5S4I2.5D1M	0.25%	80648	240.4s	335
C20T2.5S8I1.25D1M	0.33%	55484	236.9s	234
C20T5S8I2D1M	0.5%	179999	1200.8s	150

Table 2. Sequential Time and Number of Frequent Sequences

Synthetic Datasets: We used the publicly available dataset generation code from the IBM Quest data mining project [19]. These datasets mimic real-world transactions, where people buy a sequence of sets of items. Some customers may buy only some items from the sequences, or they may buy items from multiple sequences. The customer sequence size and transaction size are clustered around a mean and a few of them may have many elements. The datasets are generated using the following process. First N_I maximal itemsets of average size I are generated by choosing from N items. Then N_S maximal sequences of average size S are created by assigning itemsets from N_I to each sequence. Next a customer of average C transactions is created, and sequences in N_S are assigned to different customer elements, respecting the average transaction size of T. The generation stops when D customers have been generated. Like [6] we set $N_S = 5000$, $N_I = 25000$ and $N = 10000$. Table 1 shows the datasets with their parameter settings. We refer the reader to [5] for additional details on the dataset generation.

Table 2 shows, for the different datasets, the minimum support used in the experiments reported below, the total number of frequent sequences found, the serial time, and the number of frequent sequences enumerated per second (note: the number of intersections performed is 2-3 times higher). The distribution of frequent sequences as a function of length is plotted in Figure 13. The figure also shows the total number of frequent sequences obtained and the total number of joins performed. The number of joins corresponds to the total number of candidates evaluated during the course of the algorithm.

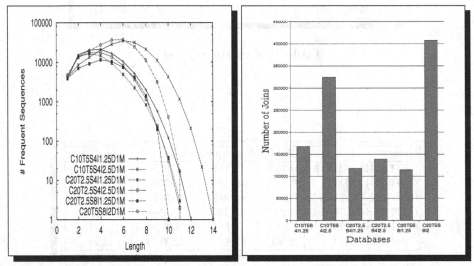

Fig. 13. Number of Frequent Sequences and Candidate Joins

6.1   Serial Performance

The performance of SPADE, the serial version of pSPADE, was studied in [4], and it was compared against GSP [6]. It was shown that SPADE outperforms GSP by more than an order of magnitude if we pre-process the data and store the supports of all frequent 2-sequences above a minimum threshold. The performance comparison of SPADE vs. GSP is shown in Figure 14.

There are several reasons why SPADE outperforms GSP:

1. SPADE uses only simple temporal join operation on idlists. As the length of a frequent sequence increases, the size of its idlist decreases, resulting in very fast joins.
2. No complicated hash-tree structure is used, and no overhead of generating and searching of customer subsequences is incurred. These structures typi-

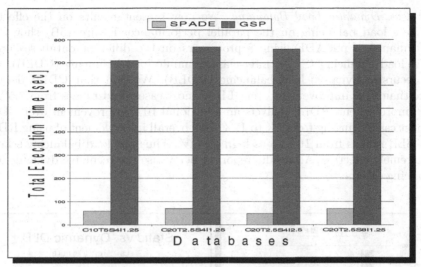

Fig. 14. Serial Performance: SPADE vs. GSP (0.25% Minimum Support; D200K)

cally have very poor locality [3]. On the other hand SPADE has good locality, since a join requires only a linear scan of two lists.

3. As the minimum support is lowered, more and larger frequent sequences are found. GSP makes a complete dataset scan for each iteration. SPADE on the other hand restricts itself to only a few scans. It thus cuts down the I/O costs.

These benefits of SPADE carry over to pSPADE. For these reasons we chose not to parallelize GSP for comparison against pSPADE. It should be noted that it is possible to optimize GSP further to reduce the number of database scans by generating candidates of multiple lengths at the same time (if memory permits). However, the base GSP, as described in [6] does not do this.

6.2 Parallel Performance

Data vs. Task Parallelism We first present the results for the level-wise idlist data parallel algorithm we described in Section 5.2. Figure 15A) shows the results for four databases on 1, 2, and 4 processors. We find that the data parallel algorithm performs very poorly, resulting in a speed-down with more processors. The level-wise approach does well initially when the number of tree nodes or classes is relatively few. However, as computation progresses more and more classes are generated and consequently more and more barriers are performed. In fact there are almost as many classes as there are frequent itemsets, requiring as many barriers. For example, for the $C20T2.5S4I2.5D1M$ dataset, the data parallel approach may have performed around 80648 barriers. Since data parallel approach doesn't perform well, we only concentrate on task parallelism in the remainder of this section.

Static vs. Dynamic Load Balancing. We now present results on the effect of dynamic load balancing on the parallel performance. Figure 15B) shows the performance of pSPADE using 8 processors on the different databases under static load balancing (SLB), inter-class dynamic load balancing (CDLB), and the recursive dynamic load balancing (RDLB). We find that CDLB delivers more than 22% improvement over SLB in most cases, and ranges from 7.5% to 38% improvement. RDLB delivers an additional 10% improvement over CDLB in most cases, ranging from 2% to 12%. The overall improvement of using RDLB over SLB ranges from 16% to as high as 44%. Thus our load balancing scheme is extremely effective. All results reported below use the recursive dynamic load balancing scheme.

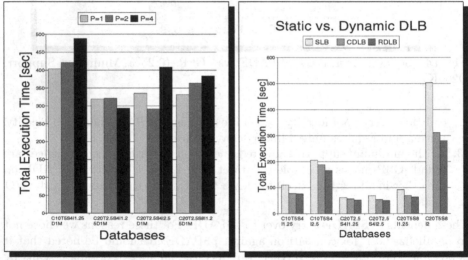

Fig. 15. A) Level-Wise Idlist Data Parallelism, B) Effect of Load Balancing

Parallel Time and Speedup. Figure 16 shows the total execution time and the speedup charts for each database using the minimum support values shown in Table 1. We obtain near perfect speedup for 2 processors, ranging as high as 1.91. On 4 processors, we obtained a maximum of 3.2, on 8 processors the maximum was 5.6, and on 12 the maximum speedup was 7.2. As these charts indicate, pSPADE achieves relatively good speedup performance. However, the speedup on C20T5S8I2D1M was not as good. If one looks at the distribution of the frequent sequence lengths for C20T5S8I2D1M in Figure 13 we see that it has many more large frequent sequences compared to other datasets, and has longer idlist sizes as well. Many frequent items imply that there is more overlap of items among the classes, and along with longer idlists this causes more disk reads. In itself this is not a problem, but since the our SGI Origin system only supports serial I/O, this results in increased disk contention, which in turn limits

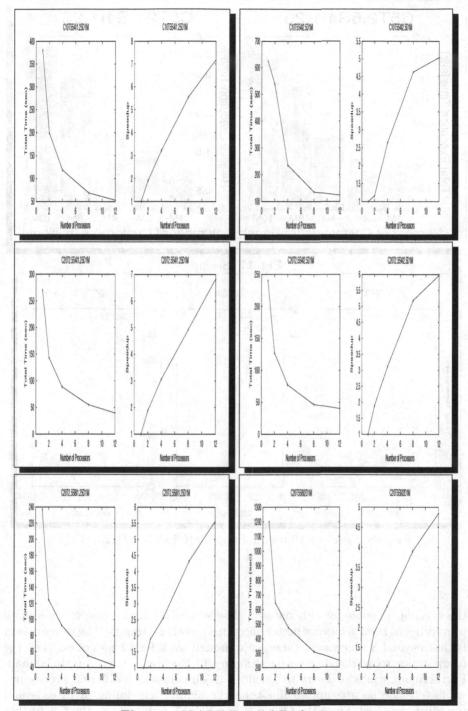

Fig. 16. pSPADE Parallel Performance

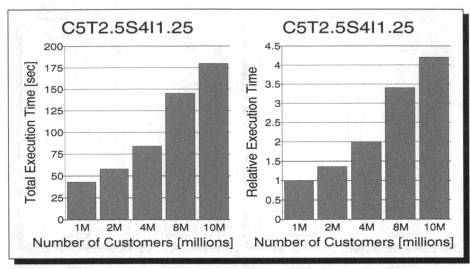

Fig. 17. Sizeup

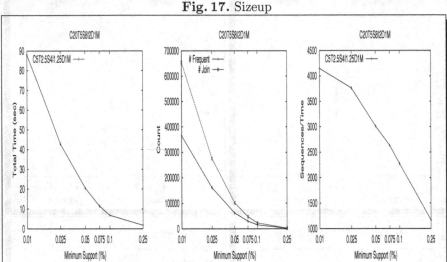

Fig. 18. Effect of Minimum Support ($C5T2.5S4I1.25D1M$)

the speedup possible for this dataset. The serial I/O is also one of the causes preventing us from achieving better speedups on other datasets. The other reason is that beyond 8 processors, there isn't enough work for 12 processors, i.e., the computation to overhead (class partitioning, disk contention, etc.) ratio is small. Furthermore, while we do try to schedule disjoint classes on different processors, we have made no attempt to fine-tune the affinity scheduling of threads and the idlists accessed. Since the Origin is has NUMA architecture, there is further scope for performance tuning by allocating groups of related classes to processors that are topologically close, or at least among the two processors on the same node board (see Figure 6).

6.3 Scaleup

Figure 17 shows how pSPADE scales up as the number of customers is increased ten-fold, from 1 million to 10 million (the number of transactions is increased from 5 million to 50 million, respectively). The database size goes from 110MB to 1.1GB. All the experiments were performed on the C5T2.5S4I1.25 dataset with a minimum support of 0.025%. Both the total execution time and the normalized time (with respect to 1M) are shown. It can be seen that while the number of customers increases ten-fold, the execution time goes up by a factor of less than 4.5, displaying super-linear scaleup.

Finally, we study the effect of changing minimum support on the parallel performance, shown in Figure 18. We used 8 processors on C5T2.5S4I1.25D1M dataset. The minimum support was varied from a high of 0.25% to a low of 0.01%. Figure 18 shows the number of frequent sequences discovered and the number of joins performed (candidate sequences) at the different minimum support levels. It also shows the number of frequent sequences enumerated per second. Running time goes from 6.8s at 0.1% support to 88s at 0.01% support, a time ratio of 1:13 vs. a support ratio of 1:10. At the same time the number of frequent sequences goes from 15454 to 365132 (1:24), and the number of joins from 22973 to 653596 (1:29). The number of frequent sequences are, in general, not linear with respect to the minimum support. In the worst case, the number of sequences increase exponentially with decreasing support. However, it appears that for the range of support values we looked at the execution time is near-linear. It is interesting to note that the efficiency of pSPADE increases with decreasing support, i.e., it lists more frequent sequences per second on lower support values.

7 Conclusions

In this paper we presented pSPADE, a new parallel algorithm for fast mining of sequential patterns in large databases. We carefully considered the various parallel design alternatives before choosing the best strategy for pSPADE. These included data parallel approaches like idlist parallelism (single vs. level-wise) and join parallelism. In the task parallel approach we considered different load balancing schemes such as static, dynamic and recursive dynamic. We adopted the recursive dynamic load balancing scheme for pSPADE, which was designed to maximize data locality and minimize synchronization, by allowing each processor to work on disjoint classes. Finally, the scheme minimizes load imbalance by exploiting both inter-class and intra-class parallelism. An extensive set of experiments was been conducted on the SGI Origin CC-NUMA shared memory system, to show that pSPADE has good speedup and excellent scaleup properties.

This work opens several research opportunities, which we plan to address in future work:

1. pSPADE works on the assumption that each class and its intermediate idlists fit in main memory. The mean memory utilization of pSPADE is less than 1% of the database size, but the maximum usage may be as high as 10% [16]. This means that on our Origin system, we can handle around 20GB datasets. One solution for handling larger datasets is to write intermediate idlists to disk when we exceed memory. This requires minimal modification to the pSPADE. However, we need to consider the case where even a single idlist may not fit in memory. In this case we bring in the portion of the two idlists that fit in memory and perform joins on the memory-resident portions, repeating the process until the two list have been joined completely. We plan to implement these techniques in the future.
2. Extending pSPADE to run on CLUMPS or clusters of SMP machines, which are becoming increasingly popular. We could utilize pSPADE on each SMP node, while message passing would be required for load balancing among nodes.
3. pSPADE uses only simple intersection operations, and is thus ideally suited for direct integration with a DBMS. We plan to implement pSPADE directly on top of a parallel DBMS.
4. Extending pSPADE for parallel discovery of *quantitative* and *generalized* sequences – where the quantity of items bought is also considered, and where we introduce time gap constraints, sliding windows, and impose a taxonomy on the items, respectively.

References

1. Zaki, M.J., Lesh, N., Ogihara, M.: PLANMINE: Sequence mining for plan failures. In: 4th Intl. Conf. Knowledge Discovery and Data Mining. (1998)
2. Hatonen, K., Klemettinen, M., Mannila, H., Ronkainen, P., Toivonen, H.: Knowledge discovery from telecommunication network alarm databases. In: 12th Intl. Conf. Data Engineering. (1996)
3. Parthasarathy, S., Zaki, M.J., Li, W.: Memory placement techniques for parallel association mining. In: 4th Intl. Conf. Knowledge Discovery and Data Mining. (1998)
4. Zaki, M.J.: Efficient enumeration of frequent sequences. In: 7th Intl. Conf. on Information and Knowledge Management. (1998)
5. Agrawal, R., Srikant, R.: Mining sequential patterns. In: 11th Intl. Conf. on Data Engg. (1995)
6. Srikant, R., Agrawal, R.: Mining sequential patterns: Generalizations and performance improvements. In: 5th Intl. Conf. Extending Database Technology. (1996)
7. Mannila, H., Toivonen, H., Verkamo, I.: Discovering frequent episodes in sequences. In: 1st Intl. Conf. Knowledge Discovery and Data Mining. (1995)
8. Mannila, H., Toivonen, H.: Discovering generalized episodes using minimal occurences. In: 2nd Intl. Conf. Knowledge Discovery and Data Mining. (1996)
9. Oates, T., Schmill, M.D., Jensen, D., Cohen, P.R.: A family of algorithms for finding temporal structure in data. In: 6th Intl. Workshop on AI and Statistics. (1997)
10. Agrawal, R., Shafer, J.: Parallel mining of association rules. IEEE Trans. on Knowledge and Data Engg. **8** (1996) 962–969

11. Cheung, D., Ng, V., Fu, A., Fu, Y.: Efficient mining of association rules in distributed databases. In: IEEE Trans. on Knowledge and Data Engg. (1996) 8(6):911–922
12. Han, E.H., Karypis, G., Kumar, V.: Scalable parallel data mining for association rules. In: ACM SIGMOD Conf. Management of Data. (1997)
13. Park, J.S., Chen, M., Yu, P.S.: Efficient parallel data mining for association rules. In: ACM Intl. Conf. Information and Knowledge Management. (1995)
14. Shintani, T., Kitsuregawa, M.: Hash based parallel algorithms for mining association rules. In: 4th Intl. Conf. Parallel and Distributed Info. Systems. (1996)
15. Zaki, M.J., Ogihara, M., Parthasarathy, S., Li, W.: Parallel data mining for association rules on shared-memory multi-processors. In: Supercomputing'96. (1996)
16. Zaki, M.J., Parthasarathy, S., Ogihara, M., Li, W.: Parallel algorithms for fast discovery of association rules. Data Mining and Knowledge Discovery: An International Journal **1(4):343-373** (1997)
17. Shintani, T., Kitsuregawa, M.: Mining algorithms for sequential patterns in parallel: Hash based approach. In: Pacific-Asia Conf. on Knowledge Discovery and Data Mining. (1998)
18. Tang, P., Yew, P.C.: Processor self-scheduling for multiple nested parallel loops. In: International Conference On Parallel Processing. (1986)
19. IBM: http://www.almaden.ibm.com/cs/quest/syndata.html. (Quest Data Mining Project, IBM Almaden Research Center, San Jose, CA 95120)

Parallel Predictor Generation

D.B. Skillicorn

Department of Computing and Information Science
Queen's University, Kingston, Canada
skill@cs.queensu.ca

Abstract. Classification and regression are fundamental data mining techniques. The goal of such techniques is to build *predictors* based on a training dataset and use them to predict the properties of new data. For a wide range of techniques, combining predictors built on samples from the training dataset provides lower error rates, faster construction, or both, than a predictor built from the entire training dataset. This provides a natural parallelization strategy in which predictors based on samples are built independently and hence concurrently. We discuss the performance implications for two subclasses: those in which predictors are independent, and those in which knowing a set of predictors reduces the difficulty of finding a new one.

1 Introduction

Many data mining algorithms generate predictors. A training dataset, consisting of a large set of input vectors and label pairs, is provided. The goal is to build a predictor that predict labels for previously unseen vectors. The error rate is the fraction of examples that are misclassified by the predictor. Predictors can be ranked by their error rate, which may be determined using a test dataset or an estimation technique. If the labels being predicted are class labels, the process is called *classification*; if the labels are numeric, the process is called *regression* [2].

In practice, the size of the training dataset is extremely large, and the number of computations needed to build a predictor large as well. It is natural to consider using parallelism to build predictors more quickly, or to make it possible to use more sophisticated predictors than would otherwise be possible.

In this paper we discuss, in an algorithm-independent way, the computation, data access, and communication requirements of two classes of predictor-building data mining algorithms. We show that parallelism can be expected to provide almost linear speedup for one class, and superlinear speedup for the second. This superlinear speedup does not depend on architectural idiosyncrasies, but on fundamental properties of the underlying algorithms.

A sequential predictor-building algorithm must perform computations, and must access the data of the training dataset. Let w denote the computation required, in units of instruction executions (or, equivalently, clock cycles). The time required for data access is the product of the number of elements accessed,

M.J. Zaki, C.-T. Ho (Eds.): Large-Scale Parallel Data Mining, LNAI 1759, pp. 190–196, 2002.

say d, and the time per access, say r. If r is also expressed in units of instruction times, then the data access time for an algorithm, dr, is in the same units as w. Note that r is typically in the range of hundreds to thousands of instruction times. The time complexity of a sequential data mining algorithm has the form $w + dr$ or $MAX(w, dr)$ or something in between depending on how data access is overlapped with computation.

2 Exploiting Parallelism in Generating Predictors

Suppose that we want to parallelize an arbitrary algorithm using p processors. The best we can hope for is that the computation has been perfectly divided between the processors, so that the parallel computation time is w/p. Similarly, the data access time could have been divided perfectly so that it is dr/p. However, any non-trivial parallel algorithm will require some communication between processors during its execution, and this will add to the overall cost of the program.

Suppose that the total amount of communication required by the parallel program is c (say c messages of fixed size for simplicity). The effect of this communication on the overall time cost of the program depends on how the communication is arranged, in particular how balanced it is. Suppose, for example, that all of the communication originated at one processor. Then the time taken to complete it would be cg, where g is the cost of sending one message (again, expressed in units of instruction times for consistency). However, if the required communication is balanced, so that each processor sends c/p messages, then the time taken for communication is cg/p.

Thus the cost of a parallel version of a sequential algorithm with computation w, data access dr, and balanced communication is at best:

$$\text{parallel cost} = \frac{w}{p} + \frac{dr}{p} + \frac{cg}{p}$$

$$= \frac{\text{seq cost}}{p} + \text{communication overhead}$$

(Possibly the maximum of these three terms could be used instead, but it makes little difference to the conclusions we draw.) The communication overhead can be reduced by (a) communicating infrequently, (b) communicating small data, or (c) communicating in a balanced way.

Parallel programs also suffer performance penalties from another kind of imbalance: of the intervals between communication. This synchronization overhead means that one processor must wait for another to reach a consistent state before both can proceed. It is reduced by dividing the work (computation and data access) evenly among the processors – but of course it is not possible in general to predict these quantities accurately in advance.

When approaching an application domain such as data mining, it is tempting to parallelize algorithms in a fine-grained way. This temptation is to be resisted since it tends to cause large volumes of communication, and a great deal of synchronization overhead (for the same reasons that humans do not perform well when 'micro-managed'). Fortunately, the structure of most predictor-building algorithms is such that coarse-grained parallelization strategies work well. In general, the following properties have been observed across a wide range of predictors:

- Using a relatively small subset (a few percent) of the training dataset produces a predictor that is fairly accurate (within a few percentage *points*);
- Using the entire training dataset produces a predictor that is more accurate, but
- Combining predictors trained on subsets of the training dataset produces the best predictors of all (combining may be done by voting, for classification; by averaging for regression; and by true merging when a technique for doing do is known).

This last technique, pasting together predictors trained on different subsets of the training dataset, naturally lends itself to parallelism. Instead of sequentially generating training data subsets and building predictors on each one, we can generate data subsets by partitioning and build predictors independently at different processors. The merging step differs depending on exactly what kind of predictor is being built, but the sequential merge implied above is easily replaced by a parallel merge, provided that the merge operation itself is associative (as voting or averaging are).

Pasting techniques tend not to be very sensitive to the size of sample used to train each predictor. Intuitively, a small sample is unlikely to represent the training data well. As the sample size increases, the sample becomes an increasingly accurate representation of the training data, from which almost all the knowledge can be extracted at reduced cost. The curve of accuracy of prediction against sample size typically shows a very sudden jump from poor accuracies to quite good ones – and often at samples whose size is both absolutely quite small (< 50, say) and a small fraction of the training dataset (a few percent).

There are two different classes of predictors for which parallelization differs slightly, while parallel performance differs a lot; when

A. The work required to build a predictor depends only on the amount of data used to build it; or
B. The work required to build a predictor depends on the amount of data used to build it, but can be reduced if other predictors are already known.

An example of the first kind of predictor is a decision tree. Decision trees are brittle in the sense that small changes in the training data give rise to very different trees. It has been shown [5,3] that generating decisions trees from subsets of the training data and then using voting to determine class labels has smaller error rates than generating a single decision tree. Here, the merge operation is the addition of each newly-generated tree to a voting pool. It is even possible to recreate the transparency of decision trees by merging this pool of trees into a single tree, called a *born-again tree* [6].

An example of the second kind is neural networks. If a neural network is trained using a deterministic technique then, after it has seen some data, it has accumulated an error vector. This error vector is an encapsulated predictor in the sense that applying it to the current weight set produces a new neural net that is a better predictor than the original. The merge operation is therefore the application of an error vector to update a set of weights. In sequential neural net learning, this updating can occur after a single example, or after a batch of any size [1]. The particular error vector produced depends on how accurate the network is already. The fixed amount of work required to learn from the next batch produces better and better error vectors, improving the speed of learning superlinearly [10].

Another example of the second kind in which predictor improvement is superlinear is inductive logic learning [8,9]. Algorithms repeatedly find hypotheses that account for the training data. Each accepted hypothesis 'covers' a part of the training data which is not examined in subsequent steps. Hence, the more hypotheses that already exist, the smaller the work required to find the remaining ones.

3 Parallelizing Independent Predictors

The essential structure of predictor-building algorithms of the first kind is:

while error rate still improving
    generate a new predictor
    merge it into the previous predictors

If the loop executes k times, then the sequential cost of such algorithms can be expressed as:

$$\text{cost} = k\left[\text{cost(predictor)} + \text{cost(merge)}\right]$$

(The test for whether the error rate is improving may itself be significant for some techniques, for example where a testing set is used. This would add another term inside the brackets.)

Provided that the merge operation is associative (and we have seen that it often consists of adding the newest predictor to a set), such algorithms can be parallelized like this:

while error rate still improving
    forall p
        generate new predictors in each processor
    merge the p predictors using a reduction

The parallel cost of this new formulation is:

$$\text{parallel cost} = \frac{k}{p}\left[\text{cost(predictor)} + \log p\,\text{cost(merge)}\right]$$

Of course, the parallel formulation will require some communication during the merge step, but the objects communicated are predictors, whose size is typically independent of the size of the data. Hence this term tends to be a small constant ($|$ predictor $|$ g) that can be folded into the cost of the merge itself.

For small p, this cost formula gives approximately linear speedup. For large p, the cost is dominated by the logarithmic term which becomes, in the limit, a single reduction over p predictors.

Notice that we have assumed that the parallel algorithm examines a pth fraction of the data at each processor. This is not necessary – as we discussed above, a much smaller sample is likely to produce a predictor of the same accuracy. Corresponding reductions in the cost(predictor) term are possible.

Two techniques for selecting the subsets of the training data used for producing each predictor have been studied in the literature: bagging, and arcing [3,4]. Bagging is uniformly random selection, while arcing (adaptive resampling and combining) increases the relative likelihood of inclusion for objects that are more likely to be misclassified. Arcing has also been called boosting [7]. The motivation for using such techniques in sequential prediction is twofold: to reduce the stiffness of some classification techniques, and to reduce the work required to build predictors. In some experiments, combining predictors built from samples of a few hundred objects produced error rates comparable to training on entire datasets with many thousands of objects.

Parallelism in training benefits from both the relative independence of training predictors in different processors (giving speedups proportional to p) and the freedom to use small samples to build each predictor (which is also, of course, available in sequential training). Because bagging requires random samples for each processor, a mechanism to ensure that the data distributed to each processor is a random sample of the whole training dataset is necessary, but this can be achieved by a 'front end' to the disk storage system that responds to requests for data with a random subset of the dataset.

Parallelizing arcing predictors is more difficult, partly because it is not yet understood how arcing works, although it is known to work well. The known arcing algorithms have an apparent sequential dependency – the sample used for training the $i + 1$st predictor depends on either the ith predictor or *all* of the previous predictors. An obvious parallelization strategy is to have all processors exchange their newly-generated predictor at the end of each phase, and therefore use all of the known predictors to generate their next data sample. It is unclear what performance to expect from this algorithm, because our understanding of arcing is still limited. It certainly does no worse than the sequential algorithm; it seems intuitive that generating p times as many predictors at each phase should provide at least linear speedup. It is even conceivable that parallel arcing might be a dependent algorithm since having access to a larger set of predictors presumably makes it easier to find 'difficult' boundaries. Arcing seems remarkably impervious to the precise structure of the algorithm, so there are grounds for optimism.

4   Parallelizing Dependent Predictors

The essential structure of predictor-building algorithms of the second kind is:

while error rate still improving and still work to do
      generate a new predictor
      merge it with the previous predictors
         (reducing the remaining work)

Suppose that the amount of work required to compute the $i + 1$st predictor is an α fraction $(0 < \alpha < 1)$ of the work required to compute the ith predictor. The loop may still execute until the error rate stops improving, but would more typically stop when there is no remaining work to be done. We express this using some minimum remaining work such that the loop terminates when $\alpha^k < min$. The sequential cost of such an algorithm can be expressed as:

$$\text{cost} = \sum_{i=0}^{k} \left[\alpha^i \text{cost(predictor)} + \text{cost(merge)} \right]$$

Especially when α is much less than 1, such algorithms tend to terminate much more quickly than those of the first kind.

The parallel version of such an algorithm has this structure:

while error rate still improving and work to do
      forall p
         generate new predictors in each processor
      merge the p predictors using a reduction
         (reducing the remaining work by the total amount
         completed by all of the processors)

When such an algorithm is parallelized, we get speedup because of the use of multiple processors. More importantly, we also get speedup because the $i + 1$st iteration of the outside loop *in all processors* uses all of the progress in the previous loop.

The parallel complexity can be expressed as:

$$\text{parallel cost} = \sum_{i=0}^{k/p} \left[\alpha^{ip} \text{cost(predictor)} + \text{cost(merge)} \right]$$

Thus on the first iteration using, say, 4 processors, each processor examines all of its data. On the second, however, each need only examine an α^4 fraction of the data, on the next an α^8 fraction, and so on. This reduces the computation component substantially, although the required communication is reduced only to the extent that the total number of iterations is reduced.

Whether or not sampling, in the sense of bagging or arcing, can be used in algorithms such as these depends on the data mining technique used. For neural network training, batch learning *is* a sampling technique. On the other hand, inductive learning is a covering technique and, as such, all training data must be seen and accounted for.

The parallelization technique discussed in this section has been applied to both neural network learning [10] and inductive logic learning (Yu Wang, unpublished work) and significant speedups from both sources do occur.

5   Discussion and Conclusions

We have presented an analysis of the parallel complexity of prediction treating sequential algorithm, in their plain or sample-based forms, as black boxes. We have shown that techniques based on pasting together predictors trained on samples have relatively small overheads when parallelized. Hence, as well as the performance gains of the pasting approach, they may be expected to demonstrate almost linear speedup. Techniques in which the work required to generate the next predictor is reduced by the existence of previous predictors allow each processor to benefit from the construction of p predictors in the time it takes to generate one. Hence, as well as the almost linear speedup due to parallelism, they exhibit another speedup due to this sharing of common progress. Our calculations suggest that there is more to be gained by parallelizing data mining at large grain, using the replicated sequential algorithm as a building block, than in trying to parallelize algorithms internally.

References

1. C. Bishop. *Neural networks for pattern recognition*. Oxford University Press, 1995. 193
2. P.S. Bradley, U.M. Fayyad, and O.L. Mangasarian. Mathematical programming for data mining: Formulations and challenges. *INFORMS Journal of Computing*, 11:217–238, 1999. 190
3. L. Breiman. Bagging predictors. *Machine Learning*, 24:123–140, 1996. 192, 194
4. L. Breiman. Arcing classifiers. *Annals of Statistics*, 26(3):801–849, 1998. 194
5. L. Breiman. Pasting bites together for prediction in large data sets and on-line. *Machine Learning*, 36(1&2), 1999. 192
6. L. Breiman and N. Shang. Born again trees. Technical report, Department of Statistics, University of California, Berkeley, 1996. 192
7. Y. Freund and R. Schapire. Experiments with a new boosting algorithm. In *Proceedings of the 13th International Conference on Machine Learning*, pages 148–156, 1996. 194
8. S. Muggleton. Inductive logic programming: Issues, results and the LLL challenge. *Artificial Intelligence*, 1999. 193
9. S. Muggleton. Scientific knowledge discovery using inductive logic programming. *Communications of the ACM*, 1999. 193
10. R.O. Rogers and D.B. Skillicorn. Using the BSP cost model for optimal parallel neural network training. *Future Generation Computer Systems*, 14:409–424, 1998. 193, 196

Efficient Parallel Classification Using Dimensional Aggregates

Sanjay Goil[1] and Alok Choudhary[2]

[1] Performance Technologies Group
Sun Microsystems Inc.
Sanjay.Goil@eng.sun.com
[2] Department of Electrical & Computer Engineering
Northwestern University
choudhar@ece.nwu.edu

Abstract. Multidimensional aggregates are frequently computed to improve query performance in Online Analytical Processing applications. We present a new method for decision tree based classification trees using the aggregates computed in the multidimensional data model. The structure imposed on data in a explicit multidimensional storage mechanism leads to efficient dimensional operations. Decision tree based classification algorithms perform computations to find the best split point at each node of the tree. Efficient computation of the split in the decision tree can be done by using the one-dimensional aggregates if the cell values are the class-id values, and counts are maintained for each class. This is used repeatedly at the nodes of the decision tree to calculate splits and manage data. Previous parallel approaches for decision-tree based classification use sorted attribute lists and hash tables to compute the split point and split the data appropriately. The amount of data communicated is proportional to the product of number of records in the training set, and the number of dimensions, at each level of the tree, in the worst case. Parallel formulation of our approach uses data communication proportional to the product of the sum of cardinality of all dimensions and the number of non-classified nodes at each level of the tree. Communication volume is greatly reduced in our approach and is done in one phase of communication at each level of the tree, by coalescing messages. Preliminary results from our experiments on a coarse-grained, distributed memory parallel machine (IBM-SP2) show good performance.

1 Introduction

Classification of large data sets has received considerable attention in the data mining literature recently. The objective of classification is to build a model of the classifying attribute based upon the other attributes of the record. A set of sample records called the training data set is given, consisting of several attributes. Attributes can either be *continuous*, if they come from an ordered domain, or *categorical*, if they are from an unordered domain. One of the attributes is the *classifying* attribute that indicates the *class* to which the record belongs. Several

M.J. Zaki, C.-T. Ho (Eds.): Large-Scale Parallel Data Mining, LNAI 1759, pp. 197–210, 2000.

classification models have been used in the past, notably neural networks [1], genetic algorithms [2], and decision trees [3,4]. Among these models, the decision tree models are considered to be the most useful in the domain of data mining because they are relatively inexpensive to construct, easy to interpret and easy to integrate with data base systems. Also, for a variety of problem domains they yield comparable or better accuracy as compared to the other models [1].

A decision tree recursively partitions the training set until each partition consists entirely or dominantly records from one class. Each *non-leaf* node of the tree contains a split point which is a test on an attribute and determines how the data is partitioned. Once the decision tree is built from the training set it can be used to classify future instances. The decision-tree based classifiers that can handle large data sets are important because use of larger data sets improves the classification accuracy [1].

Previous work in classifying large data sets has been to use sampled data sets or multiple partitions of the data set [1,5]. Recent work has focused on using the entire data set, in classifiers like SLIQ [6] and SPRINT [7]. A parallel classifier in the same spirit has been developed in ScalParC [8]. Classifiers like CART [3] and C4.5 [4] perform sorting at every node of the decision tree, which makes them expensive for large data sets since disk-based sorting is required at each node. The approach of SPRINT, SLIQ is to sort the continuous attribute once in the beginning and maintain the sorted order in the subsequent splitting steps. Separate lists are kept for each attribute which maintains a record identifier for each sorted value. In the splitting phase the same records need to be assigned to a node, which may be in a different order in the different attribute lists. A hash table is used to provide a mapping between record identifiers and the node to which it belongs after the split. This mapping is then probed to split the attribute lists in a consistent manner. A framework for instantiating several of these algorithms is presented in [9], which uses attribute value and class-label pairs (AVC-sets) to make the splitting criteria decision. It is also a greedy top-down approach as the others, except that it works on the AVC-sets at each node of the decision tree. This allows it to use memory more efficiently and perform much better than the attribute-list approaches.

Table 1. Training set data

Row-id	Age	Car-Color	Gender	Class-id
0	10	Green	F	0
1	50	Blue	M	1
2	40	Yellow	F	0
3	30	Green	F	0
4	20	Red	M	1
5	40	Blue	M	0
6	20	Yellow	M	1

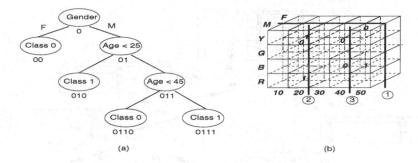

(a)   (b)

Fig. 1. (a) Classification tree for training set (b) Classification tree embedded on a cube

Table 1 is an example training set with three attributes, Age, Car color and Gender, and a class attribute. Age is a continuous attribute, whereas both Car color and Gender are categorical attribute. For a categorical attribute having c distinct classes it is assumed that the splitting decision forms c partitions, one for each of its values. Figure 1(a) shows the classification tree for it. At each node the attribute to split is chosen that best divides the training set. Several splitting criteria have been used in the past to evaluate the goodness of a split. Calculating the *gini* index is commonly used [3]. This involves computing the frequency of records of each class in each of the partitions. If a parent node having n records and c possible classes is split into p partitions, the *gini* index of the ith partition is $gini_i = 1 - \sum_{j=1}^{c}(n_{ij}/n_i)^2$, where n_i is the total number of records in partition i, of which n_{ij} records belong to class j. The *gini* index of the total split is given by $gini_{split} = \sum_{i=1}^{p}(n_i/n)gini_i$. The attribute with the least value of $gini_{split}$ is chosen to split the records at that node. The matrix n_{ij} is called the *count matrix*. The count matrix needs to be calculated for each evaluated split point for a continuous attribute.

Categorical attributes have only one count matrix associated with them, hence computation of the gini index is straightforward. For the continuous attributes an appropriate splitting value has to be determined by calculating the $gini_{split}$ and choosing the one with the minimum value. If the attribute is sorted then a linear search can be made for the optimal split point by evaluating the gini index at each attribute value. The count matrix is calculated at each possible split point to evaluate the $gini_{split}$ value. The *gini* index calculations and the node splits for the example above are given in Figure 2. At Node 0, the attribute *Gender* yields the optimal $gini_{split}$ value of 0.214. This creates a split with one partition with M values for gender and another with F values. After this split is made, two child nodes are created. The record values need to be partitioned consistently between the two nodes for the *split-attribute* and the *non-split attributes*. Splitting the split-attribute is straightforward by adjusting pointer values. The challenge is to split the non-split attributes efficiently. Ex-

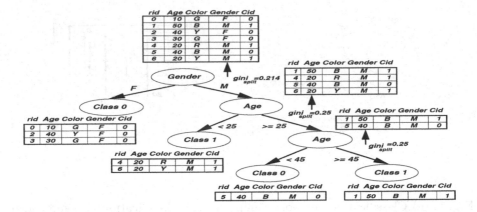

Fig. 2. Gini index calculation for the attributes and node splitting

isting implementations such as SPRINT and ScalParC maintain a mapping of the row-id and class-id with the values assigned to each node. The values are split physically among nodes, such that the continuous attribute maintain their sorted order in each node to facilitate the sequential scan for the next split determination phase. A hash list maintains the mapping of record ids to nodes. The record ids in the lists for non-splitting attributes are searched to get the node information, and perform the correct split.

2   Proposed Classification Using Multidimensional Aggregates

Multidimensional analysis, OLAP queries and association rule mining are performed efficiently using the materialized aggregates in the data cube. A multidimensional chunk based infrastructure for OLAP and multidimensional analysis for high dimensional data is developed in [10], which optimizes the building of the data cube operator [11]. In this model an attribute is treated as a dimension, and records are points in a multidimensional space. Dimensional operations can be performed more efficiently in such a model since a structure is imposed in the storage of data. Multidimensional arrays are the most intuitive and simple structures for this. However, data sets with large dimension cardinalities and a high number of dimensions cannot be handled using arrays. Also, most data sets are sparse and multidimensional arrays lead to redundant storage in such a scenario. We have used a chunk based implementation to sparse data in a bit-encoded sparse structure (BESS) which encodes the indices of the element in a chunk. Dimensional operations are efficiently performed on compressed chunks, which allow a large number of dimensions to be used.

We propose that classification trees can be built using structure imposed on data using the multidimensional data model. Gini index calculation relies on the count matrix which can be efficiently calculated using the dimensional model. Each populated cell represents a record in the array. For the base cube (which is a multidimensional representation of the records without any aggregation) the class value of the record is stored in each cell. The gini index calculation uses the count matrix which has information about the number of records in each partition belonging to each possible class.

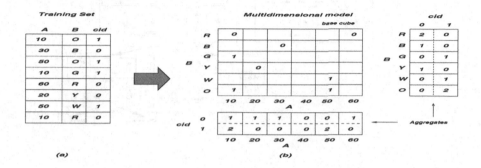

(a)   (b)

Fig. 3. (a) Training set records (b) corresponding multidimensional model

To evaluate split points for a continuous attribute the $gini_{split}$ needs to be evaluated for each possible split point in a continuous attribute and once for a categorical attribute. This means the aggregate calculations present in each of the 1 dimensional aggregates can be used if they have number of records belonging to each class. Therefore for each aggregate we store the number of records in each class. Figure 3(a) gives an example training set with two dimensions, A, a continuous dimension and B a categorical dimension and two class values 0 and 1.

Figure 3(b) is the corresponding multidimensional model. The continuous dimensions A is stored in the sorted order. The aggregates store the number of records mapping to that cell for both classes 0 and 1. To calculate the $gini_{split}$ for the continuous attribute attribute A it is now easy to look at the A aggregate and sum the values belonging to both classes 0 and 1 on both sides of the split point under consideration to get the count matrix. Gini index calculation is done on an attribute list which in the case of a multidimensional model is a dimension. Count matrix is repeatedly calculated on the sorted attribute list which is readily available in the cube structure as a higher level one dimensional aggregate. Each dimension is sorted in the dimensional structure as shown in Figure 3(b).

Figure 4 illustrates the classification tree building process using the multidimensional model and the aggregates maintained at the highest level of the cube structure, one for each dimension.

The challenge is to calculate the one dimensional aggregates efficiently and keep them updated to reflect the partitions after each split. The simple method

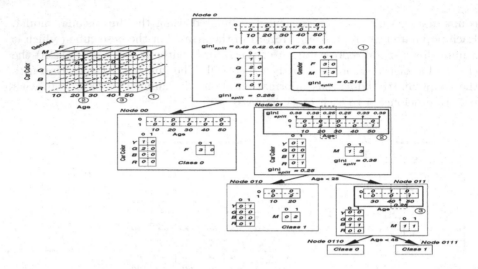

Fig. 4. Gini index calculation for the attributes and node splitting with multi-dimensional aggregates

of computing each level 1 aggregate is to do so from base data. Some alternative strategies that enumerate some intermediate values to optimize the computation of the one-dimensional aggregates have been described in [12].

3   Related Work

In this section we will briefly discuss the previous efforts in parallel classification [13,7,8] on distributed memory machines, significant of which are parallel SPRINT [7] and ScalParC [8] since they do not require resorting at each node. Classification on fine-grained shared memory machines has addressed in [14]. The issues involved on such architectures are much different than distributed memory machines and hence we do not discuss that work here.

Parallelization of tree methods, especially multidimensional binary search trees (k-d trees), quadtrees and octrees for hierarchical methods have received considerable attention in the areas of scientific processing [15]. Classification trees fall under a similar paradigm.

The parallel version of SPRINT partitions each attribute list by sorting each one using a parallel sort with probabilistic splitting. This gives approximately equal sections to each processor of each sorted attribute list. Split points are found by first doing a **prefix sum** operation for the count of values below and above the first split point on each processor followed by building the count matrices locally on each processor. After calculating the gini index locally, the processors communicate to determine which split point has the lowest value. Since there is only one count matrix for categorical attributes, they are constructed locally and one processor collects the global count and calculates the gini values.

Each processor splits its splitting attribute list locally. *rids* are collected from all processors to build the hash table on each processor. The non-splitting attribute lists then probe this table with *rids* to determine the split locally. This has a space complexity of $O(N)$ and makes it unscalable in memory requirements. ScalParC on the other hand maintains a distributed hash table for the splitting phase which has a space complexity of $O(N/P)$. However, the splitting phase is slightly different in their case. A distributed hash table, called the *node table* is maintained by hashing a *rid* with a hash function $h(rid) = (p = rid \; div \; N/P, l = rid \; mod \; N/P)$, where the first field is the processor number and the second is the local index on that processor. After the splitting decision, each processor uses the *rids* of the split attribute to construct hash buffers with $(l, child)$ entry destined for all processors p calculated by the hash function. An **all-to-all personalized** communication phase exchanges these to update the distributed node table. For each non-split attribute list, the distributed node table is queried by filling out a communication buffer with *rids* (enquiry buffer) and sending it to the processor p which then fills it with the child label and sends it back. Two **all-to-all personalized** communication phases are needed to achieve this.

The size of the node table at each level is usually of size $O(N/P)$. Also, each processor sends $O(N/P)$ elements from each of the non-splitting attribute list. However, there are cases when a processor has to hash all global *rids* at some level and the other processors need to send $O(N)$ elements to be queried by the node table on a single processor [8]. Hence, the worst case complexity is $O(N)$.

4   Parallel Classification Using Multidimensional Aggregates

Parallel classification on the multidimensional cube is similar to the sequential classification algorithm, except the fact that each processor calculates the aggregates locally and then needs to update counts for each partitioned dimension from other processors. This is done by a communication phase which calculates a **prefix sum** on the first split point for continuous attributes since each split point is evaluated by computing the $gini_{split}$. For categorical attributes, however, a processor can sum the counts for a value of the categorical dimension and calculate the gini index. Note that separate processors can compute the gini value for a categorical attribute.

4.1   Dimension Partitioning and Gini Index Calculation

Figure 5 shows a one dimensional partitioning of the multidimensional base cube and the associated local aggregate calculations. Each processor builds the aggregate locally and for each continuous attribute determines the gini index for the values that lie in its partition. For non-distributed dimensions, each processor locally calculates the aggregates and then does a **reduce all (sum)** on the aggregates for each such dimension. Each processor then works on a part of the aggregate list to calculate the gini index values. This results in computation being partitioned between processors. If the size of the dimension i is d_i, then each processor $P_j, 0 \leq j < P$, calculates the gini index from $(d_i/P)P_j$ to $(d_i/P)P_{j+1}$ for each dimension. For categorical attributes also the computation can be distributed similarly if a **reduce all** is performed on the aggregated dimensions. Otherwise a **reduce (sum)** operation gets the aggregates on a single processor which does the calculation. Since dimensions with categorical attributes are usually small we use the latter approach.

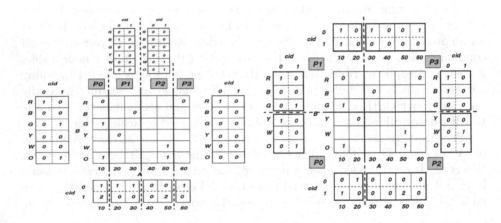

Fig. 5. One and two dimensional partitioning of dimensions

Another alternative is to perform a two dimensional partitioning by selecting the two largest dimensions and partitioning the multidimensional base cube on a 2-dimensional processor grid as shown in Figure 5. This may provide better load balancing in some cases. The communication pattern for the two distributed dimension changes but remains the same for the rest. The non-distributed dimensions get the aggregates locally and do a **reduce all (sum)** to sum each dimensional aggregate independently on each processor. Each processor then works at calculating the gini index in contiguous portions as in the one-dimensional partitioning case. For the distributed dimension A in the figure the reduce for the dimension on processor P_j is done on processor $(P_j/P_Y)P_Y$, where P the number of processors is divided into a two dimensional grid in the dimensions X and Y as $P_X \times P_Y$. The processors $P_0 + i * P_Y, i = 0, \ldots P_X$ then calculate the local sums of class ids and need a **prefix sum** to get the values updated across processor boundaries with the number above and below in each class. Each of these processors then calculates the gini index for the local dimension values.

Similarly, for dimension B a **reduce** operation is done on processor $P_j \% P_Y$ and again a **prefix sum** is done between processors $P_0 + i, i = 0, \ldots P_Y$ to calculate the gini index locally.

4.2   Node Splits

Once the $gini_{split}$ is calculated for all attributes (dimensions), each processor picks out the minimum and the attribute it is related to. A **Reduce (minimum)** gets the minimum and the attribute which is the *split* attribute. Each processor then partitions the split attribute locally. Each processor maintains a mapping of dimension indices to the node they belong to, as they are split. In other words, a global tree representation is present on each node. Each node keeps the dimensional boundaries of the dimensions split, defining a hypercube the node encapsulates. The aggregates are then calculated within the node boundaries. The communication required is for each dimension, but now there are multiple count values, one for each active node which has not yet been classified.

Let n_a be the number of attributes (dimensions) divided into n_d, the set of distributed dimensions and n_u, the set of non-distributed dimensions. For non-distributed dimensions these need to be aggregated using a **Reduce (sum)** on all processors to distribute the computation of the gini index calculation. The amount of data communicated at a level k of the classification tree is $O(\mathcal{N}_n^k |D_u|)$, where $\mathcal{N}_n^k$ is the number of active nodes at a level k, and $|D_u|$ is the sum of dimension sizes of dimensions $d_i \in n_u$. For a distributed dimension a local aggregation is done for each dimension for each node and then a **Parallel prefix (sum)** is done. The data communicated for this operation at level k is $O(\mathcal{N}_n^k n_d)$. The total data communicated at level k of the classification tree is then $O(\mathcal{N}_n^k(|D_u| + n_d)) = O(\mathcal{N}_n^k |D_a|)$, $|D_a| = |D_u| + |D_d|$, because the number of split dimensions is usually one or two. This is the case for our implementation where the optimization of message-coalescing, reduces the number of communication messages by combining the messages as one buffer.

For the scalable record based classification algorithm (ScalParC) the complexity of communication at each level is $O(n_a \frac{N}{P})$ at each level and $O(n_a N)$ in the worst case, where N is the size of the training set. The number of active nodes at any level is much smaller than the size of the training set. Also, the sum of dimension sizes, $|D_a|$, is also much smaller when compared to N. Thus, $\mathcal{N}_n^k \times |D_a| < N$, for a large N. This makes the overall communication requirement of our multidimensional classification algorithm better. Computation of the 1-D aggregates and the gini index calculations has the time complexity $O(\frac{N}{P} + \mathcal{N}_n D_a)$ in our method, whereas ScalParc requires $O(\frac{N}{P} n_a)$, to compute the gini indices and $O(N n_a)$ in the worst case.

A **broadcast** of the prefix sum from the last processor is followed by the local calculation of the gini index and a **Reduce (minimum)** for the gini value which determines the attribute used for the split. Notice that for a non-distributed categorical attribute B the calculation is distributed across processors by letting each processor work on a section since all information is available on each processor as a result of the reduce. Suppose the $gini_{split}$ results in selecting $A = 25$ as the split point in the example.

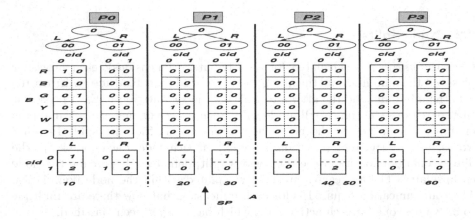

Fig. 6. Node split of dimension $A = 25$, and the count arrays for each node

Figure 6 shows the split at each processor into L and R nodes labeled 00 and 01 respectively. The counts of each dimension are done for each node on each processor. The steps for parallel gini index calculations are done for each node on every processor. Communication can be concatenated for the nodes at each level following the idea of concatenated parallelism in [15] for each active node.

4.3   Communication Optimizations

Only one collective communication operation is performed for all nodes at each level. This is due to the fact that information that needs to be communicated for all nodes is stored contiguously. Each node has the counts of class id. values for each dimension. This is combined using a **Reduce (sum)** operation across all nodes as described in a previous section. The count matrices for each dimension are allocated contiguously for each active node as shown in Figure 7. Each node allocates memory for each dimension, d_i, for each class. At each level only the unclassified nodes (active nodes) are represented and need to participate. Algorithm 1 describes the steps of the overall parallel algorithm for classification.

5   Performance Results

We use the synthetic data generator introduced by Agrawal et al. in [16]. It is a widely used synthetic set used by many others, primarily because there are no large real data sets available.

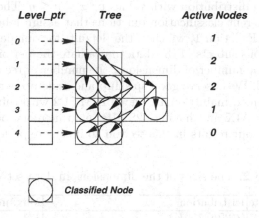

Level_ptr   Tree   Active Nodes

0   1
1   2
2   2
3   1
4   0

Classified Node

Fig. 7. Tree structure at each processor, nodes being stored contiguously to coalesce messages for communication at each level

Algorithm 1. Multidimensional Classification Algorithm

```
/* set the root node to represent the entire multidimensional space */
for i ← 0 to k
        begin_i = 0
        end_i = |d_i|
n_active_nodes = 1;
while(n_active_nodes > 0)
        For each chunk c
                Get chunk boundary values in each dimension
                For each active node j, (0 ≤ j < n_active_nodes)
                        Determine if chunk c is contained within node j,[begin_i, end_i), for all i, else if
                        it overlaps or else not in range.
                For each active node j, (0 ≤ j < n_active_nodes)
                        Compute the contribution of chunk c to 1-dimensional aggregate if the chunk is inclu-
                        sive or overlapping to the node j.
                One Reduce (sum) communication operation for consolidating k 1-dimensional aggregates
                on all processors.
                For each active node j, (0 ≤ j < n_active_nodes)
                        Check if node j is already classified within the threshold level.
                        If the node is not classified
                                For each attribute i, 0 ≤ i < k,
                                        Compute gini indices for each dimension i recording the minimum value
                                        and corresponding i (split_i) and the split point.
                                        Update for the child node, begin_i and end_i for split_i using the split point and
                                        copy the others from the parent node j.
                                        Add the number of child nodes to the count of active nodes.
                Update n_active_nodes as the count of child nodes.
end
```

The synthetic set has nine attributes as shown in Table 2. $\mathcal{U}(x:y)$ denotes the integer uniform distribution with values $v : x \le v \le y$. The data set can be generated with different classification functions that assign labels to the records produced. We use Function 1, which is the default, for our performance study. We have used various subsets of the data to evaluate the performance of our algorithm, varying the number of dimensions, the number of records and the classification threshold. We observe good speedup and scale-up performance for our experiments performed mainly on a 16 node IBM SP2 with thin nodes (120Mhz processor) running AIX and having 128 MB main memory per processor. We present a subset of our results in this section to illustrate performance.

Table 2. The sizes of the dimensions in data set used

Predictor Attribute	Distribution	Max. number of entries
Salary	$\mathcal{U}(20K, 150K)$	131
Commission	0, if(salary > 75K) else $\mathcal{U}(10K, 75K)$	66
Age	$\mathcal{U}(20, 80)$	61
Education	$\mathcal{U}(0, 4)$	5
Car	$\mathcal{U}(1, 20)$	20
Zip Code	$\mathcal{U}(\text{nine zip codes})$	9
House Value	$\mathcal{U}(0.5 \times k \times 100K, 1.5 \times k \times 100K)$ k depends on ZipCode	1351
Home Years	$\mathcal{U}(0, 30)$	31
Loan	$\mathcal{U}(0, 500K)$	501

Figure 8(a),(b) shows the time for classifying 1 million and 5 million records with 8 dimension (again without Loan attribute) and classification threshold value set to T = 0.8. The 5 million records data set is We observe that most of the time is taken for the 1 dimensional aggregate calculations and the gini computations, a small fraction taken by communication and maintenance of the classification tree.

Figure 8(c) shows the classification performance for a 9 dimensional data set with 1 million records. The major component of the computation is the 1-dimensional aggregate calculations for all nodes. This is the parallel component and we see good speedup as the number of processors is increased. The other phases of communication and gini index calculations as shown in the figure are small portions of the entire time. Communication increases slightly as number of processors increase, due to the increase in p term in the complexity of the **Reduce** global communication operation. We are currently running experiments with larger data sets and will include the results in the final version.

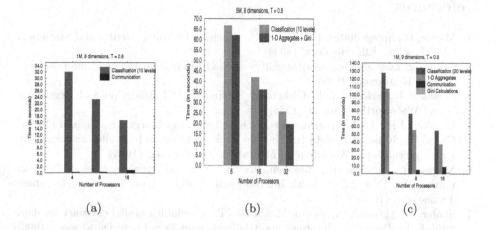

Fig. 8. Classification of a 8 dimensional data set for 10 levels, with classification threshold T = 0.8 for (a) 1M records (b) 5M records (c) Classification of a 9 dimensional data set for 20 levels, with classification threshold T = 0.8 for 1M records

6   Conclusions

In this article we introduce classification using decision trees on an explicit multidimensional storage scheme. The split point for a node in the classification tree is chosen after computing the counts of records belonging to each class for each attribute value, in each dimension. A multidimensional representation make a 1-dimensional computation for each dimension from the base cube very efficient. A parallel framework is used to parallelize this calculation, and one round of communication is required at each level of the tree by concatenating (coalescing) communication for each node together. Results on a synthetic benchmark [16], widely used for classification algorithms performance, shows good parallel performance.

Acknowledgments

This work was supported in part by NSF Young Investigator Award CCR-9357840 and NSF CCR-9509143. This work was performed when the first author was at Northwestern University.

References

1. Michie, D., Spiegelhater, D., Taylor, C.: Machine Learning, Neural and Statistical Classification. Ellis Horwood (1994)
2. Goldberg, D.: Genetic Algorithms in Search, Optimization and Machine Learning. Morgan Kaufmann (1989)
3. Breiman, L., Friedman, J., Olshen, R., Stone, C.: Classification and Regression Trees. Wadsworth, Belmont (1984)
4. Quinlan, J.R.: C4.5: Programs for Machine Learning. Morgan Kaufmann (1993)
5. Chan, P., Stolfo, S.: Meta-learning for multistrategy and parallel learning. In: Proc. International Workshop on Multistrategy Learning. (1993)
6. Mehta, M., Agrawal, R., Rissanen, J.: SLIQ: A fast scalable classifier for data mining. In: Proc. of the Fifth International Conference on Extending Database Technology. (1996)
7. Shafer, J., Agrawal, R., Mehta, M.: SPRINT: A scalable parallel classifier for data mining. In: Proc. 22th International Conference on Very Large Databases. (1996)
8. Joshi, M., Karypis, G., Kumar, V.: ScalParC: A new scalable and efficient parallel classification algorithm for mining large datasets. In: Proc. International Parallel Processing Symposium. (1998)
9. Gehrke, J., Ramakrishnan, R., Ganti, V.: RainForest - A Framework for Fast Decision Tree Construction of Large Data Sets. In: Proc. 24th International Conference on Very Large Databases. (1998)
10. Goil, S., Choudhary, A.: High performance multidimensional analysis and data mining. In: Proc. SC98: High Performance Networking and Computing Conference. (1998)
11. Gray, J., Bosworth, A., Layman, A., Pirahesh, H.: Data cube: A relational aggregation operator generalizing group-by, cross-tab, and sub-totals. In: Proc. 12th International Conference on Data Engineering. (1996)
12. Goil, S., Choudhary, A.: Parallel classification using the multidimensional data model (under preparation). Technical Report CPDC-9904-006, Northwestern University (1999)
13. Fifield, D.: Distributed Tree construction from large data sets. Bachelor's Honors Thesis, Australian National University (1992)
14. Zaki, M., Ho, C., Agrawal, R.: Scalable parallel classification for data mining on shared-memory multiprocessors. In: Proc. International Conference on Data Engineering. (1999)
15. Al-furaih, I., Aluru, S., Goil, S., Ranka, S.: Parallel construction of multidimensional binary search trees. In: Proc. International Conference on Supercomputing. (1996)
16. Agrawal, R., Imielinski, T., Swami, A.: Database mining: A performance perspective. IEEE Transactions on Knowledge and Data Engineering (1993)

Learning Rules from Distributed Data

Lawrence O. Hall[1], Nitesh Chawla[1], Kevin W. Bowyer[1],
and W. Philip Kegelmeyer[2]

[1] Department of Computer Science and Engineering, ENB 118
University of South Florida, 4202 E. Fowler Ave.
Tampa, Fl 33620
{hall, chawla, kwb}@csee.usf.edu
[2] Sandia National Laboratories
Advanced Concepts Department
P.O. Box 969, MS 9214
Livermore, CA, 94551-0969
wpk@ca.sandia.gov

Abstract. In this paper a concern about the accuracy (as a function of parallelism) of a certain class of distributed learning algorithms is raised, and one proposed improvement is illustrated. We focus on learning a single model from a set of disjoint data sets, which are distributed across a set of computers. The model is a set of rules. The distributed data sets may be disjoint for any of several reasons. In our approach, the first step is to construct a rule set (model) for each of the original disjoint data sets. Then rule sets are merged until an eventual final rule set is obtained which models the aggregate data. We show that this approach compares to directly creating a rule set from the aggregate data and promises faster learning. Accuracy can drop off as the degree of parallelism increases. However, an approach has been developed to extend the degree of parallelism achieved before this problem takes over.

1 Introduction

Training data may be distributed across a set of computers for several reasons. For example, several data sets concerning telephone fraud might be owned by separate organizations who have competitive reasons for keeping the data private. However, the organizations would be interested in models of the aggregate data.

Another example is very large datasets that will not fit in a single memory which are useful in the process of learning a classifier or model of the data. It is now possible to have training data on the order of a terabyte which will not fit in a single computer's memory. A parallel approach to learning a model from the data will solve the practical problem of how to deal with learning from large data sets.

This paper describes an approach that learns a single model of a distributed training set in the form of a set of rules. A single model may be an advantage in the case that it will be applied to a large amount of data. For example, consider

M.J. Zaki, C.-T. Ho (Eds.): Large-Scale Parallel Data Mining, LNAI 1759, pp. 211–220, 2000.

the problem of visualizing "interesting" regions of a large data set. A set of rules might be learned which can do this. These rules would then be applied to similarly large data sets to guide the user to the interesting regions.

This paper examines an approach to generating rules in parallel that is related to work by [1,2]. A set of rules will be generated from disjoint subsets of the full data set used for training. Given N disjoint subsets of the full dataset there will be N sets of rules generated. Each subset of data may reside on a distinct processor. The distributed rule sets must be merged into a single rule set. Our focus is towards using a large N with very large training sets.

The final set of merged rules should be free of conflicts and have accuracy equivalent to a set of rules developed from the full dataset used for training. We discuss an approach to building a single, accurate set of rules created from N rule sets. The question of how similar to one another rule sets developed sequentially and in parallel might be is explored. Experimental results on several small, representative datasets show that accuracy tends to decline as N increases. A method to reduce this tendency is presented.

In Section 2 the generation of rules in parallel and the combination of rule sets is discussed. Section 3 contains experimental results and a discussion of the issues shown by an analysis of them. Section 4 contains a summary of the strengths and open questions associated with the presented approach to learning in parallel.

2   Generating Rules in Parallel and Combining Them

The disjoint subsets of extremely large data sets may also be very large. In principle any approach that produces rules can be used to learn from each data set. It is possible, for example, to learn decision trees [3,4] in a fast, cost effective manner. Learning a decision tree, pruning it and then generating rules from the pruned tree will be an effective competitor from a time standpoint to other rule generation approaches such as RL [5] or RIPPER [6].

In the work reported here, rules are created directly by traversing pruned decision trees (with the obvious optimization of removing redundant tests). The process of creating rules from decision trees in a more time consuming fashion has been covered in [3,7]. In learning rules it is often the case that a default class is utilized. However, it is desirable to avoid having default classes for examples because the lack of a model for some examples cannot be resolved in a straightforward way when rule sets are merged.

Each rule that is created will have associated with it a measure of its "goodness" which is based on its accuracy and the number and type of examples it covers. We are using a normalized version of Quinlan's certainty factor [8,2] to determine the accuracy of a rule R over an example set E as:

$$acc(R, E) = (TP - 0.5)/(TP + \rho FP), \tag{1}$$

where TP is the number of true positives examples covered by R when applied to E, FP is the number of false positives caused by R when applied to E, and

ρ is the ratio of positive examples to negative examples for the class of the rule contained in the training set.

A rule, R, must have acc(R,E) $\geq t$ for some threshold t in order to be considered acceptable over a set of E examples. When a rule is built on a single subset of data, its accuracy may change as it is applied to each of the other subsets of data. The rule can be discarded whenever its accuracy is less than t or only after it has been applied to all of the distributed examples and has an accuracy below the threshold.

Discarding a rule as soon as it is below the accuracy threshold will save the testing time on other processors and some communication time required to send it and its current TP/FP count to another processor. Testing time is not likely to be very high and communication time for one rule will generally be low. So, the per rule savings may be relatively low. On the other hand a rule which performs poorly on one partition and then improves to be acceptable or quite good will be ruled out under the incremental deletion approach. Our approach will be to only delete rules after testing is complete.

2.1 Merging Rule Sets Generated in Parallel

In [9] it is shown that any rule which is acceptable, by the accuracy definition in (1), on the full training set will be acceptable on at least one disjoint subset of the full data. This suggests that a rule set created by merging sets of acceptable rules learned on disjoint subsets of a full training set will contain rules that would be found on the full training set. Earlier work on building rules in parallel and then merging them [2] found that the merged set of rules contained the same rules as found by learning on the full data set and some extras. In that work, the training set was large, over 1,000,000 examples. The same paper expressed the belief that the same rule set would be found in parallel as generated sequentially.

However, in Figure 1 we show a small illustrative data set for which the rules learned by merging disjoint rule sets built on a disjoint 2 partition of the data do not include any rules learned by training on the full data set. Information gain is used to choose the attribute test for each node in the decision tree [4].

Figure 1 shows that a merged rule set, with each of the constituent rule sets developed in parallel on a disjoint training set, may in the extreme contain no rules in common with the rules created by training on the union of all the subsets (i.e. the full training set). The final merged rule set will depend upon how the examples are partitioned. The mix of examples needs to reflect the mix of available training examples.

The example data set and results from it shown in Figure 1 suggest that the accuracy of merged rules may well be different from the accuracy of the rules created from the full training set. Our experimental results will examine how different the accuracy may be and how it is affected by the number of partitions made from the training data.

As rule sets are merged, contradictions may be introduced in the sense that an example may be classified into different classes by two rules. As an individual rule is applied to more labeled examples its accuracy may change significantly.

Examples			
name	attr. 1	attr. 2	class
A	1	1	C1
B	4	3	C1
C	3	2	C1
D	2	4	C2
E	5	2	C2
F	6	1	C2

Sorted on Attr. #1		
name	attr. 1	class
A	1	C1
D	2	C2
C	3	C1
B	4	C1
E	5	C2
F	6	C2

Sorted on Attr. #2		
name	attr. 2	class
A	1	C1
F	1	C2
C	2	C1
E	2	C2
B	3	C1
D	4	C2

Processor 1 gets examples BCD and produces the rules:

> *if attr 1 > 2 then C1.*
> *if attr 1 <= 2 then C2.*

or

> *if attr 2 > 3 then C2.*
> *if attr 2 <= 3 then C1.*

Processor 2 gets examples AEF and produces the rules:

> *if attr 1 <= 1 then C1.*
> *if attr 1 > 1 then C2.*

From the full training set we get the rules:

> *if attr 1 > 4 then C2.*
> *if attr 1 <= 4 and attr 2 <= 3 then C1.*
> *if attr 1 <= 4 and attr 2 > 3 then C2.*

Fig. 1. An example where rules built in parallel on disjoint subsets **must** be different from rules built on the full data set. Using information gain to decide the splits.

Consider two rules R1 and R2 which classify an overlapping set of examples into two different classes. As the rules are applied to all of the subsets of the original training examples, the accuracy of one of them is expected to become less than a well-chosen threshold, t. Hence, one will be removed and the conflict resolved. However, it is possible for partially conflicting rules to survive.

For example, from the Iris data set [10] using 2 partitions we get the rules shown in Figure 2. The final accuracy after they have been applied to all training examples (but learned only from the examples in one partition) is shown in the second set of brackets associated with the rule. Both rules perform quite well when the accuracy measure in (1) is applied to them. If the conflict is not resolved, then rule ordering will affect the rules' performance. A reasonable choice might be to give higher priority to the rule with a better value of acc(R,E). Alternatively, conflict can be resolved as shown in [11,1]. Essentially conditional tests can be added to one or both rules resulting in specialization of the rules. Any examples left uncovered can then be classified by a newly created rule.

Here, we will remove the lowest performing conflicting rule with any uncovered examples being assigned to the majority class.

```
if petal width in cm > 0.4 and
   petal length in cm > 4.9
then class Iris-viginica [1/23]
                         [1/40]
if  0.5 < petal width in cm <= 1.6
then class Iris-Versicolor [0/23]
                           [4/48]
```

Fig. 2. Example of two rules from 1 fold of an Iris data 2 partition which have conflicts but survive to the final set. The numbers in brackets are the false positives and number of examples covered respectively. The second set of numbers for a rule is its accuracy after it is applied to the partition on which it was not learned.

Another type of conflict occurs when two rules for the same class created from different disjoint subsets have coverage which overlaps. For example, the rules shown in Figure 3, can be combined as the second more general rule. In general when there are overlaps among rules for the same class, the more general test is used.

```
a) if x > 7  and x < 15 then Class1
b) if x > 9  and x < 16 then Class1
c) if x > 7  and x < 16 then Class1
```

Fig. 3. Two overlapping rules, a and b, can be replaced by the third, c.

3   Experiments

The experiments reported here are from two datasets from the UC Irvine database [10] both of which consist of all continuous attributes. The IRIS data set [12] has 150 examples from 3 classes and the PIMA Indian diabetes data set has 768 examples from 2 classes. We are interested in how the accuracy is affected by partitioning these small data sets into N disjoint subsets, learning decision trees on the subsets, generating rules from the decision trees and then merging the rules into a final set of rules.

Our experiments were done using 10 fold cross validation [13]. For an individual data set and a given number of disjoint subsets, N, 10 partitions of the data were made each consisting of 90% of the train data with a unique 10% held back for testing. From each fold, N disjoint subsets are created. C4.5 is applied to each of the N subsets and rules are created from the generated decision tree. The rules created from the jth subset of data are then applied to the N-1 other subsets. The accuracy of each rule must be greater than the chosen threshold, t, in order for the rule to remain in the final set of rules. The default for the threshold t was chosen as 51, just slightly better than guessing every example belongs to the class of the rule. For the Iris data we chose t=75 rather arbitrarily. Setting t in an appropriate and systematic way must still be addressed.

For the Iris data, we have done an experiment with N=2. With the default C4.5 release 8 parameters the results on Iris for 10-fold cross validation and the results from the approach described here (with 2 different choices for certainty factors or cf's for use in pruning) are given in Table 1. The average number of rules was 6.5 for the default cf=25 and 3.1 for cf=1.

The reason for decreasing the certainty factor for pruning was to make the rules produced on the data subsets more general and less likely to overfit on the small number of examples. On this dataset there was a small positive impact.

Table 1. Results on the Iris data set using 10-fold cross-validation for a 2 processor partition. sd - standard deviation.

C4.5 % Correct ± sd	Pruned (cf=25) % Correct ± sd	Pruned (cf =1)% Correct ± sd
95.3 ± 6.01	94 ± 6.96	94.7 ± 5.81

The results for the simulated parallel approach are insignificantly worse than for C4.5 with default parameters but comparable to C4.5 with the cf=1 (94.7% and std= 5.81%).

A more interesting experiment is to look at a significant number of partitions. With the larger Pima data set, experiments were run with N=2, N=4, ..., N=10, and N=12. The results of a 10-fold cross-validation experiment with C4.5 using its default pruning (cf=25) were an average accuracy of 73.90% with sd=4.26% and an average of 23.8 rules. Figure 4 shows plots of accuracy, standard deviation and the number of rules for 10-fold cross validation experiments with each of the above N disjoint partitions. The performance of rules created from the unpruned tree, the pruned tree with the certainty factor of 25 and a certainty factor of 1 are shown. It can be seen that the accuracy of the rule set generally decreases as N increases. The standard deviation tends to get large, suggesting that performance on some folds is quite poor. The number of rules that remain in the final set remains fairly constant as N is increased. There are significantly less rules, after conflict resolution, than when training is done on the full data set.

3.1   Discussion

The results obtained here come from small datasets. However, we believe the issue of rule accuracy falling off can also occur with larger datasets. Our results are consistent with those found in [14] where experiments were conducted on

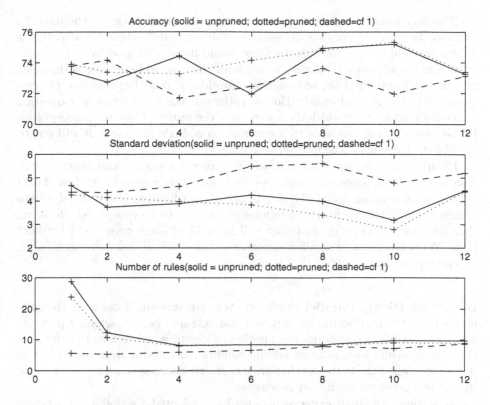

Fig. 4. Results from PIMA dataset experiments.

data sets related to the human genome project. It was found that more partitions resulted in lower performance on unseen data. Their approach to combining the classifiers was different, relying on voting among the learned set of classifiers.

Some success in mitigating the effect of learning in parallel may be gained by using a combiner or arbitrator approach to integrating multiple classifiers [15,16]. However, such approaches entail retaining all N classifiers learned in parallel and may be problematic for large N. There is not a single model of the data either.

In [2] an approach similar to ours was used on a very large dataset (over 1,000,000 examples) and there was no drop off in accuracy for partitions up to N=4. Our results suggest that accuracy would fall off as N increased.

If there are enough representative examples of each class in each of N disjoint partitions, the combined ruleset will have high accuracy. Clearly, the limit case is that each of the N subsets has an example which exactly or in the case of continuous data, almost exactly, matches each of the examples in the other subsets. So, the data really consists of only $|S_i|$ distinct examples, where $|S_i|$ is the set of examples at the ith compute node.

The very worst case is that $|S_i| = C$, the number of classes in the data. In this case each subset consists of just one example of each class. Clearly, this is an unreasonable choice for N and no one would make it in practice.

Under the approach to parallel rule generation covered here there is the usual question of how large N can be before communication costs begin to slow the rule generation process significantly. However, there is the more important question of determining an N for which the accuracy of the resultant rule set is acceptable. In datasets that are too large to learn from on a single processor, it will not be possible to know what the maximum accuracy is.

Clearly with this approach a tradeoff between accuracy and speed exists. The use of more processors promises that each can complete its task faster on a smaller training set at the usual cost of coordinating the work of all the processors and waiting for the combination of rules to be completed. However, there is a second *accuracy* cost that will be paid at some point as N becomes large. What the point of significant accuracy falloff is and how to recognize it is an open question.

Improving Highly Parallel Performance. On very small datasets, the rules learned will tend to be too general. A good rule on one dataset may prove to wrongly classify many examples on another processor which belong to a different class. Specializing such rules by adding conditional tests to them can help rule out some or all of the examples that are incorrectly classified on a given processor by a rule created on a different processor.

In a couple of small experiments, we have adopted the following strategy to improve rule performance. Any rule that is within 5% of the acceptability threshold and was created on a processor other than the current processor is a candidate for specialization. The rule is specialized by taking the examples that are classified by the rule and growing a decision tree on them. Then one takes the test(s) along the best branch and adds this to the rule to create a new specialized rule. The specialized rule as well as the original rule will be tested against the next subset of examples. The accuracy of the specialized rule is only reported on the examples available on the current processor. Both the original rule and the specialized rule can be further specialized as new data is encountered as long as their performance remains within 5% of the threshold, t.

A good feature of this approach is that there will be no decrease in performance as long as the original rule remains in the final rule set, but has a lower priority than its specializations. Any examples left uncovered by the specialized rules will still be classified by the more general rule. Of course, the general rule will only exist at the end if its accuracy value is above the threshold.

As a simple example of the potential for improvement consider the example of Figure 1. Assume you got the second set of rules using attribute 2 (Att2) from processor 1 (Proc1) and applied them to the examples held by processor 2. The rule

```
if Att2 <= 3 then C1
```

now gets only 2/5 examples correct. If it is specialized to be

```
if Att2 <= 3 and Att1 < 5   then C1
```

the rule will cover 3/3 examples correctly. Further it essentially matches the second rule obtained from the whole training set in Figure 1. This example shows how specialization would work.

On the Pima data, specialization was applied to the two partition case raising the accuracy slightly from 73.38% to 73.77%.

Rule specialization could be decided upon in other ways than in our experiment. For example, after learning, a pessimistic estimate of the rules performance [3] could be generated. For a test subset on which the classification performance of the rule was more that x% below the estimate, specialization could be carried out. To get a better estimate of the performance of a specialized rule, it might be tested against all the data on which it was not created (e.g. broadcast to all processors). This would make the conflict resolution process more accurate.

4   Summary

This paper discusses an approach to creating rules in parallel by creating disjoint subsets of a large training set, allowing rules to be created on each subset and then merging the rules. It is shown that this approach can provide good performance. It is also pointed out that the rules discovered in parallel may be different from those discovered sequentially. While it is true that rules which perform well on the full data set will perform well on at least one subset of the data, it is not necessarily the case that these rules will be discovered.

In an empirical study, it is shown that the accuracy of the merged rule sets can degrade as the number of processors, N, is increased. This raises the question of how to choose N to maximize speed and keep accuracy high. The approach discussed here uses a threshold of goodness for rules. Rules that perform below the threshold are deleted from the final rule set. The question of how to most effectively set the threshold is an open one.

It is shown that the performance of rules can be improved by further specializing those that are under performing. Conditions can be added as the rules are applied tested on data stored on other processors. Both the specialized rules and original rules remain as long as their accuracy is above the threshold.

We have pointed out issues and potential fixes to an approach that promises to provide scalable, accurate rules generated from a parallel computing system. It will enable learning from large distributed data sets.

Acknowledgments

This research was partially supported by the United States Department of Energy through the Sandia National Laboratories LDRD program, contract number DE-AC04-76DO00789. It was also partially supported by a sabbatical at the University of California, Berkeley thanks to the hospitality of Prof. Zadeh.

References

1. G. Williams, *Inducing and Combining Multiple Decision Trees*. PhD thesis, Australian National University, Canberra, Australia, 1990.
2. F. Provost and D. Hennessy, "Scaling up: Distributed machine learning with cooperation," in *Proceedings of AAAI'96*, pp. 74–79, 1996.
3. J. Quinlan, *C4.5: Programs for Machine Learning*. Morgan Kaufmann, 1992. San Mateo, CA.
4. J. Quinlan, "Improved use of continuous attributes in C4.5," *Journal of Artificial Intelligence Research*, vol. 4, pp. 77–90, 1996.
5. S. Clearwater, T. Cheng, H. Hirsh, and B. Buchanan, "Incremental batch learning," in *Proceedings of the Sixth Int. Workshop on Machine Learning*, pp. 366–370, 1989.
6. W. Cohen, "Fast effective rule induction," in *Proceedings of the 12th Conference on Machine Learning*, 1995.
7. R. Kufrin, "Generating C4.5 production rules in parallel," in *Proceedings of the Fourteenth National Conference on Artificial Intelligence (AAAI-97)*, pp. 565–570, July 1997.
8. J. Quinlan, "Generating production rules from decision trees," in *Proceedings of IJCAI-87*, pp. 304–307, 1987.
9. F. Provost and D. Hennessy, "Distributed machine learning: Scaling up with coarse-grained parallelism," in *Proceedings of the Second International Conference on Intelligent Systems for Molecular Biology*, 1994.
10. C. Merz and P. Murphy, *UCI Repository of Machine Learning Databases*. Univ. of CA., Dept. of CIS, Irvine, CA.
    http://www.ics.uci.edu/~mlearn/MLRepository.html.
11. L. Hall, N. Chawla, and K. Bowyer, "Decision tree learning on very large data sets," in *International Conference on Systems, Man and Cybernetics*, pp. 2579–2584, Oct 1998.
12. R. Fisher, "The use of multiple measurements in taxonomic problems," *Ann. Eugenics*, vol. 7, 1936.
13. S. Weiss, R. Galen, and P. Tadepalli, "Maximizing the predictive value of production rules," *Artificial Intelligence*, vol. 45, pp. 47–71, 1990.
14. P. Chan and S. Stolfo, "Scaling learning by meta-learning over disjoint and partially replicated data," in *Proceedings of the Florida Artificial Intelligence Society*, 1996.
15. S. Stolfo, A. Prodromidis, S. Tselepis, W. Lee, D. Fan, and P. Chan, "JAM: Java agents for meta-learning over distributed databases," in *Proc. KDD-97*, 1997.
16. P. K. Chan and S. J. Stolfo, "Toward scalable learning with non-uniform class and cost distributions: A case study in credit card fraud detection," in *Proc. KDD-98*, 1998.

Collective, Hierarchical Clustering from Distributed, Heterogeneous Data

Erik L. Johnson[1] and Hillol Kargupta[2]

[1] School of Electrical Engineering and Computer Science
Washington State University
erikj@wsunix.wsu.edu
http://www.eecs.wsu.edu/~ejohnso1
[2] School of Electrical Engineering and Computer Science
Washington State University
hillol@eecs.wsu.edu
http://eecs.wsu.edu/~hillol

Abstract. This paper presents the Collective Hierarchical Clustering (CHC) algorithm for analyzing distributed, heterogeneous data. This algorithm first generates local cluster models and then combines them to generate the global cluster model of the data. The proposed algorithm runs in $O(|\mathcal{S}|n^2)$ time, with a $O(|\mathcal{S}|n)$ space requirement and $O(n)$ communication requirement, where n is the number of elements in the data set and $|\mathcal{S}|$ is the number of data sites. This approach shows significant improvement over naive methods with $O(n^2)$ communication costs in the case that the entire distance matrix is transmitted and $O(nm)$ communication costs to centralize the data, where m is the total number of features. A specific implementation based on the single link clustering and results comparing its performance with that of a centralized clustering algorithm are presented. An analysis of the algorithm complexity, in terms of overall computation time and communication requirements, is presented.

1 Introduction

The field of Knowledge Discovery from Data (KDD) emerged in the recent past as a result of the dramatic evolution of the technology for information storage, access, and analysis. The ability of various organizations to collect, store and retrieve huge amounts of data has necessitated the development of algorithms which can extract useful information from these databases. The field of KDD addresses this issue.

Distributed knowledge discovery (DKD) is a result of further evolution of the KDD problem. DKD embraces the growing trend of merging computation with communication. It considers all the new dimensions of the knowledge discovery process in the context of the emerging distributed computing environments. DKD accepts the fact that data may be inherently distributed among different

M.J. Zaki, C.-T. Ho (Eds.): Large-Scale Parallel Data Mining, LNAI 1759, pp. 221–244, 2000.

loosely coupled sites connected by a network and the sites may have heterogeneous data. It offers techniques to discover new knowledge through distributed data analysis and modeling using minimal communication of data.

Account number	Amount	Location	Previous record	Unusual transaction
11992346	-42.84	Seattle	Poor	Yes
12993339	2613.33	Seattle	Good	No
45633341	432.42	Portland	Okay	No
55564999	128.32	Spokane	Okay	Yes

Table 1. Homogeneous case: Site A with a table for credit card transaction records.

Account number	Amount	Location	Previous record	Unusual transaction
87992364	446.32	Berkeley	Good	No
67845921	978.24	Orinda	Good	Yes
85621341	719.42	Walnut Creek	Okay	No
95345998	-256.40	San Francisco	Bad	Yes

Table 2. Homogeneous case: Site B with a table for credit card transaction records.

DKD must deal with different possibilities of data distribution. Different sites may contain data for a common set of features of the problem domain. In case of relational data this would mean a consistent database schema across all the sites. This is the homogeneous case. Tables 1 and 2 illustrate this case using an example from credit card transaction domain.[1] There are two data sites A and B, connected by a network. The KDD objective is to find patterns of fraudulent transactions. Note that both the tables have the same schema.

The data sites may also be heterogeneous. In other words, sites may contain data for different features. Let us illustrate this case with relational data. Table 3 shows two data-tables at site X. The table on the left contains weather-related data and the one on the right contains demographic data. Table 4 shows the content of site Y, which contains holiday toy sales data. The objective of the KDD process is to detect relations between the toy sales and the demographic and weather related features.

This paper presents an adaptation of the existing *Single Link Clustering Algorithm* to the heterogeneous case. The proposed algorithm first generates local cluster models of the data at each of the sites, and then transmits these

---

[1] Please note that the credit card domain may not always have consistent schema. The domain is used just for illustration.

City	Temp.	Humidity	Wind Chill
Pullman	20	24%	14
Spokane	32	48%	23
Seattle	63	88%	62
Portland	51	86%	46
Richland	47	52%	41

City	Size	Average earning	Proportion of small business owners
Pullman	Small	Low	0.041
Spokane	Medium	Medium	0.022
Seattle	Large	High	0.014
Portland	Large	High	0.017
Richland	Medium	Medium	0.031

Table 3. Heterogeneous case: Site X with two tables, one for weather and the other for demography.

City	Best Selling Item	Price	Number Items Sold (In thousands)
Spokane	Snarc Action Figure	47.99	23
Pullman	Power Toads	23.50	2
Richland	Light Saber	19.99	5
Seattle	Super Squirter	24.99	142
Portland	Super Fun Ball	9.99	24

Table 4. Heterogeneous case: Site Y with one table holiday toy sales.

models to a *facilitator* site, which combines the models into a global model. It will be shown that this process can be accomplished in the same asymptotic time as the existing optimal single link clustering algorithms, with a significant savings compared to naive methods in communication costs.

The rest of this paper is arranged as follows. Section 2 provides background information concerning agglomerative hierarchical clustering algorithms and a brief overview of other related efforts, including related work both in terms of clustering algorithms and DKD in general. Section 3 defines the problem of generating local models using known clustering algorithms in a heterogeneous space, and shows the flaws of a naive approach. Section 4 derives a set of bounding equations for generating a global model from a set of locally generated models, and uses these to derive the CHC algorithm. Section 5 examines the time complexity of the CHC algorithm. Section 6 provides empirical results. Ongoing and future work is discussed in Section 7. Finally, section 8 concludes this paper.

2   Background

This section presents a brief overview of agglomerative hierarchical clustering, and single link clustering in particular. Furthermore, this section presents an overview of other related efforts.

2.1   A Brief Overview of Agglomerative Hierarchical Clustering

Hierarchical clustering transforms a set of points, with an associated dissimilarity metric between two given points, into a tree structure, known as a *dendrogram* [1]. The dendrogram represents a sequence of combinations of sets of points when viewed from from the bottom of the tree. The dendrogram can also be viewed as a series of partitionings of the data into clusters when viewed from the top of the tree. Each leaf node of a dendrogram represents a single point from the data set, and each internal node represents a partitioning of the data set into two clusters. An agglomerative algorithm builds the dendrogram from the leaf nodes up, whereas a partitional algorithm builds the tree from the top down. The algorithm presented in this paper is based upon the single link clustering algorithm, which is an agglomerative hierarchical clustering method.

As noted, in addition to the set of points that form the leaves of the dendrogram, a dissimilarity metric must be selected. The dissimilarity between two points or clusters is frequently measured in terms of a distance between the points or clusters. Common distance metrics used include the Euclidean distance metric and the "city-block" distance metric. The algorithm presented in this paper is based upon the use of the Euclidean distance metric for the measure of dissimilarity; however, it is extensible to other distance metrics as well.

In general, an agglomerative hierarchical clustering algorithm consists of three primary steps [1]:

1. Initialize each individual point as a single cluster.
2. Determine the smallest measure of dissimilarity between two clusters, and merge these clusters.
3. Continue to merge the two least dissimilar clusters until all points are contained in a single cluster.

The algorithm presented in this paper focuses on single link clustering, also referred to as *nearest neighbor* clustering. This method combines two sub-clusters into a single cluster by choosing the two remaining unconnected clusters that have the shortest distance as measured by the closest pair of points between the two clusters. In the case of single link clustering, the distance between two individual sub-clusters that have been merged is stored as the internal nodes of the dendrogram.

There are a number of other related methods of clustering that differ primarily in how the distance between points within a cluster and between two separate clusters is measured. An overview of various methods of hierarchical agglomerative clustering can be found in [1].

Once the dendrogram is generated, a level of dissimilarity is chosen. All subtrees that contain either a single point or a dissimilarity measure which is less than the chosen level of dissimilarity, and whose parent node has a measure of dissimilarity greater to or equal to the chosen level of dissimilarity become individual clusters. Note that once the dendrogram has been generated, this chosen level of dissimilarity may be changed to increase and decrease the granularity of the clusters.

	Feature			
Point	f_1	f_2	f_3	f_4
p_1	1.00	1.00	1.00	1.00
p_2	1.25	1.00	1.25	1.25
p_3	1.00	1.25	2.00	2.00
p_4	3.00	3.25	2.25	2.25
p_5	3.25	3.00	3.00	3.00
p_6	3.25	3.50	3.25	3.25

Fig. 1. *Example data set consisting of 6 points, each described by four features*

	p_1	p_2	p_3	p_4	p_5	p_6
p_1	0.000	0.433	1.436	3.491	4.131	4.630
p_2	0.433	0.000	1.118	3.182	3.758	4.272
p_3	1.436	1.118	0.000	2.850	3.182	3.640
p_4	3.491	3.182	2.850	0.000	1.118	1.458
p_5	4.131	3.758	3.182	1.118	0.000	0.612
p_6	4.630	4.272	3.640	1.458	0.612	0.000

Fig. 2. *Distance matrix for points p_1 through p_6 as described in Figure 2.1, using the Euclidean distance metric.*

As an example of monolithic single link clustering, let us consider a data set consisting of set of six points, p_1 through p_6, each described by four features f_1 through f_4, as shown in Figure 2.1. Note that the values of each feature are assumed to have the same significance.

Using the Euclidean distance metric, we find that the points p_1 through p_6 have the distances as shown in Figure 2.1. Note that for large data, we would not compute these distances and store them in a matrix such as shown, as this would entail an n^2 memory requirement; however, it is useful for the purpose of illustration.

To apply single link clustering, we would first initialize each point as an individual cluster. The smallest amount of dissimilarity between two clusters at this point is between points p_1 and p_2. We would therefore join these two clusters and set the distance of the connecting node to 0.433. At this point, the smallest distance between two clusters is now between the single point clusters consisting of points p_1 and p_2, and that that distance is 0.621. We now find that the two pairs of clusters consisting of $\{\{p_1, p_2\}, \{p_3\}\}$ and $\{\{p_4\}, \{p_5, p_6\}\}$ both have a distance of 1.118, and we therefore combine these clusters. Finally, we find that the two clusters consisting of $\{p_1, p_2, p_3\}$ and $\{p_4, p_5, p_6\}$ have a shortest distance (in this case, between points p_3 and p_4, have a distance of 2.850. We merge these final two clusters, and our dendrogram is complete. By following these steps, the dendrogram shown in Figure 3 is generated.

The decision of what level of dissimilarity should be used to determine which internal nodes of the dendrogram, representing the partitioning of the data, should become the actual clusters is not firmly defined; rather, it is somewhat a

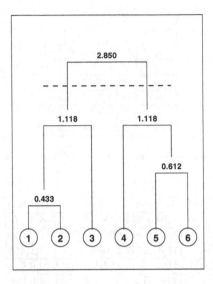

Fig. 3. *Dendrogram generated from the monolithic dataset shown in Figure 2.1.*

matter of heuristics and a matter of the desired granularity. For the purpose of this example, we will choose a level of dissimilarity somewhere between 1.118 and 2.850, as shown by the heavy dashed line in Figure 3. This results in two clusters, consisting of points $\{p_1, p_2, p_3\}$ in the first cluster, and points $\{p_4, p_5, p_6\}$.

The monolithic single link clustering algorithm has been well known for a number of years. An early version, SLINK, presented in [2], is still considered to be the standard of comparison. The SLINK algorithm runs in $O(n^2)$ time and $O(n)$ space.

2.2   Related Work

There are numerous recent efforts directed towards scaling up clustering algorithms in order to allow practical use with the huge data sets commonly associated with KDD. In [3], an adaptation of the K-Means clustering algorithm is presented that is able to cluster huge monolithic data sets with a single scan of the data. The authors show that their approach is both faster and more accurate than a sampling based approach. Another approach toward scaling up clustering algorithms is presented in [4]. The authors present an algorithm applicable to clustering in a KDD environment, which in addition to being scalable, is well suited to handling noise in the dataset. Another such approach is presented in [5]. Here the authors present the CLARANS algorithm, that is also intended to scale up clustering algorithm for KDD applications. CURE, and algorithm which utilizes a combination of both random sampling and partitioning for clustering in the KDD domain is presented in [6].

A number of recent efforts have proposed parallel based approaches to the problem of scaling clustering algorithms up for use in KDD environments. In [7], the author shows an adaptation of the SLINK [2] and other agglomerative hierarchical clustering algorithms to a multiprocessor environment to parallelize the clustering process. In [8], the authors adapt the K-Means algorithm to run in a parallel environment.

The PADMA system [9,10] achieves scalability by locating agents with the distributed data sources. An agent coordinating facilitator gives user requests to local agents that then access and analyze local data, returning analysis results to the facilitator, which merges the results. The high level results returned by the local agents are much smaller than the original data, thus allowing economical communication and enhancing scalability. The authors report on a PADMA implementation for unstructured text mining.

There exists very little literature for analyzing data from heterogeneous sites. Learning from heterogeneous data sites is discussed in [11] from the perspective of inductive bias. This work notes that such partitioning of the feature space can be addressed by decomposing the problem into smaller sub-problems when the problem is site-wise decomposable. The WoRLD system [12] addressed the problem of concept learning from heterogeneous sites by developing an "activation spreading" approach. This approach first computes the cardinal distribution of the feature values in the individual data sets. Next, this distribution information is propagated across different sites. Features with strong correlations to the concept space are identified based on this first order statistics of the cardinal distribution. The selected features are used for learning the appropriate concept. Since the technique is based on the first order statistical approximation of the underlying distribution, it may not be appropriate in general for non-convex concept space. The propagation of marker activation records from one site to another is accomplished through basic database operations. This makes the approach easily implementable in database systems. Nevertheless, a general methodology for learning functions from distributed, heterogeneous data sites with guaranteed control of accuracy and minimal communication overhead is still an open issue.

In the recent past Kargupta and his colleagues [13] considered this case and proposed the *collective data mining* (CDM) framework that makes use of orthonormal basis functions for correct local analysis. This work describes the Collective Data Mining methodology that can learn different popular data models such as regression, decision trees in a distributed environment. Interested readers may refer to [14] for additional experimental and theoretical analysis of this framework. The main motivation behind this framework is that direct application of existing machine learning and statistical algorithms to local data sites may produce partials models that are completely incorrect and possibly ambiguous. CDM makes use of orthonormal representations to guarantee accurate learning of local models and their subsequent aggregation.

To the best knowledge of the authors, there exists no published work on distributed clustering techniques for heterogeneous data sites.

The following section defines the problem of hierarchical clustering in a heterogeneous environment.

3   Problem Definition

Suppose we have some set of sites S, each of which has access to some subset of the total number of features $\mathcal{F}$, our goal is to generate a global model that is equivalent to the model that would be generated if the data were centralized; that is, we wish our dendrogram to have the same structure. In general, there are four criteria that are critical to the generation of a global model from some set of local models:

1. The dendrogram representing global model should have the same general structure as the dendrogram that would be generated if the data set was centralized and a known clustering algorithm run on this centralized data.
2. As an added constraint, it is not acceptable to transmit the entire dataset to a single site for processing; rather, local models could be generated at each of the $|S|$ sites, and these local models transmitted to a *facilitator* site, which will generate our global model. Obviously, it is not appropriate to transmit the entire dissimilarity matrix, as the cost of such transmission would be $O(|S|n^2)$.
3. Furthermore, asymptotic time complexity of the algorithm should be less than or equal to the asymptotic time complexity of generating the model on a single site from monolithic data.
4. Finally, the global model should not only indicate the sets of clusters and their membership, but also should have a metric of the dissimilarity between the points and between the clusters. We will show that there exists a naive method of generating a global model that meets some of the above requirements, but gives no information about the proximity of the points.

We shall assume in the following discussion that there is some unique key associated with each element in the overall dataset that is accessible to each of the local sites. For example, if a local telephone company and an insurance company wished to build local models on of their customers in a given area, a good choice for a unique key to identify members the elements of the dataset (customers) might be the phone number. Given that there exists a unique key of this nature to identify the rows of the database, there also must exit some function $f(key)$ that, given the set of keys, will return an linear enumeration between [0, n-1] of the keys. This fact will be utilized in the following algorithm.

As example, suppose there are two sites, $S = \{s_1, s_2\}$. We will use the data set from the previous example, shown in Figure 2.1. Suppose site s_1 has access to the subset $\{f_1, f_2\}$ of the overall feature set $\mathcal{F} = \{f_1, f_2, f_3, f_4\}$, and s_2 has access to the subset $\{f_3, f_4\}$.

If the single link clustering algorithm is applied at each of the two sites s_1 and s_2, with no interaction or information sharing between the two sites, the dendrograms shown in Figures 4 and 5 would be generated.

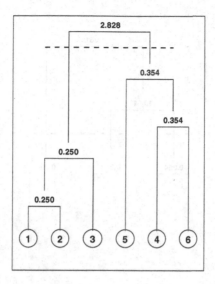

Fig. 4. *Dendrogram generated at site s_1, with access to features $\{f_1, f_2\}$ from the data set shown in Figure 2.1.*

In this example, a dissimilarity between 0.354 and 2.282 was chosen for site s_1, and between 0.354 and 1.061, shown as a bold dashed line in figures 4 and 5. Heuristically, this is somewhat a natural place to split the dendrogram into the clusters, since this is the point where the dissimilarity between the clusters begins to increase rapidly. Note that this is a common heuristic for choosing the point at which to divide the dendrogram into the various clusters. Given this choice, site s_1 has two clusters, $c_{1,1} \in \{p_1, p_2, p_3\}$ and $c_{1,2} \in \{p_4, p_5, p_6\}$. In this case, the local model agrees with our dendrogram generated from the monolithic data, with the exception that there is a difference in the hierarchical structure of cluster $c_{1,2}$. The dendrogram generated at site s_2, however, is significantly different from the monolithically generated dendrogram. At site s_2, three clusters have been generated: $c_{2,1} \in \{p_1, p_2\}$, $c_{2,2} \in \{p_3, p_4\}$ and $c_{2,3} \in \{p_5, p_6\}$ The choice of dissimilarity used to split the dendrogram is insignificant; there is no choice of the measure of dissimilarity that will result in a clustering such as was generated from the monolithic data. In other words, no matter where the dendrogram is split up to generate the boundaries between clusters, the membership of the clusters will be different from the membership of the clusters in the monolithically generated model.

Once the local models have been generated, we wish to transmit these models to a central facilitator site in order to combine them into a global model. One possible solution to this problem would be to transmit the cluster membership lists to the facilitator, that in turn would take the element-wise intersection of all of the clusters between each site. In the above example, this would result in a total of four clusters:

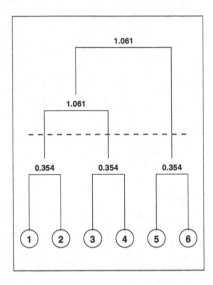

Fig. 5. *Dendrogram generated at site s_2, with access to features $\{f_3, f_4\}$ from the data set shown in Figure 2.1.*

$$\{\{p_1, p_2, p_3\}, \{p_4, p_5, p_6\}\} \cap \{\{p_1, p_2\}, \{p_3, p_4\}, \{p_5, p_6\}\} =$$

$$\{\{p_1, p_2\}, \{p_3\}, \{p_4\}, \{p_5, p_6\}\}$$

Note that this approach does indeed generate a set of clusters that, given a choice of a level of dissimilarity between 0.612 and 1.118 could have been generated by the monolithic model. Thus, the first criteria is partially met; the clusters generated from the local models are indeed a subset of those generated by the monolithically generated model. However, we do not have a dendrogram representing the structure of the clustering. The second criteria has also been met; the transmission cost for such a scheme is $O(n)$, as all that has to be transmitted are the unique keys of the points. Likewise, the third criteria has been met, as the cost of generating the local models is identical to the cost of generating the monolithically generated model; in fact, this scheme allows for parallelization of the clustering, although, there is the added cost of the intersection of the clusters. However, the fourth criteria is not met in any way; there is no more information that can be gained from the global model except which points fall into which clusters. Therefore, this scheme is not adequate given the stated criteria for generating a global model from the local models. Therefore, we will examine a technique for bounding the dissimilarity between two points and/or clusters given two or more dendrograms. The following section derives an algorithm that meets all of the listed criteria.

4   Collective Hierarchical Clustering

In this section, we will derive a lower and upper bound for the distance between two points given only the set of local models. Furthermore, we will show how these bounds can be used to generate a global model of the data. Finally, we will provide a specific implementation of the CHC algorithm that meets all of the specified criteria.

4.1   Bounding of Euclidean Distances Between Points

For the following discussion, we will assume that the Euclidean distance metric will be the measure of dissimilarity (see Section 7 for a discussion on ongoing work concerning other distance metrics). Furthermore, we will also assume that any necessary feature selection and scaling of the features have already been performed.

Given two points, p_1 and p_2, with $m = |\mathcal{F}|$ features each consisting of $\mathcal{F} \in \{f_1, f_2, ...f_n\}$, the Euclidean distance between these two points is defined as:

$$dist_{actual}(p_1, p_2) = \sqrt{\sum_{i=1}^{m} (f_{p1,i} - f_{p2,i})^2} \tag{1}$$

This can be expanded as follows:

$$dist_{actual}(p_1, p_2) = \sqrt{\sum_{i=1}^{m} \left(f_{p1,i}^2 - 2f_{p1,i}f_{p2,i} + f_{p2,i}^2\right)} \tag{2}$$

$$dist_{actual}^2(p_1, p_2) = \sum_{i=1}^{m} \left(f_{p1,i}^2 - 2f_{p1,i}f_{p2,i} + f_{p2,i}^2\right) \tag{3}$$

Hence, if the distance matrix generated at each local site were transmitted to the facilitator site responsible for generating the global model, the distances could be approximated by:

$$dist_{approx}(p_1, p_2) = \sqrt{\sum_{i=1}^{m} \left(f_{p1,i}^2 + f_{p2,i}^2\right)} \tag{4}$$

and the clustering algorithm being used could be applied to the resulting approximate distances. However, this approach does not take into account the cross terms, which in many cases are significant. Furthermore, this approach would require the transmission of the distance matrices generated at each of the $|\mathcal{S}|$ local sites, which would have a transmission cost of $O\left(|\mathcal{S}|n^2\right)|$, not to mention that these matrices can very easily be prohibitively large to be generated at the local sites, let alone gathered at the facilitator site.

We can, however, given a dendrogram in which the leaves contain only the unique key identifying the point that is represented by the leaf, generate both a minimum and a maximum bound of the distance between the two points. Noting that the transmission cost is $O(n)$ to send each of the locally generated models to the facilitator (see Section 5), such a bounding of the actual distance would allow the generation of a global model from the local models with the desired dissimilarity information and within the transmission cost constraints.

If we have more than one site, each of which has some subset of the features, we can rewrite Equation 1 as follows:

$$dist_{actual}(p_1, p_2) = \sqrt{\sum_{j=1}^{|S|}\left(\sum_{i \in \mathcal{F}_j}(f_{p1,i} - f_{p2,i})^2\right)} \tag{5}$$

We wish to find an upper and a lower bound for the $|S|$ individual summations in Equation 5.

Given any two points, the shortest distance between these two points is represented in the dendrogram as the distance value stored in the lowest root of the subtree connecting the two leaves. This follows from the definition of how the dendrogram is generated.

Given a single dendrogram representing a single link clustering, the shortest distance between two points is represented in the dendrogram as the value stored the lowest common subroot connecting the the two leaves that represent the two points. Hence, we can place a lower bound for each of the $|S|$ summation terms in Equation 5. Therefore, we may state that:

$$dist_{actual}(p_1, p_2) = \sqrt{\sum_{j=1}^{|S|}\left(\sum_{i \in \mathcal{F}_j}(f_{p1,i} - f_{p2,i})^2\right)}$$

$$\geq \sqrt{\sum_{j=1}^{|S|} d^2_{commonroot,j}} \tag{6}$$

where $d_{commonroot,j}$ is the distance value stored in the lowest connecting subroot of jth locally generated dendrogram. This leads directly to the equation for the lower bound of the distances:

$$dist_{min}(p_1, p_2) = \sqrt{\sum_{j=1}^{|S|} d^2_{commonroot,j}} \tag{7}$$

In order to generate an upper bound on the distance between two given points in a single dendrogram, we observe that the maximum possible distance between these two points is the sum of the distances on the shortest path connecting the two leaf nodes of the dendrogram. In the case that the path connecting two leaf nodes is of length one, this is obvious. However, this is not immediately intuitive when the path is longer. We will show by example why this is the case.

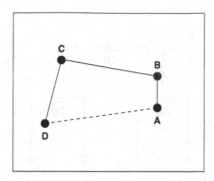

Fig. 6. *The set of points $\{A, B, C, D\}$, with $\overline{AB} < \overline{CD} < \overline{CB}$.*

Consider the set of points $\{A, B, C, D\}$ shown in Figure 6. Let $\overline{AB} < \overline{CD} <$ $\overline{CB}$. This would result in the dendrogram shown in Figure 7. Say that we were trying to find the maximum distance possible between points between points A and D with only the information provided in the associated dendrogram. Certainly, we know precisely the distance between A and B, and also, between C and D. We also know the minimum of of the four distances $\overline{AC}$, $\overline{AD}$, $\overline{BC}$ and $\overline{BD}$, represented by $\overline{BC}$ in the dendrogram. However, we do not know that this distance is in fact $\overline{BC}$. For example, the distance represented as $\overline{BC}$ in the dendrogram might actually be $\overline{AD}$, as shown by the dashed line in Figure 6. Now, if we were attempting to put an upper bound on the distance between A and D, given only the information in the dendrogram, it would make sense to sum up the distances along the shortest path in the dendrogram given the relative positions of the points in this example, as in the worst case, the points would actually lie on a straight line. However, if we were trying to find the upper distance bound between B and C, which is actually equal to the distance represented at the highest level of the dendrogram, we would still have to assume the worst case, that the points were in the straight line consisting of the sequence $\{C, D, A, B\}$. Therefore, we can bound the maximum possible distance between two points in the dendrogram as being less than the sum of the distances on the shortest path connecting the two leaf nodes of the dendrogram.

Now, consider that we have more than one dendrogram, and wish to find a total maximum distance between two points. In a manner similar to that used for the lower distance bound, we can place an upper bound on the total distance as follows:

$$dist_{actual}\left(p_1, p_2\right) = \sqrt{\sum_{j=1}^{|\mathcal{S}|}\left(\sum_{i \in \mathcal{F}_j}\left(f_{p1,i} - f_{p2,i}\right)^2\right)}$$

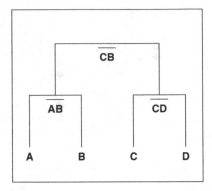

Fig. 7. *The dendrogram representing the points shown in Figure 6.*

$$\leq \sqrt{\sum_{j=1}^{|S|} \left(\sum_{shortpath,j} d_{pathnode} \right)^2} \qquad (8)$$

where $shortpath, j$ is the shortest connecting path between the two leaf nodes representing the points in j^{th} locally generated dendrogram, and $d_{pathnode}$ is the distance contained in a given node along that path. Hence, the upper distance bound is defined as:

$$dist_{max}(p_1, p_2) = \sqrt{\sum_{j=1}^{|S|} \left(\sum_{shortpath,j} d_{pathnode} \right)^2} \qquad (9)$$

Hence, a lower and upper bound have been established for the distances between any two given points when the only information available are the locally generated dendrograms, each of which have only the unique keys associated with the points for data in the leaf nodes of the dendrogram which represent those points. The next step in the process is to use these bounds to build a global dendrogram from the locally generated dendrograms that meets the stated criteria for the global model.

4.2   Generation of the Global Model

Once the local models have generated dendrograms based upon the available features at each of the local sites and have transmitted these to the facilitator site, the facilitator is responsible for combining these locally generated models into a global model. In order to do this, the facilitator will use the bounded distances described previously and some function $f(min, max)$ to generate a metric of dissimilarity between the points, and, given this metric, will build the global dendrogram.

There are a number of possible choices for the function $f(min, max)$ to generate the dissimilarity metric (see Section 7 concerning future work for more details). One choice for the dissimilarity metric is the simple mean of the minimum and the maximum distances. While this will not result in an exact equivalent measure of dissimilarity between a dendrogram generated from a monolithic data set and the global dendrogram generated from some set of local models, it will give a reasonably good approximation of the relative dissimilarities between two given points. In the case of the Euclidean distance metric, using the average of the minimum and maximum possible distances between the points yields the dissimilarity function of:

$$dist_{ave}(p_1, p_2) = \frac{\sqrt{\sum_{j=1}^{|\mathcal{S}|} d^2_{commonroot,j}} + \sqrt{\sum_{j=1}^{|\mathcal{S}|} \left(\sum_{shortpath,j} d_{pathnode} \right)^2}}{2}$$

(10)

After the function $f(min, max)$ has been chosen, the facilitator must recluster the points in the dataset using $f(min, max)$ as the measure of dissimilarity. The resulting dendrogram is the global model of the data.

4.3   CHC - Collective, Hierarchical Clustering from Distributed, Heterogeneous Data

We are now ready to state the general form of the CHC algorithm:

1. At each local site, apply the chosen hierarchical clustering algorithm to the dataset and generate a local dendrogram.
2. Transmit the locally generated dendrograms to the facilitator site.
3. Using a statistic based on the bounds (e.g., average), generate the global dendrogram.

The following discussion concerns itself with one possible implementation of the CHC algorithm.

4.4   Implementation of the CHC Algorithm for Single Link Clustering

In order to generate the global model from the local models in a reasonable amount of time and given a memory constraint, we will take advantage of the *reducibility property* [15], which allows us to perform clustering in $O(n^2)$ time and in $O(n)$ space. The reducibility property requires that when two clusters i and j are agglomerated, the new cluster $i + j$ cannot be any closer to any other clusters than either i or j were. This property is satisfied in the case of single link clustering [7]. As a consequence of the reducibility property being satisfied, we need not store the entire $n \times n$ distance matrix containing every distance between every pair of points, but, rather, only two one-dimensional arrays of

```
(0)    Function BuildLocalModel( input: LocalModels )
(1)      For each {i : 0 ≤ i < n}
(2)        For each {k : 0 ≤ k < |s|}
(3)          Traverse tree k to compute upper and lower distance bounds
             between point i and each other point j, j < i
             Store as:
             LowerBound(j, k) ← lower bound between i, j
             UpperBound(j, k) ← upper bound between i, j
(4)          Apply Equation 10 to determine average distance metric for
             each (j, k)
             While doing so track the minimum distance and store as:
             N(i) ← key of the closest point
             D(i) ← distance to closest point
(5)    Initialize array Π(n) to be pointers to each of the initial
       clusters, e.g., the set of n points
(6)    Repeat n − 1 times
(7)      Cluster1 ← indexOf(min(D))
(8)      Cluster2 ← N(Cluster1)
(9)      Agglomerate( Cluster1, Cluster2 )
(10)     Update Π, N and D as necessary
(11)   End
```

Fig. 8. *An efficient algorithm for building the global model from the local models.*

length n. Each element of the first of these arrays, $\mathcal{N}$, is initialized such that element i contains the key of the closest other point (cluster) j. Each element of the second of these arrays, $\mathcal{D}$, is initialized such that element i contains the associated distance $dist(i, j)$ for the key of j stored in $\mathcal{N}(i)$.

Determining the minimum distances does not require that the entire $n \times n$ distance matrix is generated and stored all at one point in time; rather, only one row of this matrix needs be generated at any point in time. Once this row is generated, the minimum distance between the point represented by the index of the row and all points such that their key is less than the key of the current row is found, and this value is used for the appropriate cells in $\mathcal{D}$ and $\mathcal{N}$. The algorithm for generating $\mathcal{D}$ and $\mathcal{N}$ is shown in Figure 8.

In order to demonstrate how the CHC algorithm may be applied to single link clustering, we will continue with the example started in Section 2.1. Recall that the features are heterogeneous, , $\mathcal{S} = \{s_1, s_2\}$, with the feature values given in Figure 2.1, and that site s_1 has access to the subset $\{f_1, f_2\}$ of the overall feature set $\mathcal{F} = \{f_1, f_2, f_3, f_4\}$, and s_2 has access to the subset $\{f_3, f_4\}$.

First, each of the local sites s_1 and s_2 generates a dendrogram, using the single link clustering algorithm, based upon the feature information available at that site, as shown in Figures 4 and 5. These dendrograms are transmitted to the facilitator site.

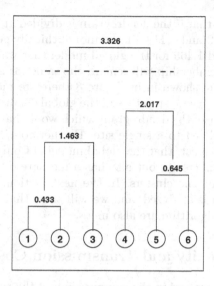

Fig. 9. *Global dendrogram as generated by the facilitator from data available from local dendrograms generated at sites s_1 and s_2, shown in Figures 4 and 5.*

Using the dissimilarity metric as given in Equation 10, the dendrogram shown in Figure 9 is generated from the two local models, using the given dissimilarity metric and the single link clustering algorithm.

The overall structure of the globally generated dendrogram is similar to the dendrogram generated from the monolithic data shown in figure 3. However, it should be noted that the dissimilarity metric stored in the internal nodes is an approximation of the dissimilarity between the partitions. In fact, the only case where an exact measure of the distance can be generated from the local models is the case where the length of the path between two given nodes in the local models is exactly one, as is the case between points p_1 and p_2. However, the measure of dissimilarity given does provide enough information to determine a level at which to split the global dendrogram into the individual clusters. In this case, the measure of dissimilarity is chosen to be between 2.017 and 3.326, as, heuristically, this is the point at which the level of dissimilarity rises most sharply. Using this level of dissimilarity to determine the individual cluster membership, the global model in this example results in two clusters, one containing the set of points $\{p_1, p_2, p_3\}$, the other containing the set of points $\{p_4, p_5, p_6\}$. This result is the desired one: the dendrogram generated from the local models is approximately equivalent to the dendrogram generated from the monolithic data set as shown in Figure 3. Furthermore, while not exact, the dissimilarity values stored in the internal nodes is allowed a division of the points into individual clusters without explicit knowledge of the exact coordinates of the points that is equivalent to the division of the points performed on the monolithically generated dendrogram. It should also be noted that, given the similarity of the structures of the two dendrograms, that if the dendrogram is divided at some lower point, for example between 0.612 and 1.118 for the monolithically generated dendrogram and between 0.645 and 1.463 for the global model that was built from the local models, the cluster membership will remain the same for both clusterings.

The CHC algorithm shown in in Figure 8 therefore meets the first requirement; that is, that the general structure of the global dendrogram generated from the local models is that of the dendrogram which would have been generated had the data been transmitted to a single site. Furthermore, the the global model meets the forth requirement, that the global model not only indicates the sets of clusters and their membership, but also has a measure of dissimilarity between the points and between the clusters. In the next section, the time complexity of the CHC algorithm is analyzed, and we will show that the second and third requirements for the algorithm are also met.

5   Time Complexity and Transmission Costs

There are two issues involved in the computation of the time complexity: 1. the cost of transmission of the local models to the facilitator site, and, 2. the computational cost of generating the global dendrogram from the locally generated dendrograms.

The first cost analysis, that of transmission of the local models to the facilitator site, turns out to be rather straight forward. Given the nature of the tree that represents the dendrogram, with a total of n points represented as the leaves of the tree, it follows that there will always be $n-1$ leaves. As it is not necessary to transmit any information about the points represented as the leaves, and as the keys of the points have been structured such that the leaves are linearly enumerated, the number of features is not relevant to the cost of transmitting the local models.

If the nodes of the tree are enumerated using a standard in-order (left-node-right) traversal of the locally generated dendrogram, the tree can be flattened into an array of length $2n-1$. This format is well adapted to transmission. When the tree is flattened, each internal node will be represented as a cell in the array, with four elements: 1. the node's number, 2. the node number of the left child, 3. the node number of the right child, and 4. the distance associated with the node. Each leaf node will contain the node number and the key, which will be used to position the node properly in the array representing the base of the dendrogram.

Given that there are $2n-1$ elements in this array, and that each element in the array contains at most 4 items, the cost of transmission of a given local model to the facilitator site is given by:

$$CT_{local} = O\left(4 \times (2n-1)\right) = O\left(n\right)$$

Therefore, the overall cost of transmission for all of the local models to the facilitator site is given by:

$$CT_{total} = O\left(|\mathcal{S}|n\right)$$

Which is effectively $O(n)$, when $|\mathcal{S}|$ is a constant and $|\mathcal{S}| \ll n$.

In order to evaluate the time and space complexity of the CHC algorithm, we first note that there are two primary loops, one represented by lines (1) through (4) in Figure 8, the other represented by lines (6) through (10). We will examine each of these separately. Line (5) is an $O(n)$ operation, and is not consequential to the overall analysis, as will be shown in the following discussion.

The first line of the first loop, line (1), iterates over each of the points in the tree in order to find the closest other point such that the key (represented by the index) of the other point is less than that of the point under consideration. Obviously, we must perform this n times; hence, the outer loop has a time complexity of $O(n)$.

Line (2) is a nested loop within the loop which began on line (1). As we must extract information from each of the local models, this will add a factor of $O(|\mathcal{S}|)$ to the overall time complexity of the first loop.

Line (3) is the process by which the bounds for the distances are determined. It is only necessary to traverse the tree once in order to determine the distance bounds between a given leaf node (point) and all other points. This traversal is an $O(n)$ operation. As this traversal is nested within the loop began on line line (2), this adds a further factor of $O(n)$ to the overall time complexity. Hence, the overall complexity of the loop began on line (2) is $O(|\mathcal{S}|n)$. Without considering line (4), then, the time complexity of the loop began on line (1) is then $O(|\mathcal{S}|n^2)$

Finally, the first primary loop contains line (4), which, it should be noted, is not contained within the loop defined on line (2). Hence, as the process of finding the minimum dissimilarity metric as defined in Equation 10 for each of the $O(n)$ elements for the under consideration, the components of which are stored in $O(|\mathcal{S}|)$ arrays of length $O(n)$ is itself $O(|\mathcal{S}|n)$. Therefore, line (4) adds nothing further to the overall time complexity of the loop began on line (1). Thus, the time complexity of the first primary loop, which began on line (1), remains $O(|\mathcal{S}|n^2)$.

Note that to this point, the total memory usage involves the following data structures:

- $2 \times |\mathcal{S}|$ reusable arrays to store the upper and lower bounds of the distances between the current point under consideration and those points whose index is less than the index of the point currently under consideration. Each of these arrays uses $O(n)$ space. Hence, the space complexity of these arrays is $O(|\mathcal{S}|n)$.
- $2 \times |\mathcal{S}|$ tree structures representing the locally generated models, each of size $2n - 1$. The space complexity for these data structures is thus $O(|\mathcal{S}|n)$.
- The arrays $\mathcal{N}$ and $\mathcal{D}$. These arrays are both of length n, and thus, have an overall space complexity of $O(n)$.

Thus, the overall space complexity of algorithm through the termination of the first primary loop, which includes lines (1) through (4) is $O(|\mathcal{S}|n)$.

Recall that line (5) is an $O(n)$ operation, and is not consequential to the overall analysis, as we have already determined that the time complexity to this point in the algorithm is of $O(|\mathcal{S}|n^2)$. Furthermore, the space involved on line (5) is $O(n)$, which is less than the $O(|\mathcal{S}|n)$ needed for the first primary loop.

The second primary loop begins on line (6) and includes the rest of the algorithm. Note that this section of the algorithm is an adaptation of the SLINK algorithm [2]. The loop that begins on (6) repeats $O(n)$ times.

Line (7) is a entails a traversal of the array $\mathcal{D}$. Note that the index of the array is the key of the point with which the element value is associated; therefore, it is not possible to sort this array and also maintain the $O(1)$ lookup time in line (8). As line (7) is nested within the second primary loop which began on line (6), and line (7) entails an $O(n)$ operation, the overall time complexity of the second primary loop to this point is $O(n^2)$.

As noted, line (8) is an $O(1)$ operation, and, therefore, adds nothing to the overall time complexity of the second portion of the algorithm.

By using the pointer representation for maintaining the current highest levels of agglomeration in the array Π, the agglomeration in line (9) becomes an $O(1)$ operation. This is also true of the updates necessary in line (10). (See [2] for details). Hence, neither of these lines add any significant amount of time to the overall time complexity of the second primary loop, and, hence, this loop remains with a time complexity of $O(n^2)$.

The space complexity of the second loop is easily shown to be $O(n)$. As the only new data element being utilized is the tree which is built using the Π array, and this dendrogram will contain, including the base nodes as initialized in the Π array, $2n - 1$ elements, the overall space complexity of the second portion of the algorithm is $O(n)$.

Given that the first loop was shown to have a time complexity of $O(|\mathcal{S}|n^2)$, line (5) a time complexity of $O(n)$, and the second loop to have a time complexity of $O(n^2)$, our overall time complexity is given by:

$$O(|\mathcal{S}|n^2) + O(n) + O(n^2) = \tag{11}$$

$$O(|\mathcal{S}|n^2) \tag{12}$$

When $|\mathcal{S}|$ is a constant and $|\mathcal{S}| \ll n$, we can rewrite Equation 12 as:

$$time = O(n^2) \tag{13}$$

This time complexity is of the same order as that shown for the SLINK algorithm [2], and, hence, is considered to be the optimal possible.

Furthermore, the overall space complexity for the first primary loop was shown to be $O(|\mathcal{S}|n)$, and $O(n)$ for the second. Once again, when when $|\mathcal{S}|$ is a constant and $|\mathcal{S}| \ll n$, we can write:

$$space = O(n) \tag{14}$$

Hence, the overall time and space requirements are equivalent to that of the SLINK algorithm, and, therefore, equivalent to those which would be required for optimal clustering using the single link method on monolithic data. However, in order to transmit all of the data from the various remote sites would take $O(n^2)$ time and bandwidth, while our method uses only $O(n)$ time and bandwidth. Therefore, the second requirement specified for the algorithm has been met, that the transmission cost be less than or equal to that of transmitting the entire data set to a single site. Furthermore, the third requirement that the algorithms asymptotic time complexity should be less than or equal to the asymptotic time complexity of generating the model on a single site from monolithic data has also been met. As noted at the conclusion of the previous section, the first and forth requirements for the algorithm have also been met; therefore, the given algorithm meets all of the requirements specified.

The following section provides empirical results generated using the algorithm.

6   Empirical Results

The data set used for testing the algorithm was the Boston Housing Data set, available from the UCI Machine Learning Repository, at
   http://www.ics.uci.edu/AI/ML/MLDBRepository.html.
This data set contains 506 instances with 14 features. All data was normalized to the range $[0, 1]$, and the feature values were considered to be of equal significance. A total of three dendrograms were generated. The first of these, B_1, was generated using the canonical single link clustering algorithm for monolithic data. The second, B_2, was generated from two local models, the first of which was built from features $[1, 7]$, the second from features $[8, 14]$. The third global model, B_3, was generated from three local models, the first of which was built from features $[1, 5]$, the second from features $[6, 10]$, the third from features $[11, 14]$.

In order to determine the accuracy of the CHC algorithm relative to the monolithic single link clustering algorithm, the dendrograms were "split" at different points resulting in different number of clusters, in a manner similar to the example followed throughout the discussion of the algorithm, in which, the monolithically generated dendrogram and the dendrogram generated in the distributed manner were split such that there were 2 clusters in each. The dendrograms were split such that there were 2, 3, 5 and 10 clusters. Figure 10 shows the accuracy for B_2 and B_3 at these levels of division. In order to measure the accuracy, a "best-fit" method was used. This method consisted of comparing the clusters generated from the monolithic data to those generated using the CHC algorithm. The clusters were compared in decreasing order of size of the monolithically generated clusters. The cluster generated from the distributed local models that contained most of the points also contained in given monolithically generated cluster was considered to be the best-fitting cluster. Any points that were not in this point-wise intersection of the best-fitting clusters were considered to be incorrectly placed. Hence, the values displayed in Figure 10 represent the ratio of points that resulted from the described intersection operation to the total number of points in the dataset. Note that the differing

	B_1 Compared To:	
Number Divisions	B_2	B_3
2	92.4%	88.7%
3	82.2%	88.5%
5	83.0%	86.5%
10	79.8%	76.8%

Fig. 10. *Comparative results at different levels of division of the dendrogram between the monolithically generated dendrogram (B_1) and the global model generated from two sites (B_2) and the global model generated from three sites (B_3).*

results are a consequence of the sequence of agglomeration at the higher levels of the dendrograms.

The following section addresses future work to be performed.

7 Future Work

This paper presented an algorithm for distributed single link clustering of heterogeneous data. The general method for bounding of the distances presented in this paper are specific to the Euclidean distance metric and single link clustering. Therefore, future work will include the following activities:

– Expansion of the method of bounding distances to handle other agglomerative, hierarchical clustering methods, such as average link and complete link clustering.
– Expansion of the general form of the algorithm to handle other distance metrics, such as the Manhattan distance metric.
– Expansion of the general form of the algorithm to cover clustering methods such as density based clustering in a similar manner, with the same requirements as specified in Section 3.
– Inclusion of the algorithm into the existing Collective Data Mining (CDM) [13] system BODHI, a Java based communication and interface package.
– Further generation of results on larger data sets.
– Examination of the statistic given in Equation 10 to determine if a better metric of dissimilarity is achievable. This would result in a higher accuracy of classification for the distributed models when compared to the monolithically generated model.

The following section concludes this paper.

8 Conclusion

This paper has presented a set of requirements for a distributed clustering algorithm which operates on heterogeneous data, and the Collective Hierarchical Clustering (CHC) algorithm which meets, and in some cases, exceeds those requirements. The time complexity of this algorithm has been shown to be $O(|\mathcal{S}|n^2)$, and the space requirements of this algorithm have been shown to be $O(n)$. This indicates that the CHC algorithm is capable of performing the analysis of the data in the same order of time and space as the equivalent centralized version of the algorithm.

The transmission cost for assembling the local models at a central facilitator site have been shown to be independent of the number of features at each site, with an overall communication requirement of $O(n)$ and a time complexity for transmission of $O(n)$. This is a significant improvement over centralizing the data to a single site, which has a communication cost of $O(nm)$, when there are n elements and m features in the data set. Furthermore, the CHC algorithm has both significantly lower communication costs and lower time complexity than transmitting the entire distance matrix to a centralized cite, which has an $O(n^2)$ communication cost and time complexity.

The empirical results and examples shown in this paper demonstrate that the CHC algorithm is indeed a feasible approach to distributed, heterogeneous clustering.

Finally, the bounding metrics presented in this paper are adaptable by their nature to other hierarchical clustering algorithms. This indicates that this algorithm is adaptable to other clustering methods. Efforts are being directed to this end.

Acknowledgments

The authors would like to acknowledge support from the National Science Foundation Grant IIS-9803360 and the American Cancer Society.

References

1. Dubes, R., Jain, A.: Clustering methodologies in exploratory data analysis. Advances In Computers **19** (1980) 113–228
2. Sibson, R.: Slink: An optimally efficient algorithm for the single-link cluster method. The Computer Journal **16** (1973) 30–34
3. Bradley, P., Fayyad, U., Reina, C.: Scaling clustering algorithms to large databases. In: Proceeding of the Fourth International Conference on Knowledge Discovery and Data Mining, AAAI Press (1998) 9–15
4. Zhang, T., Ramakrishnan, R., Livny, M.: Birch: An efficient data clustering method for very large databases. In: Proceedings of the 1996 ACM SIGMOD International Conference on Management of Data, ACM Press (1996) 103–114
5. Ng, R., Han, J.: Efficient and effective clustering methods for spatial data mining. In: Proceedings of 20th International Conference on Very Large Data Bases, Morgan Kaufmann (1994) 144–155
6. Guha, S., Rastogi, R., Shim, K.: Cure: An efficient clustering algorithm for large databases. In: Proceedings ACM SIGMOD International Conference on Management of Data, ACM Press (1998) 73–84

7. Olson, C.: Parallel algorithms for hierarchical clustering. Parallel Computing **8** (1995) 1313–1325
8. Dhillon, I., Modha, D.: A data clustering algorithm on distributed memory multi-processors. In: Workshop on Large-Scale Parallel KDD Systems. (1999)
9. Kargupta, H., Hamzaoglu, I., Stafford, B., Hanagandi, V., Buescher, K.: PADMA: Parallel data mining agent for scalable text classification. In: Proceedings Conference on High Performance Computing '97, The Society for Computer Simulation International (1996) 290–295
10. Kargupta, H., Hamzaoglu, I., Stafford, B.: Scalable, distributed data mining using an agent based architecture. In Heckerman, D., Mannila, H., Pregibon, D., Uthurusamy, R., eds.: Proceedings of Knowledge Discovery And Data Mining, Menlo Park, CA, AAAI Press (1997) 211–214
11. Provost, F.J., Buchanan, B.: Inductive policy: The pragmatics of bias selection. Machine Learning **20** (1995) 35–61
12. Aronis, J.M., Kolluri, V., Provost, F.J., Buchanan, B.G.: The world: Knowledge discovery from multiple distributed data bases. Technical Report ISL-96-6, Intelligent Systems Laboratory, Department of Computer Science, University of Pittsburgh, Pittsburgh, PA (1996)
13. Kargupta, H., Park, B., Hershbereger, D., Johnson, E.: Collective data mining: A new perspective toward distributed data mining. Accepted in the Advances in Distributed Data Mining, Eds: Hillol Kargupta and Philip Chan, AAAI/MIT Press (1999)
14. Hershberger, D., Kargupta, H.: Distributed multivariate regression using wavelet-based collective data mining. Technical Report EECS-99-02, School of EECS, Washington State University (1999)
15. Murtagh, F.: Multidimensional Clustering Algorithms. Physica-Verlag (1985)

A Data-Clustering Algorithm
on Distributed Memory Multiprocessors

Inderjit S. Dhillon[1] and Dharmendra S. Modha[2]

[1] Department of Computer Science, University of Texas, Austin, TX 78712, USA
inderjit@cs.utexas.edu
http://www.cs.utexas.edu/users/inderjit
[2] IBM Almaden Research Center, 650 Harry Road, San Jose, CA 95120, USA
dmodha@almaden.ibm.com
http://www.almaden.ibm.com/cs/people/dmodha

Abstract. To cluster increasingly massive data sets that are common today in data and text mining, we propose a parallel implementation of the k-means clustering algorithm based on the message passing model. The proposed algorithm exploits the inherent data-parallelism in the k-means algorithm. We analytically show that the speedup and the scaleup of our algorithm approach the optimal as the number of data points increases. We implemented our algorithm on an IBM POWERparallel SP2 with a maximum of 16 nodes. On typical test data sets, we observe nearly linear relative speedups, for example, 15.62 on 16 nodes, and essentially linear scaleup in the size of the data set and in the number of clusters desired. For a 2 gigabyte test data set, our implementation drives the 16 node SP2 at more than 1.8 gigaflops.

1 Introduction

Data sets measuring in gigabytes and even terabytes are now quite common in data and text mining, where a few million data points are the norm. For example, the patent database (www.ibm.com/patents/), the Lexis-Nexis document collection containing more than 1.5 billion documents (www.lexisnexis.com), and the Internet archive (www.alexa.com) are in multi-terabyte range. When a sequential data mining algorithm cannot be further optimized or when even the fastest available serial machine cannot deliver results in a reasonable time, it is natural to look to parallel computing. Furthermore, given the monstrous sizes of the data sets, it often happens that they cannot be processed *in-core*, that is, in the main memory of a single processor machine. In such a situation, instead of implementing a disk based algorithm which is likely to be considerably slower, it is appealing to employ parallel computing and to exploit the main memory of *all* the processors.

Parallel data mining algorithms have been recently considered for tasks such as association rules and classification, see, for example, Agrawal and Shafer [1], Chattratichat et al. [2], Cheung and Xiao [3], Han, Karypis, and Kumar [4], Joshi, Karypis, and Kumar [5], Kargupta, Hamzaoglu, and Stafford [6], Shafer, Agrawal, and Mehta [7], Srivastava, et al. [8], Zaki, Ho, and Agrawal [9], and

M.J. Zaki, C.-T. Ho (Eds.): Large-Scale Parallel Data Mining, LNAI 1759, pp. 245–260, 2002.

Zaki et al. [10]. Also, see Stolorz and Musick [11] and Freitas and Lavington [12] for recent books on scalable and parallel data mining.

In this paper, we consider parallel clustering. Clustering or *grouping of similar objects* [13] is one of the most widely used procedures in data mining [14]. Practical applications of clustering include unsupervised classification and taxonomy generation [13], nearest neighbor searching [15], scientific discovery [16,17], vector quantization [18], time series analysis [19], and multidimensional visualization [20,21].

Our interest in clustering stems from the need to mine and analyze heaps of unstructured text documents. Clustering has been used to discover "latent concepts" in sets of unstructured text documents, and to summarize and label such collections. Clustering is inherently useful in organizing and searching large text collections, for example, in automatically building an ontology like Yahoo! (www.yahoo.com). Furthermore, clustering is useful for compactly summarizing, disambiguating, and navigating the results retrieved by a search engine such as AltaVista (www.altavista.com). Conceptual structure generated by clustering is akin to the "Table-of-Contents" in *front* of books. Finally, clustering is useful for personalized information delivery by providing a setup for routing new information such as that arriving from newsfeeds and new scientific publications. For experiments describing a certain syntactic clustering of the whole web and its applications, see [22]. For detailed review of various classical text clustering algorithms such as the k-means algorithm and its variants, hierarchical agglomerative clustering, and graph-theoretic methods, see [23,24]. Recently, there has been a flurry of activity in this area, see [25,26,27,28,29]. For our recent work on matrix approximations using a variant of the k-means algorithm applied to text data, see [30]. Our results have been extremely promising; their applicability to extremely large collections of text documents requires a highly scalable implementation, and, hence, the motivation for this work.

In this paper, as our main contribution, we propose a parallel clustering algorithm on distributed memory multiprocessors, that is, on a shared-nothing parallel machine, and analytically and empirically validate our parallelization strategy. Specifically, we propose a parallel version of the popular k-means clustering algorithm [31,13] based on the message-passing model of parallel computing [32,33]. To the best of our knowledge, a parallel implementation of the k-means clustering algorithm has not been reported in the literature. In this paper, our focus in on parallelizing the classical direct k-means algorithm.

We now briefly outline the paper, and summarize our results. In Section 2, we present the k-means algorithm. In Section 3, we carefully analyze the computational complexity of the k-means algorithm. Based on this analysis, we observe that the k-means algorithm is inherently data-parallel. By exploiting this parallelism, we design a parallel k-means algorithm. We analytically show that the speedup and the scaleup of our algorithm approach the optimal as the number of data points increases. In other words, we show that as the number of data points increases the communication costs incurred by our parallelization strategy are relatively insignificant compared to the overall computational complexity. Our parallel algorithm is based on the message-passing model of parallel computing; this model is also briefly reviewed in Section 3. In Section 4, we empirically study the performance of our parallel k-means algorithm (that is, speedup and scaleup) on an IBM POWERparallel SP2 with a maximum of 16 nodes. We empirically establish that our parallel k-means algorithm has nearly linear speedup, for example, 15.62 on 16 nodes, and has nearly linear scaleup behavior. To capture the effectiveness of our algorithm in a nutshell, note that we are able to to drive the 16 node SP2 at nearly 1.8 gigaflops (floating point operations) on a 2 gigabyte test data set. In Section 5, we include a brief discussion on future work.

Our parallelization strategy is simple but very effective; in fact, the simplicity of our algorithm makes it ideal for rapid deployment in applications.

2 The k-Means Algorithm

Suppose that we are given a set of n data points $X_1, X_2, \cdots, X_n$ such that each data point is in R^d. The problem of finding the *minimum variance* clustering of this data set into k clusters is that of finding k points $\{m_j\}_{j=1}^k$ in R^d such that

$$\frac{1}{n} \sum_{i=1}^{n} \left(\min_j d^2(X_i, m_j) \right), \tag{1}$$

is minimized, where $d(X_i, m_j)$ denotes the Euclidean distance between X_i and m_j. The points $\{m_j\}_{j=1}^k$ are known as *cluster centroids* or as *cluster means*. Informally, the problem in (1) is that of finding k cluster centroids such that the average squared Euclidean distance (also known as the mean squared error or MSE, for short) between a data point and its nearest cluster centroid is minimized. Unfortunately, this problem is known to be NP-complete [34].

The classical k-means algorithm [31,13] provides an easy-to-implement approximate solution to (1). Reasons for popularity of k-means are ease of interpretation, simplicity of implementation, scalability, speed of convergence, adaptability to sparse data, and ease of out-of-core implementation [30,35,36]. We present this algorithm in Figure 1, and intuitively explain it below:

1. (**Initialization**) Select a set of k starting points $\{m_j\}_{j=1}^k$ in R^d (line 5 in Figure 1). The selection may be done in a random manner or according to some heuristic.
2. (**Distance Calculation**) For each data point X_i, $1 \le i \le n$, compute its Euclidean distance to each cluster centroid m_j, $1 \le j \le k$, and then find the closest cluster centroid (lines 14-21 in Figure 1).
3. (**Centroid Recalculation**) For each $1 \le j \le k$, recompute cluster centroid m_j as the average of data points assigned to it (lines 22-26 in Figure 1).
4. (**Convergence Condition**) Repeat steps 2 and 3, until convergence (line 28 in Figure 1).

The above algorithm can be thought of as a gradient-descent procedure which begins at the starting cluster centroids and iteratively updates these centroids to decrease the objective function in (1). Furthermore, it is known that k-means will always converge to a local minimum [37]. The particular local minimum found depends on the starting cluster centroids. As mentioned above, the problem of finding the global minimum is NP-complete.

Before the above algorithm converges, steps 2 and 3 are executed a number of times, say $\mathfrak{I}$. The positive integer $\mathfrak{I}$ is known as the *number of k-means iterations*. The precise value of $\mathfrak{I}$ can vary depending on the initial starting cluster centroids even on the same data set.

In Section 3.2, we analyze, in detail, the computational complexity of the above algorithm, and propose a parallel implementation.

3 Parallel k-Means

Our parallel algorithm design is based on the Single Program Multiple Data (SPMD) model using message-passing which is currently the most prevalent model for computing on distributed memory multiprocessors; we now briefly review this model.

3.1 Message-Passing Model of Parallel Computing

We assume that we have P processors each with a local memory. We also assume that these processors are connected using a communication network. We do not assume a specific interconnection topology for the communication network, but only assume that it is generally cheaper for a processor to access its own local memory than to communicate with another processor. Such machines are commercially available from vendors such as Cray and IBM.

Potential parallelism represented by the distributed-memory multiprocessor architecture described above can be exploited in software using "message-passing." As explained by Gropp, Lusk, and Skjellum [32, p. 5]:

> The message-passing model posits a set of processes that have only local memory but are able to communicate with other processes by sending and receiving messages. It is a defining feature of the message-passing model that data transfers from the local memory of one process to the local memory of another process require operations to be performed by both processes.

MPI, the Message Passing Interface, is a standardized, portable, and widely available message-passing system designed by a group of researchers from academia and industry [32,33]. MPI is robust, efficient, and simple-to-use from FORTRAN 77 and C/C++.

From a programmer's perspective, parallel computing using MPI appears as follows. The programmer writes a single program in C (or C++ or FORTRAN 77), compiles it, and links it using the MPI library. The resulting object code is loaded in the local memory of every processor taking part in the computation; thus creating P "parallel" *processes*. Each process is assigned a unique identifier

```
1:
2:
3: MSE = LargeNumber;
4:
5: Select initial cluster centroids {m_j}_{j=1}^k;
6:
7:
8: do {
9:     OldMSE = MSE;
10:    MSE' = 0;
11:    for j = 1 to k
12:        m'_j = 0; n'_j = 0;
13:    endfor;
14:    for i = 1 to n
15:        for j = 1 to k
16:            compute squared Euclidean
                   distance d^2(X_i, m_j);
17:        endfor;
18:        find the closest centroid m_ℓ to X_i;
19:        m'_ℓ = m'_ℓ + X_i; n'_ℓ = n'_ℓ + 1;
20:        MSE' = MSE' + d^2(X_i, m_ℓ);
21:    endfor;
22:    for j = 1 to k
23:
24:
25:        n_j = max(n'_j, 1); m_j = m'_j/n_j;
26:    endfor;
27:    MSE = MSE';
28:} while (MSE < OldMSE)
```

```
1:
2:
3: MSE = LargeNumber;
4:
5: Select initial cluster centroids {m_j}_{j=1}^k;
6:
7:
8: do {
9:     OldMSE = MSE;
10:    MSE' = 0;
11:    for j = 1 to k
12:        m'_j = 0; n'_j = 0;
13:    endfor;
14:    for i = 1 to n
15:        for j = 1 to k
16:            compute squared Euclidean
                   distance d^2(X_i, m_j);
17:        endfor;
18:        find the closest centroid m_ℓ to X_i;
19:        m'_ℓ = m'_ℓ + X_i; n'_ℓ = n'_ℓ + 1;
20:        MSE' = MSE' + d^2(X_i, m_ℓ);
21:    endfor;
22:    for j = 1 to k
23:
24:
25:        n_j = max(n'_j, 1); m_j = m'_j/n_j;
26:    endfor;
27:    MSE = MSE';
28:} while (MSE < OldMSE)
```

Fig. 1. Sequential k-means Algorithm.   **Fig. 2.** Parallel k-means Algorithm. See Table 1 for a glossary of various MPI routines used above.

MPI_Comm_size()	returns the number of processes
MPI_Comm_rank()	returns the process identifier for the calling process
MPI_Bcast(message, root)	broadcasts "message" from a process with identifier "root" to all of the processes
MPI_Allreduce(A, B, MPI_SUM)	sums all the local copies of "A" in all the processes (reduction operation) and places the result in "B" on *all* of the processes (broadcast operation)
MPI_Wtime()	returns the number of seconds since some fixed, arbitrary point of time in the past

Table 1. Conceptual syntax and functionality of MPI routines which are used in Figure 2. For the exact syntax and usage, see [32,33].

between 0 and $P - 1$. Depending on its processor identifier, each process may follow a distinct execution path through the same code. These processes may communicate with each other by calling appropriate routines in the MPI library which encapsulates the details of communications between various processors.

Table 1 gives a glossary of various MPI routines which we use in our parallel version of k-means in Figure 2. Next, we discuss the design of the proposed parallel algorithm.

3.2   Parallel Algorithm Design

We begin by analyzing, in detail, the computational complexity of the sequential implementation of the k-means algorithm in Figure 1.

We count each addition, multiplication, or comparison as one floating point operation (flop). It follows from Figure 1 that the amount of computation within each k-means iteration is constant, where each iteration consists of "distance calculations" in lines 14-21 and a "centroid recalculations" in lines 22-26. A careful examination reveals that the "distance calculations" require roughly $(3nkd + nk + nd)$ flops per iteration, where $3nkd$, nk, and nd correspond to lines 15-17, line 18, and line 19 in Figure 1, respectively. Also, "centroid recalculations" require approximately kd flops per iteration. Putting these together, we can estimate the computation complexity of the sequential implementation of the k-means algorithm as

$$(3nkd + nk + nd + kd) \cdot \mathfrak{I} \cdot T^{\text{flop}}, \tag{2}$$

where $\mathfrak{I}$ denotes the number of k-means iterations and T^{flop} denotes the time (in seconds) for a floating point operation. In this paper, we are interested in the case when the number of data points n is quite large in an absolute sense, and also large relative to d and k. Under this condition the serial complexity of the k-means algorithm is dominated by

$$T_1 \sim (3nkd) \cdot \mathfrak{I} \cdot T^{\text{flop}}. \tag{3}$$

By implementing a version of k-means on a distributed memory machine with P processors, we hope to reduce the total computation time by nearly a factor of P. Observe that the "distance calculations" in lines 14-21 of Figure 1 are inherently data parallel, that is, in principle, they can be executed asynchronously and in parallel for each data point. Furthermore, observe that these lines dominate the computational complexity in (2) and (3), when the number of data points n is large. In this context, a simple, but effective, parallelization strategy is to divide the n data points into P blocks (each of size roughly n/P) and compute lines 14-21 for each of these blocks in parallel on a different processor. This is the approach adopted in Figure 2.

For simplicity, assume that P divides n. In Figure 2, for $\mu = 0, 1, \cdots, P - 1$, we assume that the process identified by "μ" has access to the data subset $\{X_i, i = (\mu) * (n/P) + 1, \cdots, (\mu + 1) * (n/P)\}$. Observe that each of the P processes can carry out the "distance calculations" in parallel or asynchronously, if the centroids $\{m_j\}_{j=1}^k$ are available to each process. To enable this potential parallelism, in Figure 1, a local copy of the centroids $\{m_j\}_{j=1}^k$ is maintained for each process, see, line 7 and lines 22-26 in Figure 2 (see Table 1 for a glossary of the MPI calls used). Under this parallelization strategy, each process needs to handle only n/P data points, and hence we expect the total computation time for the parallel k-means to decrease to

$$T_P^{\text{comp}} = \frac{T_1}{P} \sim \frac{(3nkd) \cdot \mathfrak{I} \cdot T^{\text{flop}}}{P}. \tag{4}$$

In other words, as a benefit of parallelization, we expect the computational burden to be shared equally by all the P processors. However, there is also a price attached to this benefit, namely, the associated communication cost, which we now examine.

Before each new iteration of k-means can begin, all the P processes must communicate to recompute the centroids $\{m_j\}_{j=1}^k$. This global communication (and hence synchronization) is represented by lines 22-26 of Figure 2. Since, in each iteration, we must "MPI_Allreduce" roughly $d \cdot k$ floating point numbers, we can estimate the communication time for the parallel k-means to be

$$T_P^{\text{comm}} \sim d \cdot k \cdot \mathfrak{I} \cdot T_P^{\text{reduce}}, \tag{5}$$

where T_P^{reduce} denotes the time (in seconds) required to "MPI_Allreduce" a floating point number on P processors. On most architectures, one may assume that $T_P^{\text{reduce}} = O(\log P)$ [38].

Line 27 in Figure 2 ensures that each of the P processes has a local copy of the total mean-squared-error "MSE", hence each process can independently decide on the convergence condition, that is, when to exit the "do{ $\cdots$ }while" loop.

In conclusion, each iteration of our parallel k-means algorithm consists of an asynchronous computation phase followed by a synchronous communication phase. The reader may compare Figures 1 and 2 line-by-line to see the precise correspondence of the proposed parallel algorithm with the serial algorithm. We stress that Figure 2 is optimized for understanding, and not for speed! In particular, in our actual implementation, we do not use $(2k+1)$ different "MPI_Allreduce" operations as suggested by lines 23, 24, and 27, but rather use a single block "MPI_Allreduce" by assigning a single, contiguous block of memory for the variables $\{m_j\}_{j=1}^k$, $\{n_j\}_{j=1}^k$, and MSE and a single, contiguous block of memory for the variables $\{m_j'\}_{j=1}^k$, $\{n_j'\}_{j=1}^k$, and MSE'.

We can now combine (4) and (5) to estimate the computational complexity of the parallel k-means algorithm as

$$T_P = T_P^{\text{comp}} + T_P^{\text{comm}} \sim \frac{(3nkd) \cdot \mathfrak{I} \cdot T^{\text{flop}}}{P} + d \cdot k \cdot \mathfrak{I} \cdot T_P^{\text{reduce}}. \tag{6}$$

It can be seen from (4) and (5) that the relative cost for the communication phase T_P^{comm} is insignificant compared to that for the computation phase T_P^{comp}, if

$$\boxed{\frac{P \cdot T_P^{\text{reduce}}}{3 \cdot T^{\text{flop}}} \ll n} . \tag{7}$$

Since the left-hand side of the above condition is a machine constant, as the number of data points n increases, we expect the relative cost for the communication phase compared to the computation phase to progressively decrease.

In the next section, we empirically study the performance of the proposed parallel k-means algorithm.

4   Performance and Scalability Analysis

Sequential algorithms are tested for correctness by seeing whether they give the right answer. For parallel programs, the right answer is not enough: we would like to decrease the execution time by adding more processors or we would like to handle larger data sets by using more processors. These desirable characteristics of a parallel algorithm are measured using "speedup" and "scaleup," respectively; we now empirically study these characteristics for the proposed parallel k-means algorithm.

4.1   Experimental Setup

We ran all of our experiments on an IBM SP2 with a maximum of 16 nodes. Each node in the multiprocessor is a Thin Node 2 consisting of a IBM POWER2 processor running at 160 MHz with 256 megabytes of main memory. The processors all run AIX level 4.2.1 and communicate with each other through the High-Performance Switch with HPS-2 adapters. The entire system runs PSSP 2.3 (Parallel System Support Program). See [39] for further information about the SP2 architecture.

Our implementation is in C and MPI. All the timing measurements are done using the routine "MPI_Wtime()" described in Table 1. Our timing measurements ignore the I/O times (specifically, we ignore the time required to read in the data set from disk), since, in this paper, we are only interested in studying the efficacy of our parallel k-means algorithm. All the timing measurements were taken on an otherwise idle system. To smooth out any fluctuations, each measurement was repeated five times and each reported data point is to be interpreted as an average over five measurements.

For a given number of data points n and number of dimensions d, we generated a test data set with 8 clusters using the algorithm in [40]. A public domain implementation of this algorithm is available from Dave Dubin [41]. The advantage of such data generation is that we can generate as many data sets as desired with precisely specifiable characteristics.

As mentioned in Section 2, each run of the k-means algorithm depends on the choice of the starting cluster centroids. Specifically, the initial choice determines the specific local minimum of (1) that will be found by the algorithm, and it determines the number of k-means iterations. To eliminate the impact of the initial choice on our timing measurements, for a fixed data set, identical starting cluster centroids are used–irrespective of the number of processors used.

We are now ready to describe our experimental results.

4.2   Speedup

Relative speedup is defined as the ratio of the execution time for clustering a data set into k clusters on 1 processor to the execution time for identically clustering the same data set on P processors. Speedup is a summary of the efficiency of the parallel algorithm.

Using (3) and (6), we may write relative speedup of the parallel k-means roughly as

$$\text{Speedup} = \frac{(3nkd) \cdot \mathfrak{I} \cdot T^{\text{flop}}}{(3nkd) \cdot \mathfrak{I} \cdot T^{\text{flop}}/P + d \cdot k \cdot \mathfrak{I} \cdot T_P^{\text{reduce}}}, \tag{8}$$

which approaches the linear speedup of P when condition (7) is satisfied, that is, the number of data points n is large. We report three sets of experiments, where we vary n, d, and k, respectively.

Varying n: First, we study the speedup behavior when the number of data points n is varied. Specifically, we consider five data sets with $n = 2^{13}, 2^{15}$, $2^{17}, 2^{19}$, and 2^{21}. We fixed the number of dimensions $d = 8$ and the number of desired clusters $k = 8$. We clustered each data set on $P = 1, 2, 4, 8$, and 16 processors. The measured execution times are reported in Figure 3, and the corresponding relative speedup results are reported in Figure 4. We can observe the following facts from Figure 4:

- For the largest data set, that is, $n = 2^{21}$, we observe a relative speedup of 15.62 on 16 processors. Thus, for large number of data points n our parallel k-means algorithm has nearly linear relative speedup.
  But, in contrast, for the smallest data set, that is, $n = 2^{11}$, we observe that relative speedup flattens at 6.22 on 16 processors.
- For a fixed number of processors, say, $P = 16$, as the number of data points increase from $n = 2^{11}$ to $n = 2^{21}$ the observed relative speedup generally increases from 6.22 to 15.62, respectively. In other words, our parallel k-means has an excellent *sizeup* behavior in the number of data points.

All these empirical facts are consistent with the theoretical analysis presented in the previous section; in particular, see condition (7).

Varying d: Second, we study the speedup behavior when the number of dimensions d is varied. Specifically, we consider three data sets with $d = 2, 4$, and 8. We fixed the number of data points $n = 2^{21}$ and the number of desired clusters $k = 8$. We clustered each data set on $P = 1, 2, 4, 8$, and 16 processors. For the sake of brevity, we omit the measured execution times, and report the corresponding relative speedup results in Figure 5.

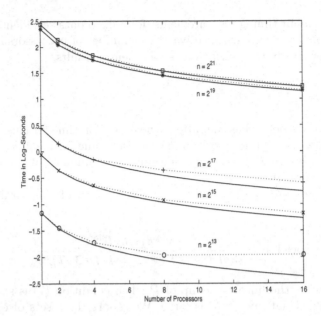

Fig. 3. Speedup curves. We plot execution time in $\log_{10}$-seconds versus the number of processors. Five data sets are used with number of data points $n = 2^{13}, 2^{15}, 2^{17}, 2^{19}$, and 2^{21}. The number of dimensions $d = 8$ and the number of clusters $k = 8$ are fixed for all the five data sets. For each data set, the k-means algorithm required $\mathfrak{I} = 3, 10, 8, 164$ and 50 number of iterations, respectively. For each data set, a dotted line connects the observed execution times, while a solid line represents the "ideal" execution times obtained by dividing the observed execution time for 1 processor by the number of processors.

Varying k: Finally, we study the speedup behavior when the number of desired clusters k is varied. Specifically, we clustered a fixed data set into $k = 2, 4, 8$, and 16 clusters. We fixed the number of data points $n = 2^{21}$ and the number of dimensions $d = 8$. We clustered the data set on $P = 1, 2, 4, 8$, and 16 processors. The corresponding relative speedup results are given in Figure 6. In Figure 5, we observe nearly linear speedups between 15.42 to 15.53 on 16 processors. Similarly, in Figure 6, we observe nearly linear speedups between 15.08 to 15.65 on 16 processors. The excellent speedup numbers can be attributed to the fact that for $n = 2^{21}$ the condition (7) is satisfied. Also, observe that all the relative speedup numbers in Figures 5 and 6 are essentially independent of d and k, respectively. This is consistent with the fact that neither d nor k appears in the condition (7).

4.3   Scaleup

For a fixed data set (or a problem size), speedup captures the decrease in execution speed that can be obtained by increasing the number of processors. Another figure of merit of a parallel algorithm is *scaleup* which captures how well the parallel algorithm handles larger data sets when more processors are available. Our

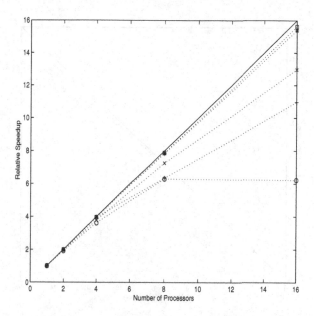

Fig. 4. Relative Speedup curves corresponding to Figure 3. The solid line represents "ideal" linear relative speedup. For each data set, a dotted line connects observed relative speedups.

scaleup study measures execution times by keeping the problem size per processor fixed while increasing the number of processors. Since, we can increase the problem size in either the number of data points n, the number of dimensions d, or the number of desired clusters k, we can study scaleup with respect to each of these parameters at a time.

Relative scaleup of the parallel k-means algorithm with respect to n is defined as the ratio of the execution time (per iteration) for clustering a data set with n data points on 1 processor to the the execution time (per iteration) for clustering a data set with $n \cdot P$ data points on P processors–where the number of dimensions d and the number of desired clusters k are held constant. Observe that we measure execution time per iteration, and not raw execution time. This is necessary since the k-means algorithm may require a different number of iterations $\mathfrak{I}$ for a different data set. Using (3) and (6), we can analytically write relative scaleup with respect to n as

$$\text{Scaleup} = \frac{(3nkd) \cdot T^{\text{flop}}}{(3nPkd) \cdot T^{\text{flop}}/P + d \cdot k \cdot T_P^{\text{reduce}}}. \tag{9}$$

It follows from (9) that if

$$\boxed{\frac{T_P^{\text{reduce}}}{3 \cdot T^{\text{flop}}} \ll n}, \tag{10}$$

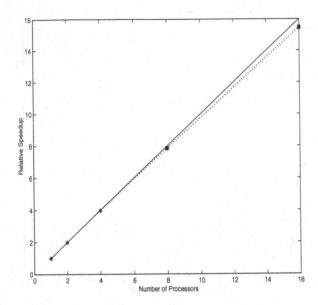

Fig. 5. Relative speedup curves for three data sets with $d = 2, 4$, and 8. The number of data points $n = 2^{21}$ and the number of clusters $k = 8$ are fixed for all the three data sets. The solid line represents "ideal" linear relative speedup. For each data set, a dotted line connects observed relative speedups. It can be seen that relative speedups for different data sets are virtually indistinguishable from each other.

then we expect relative scaleup to approach the constant 1. Observe that condition (10) is weaker than (7), and will be more easily satisfied for large number of data points n which is the case we are interested in. Relative scaleup with respect to either k or d can be defined analogously; we omit the precise definitions for brevity. The following experimental study shows that our implementation of parallel k-means has linear scaleup in n and k, and surprisingly better than linear scaleup in d.

Scaling n: To empirically study scaleup with respect to n, we clustered data sets with $n = 2^{21} \cdot P$ on $P = 1, 2, 4, 8, 16$ processors, respectively. We fixed the number of dimensions $d = 8$ and the number of desired clusters $k = 8$. The execution times per iteration are reported in Figure 7, from where it can be seen that the parallel k-means delivers virtually constant execution times in number of processors, and hence has excellent scaleup with respect to n. The largest data set with $n = 2^{21} \cdot 16 = 2^{25}$ is roughly 2 gigabytes. For this data set, our algorithm drives the SP2 at nearly 1.2 gigaflops. Observe that the main memory available on each of the 16 nodes is 256 megabytes, and hence this data set will not fit in the main memory of any single node, but easily fits in the combined main memory of 16 nodes. This is yet another benefit of parallelism–the ability to cluster significantly large data sets *in-core*, that is, in main memory.

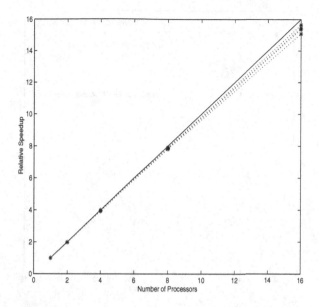

Fig. 6. Relative speedup curves for four data sets with $k = 2, 4, 8$, and 16. The number of data points $n = 2^{21}$ and the number of dimensions $d = 8$ are fixed for all the four data sets. The solid line represents "ideal" linear relative speedup. For each data set, a dotted line connects observed relative speedups. It can be seen that relative speedups for different data sets are virtually indistinguishable from each other.

Scaling k: To empirically study scaleup with respect to k, we clustered a data set into $k = 8 \cdot P$ clusters on $P = 1, 2, 4, 8, 16$ processors, respectively. We fixed the number of data points $n = 2^{21}$, and the number of dimensions $d = 8$. The execution times per iteration are reported in Figure 7, from where it can be seen that our parallel k-means delivers virtually constant execution times in number of processors, and hence has excellent scaleup with respect to k.

Scaling d: To empirically study scaleup with respect to d, we clustered data sets with the number of dimensions $d = 8 \cdot P$ on $P = 1, 2, 4, 8, 16$ processors, respectively. We fixed the number of data points $n = 2^{21}$, and the number of desired clusters $k = 8$. The execution times per iteration are reported in Figure 7, from where it can be seen that our parallel k-means delivers better than constant execution times in number of processors, and hence has surprisingly nice scaleup with respect to d. We conjecture that this phenomenon occurs due to the reduced loop overhead in the "distance calculations" as d increases (see Figure 2). The largest data set with $d = 8 \cdot 16 = 128$ is roughly 2 gigabytes. For this data set, our algorithm drives the SP2 at nearly 1.8 gigaflops.

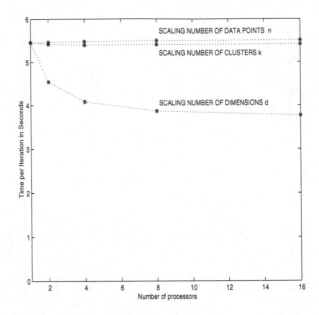

Fig. 7. Scaleup curves. We plot execution time per iteration in seconds versus the number of processors. The same data set with $n = 2^{21}$, $d = 8$, and $k = 8$ is used for all the three curves–when the number of processors is equal to 1. For the "n" curve, the number of data points is scaled by the number of processors, while d and k are held constant. For the "k" curve, the number of clusters is scaled by the number of processors, while n and d are held constant. For the "d" curve, the number of dimensions is scaled by the number of processors, while n and k are held constant.

5   Future Work

In this paper, we proposed a parallel k-means algorithm for distributed memory multiprocessors. Our algorithm is also easily adapted to shared memory multiprocessors where all processors have access to the same memory space. Many such machines are now currently available from a number of vendors. The basic strategy in adapting our algorithm to shared memory machine with P processors would be the same as that in this paper, namely, divide the set of data points n into P blocks (each of size roughly n/P) and compute distance calculations in lines 14-21 of Figure 1 for each of these blocks in parallel on a different processor while ensuring that each processor has access to a separate copy of the centroids $\{m_j\}_{j=1}^{k}$. Such an algorithm can be implemented on a shared memory machine using threads [42].

It is well known that the k-means algorithm is a hard thresholded version of the expectation-maximization (EM) algorithm [43]. We believe that the EM algorithm can be effectively parallelized using essentially the same strategy as that used in this paper.

References

1. Agrawal, R., Shafer, J.C.: Parallel mining of association rules: Design, implementation, and experience. IEEE Trans. Knowledge and Data Eng. **8** (1996) 962–969
2. Chattratichat, J., Darlington, J., Ghanem, M., Guo, Y., Hüning, H., Köhler, M., Sutiwaraphun, J., To, H.W., Yang, D.: Large scale data mining: Challenges and responses. In Pregibon, D., Uthurusamy, R., eds.: Proceedings Third International Conference on Knowledge Discovery and Data Mining, Newport Beach, CA, AAAI Press (1997) 61–64
3. Cheung, D.W., Xiao, Y.: Effect of data distribution in parallel mining of associations. Data Mining and Knowledge Discovery (1999) to appear.
4. Han, E.H., Karypis, G., Kumar, V.: Scalable parallel data mining for association rules. In: SIGMOD Record: Proceedings of the 1997 ACM-SIGMOD Conference on Management of Data, Tucson, AZ, USA. (1997) 277–288
5. Joshi, M.V., Karypis, G., Kumar, V.: ScalParC: A new scalable and efficient parallel classification algorithm for mining large datasets. In: Proceedings of the First Merged International Parallel Processing Symposium and Symposium on Parallel and Distributed Processing, Orlando, FL, USA. (1998) 573–579
6. Kargupta, H., Hamzaoglu, I., Stafford, B., Hanagandi, V., Buescher, K.: PADMA: Parallel data mining agents for scalable text classification. In: Proceedings of the High Performance Computing, Atlanta, GA, USA. (1997) 290–295
7. Shafer, J., Agrawal, R., Mehta, M.: A scalable parallel classifier for data mining. In: Proc. 22nd International Conference on VLDB, Mumbai, India. (1996)
8. Srivastava, A., Han, E.H., Kumar, V., Singh, V.: Parallel formulations of decision-tree classification algorithms. In: Proc. 1998 International Conference on Parallel Processing. (1998)
9. Zaki, M.J., Ho, C.T., Agrawal, R.: Parallel classification for data mining on shared-memory multiprocessors. In: 15th IEEE Intl. Conf. on Data Engineering. (1999)
10. Zaki, M.J., Parthasarathy, S., Ogihara, M., Li, W.: New parallel algorithms for fast discovery of association rule. Data Mining and Knowledge Discovery **1** (1997) 343–373
11. Stolorz, P., Musick, R.: Scalable High Performance Computing for Knowledge Discovery and Data Mining. Kluwer Academic Publishers (1997)
12. Freitas, A.A., Lavington, S.H.: Mining Very Large Databases with Parallel Processing. Kluwer Academic Publishers (1998)
13. Hartigan, J.A.: Clustering Algorithms. Wiley (1975)
14. Fayyad, U.M., Piatetsky-Shapiro, G., Smyth, P., Uthurusamy, R.: Advances in Knowledge Discovery and Data Mining. AAAI/MIT Press (1996)
15. Fukunaga, K., Narendra, P.M.: A branch and bound algorithm for computing k-nearest neighbors. IEEE Trans. Comput. (1975) 750–753
16. Cheeseman, P., Stutz, J.: Bayesian classification (autoclass): Theory and results. In Fayyad, U.M., Piatetsky-Shapiro, G., Smyth, P., Uthurusamy, R., eds.: Advances in Knowledge Discovery and Data Mining, AAAI/MIT Press (1996) 153–180
17. Smyth, P., Ghil, M., Ide, K., Roden, J., Fraser, A.: Detecting atmospheric regimes using cross-validated clustering. In Pregibon, D., Uthurusamy, R., eds.: Proceedings Third International Conference on Knowledge Discovery and Data Mining, Newport Beach, CA, AAAI Press (1997) 61–64
18. Gersho, A., Gray, R.M.: Vector quantization and signal compression. Kluwer Academic Publishers (1992)
19. Shaw, C.T., King, G.P.: Using cluster analysis to classify time series. Physica D **58** (1992) 288–298
20. Dhillon, I.S., Modha, D.S., Spangler, W.S.: Visualizing class structure of multidimensional data. In Weisberg, S., ed.: Proceedings of the 30th Symposium on the Interface: Computing Science and Statistics, Minneapolis, MN. (1998)
21. Dhillon, I.S., Modha, D.S., Spangler, W.S.: Visualizing class structure of high-dimensional data with applications. Submitted for publication (1999)

22. Broder, A.Z., Glassman, S.C., Manasse, M.S., Zweig, G.: Syntactic clustering of the web. Technical Report 1997-015, Digital Systems Research Center (1997)
23. Rasmussen, E.: Clustering algorithms. In Frakes, W.B., Baeza-Yates, R., eds.: Information Retrieval: Data Structures and Algorithms, Prentice Hall, Englewood Cliffs, New Jersey (1992) 419–442
24. Willet, P.: Recent trends in hierarchic document clustering: a critical review. Inform. Proc. & Management (1988) 577–597
25. Boley, D., Gini, M., Gross, R., Han, E.H., Hastings, K., Karypis, G., Kumar, V., Mobasher, B., Moore, J.: Document categorization and query generation on the World Wide Web using WebACE. AI Review (1998)
26. Cutting, D.R., Karger, D.R., Pedersen, J.O., Tukey, J.W.: Scatter/gather: A cluster-based approach to browsing large document collections. In: ACM SIGIR. (1992)
27. Sahami, M., Yusufali, S., Baldonado, M.: SONIA: A service for organizing networked information autonomously. In: ACM Digital Libraries. (1999)
28. Silverstein, C., Pedersen, J.O.: Almost-constant-time clustering of arbitrary corpus subsets. In: ACM SIGIR. (1997)
29. Zamir, O., Etzioni, O.: Web document clustering: A feasibility demonstration. In: ACM SIGIR. (1998)
30. Dhillon, I.S., Modha, D.S.: Concept decompositions for large sparse text data using clustering. Technical Report RJ 10147 (95022), IBM Almaden Research Center (July 8, 1999)
31. Duda, R.O., Hart, P.E.: Pattern Classification and Scene Analysis. Wiley (1973)
32. Gropp, W., Lusk, E., Skjellum, A.: Using MPI: Portable Parallel Programming with the Message Passing Interface. The MIT Press, Cambridge, MA (1996)
33. Snir, M., Otto, S.W., Huss-Lederman, S., Walker, D.W., Dongarra, J.: MPI: The Complete Reference. The MIT Press, Cambridge, MA (1997)
34. Garey, M.R., Johnson, D.S., Witsenhausen, H.S.: The complexity of the generalized Lloyd-Max problem. IEEE Trans. Inform. Theory 28 (1982) 255–256
35. SAS Institute Cary, NC, USA: SAS Manual. (1997)
36. Zhang, T., Ramakrishnan, R., Livny, M.: Birch: An efficient data clustering method for very large databases. In: Proceedings of the ACM SIGMOD Conference on Management of Data, Montreal, Canada. (1996)
37. Bottou, L., Bengio, Y.: Convergence properties of the k-means algorithms. In Tesauro, G., Touretzky, D., eds.: Advances in Neural Information Processing Systems 7, The MIT Press, Cambridge, MA (1995) 585–592
38. Culler, D.E., Karp, R.M., Patterson, D., Sahay, A., Santos, E.E., Schauser, K.E., Subramonian, R., von Eicken, T.: LogP: A practical model of parallel computation. Communications of the ACM 39 (1996) 78–85
39. Snir, M., Hochschild, P., Frye, D.D., Gildea, K.J.: The communication software and parallel environment of the IBM SP2. IBM Systems Journal 34 (1995) 205–221
40. Milligan, G.: An algorithm for creating artificial test clusters. Psychometrika 50 (1985) 123–127
41. Dubin, D.: clusgen.c. http://alexia.lis.uiuc.edu/~dubin/ (1996)
42. Northrup, C.J.: Programming with UNIX Threads. John Wiley & Sons (1996)
43. McLachlan, G.J., Krishnan, T.: The EM Algorithm and Extentions. Wiley (1996)

Author Index